THE FAITHFUL

The Faithful

A HISTORY OF CATHOLICS
IN AMERICA

James M. O'Toole

The Belknap Press of Harvard University Press

Cambridge, Massachusetts, and London, England

A Caravan book. For more information, visit www.caravanbooks.org

First Harvard University Press paperback edition, 2009

Library of Congress Cataloging-in-Publication Data

O'Toole, James M., 1950–
   The faithful : a history of Catholics in America / James M. O'Toole.
      p.   cm.
   Includes bibliographical references and index.
   ISBN 978-0-674-02818-0 (cloth : alk. paper)
   ISBN 978-0-674-03488-4 (pbk.)
   1. Catholic Church—United States—History—20th century.   2. Catholics—
United States—History—20th century.   3. United States—Church history—
20th century.   I. Title.
   BX1406.3.O79   2008
   282′.73—dc22   2007038343

For

Pat Byrne, Pat Casey, Richard Moynihan, Clare Walsh

Amici in Domino

Contents

Introduction   I

1   The Priestless Church   II

2   The Church in the Democratic Republic   50

3   The Immigrant Church   94

4   The Church of Catholic Action   145

5   The Church of Vatican II   199

6   The Church in the Twenty-first Century   266

Notes   311

Acknowledgments   369

Index   371

Introduction

Two scenes play out within a few hundred yards of each other on a beautiful midsummer day. In the first, more than four thousand people gather for an impromptu day-long convention to protest a spreading scandal in their church. They have come from around the country for prayer and sober reflection. There are panel discussions that try to make sense of the shocking accounts of sexual abuse of children by priests, stories that have been filling the newspapers for half a year. There are a few angry speeches: the church leaders who failed to protect those children must be held to account. The participants, mostly white and middle-aged, are unlikely revolutionaries, but some speakers call for a thorough reordering of the church, with greater involvement from its members, the people like them who fill the pews of their suburban parishes week after week, who oversee the religious instruction of the young, who volunteer at the local homeless shelter. The convention ends with the celebration of a Mass for the huge crowd, and then a march through the city streets to confront one church leader who has been judged particularly callous in tolerating the criminal, not to mention sinful, abuse.

The second scene takes place at the very same moment, in a

small chapel located in the shopping mall adjacent to the convention center. Here, about fifty people gather for Sunday Mass. They are a more mixed group—white, black, Hispanic, Asian— and they represent all ages and social classes. Some carry shopping bags, the product of a day spent hunting for necessities, luxuries, and bargains. They are not unaware of the scandal that has been swirling around them for months, and some are no doubt sympathetic with the protestors in another part of the complex. But they are in this chapel for a simpler purpose: to attend the weekly Mass for what the church calendar identifies as the Sixteenth Sunday in Ordinary Time. "Ordinary time": a period of routine, when the Sundays follow one another in order without the interruption of major feasts, like Christmas or Easter. The young priest presiding at the Mass makes no reference to the convention nearby, focusing instead on the gospel reading assigned for the day, a parable about how wheat and weeds may grow together in the same field. This service takes less than an hour, and afterward the small congregation disperses.

The participants in both of these scenes—which took place in Boston, Massachusetts, on July 20, 2002—were Catholics, members of the aggregate body of their church known as "the Faithful." This book is about them. What had brought them, individually and collectively, to this point? What experiences had shaped them and their church, the Roman Catholic Church in the United States? If the past is prologue, as Antonio says in Shakespeare's *Tempest,* their history is the prologue to their differing experiences that day: the one, an extraordinary gathering that challenged the church's hierarchy; the other, an entirely ordinary group seeking only the church's traditional rituals and sacraments. To call all of them the Faithful is appropriate, for they literally remained faithful to the church in which they claimed membership, even in the face of challenges at the beginning of a new century. The term was an ancient one, originally used to distinguish those who became Christians from those who still worshiped the pagan gods of their ancestors. Now it had an additional resonance, for both groups of Catholics were sticking with the church in spite of all the flaws manifest in the scandal. The bonds of loyalty were stretched but not broken.

Reimagining the history of the Catholic Church in the United States as a story of its people—the Faithful, the laity—rather than its leaders and institutions requires a shift in perspective. The term "laity," derived from the Greek word *laos* ("people"), is an unusual one, more likely to turn up in crossword puzzles than in everyday speech. For centuries, the laity were defined principally by who they were *not:* they were not priests. This formulation was curious, since it meant that nearly all Catholics (perhaps 99 percent of them) were characterized by who they were not rather than who they were. Today, this way of thinking seems inadequate and even faintly insulting. The British cardinal John Henry Newman's wry comment about the laity—that the church would look pretty silly without them—still has an irreducible logic a century and a half after he said it. The story of Catholicism in America must always be the story of these people, the men and women in the pews. Especially in a time of crisis in the church, a look back may help light the way forward. The backward look offered here sees the history of the American church as falling into a series of successive eras or ages. Six American Catholic lay people will mark the boundaries of these ages.

History is always dynamic. Change is constant even when imperceptible, and American Catholics have been changing from the very beginning. Their experience has been varied, not uniform or monolithic. No one experience has been more authentic or defining than all others. No one way, here or elsewhere in the world, has been right and all the others wrong: an institution that has existed for two thousand years has done a lot of changing. History is also contingent. Things did not have to turn out the way they did; they might just as well have been very different and yet remained no less authentic. Remembering that history is dynamic and contingent may be especially important for the Catholic Church, which often seemed to think that it had escaped history. The passing world might change, but the church went on serenely (in its own phrase) *per omnia saecula saeculorum*— through all the ages of ages. The Baltimore Catechism, from which I learned my Catholicism as a child, told me that the church was endowed with a "miraculous strength, permanence, and unchangeableness." Permanence, unchangeableness (not just unchanging, but unchangeable)—these characteristics remained unaffected by the contingencies of history. But of course the church did change. Understanding the varied circumstances in which it has flourished and floundered but nonetheless endured can lead to an appreciation of its resilience and perhaps its meaning.

The six ages described here span more than three centuries, from a time when America was merely the colonial outpost of an older European civilization until the present. The length of each age is approximate and should not be read too literally. Moreover, the ages sometimes overlap. Even so, the six ages encompass the shared experiences of American Catholics, and these help order and frame an otherwise disjointed history.

As different as the ages may have been from one another, several themes run through them. One is the size and structure of the American Catholic community in each age. How many Catholics were there in the United States, and where did they live? What was the balance of race, gender, and social class within the church? How many priests and religious sisters (the "church professionals," if we may call them that) served the laity, and how did this supply affect the presence of the church in their lives? What were the parishes, schools, and social welfare agencies that embodied the church and did its work? For a long time, Catholic history in America looked like a story of unimpeded "progress": the institution always seemed to be getting bigger and better. More recently, that has changed. Whatever the ups and downs, the demographics of Catholicism in America provide the foundation for describing the characteristics of the Faithful in all eras.

Beyond their numbers, however, American Catholics have found various ways to "be Catholic." Thus religious and devotional life, as practiced by ordinary church members, is another theme at the center of this story. Joining a church or remaining a part of it is not like joining the Rotary Club or the Democratic Party; such organizations do not demand the same commitment to regular, personal practice of their principles. For Catholics, though they are members of an institutional church, the underlying loyalty is to a way of seeing the world (both this one and the one that is believed to come after it) no less than to an ecclesiastical structure. This vision requires nurturing through religious practice: sacraments, liturgy, and prayer, both individual and communal. What was it like for Catholics when they went to church? What happened there, and what did it mean to them? This devotional and prayer life has been quite varied indeed, and it has changed considerably over time. Some practices spoke meaningfully to Catholics in one period but not in another. How the fortunes of the various devotions changed, and what that tells us about Catholics' inner spiritual lives, is examined in each of these ages.

The relationship of individual Catholics to the papacy is also a critical part of the story. Catholics in the United States have had to define themselves in relation to the church's leadership and authority in Rome, beginning with the pope. This was never simple. The position of the popes was changing in these ages, and more than once, the disappearance of the papacy was a genuine possibility. One pope died a prisoner of Napoleon, and it seemed unlikely that a successor could be chosen. American churchmen considered the possibility that there might not be a pope anymore, but they were sure that the faith would survive anyway. Later, another pope was driven from Rome by a popular uprising, and yet others became self-declared "prisoners of the Vatican." Despite (or maybe because of) these shifting political fortunes, popes solidified their authority within the church. "Looking Romeward" (as one American churchman put it) in all things, even relatively insignificant ones, became common practice. Whereas medieval popes had always had to negotiate with powerful local barons and kings, the popes of recent centuries established the spiritual supremacy of their office. Their power in all churchy things was summarized in a handy aphorism: *Roma locuta est, causa finita est*—Rome has spoken, the case is settled.

As American Catholics watched these developments from their distant country, they grew increasingly attached to the pope. Protest meetings condemned each perceived insult by his secular opponents, and a new cult of the papacy took root. American Catholics became the most generous contributors to the so-called Peter's Pence, a collection taken up worldwide to support the pontiff and his work. They filled their homes with his image, and soon they flocked to Rome on pilgrimages to catch a glimpse of him. American priests and bishops sought his favor, delighting in the honorific titles of symbolic nobility that he bestowed. Parishioners, too, gloried vicariously in signs of papal approbation. A priest might be "elevated" by the pope to the rank of monsignor, for instance, and lay people were as pleased with such distinctions as the cleric himself. To have a monsignor as one's pastor was to be just a cut above the parishioners down the street who were presided over by a mere priest. In later years, as popes began to travel the world, American Catholics turned out in huge crowds to see them, filling baseball stadiums and even the Mall in Washington, D.C., waving and cheering. Even so, by the end of the twentieth century the relationship of American Catholics to their spiritual leader had become more complicated. Most of them disagreed with or rejected some of his teachings on particular subjects, and they made no secret of it. Still, they looked to him as a moral leader, and those conflicting views of the pope persisted.

If Catholics had to define themselves in relation to the distant pontiff, they faced a parallel need to situate themselves in their own American context. While affirming religious allegiance to their foreign pope, they were unmatched in their political loyalty to their own nation. Anti-Catholic nativists often charged that this was simply impossible, and so accused Catholics of divided loyalties. Political cartoons depicted hordes of simian-looking Catholics, manipulated by scheming mitred prelates (sometimes transformed into crocodiles, slithering up onto American shores) and ready to do the dirty work of undermining American principles. The first time a Catholic ran for president, he was defeated in part by the charge that he would take his marching orders from the Vatican; he would even, it was said, build a tunnel from Rome to Washington to make it easier for the pope to have his way with Lady Liberty. Not until 1960 were such fears laid to rest, but only after another Catholic candidate promised to keep the principles of his faith entirely out of his policy decisions. Before that, ordinary Catholics had been similarly eager to show their patriotism. They joined the armed forces in numbers higher than their proportion of the population and filled their churches with American flags. American Catholics might be, as one joke had it, more Catholic than the pope, but at times they also seemed more American than Americans.

Catholic participation in American politics is by now the stuff of legend, particularly in the early years of the twentieth century, but the Catholic role in American life has been broader than that. The impact on education and social welfare was particularly striking. As soon as they were able, Catholics built a network of schools, from the elementary grades through college and professional schools, that few would have thought possible. At the same time, they opened hospitals, orphanages, vocational schools, employment bureaus, homes for the poor and the aged, immigrant aid services, and other agencies until the church had constructed the largest private social service system in the world. All these efforts were supported by the financial generosity of people who were often least able to afford it. Moreover, the doors of these institutions were open to all comers, regardless of religion: by the end of the twentieth century, the desks in many inner-city parochial elementary schools were filled largely with non-Catholic pupils, without any expectation of their conversion.

Precisely because Catholics participated so fully in all aspects of American public life, public perceptions of the church in the United States varied considerably. What did other Americans, those who went to different churches or to none, think of their Catholic neighbors? From the Catholic side of the street, this story has often been told as one of persistent hostility, and there have been enough examples of anti-Catholic bigotry to support that view. A woman with the too-apt pseudonym of Maria Monk, for instance, made a sensation on the lecture circuit in the 1830s with tales of the deflowering of young women that was, she insisted, going on behind the walls of Catholic convents. A hundred years later, a northern version of the Ku Klux Klan, temporarily focusing its intimidation on Catholics and Jews as well as African Americans, won political power in several states. To highlight only such episodes, however, is to misread the enduring tolerance of non-Catholic Americans toward the Roman Church. In novels, movies, and other media, the public perceptions of Catholicism have been mostly benign. Any society in which Father Chuck O'Malley (Bing Crosby's handsome singing priest in *Going My Way*) is a cultural hero cannot be understood solely in terms of anti-Catholic bigotry.

Studying the past may sometimes be merely a way of avoiding

the present. Like Miniver Cheevy, "born too late" and sighing for what is not in Edwin Arlington Robinson's poem, some may want to make the past a refuge. Properly understood, however, history is like our own individual memory: without it, we would be lost, uncertain of who we are. In times of crisis, such as those that the Catholic Church in the United States continues to face, the intellectual and even psychological grounding of history makes it a supremely relevant study. History *matters* now more than ever, both to American Catholics themselves and to the nation in which they live. For Catholics, understanding the successive ages of their church may open them to accepting change that will continue whether they want it to or not. The church and its people have never stood still in changing times, and they cannot do so now.

A new age of the church in America has begun, and what form that church will take, what combination of old and new, will be up to its people to decide. As they do, history offers a standard against which to measure the many possible futures. Expressions of faith that are two thousand years old are essential and permanent; practices that are only two hundred years old may be something less than that. "Prudence, indeed, will dictate that governments long established should not be changed for light and transient causes," as Thomas Jefferson (hardly sympathetic to Catholicism or to any other organized religion) wrote in the Declaration of Independence, and his political insight might just as readily be applied to churches. Still, knowing their own history is important for American Catholics no less than knowing their own family story.

For non-Catholics in America—and that of course is the majority of Americans—knowing something about the history of the Catholic people tells them something significant about their neighbors. It may also tell them much about their own religious practices and sentiments, or lack thereof. Other denominations face many of the same issues that Catholics are now facing, and all Americans live in a country—a nation with the soul of a church, G. K. Chesterton called it—in which religion matters as in few other places in the West. The Catholic Church is a public institution, and it continues to have an impact on a host of issues in American life. Some of these issues are political and, as a result, highly contentious. The church has articulated positions on these and other questions, and individual American Catholics have both accepted and rejected them. But Catholics and their church also influence other realms of American life. What will be our collective national culture and ethos? How shall we behave toward each other, and especially toward the more unfortunate among us? What kind of discourse will we have with one another about what really matters to us as individuals and as a nation? In addressing such questions as these, we ensure that the history of the American Catholic people continues to be a part of the larger conversation that is American life. So let's meet those people.

I

The Priestless Church

Roger Hanly lived with his wife and six children in Bristol, Maine, at the time of the American Revolution. Located on some of the rockiest stretches of the state's famously craggy coast about fifty miles (as the seagull flies) "down east" from Portland, Bristol is not a very big town today, and it was even smaller then. Its life centered on the maritime trades. Although it was not right on the water, it served a long peninsula as a market town and a place where weary seamen could rest between voyages. Roger and his brother Patrick had come there from Ireland about 1770, and they found community with other Irish families, the Kavanaghs and the Cottrills. They wanted to preserve their ancestral Catholic faith, but that was not easy. Much later, they were able to erect a small brick church, described as "dignified," a few miles up the road, just outside the town of Damariscotta. Building it was a genuine act of faith, maybe a foolhardy one, for it was rare that a priest wandered through the region to conduct any services.

One such occasion came in August 1797, when a young priest named Cheverus visited Bristol for a few days. Jean Louis Anne Madeleine Lefebvre de Cheverus was the scion of a minor French noble family who had been ordained a priest in Paris just as the

French Revolution turned in a violently anticlerical direction. Fleeing his homeland, he made his way to Boston in the new United States, where he promptly anglicized his name to John Cheverus. He was polished, witty, and urbane. John Adams, always wary of what he considered Catholicism's capacity to "charm and bewitch the simple and the ignorant," found in Cheverus a cultured and agreeable conversation partner. "No person," a friend of Adams's said of the young priest, "could have been better adapted to establish the Church of Rome in the city of the Puritans." Cheverus's real devotion, however, was to the unglamorous and often arduous work of his ministry. He not only served the small parish in Boston itself but also traveled regularly into the wilds of Maine and New Hampshire in search of scattered Catholics.

It was on his first such trip during that summer of 1797 that he met the Hanlys and their neighbors. They still thought of themselves as Catholics even though they sometimes attended the local Congregational meetinghouse (the only church in town) on Sundays. Cheverus discouraged that practice, said Mass for them in Roger's living room, heard their confessions, and baptized children and adults in the extended families. On departing for Portland, he left behind several prayer books, and when he got back to Boston, he wrote the family an affectionate letter, urging them to sustain their faith until his next visit. "Every day, say your prayers on your knees, morning and evening with attention and devotion," Cheverus advised. "Every Lord's day and Holy day" the Hanlys and nearby Catholics should gather in someone's home and conduct their own ad hoc worship. Someone should read the gospel assigned for the Mass that day, and other prayers should be recited in common. The children were to be quizzed on a catechism lesson and asked to recite a "paraphrase on the Lord's prayer, or some other prayers." These home services were not the same as attending Mass every week, of course, but they would have to do until "the next time that you will have a priest with you." How faithfully the Catholics of Bristol followed this weekly routine is unknown, though they were probably more regular than not, for they remained close to Cheverus until he returned home to France in 1823. One of the prayer books they used was handed down in the family and still survives.[1]

Today, the most striking thing about the Hanly family is this self-directed way they preserved their Catholic religion. Lacking sustained contact with the institutions of their church, they took on the task of maintaining their faith on their own. Necessity had made them independent—not autonomous, for they still very much wanted to be a part of their church. But circumstances prevented what would have otherwise defined them as Catholics: weekly Mass in a "dignified" church and other routine devotional practices. So they had to make do, holding onto their religious identity as best they could on their own, guided only in the most general way by a distant clergyman. This is what it was like to be an American Catholic in the priestless church.

The experience of the Hanlys was not unique. Across the country, the shortage of clergy was stark. In Maryland, according to a report to Rome in 1780, there were almost sixteen thousand Catholics (including three thousand slaves) but only nineteen priests; in Pennsylvania, there were seven thousand Catholics and five priests; in New York City, fifteen hundred Catholics and not a single priest. Worse, two of the priests in America were already over seventy years of age, and three more were approaching that biblical landmark of three score and ten: "thus," the report concluded, "they are incapable of sustaining the labor necessary for cultivating this vineyard of the Lord." It was easy to be pessimistic about it all. "The prospect before us is immense," wrote John Carroll, appointed in 1789 as the first Catholic bishop for the United States. "I receive applications from every part of the U. States, North, South & West, for Clergymen . . . but it is impos-

sible & cruel to abandon the Congregations already formed to go
in quest of people who wish to be established into new ones."
Carroll himself was constantly on the move. Based in Baltimore,
he had "a very large cong[regatio]n" in the city itself, he told an
English friend, but he had "often to ride 25 or 30 miles to the
sick." Beyond that, "I go once a month between 50 & sixty miles
to another cong[regatio]n in Virginia." One year, he spent the
entire months of April and May traveling up one side of the
Chesapeake Bay and down the other, "a very fatiguing service."[2]

With the institutions and personnel of the church so remote
most of the time, how did American Catholic lay people sustain
any meaningful sense of connection to their church? Many of
them did not. Some joined local Protestant churches, while others slipped off into the uncounted ranks of the "unchurched,"
a nicely succinct word. Many others stubbornly retained their
Catholic identity, however, and doing so required personal initiative. They relied on themselves as much as on a priest in the long
or short gaps between his visits. Priests still remained important to them; after all, these clergymen derived their powers
from God, Catholics believed, mediated through the authorita-
tive structures of the hierarchy. But there was no sense in merely
hoping for a priest if one was unlikely to turn up. In his absence,
lay people found that they had to do more on their own to nurture their faith. How they did so characterized this first age of the
church in America.

The experience of priests who traveled around to dispersed clus-
ters of remote Catholics was repeated in every part of the country.
Cheverus's visit with Roger Hanly and his family in 1797 fit the
pattern. The priest had gone up the coast from Boston, originally
looking for tribes of American Indians who had been converted
to Catholicism more than a century before by French missionar-

ies from Canada. These natives still thought of themselves as Catholics, even though it had been several generations since they had seen a priest. Protestant ministers would sometimes "pay them a visit in the hope of seducing them from the faith and of inocculating [sic] them with their various errors," a contemporary Catholic chronicler said. "Their invariable answer to them on these occasions was: 'We know our religion and cherish it; we know nothing of you or of yours.'" Cheverus spent several months in the native villages at Old Town (near Orono) and Pleasant Point (on Passamaquoddy Bay at the end of the coastline). He also sought out Irish immigrants and others in the seaport towns of Maine, New Hampshire, and Massachusetts. By comparison, the 120 Catholics who lived in Boston itself, his base of operations, seemed quite a crowd indeed. Even there, however, "it is probable there are more concealed & who, in consequence of intermarriages, long disuse and worldly motives, decline making an acknowledgement of profession of their faith."[3]

In South Carolina and Georgia a few years later, irregularity remained the best that most Catholics could hope for in the formal practice of their religion. One cleric rode a wide circuit. He arrived in Savannah from Charleston one January, for instance, and was told that the last time a priest had visited there was the previous October. As a result, he had a lot to do. He celebrated Mass every day, and the local Catholics took advantage of his presence to attend services that had otherwise been unavailable. Twelve people received Communion his first morning in town (a Saturday), twenty-seven the next day, and fifteen over the next two days. He spent hours hearing the parishioners' confessions, and he administered the sacrament of confirmation to fifteen. On the following Wednesday, he left Savannah aboard the four A.M. stage for Augusta, arriving two days later—"the first day very wet, the second excessively cold." There, the routine was the same: thirty Communions, almost fifty confirmations, uncounted numbers of confessions. Two days later, it was on to the town of Warrenton, then to Wilkes County, then to Locust Grove, before he finally retraced his steps slowly back to Charleston, where he arrived a full month after setting out. By that time, the priest explained, he was "so ill with Rheumatism in my left arm and shoulder and neck as to be unable to celebrate Mass."[4]

Priests in what were still the wilds of Pennsylvania were similarly itinerant. A Jesuit originally from Alsace came through in the spring of 1807, and he was particularly welcome because he could work with German-speaking Catholics. Starting from Philadelphia, he made his way through Haycock, Goshenhopen, and Reading, and from there to Lancaster and York. Turning south toward Frederick, Maryland, he found no German speakers and so pressed on to Washington, D.C., where there were some Germans living in Georgetown. A few years later, priests in central Pennsylvania were still on the road as much as they were at home. Father Patrick Leavy lived at a church in the town of Huntingdon, near Altoona, but he said Mass there only once a month. On the other Sundays he made several stops in regular rotation: one week at Lewistown, the next at Bellefonte, the next at Clearfield. His colleague Father Michael Dougherty had the same sort of routine, traveling between Gettysburg, Littlestown, Mountain Creek, and Conewago. But Father James Bradley probably took the prize for travels. He was able to say Mass twice a month in two different towns (Ebensberg and a village called simply "Hart's Sleeping Place" in Cambria County), but in those months when, given the way the calendar fell, there was a fifth Sunday, he traveled to yet another place, Cameron's Bottom in Indiana County. Catholics in this last place thus had the chance to attend Mass only about four times a year.[5]

Missionary priests farther west had even longer to go between stops. In the 1820s, a priest named John Timon, based south of St. Louis in Perry County, Missouri, regularly ventured into the surrounding countryside on both banks of the Mississippi. At Apple Creek in an area with a less attractive name ("The Barrens"), Timon said Mass in what he called "a pretty large hog pen." The locals had "dug out the dung, cleaned as well as possible the wretched cabin" nearby, and then "adorned it with green branches, built a rustic altar, which was for its beauty the wonder and admiration of the neighborhood." Timon's story of these rough-and-ready circumstances probably got better every time he told it, but he nonetheless took comfort in his success at reconnecting isolated Catholics with their church. At New Madrid, still farther down the river, he baptized six children and was then followed out of town on horseback by an old man who told him, "in accents that showed him to be an Irishman," that he and his wife were Catholics but had never been married by a priest. Timon went home with the man, married the two according to the rites of the church, and baptized their several children. Most traveling priests had similar experiences. One "blessed the marriage of two Roman Catholics who had been contracted to each other before a [civil] magistrate, and were living together in virtue thereof, this being the first opportunity which offered them of having their marriage celebrated according to the ritual of their church." Virtually no community was too small to attract the services of a missionary priest if he could get to it. Once, a southern priest detoured from a trip elsewhere through Georgia to visit St. Simon's Island off the coast because he had heard that as many as twelve Catholics might be living there.[6]

However occasional, the visits of these itinerant priests were important to lay people because, according to the tenets of their religion, there were certain things that only a priest could do for them. Church law and tradition had defined a sharp distinction between the clergy and the laity. Priests were empowered by the sacrament of ordination (officially known as "holy orders") to perform the central rites and ceremonies of the church. Only a priest could preside at Mass, for example; he alone could say the words of consecration that transformed the bread and wine of the Eucharist into the body and blood of Christ. Only a priest could hear the confessions of ordinary Catholics and forgive their sins in God's name. Catholics might legally marry before a civil official, as the couple in Missouri had done, but a priest was needed to bless the marriage in the eyes of the church. Protestant ministers, who also traveled widely throughout the hinterland, preaching to scattered communities and seeking converts from among the unchurched, might leave "lay preachers" behind as they moved on to their next stop, but priests were essential to proper Catholic practice.[7] It was for that reason that priests so actively sought out groups of Catholics, providing even infrequent connection to the church.

The life of a circuit-riding priest in America was hard, and the quality of the men who sought to work in the "vineyard" could vary considerably. John Carroll complained privately about the "medley of clerical characters" that lay people might encounter. On one occasion, he was distressed to learn that a certain missionary could not actually read or write and, worse, showed little interest in acquiring either skill. Most priests came from abroad, and some of these foreigners, dazzled by stories of wealth and opportunity in the United States, seemed more interested in advancing their own fortunes than in promoting the spiritual welfare of their people. A handful of priests who converted from Protestant churches seemed more intent on extended polemical campaigns against their former denominations, thereby distracting them from their real work.[8] Such men, however, were exceptions. Most priests were committed to their calling and endured significant adversity: theirs was far from an easy life. Still, their inadequate supply and their widely varying abilities made any sort of priestly domination of the church impossible in these years. What would later be identified as the problem of clericalism had little effect when there were so few clerics.

Tales of wandering priests who sought out "lost sheep" are usually told from the missionaries' perspective. They were the ones who recorded the accounts that have survived the intervening years, and these men are, understandably, the principal characters in their own stories. There were many examples of hardship and even nobility in the way they sought out tiny numbers of Catholics, unaided by the conveniences of modern transportation. Rheumatism was presumably not the most serious ailment to which they fell victim. But one wonders what happened to the Catholic lay people who remained behind in any given locality once the missionary had moved on to his next stop. After each visit, they knew that they might not see a priest again for a month or two—or six. What did they do that next Sunday, when they wanted to go to Mass but could not? "The week is spent in labour," a group of Catholics near Albany, New York, pointed out sadly, "but when Sunday comes it is not the day of prayer, no Priest attends, no church is opened, no bell tolls to summon them to the house of God." The dangers were real: "Is it any wonder then under such circumstances that the Catholic should become depraved, that he should spend in the haunts of dissipation the day that should be devoted to prayers, that he should . . . sink to the grave the premature victim of intemperance and folly?"[9] Catholics had to find a way to counteract those evil influences and to promote their own religious community.

One way of doing this was to build small chapels, even though they might not get much use during the fallow periods of priestlessness. This practice had been established in early Maryland, and it was copied elsewhere. In that colony, the number of chapels had grown from twenty-two in the 1720s to more than fifty by the time of the Revolution, and wealthy planters often endowed them in their wills. Lay people's willingness to donate sizable plots of land on which churches might be constructed, together with surrounding fields that could be farmed to provide income for their upkeep, was a measure of commitment. One settlement in Kentucky with less than twenty Catholic families acquired a site, built a "small, well furnished church," and even a little cabin for a priest to stay in when he came to town, though that was not often. In Georgia, the son of an original settler in a rural county donated a farm of 130 acres, inherited from his father, to help support a priest there and in the adjacent towns.

Some benefactions were more personal. In Newbern, North Carolina, Margaret Gaston, the widow of a hero of the Revolution in those parts and mother of a justice of the state's supreme court, "fitted up one of the rooms of her house as a little chapel," according to a contemporary report. Whenever a priest came through the area—years might pass between such visits—she opened her doors to her neighbors. The people may have used the chapel at other times, too, in the absence of a priest. Services there were not always successful. A priest from Ireland came through once, but since he spoke only Irish he was "not well qualified to give public instruction in English." The Catholic community in Newbern never grew very big, but the "calm, steady, persevering exertions of one good woman" were praised for a long time afterward.[10]

Although such pockets of Catholics might flourish, they might also disappear virtually overnight. John Carroll sadly noted a place in Maryland with the picturesque name of Bohemia Manor. This had once been a thriving Catholic settlement, and it had even had a school that he himself attended as a boy. By 1812, however, the place was in "a most deplorable condition." The chapel was still standing, but its windows were broken; swallows were roosting in its rafters, even above the altar, making use of the facility hazardous to those below. Mass was "scarce celebrated," and everything "appertaining to divine service" was in a "deplorable state. Vestments [were] neglected & altar linen scanty and ragged." The congregation had "dwindled to nothing," no more than a dozen people. Another missionary found similar decay in

South Carolina. Coming into the town of Newberry, he discovered that the few Catholics who remained were astonished to see him and did not know quite what to do. "The appearance of a clergyman of their own church amongst them," he said, "was as great a novelty to the catholics as to their fellow-citizens of other denominations." Try as he might, this priest was not optimistic that he could reverse their "unfortunate habit of negligence."[11]

To the scrupulous, habits of negligence were everywhere. Given the infrequency of their contact with a priest, early American Catholics did not always toe the church's line as closely as they might have. Wise missionaries applied church law leniently more often than not, and they were impatient with criticism on this score. "Are there not, my dear Sir," one priest wrote sharply to an English Jesuit who had relayed complaints about American laxity, "some on your side of the water . . . who, brooding over undigested scraps of theology, & never studying any degree of liberality to enlarge their minds, throw indiscriminate censure on every person departing ever so little from the rules of thinking & acting they have laid down for themselves?" In America, flexibility had to be the watchword and "excessive rigor" avoided. Carroll unilaterally decided, for example, to change the requirement mandating that Sunday Mass had to begin before noon, pushing back the last possible starting time for services to one in the afternoon. There had been a sensible enough reason for the original rule: at the time, Catholics (including the priest himself) who wanted to take Communion at Mass had to fast from all food and drink, even water, from midnight the night before. Waiting too long to break this fast not only risked health but also effectively reduced the number of communicants to almost zero, since only the single-minded could hold out that long. Conditions in largely priestless America, however, argued for bending the rule. When a priest arrived in a place on a Sunday morning, he often had to spend three or four hours hearing the accumulated confessions of the residents, Carroll noted. To cut them off without confession just so the liturgy could start on time was counterproductive at best. Many people "with great difficulty and inconvenience had come twenty or thirty miles and even further," and it made no sense to send them home spiritually empty.[12]

The rules on marriage demanded similar acknowledgment of the gap between the ideal and the actual. Few areas of church law were as complicated as this one, much of it devoted to regulating (and trying to discourage) marriage between Catholics and Protestants. This was less of a problem in Europe, where most young Catholics were likely to marry "one of their own." In America, however, "Catholics are so mixed with Protestants in all the intercourse of civil Society & business" that "no general prohibition can be enacted, without reducing many of the faithful to live in a state of celibacy, as in sundry places there would be no choice for them of Catholic matches." Moreover, the demand that Catholics marrying non-Catholics obtain church permission to do so beforehand was impossible to enforce in most cases. Few Catholics could consult a priest about the matter, simply because they never saw one. Carroll knew something of this problem from personal experience. One of his own kinsman, the son of his cousin, Charles Carroll of Carrollton (the only Catholic to have signed the Declaration of Independence), was involved in a complicated marriage case with a young Protestant woman from Philadelphia. Bishop Carroll traveled there, intending to perform the wedding, until he learned that the couple wanted to exchange vows before him one morning and then to be married again that evening "in a more ceremonious style" by an Episcopal clergyman. He refused to participate under such circumstances, and other family members backed him up, opening a permanent rift between the young groom and the rest of the clan.[13] The case highlighted what happened when church law met the realities of life in early Catholic America.

Personal devotional behavior among Catholics might likewise demand considerable leeway. "The necessities of Catholics in that country will justify a deviation from settled rules," one missionary was told in 1785 before setting out down the Ohio River from Pittsburgh to Louisville. Observance of Lent, for instance, the period of forty days immediately before Easter in the spring, had for centuries emphasized penitence and self-denial, and Catholics paid particular attention to dietary practices during those weeks. Some foods were prohibited, and Catholics were urged to limit their intake of all food and drink as a reminder of the sufferings of Jesus during his last days on earth. The normal expectation at the time was that Catholics would refrain from eating any meat at all during the whole of Lent, but this rule was eased in the 1790s to permit meat on five of the six Sundays of the period. Dinner at noontime was presumed to be the main meal of the day, and the amount consumed at the other "collations," morning and evening, was not supposed to exceed it in volume. In Europe, there might be precise measures for determining the size of the meal, but in America there was no general rule: in moderation, "fruit, sallads, vegetables, and fish" were acceptable. More generally throughout the year, the divine commandment to rest on the Sabbath might also have to be set aside as circumstances warranted. In the summer, for instance, when the crop was "on hand" and "urgent necessity" required hard labor to bring it in before it spoiled, Catholics could tend to business on Sunday without jeopardizing their spiritual welfare.[14]

While priests worried about how to reach far-flung Catholics, lay people devised their own means of staying connected to the church. Those who wanted to hold onto their religious identity found a number of ways to do so, ways their families had been practicing since they first came to British North America. Maryland had been founded under Catholic auspices in the 1630s as a venture of the Catholic Calvert family, but the colony's population had never been predominantly Catholic. No more than 10 percent of Marylanders were Catholics throughout the colonial period, though Catholicism claimed something approaching half the population of St. Mary's County, located on a peninsula on the western shore of the Chesapeake. Priests of the Jesuit order owned several farms in the county, and these men traveled to other parts of the colony when they could. For most Maryland Catholics, however, religious practice was based primarily in the home, usually in services they conducted themselves. This home worship replicated practices that lay Catholics in England had been accustomed to for some time. Since the Reformation, Catholics had been politically and religiously suspect in England, and the public practice of their faith had been prohibited by law, though these laws were unevenly enforced. Still, those who did not follow Henry VIII out of the Church of Rome into the Church of England worshiped in private. Mass could be said whenever a renegade priest was available, but Catholics also gathered on their own for pious reading and independent prayer. The manor house of a wealthy local Catholic became, in effect, the church of these parishioners, where they could attend to their religious duties away from public scrutiny.[15]

Catholic settlers in Maryland relied less on wealthy grandees and more on the ranks of small planters and middling sorts. People who lived near one of the Jesuit "plantations" might be able to attend Mass relatively often, while lay Catholics elsewhere took care that everything needed for the service was ready whenever a priest arrived in their vicinity. One planter in St. Mary's County bequeathed to the local chapel various "Church Stuff" (as the inventory of his estate described it) that he had been holding for safekeeping: three sets of liturgical vestments, a portable tabernacle to set up on a makeshift altar, and even a set of iron "bread cutters" for making Eucharistic hosts when needed. Catholics who lived where priests seldom visited, however, got into the habit of conducting their own informal worship. Family mem-

bers, servants, and slaves, along with nearby families, assembled
to recite prayers together; the children were instructed in the catechism by their mother or father. Such rites might be performed
"imperfectly," as Carroll would note, yet "notwithstanding all
these difficulties," some Catholics "were regular in their habits,
and at peace with all their neighbors." The Jesuits maintained informal lending libraries to put devotional texts into the hands of
those who wanted but could not afford them. Each Sunday's service might not last very long, but it was sufficient to reassure
the participants that they were doing their best to practice their
faith.[16]

The social cohesion that developed from this kind of self-suf-
ficient religious practice was real. The record books of one settlement paint a picture of a small group of Maryland Catholics who
held together in spite of the obstacles. St. Inigoes was an odd
name for an American place. It lay on the western edge of the
Chesapeake, and it had been named for the Basque founder of
the Jesuit order, Inigo (usually rendered into Latin as "Ignatius")
Loyola. By 1768, there were 162 names on the church roster there;
the next year, 97 more Catholics were also identified as living
nearby. Women outnumbered men (138 to 112, with 9 names
of indeterminate gender), and there were several interconnected
family groups: 3 distinct clans of Fenwicks, for instance. There
were also 33 slaves, 14 of whom were owned by the Jesuit priests,
who used the revenue from tobacco production to support missionary activity. The other slaves were distributed among owners
here and there: Ignatius Fenwick owned 5 and a woman identified only as "Mrs. Heard" owned 3, but most masters had just a
single slave. The community was stable, growing slowly. In the
two decades just before the American Revolution, there were 17
marriages and only 16 baptisms. Priests performed these rites
when they could, and the sacraments thus tended to cluster on
certain days. In early 1768, for instance, there was 1 baptism and 1

marriage on January 10 (a Sunday), 2 marriages nine days later (a Tuesday), and 3 baptisms on February 16 (also a Tuesday).[17] Parishioners did not have the luxury of choosing wedding or baptismal dates to suit their own convenience; they had to schedule these rites whenever a priest was available.

The population of the town expanded rapidly after independence, surpassing 400 by the century's end. Between 1786 and 1794, the annual number of baptisms in St. Inigoes rose from 33 to 47, and it had been as high as 86 in 1789. In each year, slaves constituted at least half of those baptized, the result of a concerted effort by the clergy to convert African Americans in bondage. Protestant ministers were particularly successful at slave conversions, but Catholic priests joined the effort, too. Wherever masters permitted evangelization of their chattel—some did not, thinking that conversion made slaves more likely to rebel or run away—slaves usually adopted the religion of the master, and so some of them in St. Inigoes and elsewhere became Catholics. Their conversions were seldom as complete as their white owners thought; in most cases African and Caribbean folk traditions survived and melded with Christian practices. Still, blacks were members of the St. Inigoes religious community no less than white farmers, and distinctions sometimes disappeared in the name of their common religion. Although it was rare, Catholic slaves might even serve as godparents to their masters' children. Robert and Elizabeth Jarboe—he had been active in the patriot cause during the Revolution—saw to it that all their slaves were baptized, for example, and they later asked one of them to serve as godmother to one of their own daughters. There were limits to Christian fellowship, of course. In that instance, the Jarboe daughter's name (Rachel) was recorded, while her slave godmother's name was not considered important enough to write down; she appears in the records only as "nig." The community also welcomed white converts who embraced Catholicism for a variety of reasons, with marriage to a Catholic spouse the most likely cause.[18]

In other times and places, small Catholic communities gathered in towns and cities. Boston had almost 300 Catholics by 1800, with close to 80 baptisms and a dozen marriages every year, a circumstance that a visitor described as "wonderful to tell." The Catholic population in New York was larger by then, already fed by immigration from foreign shores, and ethnic divisions among Catholics were beginning to appear. Two-thirds of those who eventually came together in 1785 to form Saint Peter's parish, at the lower tip of Manhattan, were Irish, but at least 15 percent of them were French speakers and another 5 percent were Germans. Inland at Cincinnati, the rapidly emerging "Queen City of the Ohio," the growth of Catholic communities was also impressive after an inauspicious start. The first missionaries found only about 150 Catholics in 1816, and five years later there were still just 11 who managed to receive Communion on Easter Sunday. Five years after that, however, the number of Catholics had jumped to more than 200, and the priests were hopeful for the future. Similar progress was evident in other parts of the state, too: Catholics in Canton and five nearby towns had grown rapidly from 20 to about 100 families in just a few short years.[19] By relying on a priest when they could and on themselves when they had to, lay Catholics found ways to maintain their connections to the church.

With time, Catholic communities grew sufficiently in size and resources to establish permanent parishes with resident clergy, but there were still too few priests to go around. Thus lay people often had to continue overseeing their own religious practice. Traditions of home and family worship persisted among American Catholics well into the nineteenth century. In response, church leaders prepared and distributed prayer books and devotional handbooks for the laity to use in shaping these informal services. In this way, a distinctive religious and devotional worldview took shape among the laity.

Longstanding English Catholic traditions once again provided the model, and the works of several writers were successfully transplanted to America. The three most popular were Richard Challoner (1691–1781), John Gother (died 1704), and Pacificus Baker (1695–1774). Bishop Challoner was based in London, where he published several volumes; his book *The Garden of the Soul* was probably the single most widely used collection of prayers, available for decades. Gother, who had converted from Protestantism, worked with Catholics in the English midlands, while Baker was a Franciscan friar. Just as their American priestly counterparts would later do, these three traveled the countryside, and they knew that there might be long gaps in lay religious practice. "It often happens," Challoner wrote, "that Christians thro' distance of place, indisposition or other unavoidable impediments, are hindered from being present at the great sacrifice of the mass, in which case it is proper they should endeavor to assist thereat, at least in spirit, which may be done with great fruit to their souls."[20] Prayer books helped organize private worship when there were no other options, and a number of them stayed in print in Britain before making the jump across the Atlantic. American editions began to appear in the 1770s and were popular among American Catholics thereafter.

To help lay people attend Mass "in spirit," the manuals were often structured around the unfolding pattern of the church year. From ancient times, Catholic worship had run in an annual cycle, beginning in late November or early December with the season of Advent. This was a time of looking forward to the coming (literally, the "advent") of Jesus at Christmas. The several weeks after that festival gave way in February to Lent, a penitential period beginning with Ash Wednesday, commemorating Jesus' suffering and climaxing with the celebration of his resurrection on Easter Sunday later in the spring. In a few weeks came Pentecost, often called "Whitsunday" because the newly baptized wore white robes on that day; this feast day marked the injunction Jesus had given his followers to spread his message, thereby earning it designation as the "birthday of the church." The summer and fall were "ordinary time," in which the Scripture readings at Mass retold the stories of the miracles and teachings of Jesus from the Gospels. As the calendar year approached its end, the church year too concluded and then started over again with another Advent. Moving steadily through the year thus gave Catholic practice an internal logic and a rhythm that lay people could feel, even if they could not always explain it fully.

Challoner and the others assembled devotions to keep readers abreast of this annual cycle. Lay people could gather on their own to observe the second Sunday in Lent (for example), even if they could not get to church on that day. Celebrating together connected them, at least imaginatively, to other Catholics around the world. Each Sunday in Gother's *Prayers for Sundays & Festivals, Adapted to the Use of Private Families and Congregations* began with a citation to the day's gospel; Gother did not reproduce the gospel itself, apparently assuming that users of his manual would also own a Bible and could locate the passage on their own. Then he included a short explanatory paragraph, highlighting themes in the gospel or explaining parts of it that were difficult to understand. Next came anywhere from half a dozen to twenty-five short prayers. Small gatherings of families and neighbors could say as many or as few of these as they wanted. Each prayer was to be read aloud by "the head of the family" or anyone else "who reads freely and distinctly," presumably including (though Gother did not say so explicitly) a woman. Then came a short response to each prayer that all were expected to recite.

Baker took Gother's model further, eventually producing three separate volumes to cover the church year, including the full gospel text for each week, "reflections" to be read aloud, and some short "aspirations" to be recited. For the especially fervent, he also included services for every Wednesday and Friday of the year, every day during Lent, and a number of spiritual "entertainments" for Christmas week. Each Sunday's devotion was designed to last about three-quarters of an hour—"not too much for so important a purpose," Gother thought. Not coincidentally, this was roughly the amount of time a Mass would have taken, had the group been able to attend one.[21]

If Catholics had been at an actual Mass, however, they would also have had the chance to receive the Eucharist. In its absence, these prayer books highlighted the virtues of "spiritual communion." A prayer in one of them said, "Make me partaker of that grace which they are sensible of who devoutly and worthily receive thee." As a general rule, Baker recommended monthly Communion, but when priests were absent this was simply not possible. Traveling missionaries never left behind a supply of consecrated Communion bread for lay people to use after they had moved on. The bread had been transformed into the actual body of Christ, Catholics believed, and leaving it unattended invited desecration. Accordingly, the authors of prayer books devised spiritual substitutes for the laity to perform on their own. Baker, for example, provided three days of prayers to be said before receiving Communion and three afterward—it was a rare enough event that essentially dedicating an entire week to reflecting on it did not seem excessive—and such meditations could be adapted when one was receiving the sacrament only spiritually.[22]

Confessing their sins was also something that lay people could do only with a priest, so without one they had to approximate the practice on their own. Virtually every prayer book offered what was called an examination of conscience, in which sinners could review their wrongful thoughts and actions, feel contrite, and ask God's forgiveness. This "examen" usually approached the task systematically by reviewing the Ten Commandments, the "Commandments of the Church" (including such things as fasting on the required days), and the traditional "deadly" sins, such as gluttony, pride, lust, and sloth. When a priest was available, penitents used these forms to prepare themselves to talk with him in confession, but when he was not, they could still derive spiritual benefit from the exercise. A devotional manual published in Philadelphia in 1774 included a "form of confession" in which Catholics privately took responsibility for their "divers ways" of offending God. They did so by reciting a mental list, beginning each item with the phrase "I accuse myself": of not exercising charity toward their neighbors, of not putting evil thoughts out of mind, and so on. After each offense had been specified, the penitent concluded with the simple statement, "I ask God pardon for it." These exercises were not as good as sacramental confession before a priest, of course, and that is why missionaries heard so many confessions in every town they visited. It also explains why priests sometimes heard confessions in unusual places. One lay man confessed to a circuit-rider in Missouri as the two rode along on horseback to visit the penitent's sick wife.[23] As with spiritual Communion, spiritual confession served as an alternative when nothing else was possible.

Prayer books also helped American Catholics pass the faith on to their children. So irregular was any kind of official religious instruction that church leaders devoted considerable energy to preparing catechisms, which used a simple question-and-answer format. Some of these lesson books were "historical" in their approach, presenting the doctrines of the church on topics arranged chronologically from the creation of the world to the present. More common were catechisms like the one John Carroll first published in 1793, which went through fifteen editions in the

next five years. It began with fundamental matters: "Q. Who
made you? A. God. Q. Why did God make you? A. That I might
know him, love him, and serve him in this world, and be happy
with him forever in the next." It then moved through the arti-
cles of the creed, the sacraments, "the virtues, and vices, &c."
Studying the catechism became a regular part of family religious
practice. One priest urged parents to give children a weekly as-
signment. To be sure they had absorbed the lesson, they were to
"write by heart, every Sunday," the answers to several designated
questions. Much of this content would have been familiar to any
Christian, but distinctively Catholic doctrines got special emphasis, thereby distinguishing Catholics from their Protestant neighbors. That the true "body and blood of Christ" were present in
the Eucharist was affirmed, for instance, an explicit contrast to
the teaching of other Christian denominations, which emphasized the symbolic nature of the sacrament.[24]

The mere existence of prayer books and catechisms does not,
of course, tell us how widely they were used. For that, we must
look to other evidence, much of it admittedly circumstantial.
Cheverus's letters to the Hanly family in Maine seem characteris-
tic, and though only his side of the correspondence survives, it is
clear that the small congregation consistently followed his advice. In one letter, Cheverus acknowledged the core group: "your
son Roger, his dear wife & children, your respectable Sister [in-
law] Mrs. Hanly & family, old Mr. & Mrs. McGuire, Capt.
Aikins & his family." In another, he was pleased to hear that a
child was ready for her First Communion, even though Cheverus
doubted that he could visit her for that purpose for another several months. Small communities of Catholics often selected someone to take the lead during those periods when a priest was not
present, and sometimes missionaries designated a specific person
to conduct services between visits. In the 1820s, John Dillon of
Savannah, Georgia (of whom nothing else is known), was ap-

pointed "to read the prayers for Mass on Sundays" until a priest next visited the area. In another place, a missionary noted that a group regularly "prayed together on the Sundays and Holidays, until the sickly season, when they fell off." In this way, lay Catholics tried to follow Challoner's suggestion that they gather together and attend Mass "in spirit."[25]

The wide distribution of devotional manuals also testifies to their use. What scholars have come to call a "print culture," grounded in printing and distribution networks, supported the religious practice of Catholic lay people in the priestless age. At first, volumes printed in England and Ireland made their way to America: the Hanly family owned at least one prayer book that had been published in Dublin. Printers specializing in Catholic titles also opened for business in the United States almost immediately after independence, and the market for their output was big enough to keep them at it. Bernard Dornin, for example, an Irish immigrant, set up print shops in New York, Philadelphia, and Baltimore shortly after 1800. The printing business was always a dicey one—it required heavy capital outlay at the beginning and depended on highly skilled labor—but he produced a range of titles to satisfy the growing demand. In South Carolina by the 1820s, a printer named James Haly was publishing titles of his own and, like most other printers of the era, selling the work of others in his shop. Prices were set to appeal to a broad market. One catechism sold for fifty cents, for instance, and several of Challoner's thick volumes were similarly priced at less than a dollar.[26]

By far the most successful publisher of American Catholic texts was Mathew Carey of Philadelphia. Born in Dublin, Carey had been caught up as a young man in Irish nationalist politics before fleeing to America just after the Revolution. Having picked up the printer's trade—a childhood accident had left him lame and unsuited for more strenuous labor—he set up shop and produced a steady output in spite of persistent economic troubles. "I have owed for months together from 3 to $6000, borrowed from day to day," he recalled in old age, "and sometimes in the morning to be paid at 1 o'clock the same day, to meet checks issued the preceding day." In 1790 he published the first American edition of the Douay-Rheims Bible, a translation by English priests working in France. Catholics preferred this English translation, which differed in many respects from the King James Version favored by most Protestants. Producing a Bible was a major undertaking for any printer. It was obviously a big book, requiring lots of type and other supplies, and the opportunity for errors to creep into the text was virtually unlimited. (One early Bible in England had accidentally left out the crucial word "not" in the commandment pertaining to adultery, thereby changing its meaning significantly.) Still, the Carey edition was a success and spurred publication of other Catholic Bibles. These were expensive, between five and ten dollars each, but there was sufficient demand that Catholics soon joined Protestants in contributing to what one scholar has called an "American Bible Flood."[27]

Carey was a shrewd enough businessman not to pin all his hopes on the Bible, and the range of other titles he produced for a Catholic readership is a measure of the growing size and stability of that market. By 1792 he was producing his own editions of Challoner and other writers, together with such traditional Catholic favorites as *The Imitation of Christ* and half a dozen different catechisms. His business sense was sharper still. Although an active Catholic throughout his life, he also produced volumes for other denominations: sermons by Protestant clergymen, the allegorical classics (including *Pilgrim's Progress*) of the Puritan John Bunyan, and prayer books for the just-formed Protestant Episcopal Church in the United States. Nor was religion his only focus. His catalogs always began with law books—*Cooke's Compendious System of the Bankruptcy Laws* presumably had steady sales—and included medical books (*Hamilton's Treatise of Midwifery, for Female Practitioners*), adventure tales (*Bruce's Travels to Discover the Source of the Nile*), and novels (*Gulliver's Travels* and the several imitators it inspired). He also printed school books, valuable for their annual repeat sales, and even sold stationery supplies such as ink, pencils, and blank account books.[28] Without such diversification, he probably could not have afforded to meet the demand for Catholic books; with it, he could supply texts for American Catholics to support their faith in the age of the priestless church.

The spirituality that these devotional manuals promoted among lay people differed in important respects from the religious approaches that would be popular with later American Catholics. These volumes expressed an "Enlightenment spirituality," emphasizing the reasonableness of belief and the fundamental harmony between human desires and divine intentions. Like their Protestant counterparts, Catholic clergymen in America were squarely in what was called the "evidential," Baconian tradition of theology. They were confident that the rational mind could lead one to the truths of divine revelation, and they conveyed this tradition to lay people. Moreover, God was not a God of wrath who punished according to his own exacting but ultimately inscrutable standards. Examinations of conscience encouraged Catholics to reflect on their sins, but this process was neither morbid nor an end in itself. Rather, it was a way to move Catholics beyond their own inadequacies to a realization of God's love and forgiveness, particularly as expressed through the person of Jesus. Religious fervor was marked less by extravagant outward displays than by internal commitment, an effort to "transfuse into our hearts," some of John Carroll's sermon notes said, "the sentiments and affections of J. Christ." The real work of religion was done in the heart and mind of the believer, and it was work that all Catholics could successfully undertake.[29]

Almost no lay people left a record of how they internalized this sort of religious outlook. One who did must be allowed to speak for his fellow Catholics. Charles Carroll of Carrollton was no ordinary lay man. One of the richest men in America by the time he signed on to the Revolution, he was descended from an old Maryland family that included John Carroll, whom he knew as his cousin "Jacky." As a young man of twenty-one, studying in Europe, Charles wrote a letter home to his father. Discussion of religion was rare between the two, and perhaps for that reason, the son's spiritual sentiments were concisely expressed. "I dont aim nor ever did at canonization," he wrote in 1759. "I detest scrued up devotion, distorted fa[c]es, & grimace[s]. I equally abhor those, who laugh at all devotion, look upon our religion as a fiction, & its holy misteries as the greatest absurdities. I observe my religious duties, I trust in the mercy of God not my own merits, which are none, & hope he will pardon my daily offences. I retain as yet that salutary fear of his Justice which by the wisest of men is stiled initium sapientiae [that is, the beginning of wisdom]." Here was a religion neither of extreme emotions—the screwed up faces and grimaces of enthusiastic revivals held little appeal—nor of so bloodless a rationalism that God disappeared altogether and faith became mere fiction. The young man had his devotional obligations, and he attended to them faithfully, without thinking that they qualified him for sainthood. He was conscious of his own shortcomings without dwelling on them, and he sought to achieve "a good conscience & a virtuous life," which together were "the greatest blessings we can enjoy on earth."[30]

This kind of spirituality was encouraged by the prayers and devotions of the popular manuals. *Practical Reflections for Every Day Throughout the Year,* an English Catholic staple that appeared in an American edition in 1808, urged meditation on "the dignity of a Christian" in "serving God," which was the most noble "end of Man." A *Manual of Catholic Prayers* offered several "little offices," collections of psalms to be said at various times during the day, consciously modeled on the "hours" chanted in monasteries. These prayers stressed an intimate connection between believers and God. Jesus was the mediator between them, and the focus of prayer was almost always on him. Devotion to his "Holy Name" was the theme of several sets of prayers, for example, and this manual also devoted more than fifty of its three hundred pages to the "Jesus Psalter," a now largely forgotten devotion consisting of a cycle of prayers patterned after the Psalms of David in the Hebrew Bible. The *Catholic Christian's Daily Companion,* one of the texts used in family worship by the Hanlys in Maine, had a long "Litany of Our Lord and Saviour": in it, participants responded with the phrase "Have mercy on us" to the invocation of Jesus' name under his various titles (King of Glory, Good Shepherd, Sun of Justice), his attributes (most powerful, most patient, most obedient), and for delivery from every kind of danger (from all evil, from all sin, from everlasting death). Although focused on the divine, these manuals also connected Catholics to the world of the here and now and included prayers that might be said "according to the diversity of times and occasions": for rain, for women in childbirth, for safety on a journey, and for other immediate needs.[31]

Also noteworthy are the prayers that are absent from these devotional manuals. Religious emphases that would become significant in subsequent ages of Catholicism in America were conspicuous by their relative unimportance in this early period. Prayer to the saints, for example, got comparatively little attention. Many prayer books did include litanies to saints—repeated requests for prayers from named saints—but these often seem to be afterthoughts. One thick American prayer book contained a mere nine pages of saints' litanies, for example, and these were near the back, lost among other practices. In the same way, devotion to Mary, the mother of Jesus, was less important than it would later be. Instructions for saying the rosary, a devotion that consisted of repeating prayers to Mary with the assistance of a string of beads, were usually included, but this devotion was seen as a way of focusing mental attention on Jesus himself rather than on his mother. "Why say you the Hail Mary?" Carroll's catechism asked, and the answer was: "To put us in mind of the Son of God being made man for us"; only secondarily was this prayer a way "to honour the blessed virgin." Most manuals included a prayer to an individual's guardian angel—who in popular (though never official) Catholic belief was thought to be assigned to every person as a special protector—but such a prayer was simply one among many in morning or evening devotions that covered other spiritual matters.[32] All prayer and spirituality can sometimes seem undifferentiated, but a closer examination of the religious outlook of early Catholic lay people shows it to have been different from that of later ages of the church's history.

To no small extent, these religious emphases derived from the sense that early American Catholics had of themselves as Americans. The end of the eighteenth century was a heady time, for a brand-new nation was coming into being. Together with their fellow citizens, Catholics in the United States were engaged in determining just what it meant to be an American. No longer colonists, no longer part of the larger British nation, they were something new. In that context, Catholics in particular had to define themselves in relation to their larger political and social surroundings. What would it mean to be both Catholic and American? What treatment could they expect from, and how would they interact with, other Americans who did not share their beliefs?

Those tasks were daunting, given the tradition of suspicion toward Catholics. Most of the English settlers who had planted colonies in North America had brought with them a deeply ingrained hostility toward the Roman Church. Its most virulent form was evident in Massachusetts, whose Puritan founders thought the Church of England insufficiently purged of "popery." To keep any such influences from corrupting their own godliness, the Massachusetts General Court went so far as to pass an "anti-priest" law in 1647. "No Jesuit or ecclesiastical person ordained by the authority of the pope shall henceforth come within our jurisdiction," the law declared. Anyone suspected of being a Catholic priest was to be apprehended. "If he cannot free himself of such suspicion," he was to be banished from the colony; if he came back, he was to be put to death. Fifty years later, a second statute declared that any priest was by definition "an incendiary and disturber of the publick peace and safety, and an enemy to the true Christian religion." No priest ever tested these laws, so we cannot know whether the colony would actually have carried out the death sentence. It very well may have: four Quakers who challenged a similar statute barring them from Massachusetts were hanged on Boston Common. The first Mass would not be said in Boston until the 1770s, but by then the priest who did so was more welcome, since he was the chaplain aboard a French warship, there to assist in the revolt against Britain.[33] Still, the earlier laws show how hard American Catholics might have to work to overcome the hostility of their neighbors.

The situation in Maryland was not quite as stark. The colony had begun with a commitment to toleration for all Christians. "Noe person or persons whatsoever within this Province," a law passed in 1649 said, "professing to believe in Jesus Christ, shall from henceforth bee any waies troubled, molested, or discountenanced for or in respect of his or her religion nor in the free exercise thereof." The Catholic Calvert family lost political control of the colony, however, and this open-minded attitude was replaced by a more familiar English anti-Romanism. By 1700 the settlement's governor was denouncing the "gawdy shows and serpentine policy" of Catholics—the former a derision of the Mass, the latter a reference to the supposed political intrigues of priests. The governor could not simply hound Catholics out of the colony, as the leaders of Massachusetts had hoped to do; there were just too many of them. He could, however, restrict their influence. The Church of England became the established church in Maryland, supported by the taxes of all residents, regardless of their religious affiliation. By the time the Calverts regained jurisdiction over the enterprise in 1715, they themselves had converted to Protestantism.[34]

Rhode Island alone among the American colonies embraced a broader view of religious toleration that included Catholics. There were virtually no Catholics in the tiny settlement until after the Revolution, but the principle of official neutrality toward religion set a precedent that would eventually gain wide acceptance. No Rhode Islanders, the colony's charter of 1663 had said, would be "punished, disquieted, or called in question, for any differences of opinion in matters of religion," so long as they did not "actually disturb the civil peace" or contribute to the "outward disturbance of others." The colony's leaders were willing to overlook differences of "opinion" about religion, but they were less keen on the idea of competing forms of actual religious practice. These, they thought, would almost inevitably disturb the harmony of the community. As a result, few Catholic settlers were attracted there, and, as in Massachusetts, the Mass was not said publicly until the Revolution, when a French chaplain presided at the funeral of the captain of his ship, anchored off Newport.[35]

Rhode Island's singular willingness to accept religious pluralism took on a new life with the American fight for independence, and the idea was transformed into a distinctively American approach to the role of churches in the community. The implications for Catholics were profound. Virginia took the lead, prompted by Thomas Jefferson, whose own lack of interest in organized religion made him an unlikely champion. He drafted a statute of religious freedom that the state's General Assembly finally adopted in 1786. All attempts by the civil government to coerce citizens into certain religious beliefs or to force them to support particular churches were "sinful and tyrannical," the statute declared. To deny certain civil rights, such as voting or office holding, on the basis of religious affiliation was mere "hypocrisy and meanness," a product of "impious presumption." Accordingly, "no man shall be compelled to frequent or support any religious worship, place, or ministry whatsoever . . . nor shall otherwise suffer on account of his religious opinions or belief." All citizens were "free to profess, and by argument to maintain, their opinion."[36]

Neutrality toward religion was a radical notion not immediately accepted beyond the borders of the Old Dominion. John Jay, later chief justice of the U.S. Supreme Court, had drafted a provision for the New York state constitution that expressly excluded "the professors of the religion of the Church of Rome" from voting and even from owning land in the state until they swore in court that they had renounced the authority of the pope. Jay's harsh proposal was narrowly defeated, though the New York legislators passed a nonbinding resolution decrying "that spiritual aggression and intolerance wherewith the bigotry and ambition of weak and wicked priests" had worked their mischief. Even so, the trend toward religious toleration proved irresistible and was enshrined finally in the First Amendment to the United States Constitution in 1791. Its provisions barred any law "respecting an establishment of religion, or prohibiting the free exercise thereof." Rejecting a religious "establishment" meant that no church could be declared the official church of the nation, though (as many commentators have pointed out) this left in place the laws of individual states, such as Massachusetts and Connecticut, which still provided public support for Protestant churches. Still, the new principle sounded the death knell for state churches, and all American jurisdictions with religious establishments abolished them by the 1830s. Just as important, the First Amendment's guarantee of "free exercise" meant that citizens could join any church they wanted or none at all. Now, those who had once been "disturbers of the publick peace" were able to practice their faith as full citizens.[37]

For American Catholics, this end to legal "discountenancing" coincided with a broader rapprochement with their Protestant neighbors. Even wary observers like John Adams came to the conclusion that Catholics could indeed be part of the American community. It had not always been so. In 1774, while serving as a delegate to the First Continental Congress, Adams had regaled his wife, Abigail, with a description of a Catholic Mass he attended, prompted solely by "Curiosity and good Company." The "poor wretches" in the congregation in Philadelphia were pitiful, the crusty Adams thought, "fingering their Beads [and] chanting Latin, not a Word of which they understood." Their "Pater Nosters and Ave Marias; Their holy Water; their Crossing themselves perpetually . . . their Bowings, and Kneelings, and Genuflections" provided a very curious "Entertainment," leading him to wonder "how Luther ever broke the spell." A quarter-century later, Adams had mellowed. Enthusiasm for the Revolution on the part of Catholics in Maryland and Pennsylvania had been welcome, and support from the Catholic king of France suggested the wisdom of overlooking religious practices, however superstitious he might find them. In 1802 the by-then former president contributed $100 (the largest amount from any donor) to construct a Catholic church in Boston.[38] Perhaps, Adams concluded, Catholics might not be so bad or so dangerous after all.

For their part, Catholics embraced the notion that a citizen's religion was a matter of legal indifference. Charles Carroll, for instance, who had been with Adams at the Congress in Philadelphia, had expressed the wish that "the unhappy differences & disputes on speculative points of Theology had been confined to divines," far removed from politics and government. "The savage wars & cruel Massacres, the deliberate murders committed by law, under the sanction of Religion have not reformed the morals of men," he maintained, but had rather "answered the purposes of ambition." Nor did he exempt his own church from criticism on this score. "I execrate the intollerating [sic] spirit of the Church of Rome," he said bluntly, adding, "and the other Churches—for she is not singular in that." Excluding some people from the political community because of their religious beliefs seemed to him at best a matter for sarcasm. "If my countrymen judge me incapable of serving them in a public station for believing the moon to be made of green cheese," he had told a British friend, "their conduct (if not wicked) is not less absurd than my belief." Better to allow "an unlimited toleration" in which "men of all sects were to converse freely with each other."[39]

The population of Catholics in the new nation remained small, and this, too, no doubt eased acceptance by their fellow citizens. Precise figures are hard to come by, but the general belief is that Catholics in the United States numbered at most 40,000 in 1790, less than 1 percent of the total population counted that year by the first federal census. Even by 1830, the Catholic share of the population still hovered at just over 2 percent.[40] The dramatic increase of their numbers that came with massive immigration was still in the future. The few Catholics scattered here and there across the landscape represented little challenge to the hegemony of American Protestant churches. At the same time, the social standing of many lay Catholic leaders, the extended Carroll clan foremost among them, seemed proof that adherents of the Roman Church were not so different after all. Émigré priests also underlined this sense of commonality. John Adams could converse in French with Boston's Father Cheverus: just how bad could such a refined and well-educated gentleman be? Toleration of Catholics in America had once seemed unlikely at best. By the time the Church of Rome began to grow at the end of the eighteenth century, the persistence of Catholics in America could be taken for granted.

The steadily declining fortunes of the papacy also helped reduce tensions between Catholics and other Americans. Since the Reformation, no figure had been the focus of more controversy among Christians than the bishop of Rome. For Catholics, he was at the top of the hierarchical pyramid, the leader of the church worldwide to whom they were, at least in theory, loyal and obedient. Protestant polemic had long made much of their supposed subservience to the pontiff. On meeting him, Catholics were supposed to abase themselves by kissing his toe, one old canard had it. In fact, for most American Catholics until well into the nineteenth century, the pope was a distant figure, largely irrelevant to their own faith and its practice. At any given time, most lay Catholics could probably have named the pope, but few were likely to know much about him. It was surely important to them that there was a pope: the institution of the papacy and the historical continuity it offered gave them a link back through time to Saint Peter and thus to Jesus himself. But the practical impact that any pope had on their faith or their struggle to maintain it was negligible.

In this regard, Americans were not unlike Catholics worldwide, for these centuries were hard times for the popes, then in the middle of a long slide of declining influence. The papacy was adrift in the treacherous currents of international power politics, whose real forces were controlled by the absolute monarchs of Europe. These rulers were constantly maneuvering around one another for advantage on the Continent itself and in their expanding overseas empires. The pope was a king, too, ruling the sovereign nation that was the Papal States, a swath of central Italy whose precise borders changed frequently. But he was only a minor player in geopolitical games, unable to command the resources or the armies the other monarchs had, and thus he was often at their mercy. France's infinitely cynical Cardinal Richelieu, the chief minister to Louis XIV, had summed it all up succinctly. "We must kiss the pope's feet," he was reported to have said, "and bind his hands." More often than not, that was precisely the position in which the pontiff found himself.[41]

Popes were similarly weak within the church, unable to exercise much direct control over institutions or personnel. In most countries, local bishops were chosen by the king, with the pope merely confirming selections once they were made. In France beginning in the seventeenth century, the king appointed all bishops and took the revenues of their dioceses after they died, often delaying choice of a successor so as to increase the profit to the state. In Spain in the 1750s, the king appointed more than twelve thousand Catholics to church positions, from bishoprics to local parish churches; the pope was responsible for exactly fifty-two. Most telling of all, the national monarchs had veto power over selection of the pope himself, and they let it be known to the cardinals who assembled to elect a new pope that certain candidates were unacceptable. As a result, nearly every papal election dragged on, leaving the office vacant until a compliant candidate could be identified. In 1669 and again in 1775, the papal conclave had lasted four months; in 1740, it had taken six months. Popes thus had to get used to the idea that they would be routinely pushed around by more powerful forces, sometimes literally: one pope had tried abruptly to end an unpleasant interview with the French ambassador (himself a cardinal), but the diplomat shoved him back into his chair until he had finished.[42]

Popes wanted to emphasize their spiritual role within the

church, but this too had limits. Their authority was likely to be understood in symbolic or ceremonial terms, largely without practical implications. The idea that the pope was "the universal administrator" of the church, John Carroll wrote to another priest, was absurd, one of "those claims which Rome has always kept up, tho' universally disregarded." Instead, he said on another occasion, "Clergy & Laity here know that the only connexion they ought to have with Rome is to acknowledge the pope as the Spir[itua]l head of the Church." For Carroll, "the Extent and Boundaries of the Spiritual Jurisdiction of the Holy See" were narrowly drawn. The expansive powers that Protestants accused Catholics of asserting—that the pope was infallible, for instance—were specifically rejected. In Boston in 1800, Father Cheverus wrote an open letter to a newspaper, expressly stating that "to believe the Pope infallible is no part of our Creed, & no Roman Catholick ever pretended that he is." (At the time this was a correct statement, and it would remain so until 1870, when papal infallibility was defined as church dogma at the First Vatican Council.) None of this meant that the pope's spiritual supremacy was meaningless. As "the center of Ecclesiastical unity," he helped maintain the consistency of Catholic religious practices. Carroll had long hoped, for example, that the Mass could be celebrated in English rather than in Latin, but he did not think that he had the power to mandate this change unilaterally unless authorized by "the Holy See & first Pastors of the Church."[43]

Still, Carroll thought that the role of the pope ought to be strictly limited. In particular, he was wary of a department in the church's Roman bureaucracy known as the Congregation de Propaganda Fide (literally, "for the spreading of the faith"), a name usually clipped to "the Propaganda." This office had been established in the 1560s to coordinate missionary work in the Far East and in the New World. Many of the first priests in America had

come under its auspices. As time went on, however, Carroll believed that this Roman agency should leave the American church
to run its own affairs. What troubled him most was that the Propaganda was a "foreign jurisdiction"—the phrase appears repeatedly in his correspondence—essentially a cabinet department of
the Papal States. As such, he thought, it would never be acceptable to citizens of the United States, Catholic or non-Catholic—
nor should it be. Had they not just fought a revolution to free
themselves from supervision by the British Colonial Office? How
could they now submit to a comparable agency of another foreign government? "The dependence of the R[oman] Cath[olics]
of this country on any foreign tribunal or office," Carroll wrote
to a fellow priest, "will not be tolerated." A "subjection to His
Holiness incompatible with the independence of a sovereign state"
was unacceptable. In private he could be waspish, expressing dismay that church bureaucrats in Rome, though "men whose institution was for the service of Religion," were actually inclined to
"bend their thoughts so much more to the grasping of power."[44]

For the rest of his life, Carroll continued to resist (though not
always successfully) Propaganda's efforts to assert its influence. In
the meantime, however, the French Revolution of 1789 and the
twenty-five years of turmoil following it only further eroded the
power of the papacy. Now buffeted even more by forces over
which they had no control, popes devoted their attention to the
very survival of their office. Pius VI, elected in 1775, ended his
days ignominiously as Napoleon's captive in the century's last
year. The emperor dragged the poor man across the Alps toward
Paris; when the dying pontiff pleaded to be allowed to return to
Rome for his final days, the French general in charge sneered, "A
man may die anywhere." Nine months passed before a sufficient
number of cardinals could be assembled to choose a new pope,
and their deliberations then stalled for another three months
before a successor was finally elected. The lessons of these events

were not lost on Catholics worldwide. A decade later, John Carroll was still noting that regular communication with Rome was "well nigh impossible." In 1808 a new bishop was appointed to lead the Catholics of New York, but the designee, an Irishman named Concanen, was stranded in Rome, unable to secure passage across the Atlantic. He died before ever making his way to America. In such circumstances, local churches around the world seemed better advised to look after their own interests.[45]

With the papacy so weakened, lay Catholics in America grounded their faith and practice in other ways. If theirs was a largely priestless church, it was also effectively a popeless church. Popes usually went unmentioned in Catholic prayer and preaching. In a catechism published in 1793, the pope merited precisely 1 of the 250 questions in its closely packed pages. The church consisted of "all the faithful under one head," the catechism said, and that head was unambiguously "Christ Jesus our Lord." Only then did the catechism ask, "Has the church any visible head on earth?" and the reply was, "Yes; the Bishop of Rome, who is the Successor of St. Peter, and commonly called the Pope." That was all the attention the pontiff got. In the same way, none of the popular prayer books mentioned the pope at all: the word did not even appear in their texts. It would have been idolatrous, of course, for anyone to think of praying *to* the pope: that had never been done. But ordinary Catholics were not even encouraged to pray *with* him for common concerns or, perhaps more to the point, *for* him in his troubles. No spiritual indulgences or benefits, sanctioned by the papacy and attached to the recitation of certain prayers, were enumerated, as they would be in later prayer books. None of the notable popes of history were called back from the past as exemplars to be followed or even, apparently, remembered.[46] The attachment of American Catholics to the pope would become more robust in subsequent generations, but for the laity in the priestless age, that relationship was a tenuous one.

In this way as in so many others, early American Catholic lay people were very different from those who would come after them. The institutional presence of their church was always thin and uncertain. Priests and parishes were few in number and widely scattered. Catholics' connection to their church was less than they might have thought ideal. An unknowable number of Catholics no doubt gave up the struggle and joined other denominations or abandoned religious practice altogether. Those who stayed, however, found that they could still be Catholics in the absence of regular contact with the official church. By assuming a greater measure of responsibility for their own faith, sustaining it through private worship with family and neighbors, they were able to retain their religious identity and to hand it on to their children until such time as the church caught up with them.

That would begin to happen in the next age of the church in America, but there would be new concerns. Since its foundation in ancient times, Catholicism had survived in empires and monarchies; it had shown its compatibility with aristocratic societies, in which some people were presumed to be better than others. The church had not yet shown that it could flourish in a society that rejected those hierarchical principles and presumed instead an equality among citizens. Could it flourish in a country founded on the idea that the people had the right, given them directly by God, to form their own government and to have charge of their own affairs? America would be the place where the Catholic Church would have to learn to live in a democratic republic.

2

The Church in the Democratic Republic

Doctor James C. McDonald was one of the most prominent men in Beaufort, South Carolina. This was rice country, and the doctor (whose name was spelled variously McDonnald, McDonnell) found his medical skills in great demand among the planters and their slaves, who were probably the most harshly treated of all those in bondage in the American South. McDonald was also a Catholic, but like Roger Hanly a generation before him, he saw a priest only rarely. At best, a pastor from Charleston made the trip down the coast four times a year, giving "due notice" beforehand so that McDonald and his Catholic neighbors could be ready for him. Beaufort would not have its own resident priest for another seventy years, but the general prospects for Catholicism were beginning to look up in the early 1820s, when McDonald was summoned to an unusual meeting of Catholics from across South Carolina.

On its face, the Catholic Church seemed a necessarily monarchical institution. It had a well-defined hierarchy, with a pope at the top of the pyramid and then bishops and clergy, comparable perhaps to an aristocracy, in a clear chain of command beneath him. But the bishop in charge of South Carolina, who was based in Charleston, wanted to conform the church's structure to what he saw as the genius of the American political system, and so he had drafted a constitution for his diocese. Under its provisions, the spiritual affairs of the church would always remain the purview of the clergy, but lay people would have their own role in managing such practical affairs as fundraising and building new churches. To ensure cooperation between priests and people, the constitution provided for an annual meeting, or "convention," run essentially like a bicameral legislature. All priests sat in a house of the clergy, and the scattered parishes elected representatives to sit in a house of the laity. The two houses would deliberate separately, just as Congress and state legislatures did, and then submit proposals for the bishop's approval. This seemed the perfect way to tie the interests of clergy and laity together in advancing their faith.

The first convention opened on the evening of Tuesday, November 24, 1823, in Saint Finbar's Cathedral—a tiny place, belying the grandeur usually associated with the word "cathedral"— in Charleston, and Doctor McDonald from Beaufort was unanimously elected president of the house of the laity. There were only nine other men serving as lay delegates and just four priests in the house of the clergy, but for the next two days they discussed the pressing needs of their church. These were summarized by a later chronicler: "Catholic education, elementary and secondary; seminary training and the formation of a national (that is, American) clergy; social welfare work among the laboring classes; the care of the poor, the ailing, and the immigrant; watchfulness over legislation during anti-Catholic movements; the spread of Catholic literature and the support of the Catholic press." After each house had debated and passed its resolutions, they reconvened jointly and presented them to the bishop, who endorsed them all with his thanks. The system seemed to work smoothly. "Never," a participant wrote afterward, "did there exist more affectionate attachment between clergy and laity . . . Nothing was so striking as the delicacy observed on all sides to avoid the semblance of the interference with the rights of others. The peculiar duties and special rights of each were so distinctly marked." Looking ahead, the convention also "established the principle of unity of action, and brought together as acquaintances respectable men, who had no other opportunity of meeting to consult upon a subject highly interesting to them all," namely, the survival and growth of their church.[1] This convention, together with those that would be held every year for the next two decades, helped define what it was like to be an American Catholic in the church in the democratic republic.

The concern for "delicacy" lest either priests or lay people "interfere" in the affairs of the other was not out of place, for disputes between clergy and laity had begun to appear in many places around the country. Charleston itself had been the scene of rancorous argument, but the worst of it was in Philadelphia. At Saint Mary's Church in that city, the congregation split into two factions, one supporting their pastor, the other opposing him. Fistfights occasionally broke out in front of the church, and once the police had to be called to restore order. Personalities aside, an underlying cause of tension derived from the way parishes had been formed. Lacking the pre-existing network of churches in Europe, there from time immemorial, parishes in the United States had to be created from scratch, and some very practical questions had to be resolved in the process. When a small community of Catholics got together to buy the land for a church in their town, whose name would be on the deed? Who would collect and manage the money? Who would pay the man who brought the firewood to heat the building on Sunday mornings in the winter or the woman who played the organ at Mass? In the absence of a resident priest, lay men—always men only, not women—took on these tasks themselves. Typically, they formed a small corporation according to the laws of their state, and, as in any corporation, the "stock-holders" (in this case, the parishioners) elected trustees to act in the best interests of them all.[2]

This system, which church officials later disapprovingly called "trusteeism," had arisen from necessity, but it also raised some broader questions. What part would lay people continue to play in their church, especially once the number of clergy began to increase? Moreover, if the laity could take the lead in such mundane affairs as care of the building and the land, why exactly could they not have some role in overseeing the more important religious affairs of the parish? Could they, for example, have anything to say about who their pastor would be? As citizens, they were accustomed to the ways of a democratic republic in which elected representatives oversaw the business of the community, representatives whom they themselves chose and might turn out of office if they wished. Might it not be possible to organize their church along the same lines?

American Catholics grappled with these questions in the years before the Civil War, and their struggle often underscored the distinctions between lay people and the leaders of their church. The laity rejoiced when the church expanded into new areas; they were happy that, in contrast to earlier generations, they could attend services every week, or even more often. Catholic lay people became regular churchgoers in these decades, and they came to expect that the institution would always be available to them. They enjoyed access to the Mass and the sacraments to an extent that had not been possible before. But this welcome growth did not entirely overcome some enduring tensions between the laity and the institutions and leadership of their church. Even as they became outwardly more faithful, lay people retained a sense of their own role in the church.

From one perspective, conflict between clergy and laity should have been expected in the early decades of the new century. By then, the Catholic Church in the United States was becoming a big enough institution to be worth fighting over. Catholics remained a small minority in the national population—at most 2.5 percent in 1830—but with a membership of 300,000 that year, the church had become a noticeable presence. There were still many places visited only occasionally by traveling priests, but in many other areas the church was now well established. In addition to four parishes in Philadelphia, for example, Pennsylvania boasted forty-eight, including two in the thriving river town of Pittsburgh. Mobile, Alabama, had enough Catholics to support a parish with three priests, and there were eight churches with as many priests on the Illinois frontier. Kentucky had twenty-five parishes, enough that some called the area around Bardstown, southeast of Louisville, an "American Holy Land." In Washington, D.C., there were two Catholic parishes—one at the corner of F and 10th Streets, one on Capitol Hill—with another in Georgetown and a fourth across the Potomac in Alexandria. In the country as a whole, new parishes were opening at the rate of about nine every year, a number that was modest but impressive in its regularity.[3] Nearly everywhere Catholics looked, they could see encouraging signs of growth.

As they spread, churches organized themselves so as to guarantee that a parish, once established, could continue its work after the founders died or moved away. This process was a relentlessly local one, with the laws of the individual states producing a legal and administrative patchwork. Priests or bishops could hold the deeds to parish property in their own names in some states but not in others. In New York, for example, the law required every local church to be organized as a distinct corporation governed by a board—no fewer than three members, no more than nine—elected by the "male persons of full age" in the congregation. Such officers could transact all business, though they had no authority to "alter or change the Religious Constitutions or Governments" of their church or to interfere in the "Doctrine, Discipline, or Worship" of their denomination. Catholics organized churches along these lines no less than Protestants, and the law seemed to take proper account of the distinction between temporal and spiritual concerns. Setting up such boards of trustees was a practical solution to the problems of maintaining a parish.[4]

In the vast majority of cases, this trustee system created few difficulties, and examples of cooperation between laity and clergy were legion. On the surface, the rules governing a parish in Virginia, for instance, seemed restrictive, for they mandated that the pastor communicate with the officers only in writing or when summoned to attend their meetings; if he did attend, he was supposed to play the part of a well-behaved child and speak only when spoken to. In practice, however, the pastor was often elected a member of this board, and in at least one year he was chosen as its president. German-speaking congregations in Pennsylvania and French-speaking parishioners in Louisiana could look back to long traditions of involvement in Europe and Canada, where lay boards managed local churches. Almost everywhere, collaboration between laity and clergy was the watchword. In Boston, three elected church wardens met with the pastor on the evening of the first Sunday of every month "to consider and regulate what may be necessary, and to advise in common on whatever may concern the good of the church."[5] By "advising in common," pastor and parishioners usually worked to advance their mutual goals.

Because they were all human, however, lay people and priests sometimes found it hard to get along. Besides Philadelphia, churches in Buffalo, New Orleans, Norfolk, Virginia, and other cities saw extended trustee disputes. Each of these had its own complicated story, and trying to untangle the issues from a historical distance can be difficult. But significantly, these battles were usually fought in public, with the participants eager to put their case before the citizenry at large, not merely their fellow Catholics. Extended pamphlet wars broke out between the contending parties. In 1822 alone, the dispute in Philadelphia led to the publication of an *Address to the Right Reverend, the Bishop of Philadelphia,* written by a lay member of the parish, followed soon after by a priest's *Reply to a Catholic Layman.* That called forth from the original author a *Rejoinder to the Reply,* and that in turn produced *A Reply to the Catholic Layman's Rejoinder;* next came the *Desultory Examination of the Reply . . . to a Catholic Layman's Rejoinder,* followed inevitably by *Remarks on the Catholic Layman's Desultory Examination.* By then, both sides might well have collapsed in exhaustion, but in fact the publishing and counterpublishing continued into subsequent years. All the participants were convinced that important issues were at stake.[6]

Disputes between priests and lay trustees were usually sparked by one or more common causes. The first was the congregation's simple dissatisfaction with their pastor. The "medley of clerical characters" of which John Carroll had spoken was sufficiently varied that some priests and people simply could not live together peaceably. One "turbulent and domineering clergyman," a parishioner said of his pastor, was given to delivering "inflammatory sermons," during which he apparently denounced parishioners by name from the pulpit. "No malignant, rancorous slanderer, whether clothed in ermine or decorated with clerical robes, shall assail me with impunity," the equally belligerent target of one such denunciation wrote. The trustees of a parish in Cincinnati reciprocated what they took to be their pastor's condescending attitude, sarcastically accusing him of thinking that "stupid laymen" were "unworthy to decide" matters more properly "taken before the higher tribunal of the Right Reverend Clergy." A priest in Boston, resident there before the amicable Sunday night meetings, raised eyebrows by publishing an open letter in which more effort seemed to be given to listing his various titles than to refining his spiritual message: the letter identified him as "Doctor of Divinity, Prothonotary of the Holy Church and the Holy See of Rome, Apostolic Vice-Prefect and Missionary, Curate of the Catholick Church at Boston in North America."[7] Priests of that kind seemed just a little too full of themselves for the taste of many parishioners, imbued as they were with an American faith in the virtues of the "common man."

Lay men, too, could be prickly and hard to get along with. John Oliveira Fernandez, trustee of a parish in Virginia, had been a confidant of the royal court in Portugal before political turmoil there had driven him to the New World, where he lost few occasions to remind both his pastor and his fellow parishioners that he was a cut above them. During a dispute in 1815 and 1816, he periodically lapsed into French when it suited his argumentative purposes, and he haughtily suggested passages in Saint Augustine that the priest might study so as to improve his sermons. He joined the pamphlet wars enthusiastically, contributing one that ran to forty-four pages of text with a forty-eight-page appendix of excerpts from noted theologians. "Arrogant, wicked, or ambitious Priests" were the great problem for the American church, he thought, especially owing to their influence over the "weak, superstitious, or ignorant persons" who occupied the pews. Since trustees were generally selected from among the more successful and better-off members of the parish, social tension might also surface at any time. The lay board members of a parish in Buffalo in the 1850s were all substantial figures in their community: well over half of them owned their own businesses, and an equal number held real estate valued at more than $3,000, a considerable sum for the time.[8] These were men who were used to being in charge of things. It did not take much personal volatility on either side to set off clashes between laity and clergy.

Ethnic distinctions also fueled trustee disputes. Where a pastor was of one nationality and the congregation another, deeply rooted cultural differences exacerbated personality clashes. The trouble usually began with language, but it was also broader than that.

The aristocratic "prothonotary" in Boston, who was French, was a bit much for his mostly Irish parishioners. In the same way, the Irish of several churches in Virginia and South Carolina came to feel "an insurmountable personal dislike" for a French priest traveling among them. "None but a person capable of preaching clearly and distinctly in the English language" would be acceptable, they insisted. German parishioners in New York City were complaining well into the 1840s about unspecified "insults" from their Irish neighbors during funeral processions to the local Catholic cemetery. The Germans formed a corporation to buy a separate burial ground for themselves, but the bishop (an Irish immigrant) refused to sanction its use and even threatened to close their church if they did not relent; bowing to his threat, they did so, though the incident continued to rankle. Sometimes disputes occurred within ethnic groups. French priests working among Irish parishioners could have trouble, but priests from one county in Ireland might be equally unacceptable to people from another county. A priest from Cork was perhaps just as likely as a non-Irish clergyman to get into trouble with lay people from Clare, one observer of churches in upstate New York noted.[9]

By far the most contentious issue was the right to hire and fire local pastors. Turmoil in the Catholic parish of Norfolk, Virginia, that spanned two decades offers the clearest case. From colonial times, Norfolk had been the busiest port city between Baltimore and Charleston, and a small group of Catholics had bought land for a church there as early as 1794. A priest was permanently assigned in 1815, and though the parishioners found him less than fully satisfactory, they swallowed hard and accepted him. This pastor chafed under restrictions the trustees put on him, however—they did not want him traveling up to Richmond to say Mass periodically because it took him away from his duties with them—so he proposed to remove some of the trustees and replace them with men of his own choosing. The rest of the board objected, and for a while they locked him out of the church; eventually, they withdrew into their own private chapel and invited another priest from New York to come to serve them. When the archbishop of Baltimore (who had jurisdiction over Virginia's Catholics) heard of the dispute, he threatened to excommunicate everyone involved. "Their pretended right of choosing their Priest . . . is perfectly unfounded," he wrote. Even so, by the summer of 1819 there were two priests and two congregations in Norfolk, each claiming to be the rightful one. Only the departure of the priest from one faction and a leading trustee from the other allowed things to cool down.[10]

In pressing to control the appointment of their pastors, Catholic lay people were influenced by broader American notions of authority. They were accustomed to the republican idea that ordinary people such as themselves were the source of power in civil society—after all, did they not even have the right to choose the president of the United States?—and they could not understand why the same theory did not apply to their church. "It is a primary principle among them," one bishop explained to a European churchman, "that absolutely all magistrates, whether high or low, at stated times of the year should be elected by popular vote." Thus, he concluded, lay people were "exposed to the danger of admitting the same principles of ecclesiastical rule." Moreover, the religious freedom guaranteed by the First Amendment to the Constitution had a double effect. On the one hand, it meant that the government could not force anyone to support a particular church, but on the other, it meant that all citizens were free to join whatever church they wanted. And if church membership was voluntary, how could members be excluded from decision-making? Finally, Catholics also had the example of the Protestant churches that their neighbors attended. Beginning in the seventeenth century with the Congregational churches of Puritan New England, most American denominations let local congregations hire and fire their own ministers.[11] American Catholics saw nothing wrong and much that was right with this approach.

They also thought it fully in line with Catholic tradition. Some learned trustees were clever enough to cite precedents from canon law, particularly a principle known as the *ius patronatus*— literally, the right of patronage. In medieval Europe, this practice had given to the nobleman who built a church the right to appoint its priest, together with the duty to support him. "If anyone builds a church with the consent of the diocesan bishop," Pope Innocent III had decreed at the beginning of the thirteenth century, "by that fact he acquires the *ius patronatus.*" Later popes reaffirmed this principle, and some even threatened to excommunicate anyone who tried to usurp the appointing authority. Several centuries later, lay trustees in America argued that this principle applied to them. There were no noblemen in sight, but since they had built their churches, Innocent's rule applied to them, did it not? And if they had the right to appoint a pastor, they thought, surely they had the right to remove him and to find another who they felt might better serve their needs.

Some lay Catholics tried to push this argument too far: a pastor was the "property" of his flock, one Philadelphia pamphleteer asserted, strong language in a country where slavery was still legal. Most trustees, however, made a more moderate case. "It is for the benefit of lay men, who are the great body of the church, that priests are ordained," another Philadelphian wrote in 1822. Since it was in their own interest "to procure the very best[,] there is little danger of our erring in the choice of pastors." The people were competent to choose their own doctors, lawyers, and legislators, the argument went; surely they would be no less careful in choosing their pastors.[12]

By the 1820s, the growing ranks of the hierarchy—there were eleven dioceses in the country, each with its own bishop—considered this principle potentially dangerous. Questions of authority were clearly at stake. "I will suffer no man in my diocese whom I cannot control," New York's Bishop John Hughes (whose no-nonsense personality earned him the nickname "Dagger John") was supposed to have said, and he probably spoke for other bishops as well. But there were additional grounds for the hierarchy's defense of their own powers. Practically speaking, bishops feared that lay control over pastors would induce priests to curry favor by soft-pedaling their religious and moral demands. "A zealous Clergyman performing his duty courageously & without respect of persons," John Carroll had worried as early as 1784, "would always be liable to be the victim of his earnest endeavors to stop the progress of vice and evil example." A pastor whose sermons too strenuously reminded his people of their need for repentance might find himself out of a job, replaced by a more easy-going spiritual guide. This did not mean, Carroll insisted, that priests should be imposed on churches where they were unwelcome and thus ineffective; he himself promised that "a proper regard, and such as is suitable to our Governments will be had to the rights of the Congregation." In assigning priests, he said, he would pay "every deference" to the wishes of the people, "consistent with the general welfare of Religion." Later on, trustees in Philadelphia happily quoted another bishop as saying that "no priest to whom the congregation has a repugnance that is unconquerable ought to be forced on them."[13]

Bishops also thought they had theology on their side. They believed that they and their priests had been granted distinctive spiritual authority as a result of their ordination, and this fostered the conviction that they had jurisdiction over lay people in virtually all matters connected with the church. The idea that the laity might control some aspects of parish life led bishops to conclude that trustee arrangements were inherently un-Catholic. The parallel with Protestant churches was, in the bishops' minds, precisely what was wrong with the lay appointment of pastors. "The

Catholic Church will never admit the principles and practice [of the] Presbyterians," Carroll had insisted, and one can almost see him shudder at the last word. Trustees who claimed the *ius patronatus* were trying to reshape the Catholic Church "upon the model of those who have separated from us," and such an attempt was obviously unacceptable. Trustees, another bishop would say later, "had as their guide, not a knowledge of the laws of their own church, but the example of churches which protested against its doctrines." Worse, the turbulence surrounding too many internal parish disputes inevitably caused public "scandal," always a serious matter in moral theology, and cast the church in a bad light. With all these motives, the emerging forces of hierarchical authority sought to stop the spread of trusteeism.[14]

To this end, the bishops of the United States held a general meeting in Baltimore over two weeks in October 1829. They transacted routine business on such matters as the recruitment of new priests and the religious instruction of children, but they also considered how to limit the potential damage of trusteeism. Regardless of past practices, they ruled, all local parish property was now to be held solely in the name of each bishop, wherever state law permitted such a practice. Bishops were given the right to remove any priest who abetted "lay interference in the spiritual concerns of the Church" and to close down any parish that tried to recruit an unauthorized pastor on its own. In a letter addressed to the nation's Catholics, the bishops based their position on what they saw as the unalterable "constitution of our church." In particular, they noted, it is "our duty to declare to you, that in no part of the Catholic Church does the right of instituting or dismissing a clergyman . . . exist in any one" other than the diocesan bishop himself. "We further declare to you," they went on, "that no right of presentation or patronage . . . has ever existed or does now exist canonically, in these United States." They even cited a recent statement from the pope, made in response to a trustee dispute in New Orleans, which asked incredulously: "Did Christ commit His Church to be ruled by the Trustees or by the Bishops? Shall sheep lead the shepherd?" Lay people could be assured, the bishops wrote, "that in the discharge of this most important and delicate duty, we shall always meet with your support, as our only object can be your spiritual welfare."[15] Nevertheless, it had to be clear who was the shepherd and who were the sheep.

Bishops looked to their priests for support in this effort to control trustees, and they generally got it. "With your zealous cooperation," the bishops wrote in a companion letter to the clergy, "we now expect to make considerable progress towards a more orderly and efficient state of being." Priests and bishops might experience tensions of their own, but in subsequent years a sense of solidarity within the clergy, drawn in distinction to lay people, was strengthened. Increasingly, bishops recruited and trained local men for the priesthood, thereby reducing dependence on those who wandered in from abroad. The bishops were able to form these new clerics with what they considered proper ideas, and a new ideology of the priesthood grew, characterized by a belief that bishops and priests together were "the recognized authorities" in the church. Lay people, by contrast, had a subordinate role. This emerging viewpoint was evident even in the way churchmen spoke, and "sheep" was not the only metaphor applied to Catholic parishioners. The letters that the bishops addressed to the laity began with a salutation to their "children in Christ"; letters addressed to priests began with a greeting to the bishops' "reverend co-operators and Brethren in Christ."[16] The language said it all. Lay people were the bishops' children; priests were their brothers.

Trustee disturbances in local parishes declined steadily in the years after the council of 1829. Lay "interference" in parish affairs effectively disappeared. State laws governing the ownership of church property were gradually modified until, by the end of the century, many American Catholic dioceses assumed the form of a "corporation sole": the bishop himself was the legal entity that was the church, and all property was held in his name. Moreover, the bishops also won the historical argument over trusteeism, successfully characterizing it to subsequent generations as an abuse incompatible with the true structure of the church. Trustees were always described as "rebellious laymen," sometimes "duped by . . . recalcitrant clergymen" and always practicing a form of "insubordination" and an "encroachment" on the hierarchy that was nothing short of "obnoxious." The "disease of trusteemania" was "wholly cheap, wholly mean," and motivated by "pride, envy, and greed." This "evil stalked step-by-step with the progress of the Faith," and it had to be suppressed.[17] Reconsideration of the role of the laity in the church, which came with the Second Vatican Council of the mid-twentieth century, would undercut these interpretations, but that is a story for later. In the meantime, the attempt by lay people to exercise broad responsibility in their own parishes stands out as a path not taken in the church of the democratic republic.

Even as bishops were stamping out lay "interference" in church affairs, one bishop sought to foster cooperation between clergy and laity. John England, the bishop of Charleston, South Carolina, had jurisdiction over Catholics in that state and in North Carolina and Georgia as well. England had an odd name for an Irishman, but on his immigration to the United States in 1820, he immediately fell in love with his adopted country. Charleston had been troubled by its own tensions between clergy and laity, so he set out to apply what he considered the best of the American political system to the organization and management of the church. He had, he wrote to his parishioners less than a month after taking office, "for a long time admired the excellence of your Constitution." The "sun of rational freedom" shone brightly in America, he enthused, even "as it departs from the nations of the East"—by which he meant the countries "back east" across the Atlantic in Europe. The Catholic Church in this rising nation required new forms based on "the wisdom, the moderation, and the fortitude of your government." Applying this "excellence" and "wisdom" to religious institutions no less than to civic institutions seemed the sensible course, one that would draw all church members together. His open letters to his church usually began with a greeting to "our beloved brethren of the Diocess [sic] of Charleston."[18] For England, priests and people were equally his siblings.

Accordingly, England drafted a constitution for the diocese, and in the fall of 1823 he assembled laity and clergy to approve it. He read it out to them, article by article, asking for ratification of each one; the votes in favor were unanimous. Officials in Rome had already examined a draft and found nothing contrary to church teaching, so it went into effect immediately. From almost any perspective, this was a remarkable document. Its title page noted that it had been "fully agreed to, and accepted, after repeated discussion, by the clergy and the several congregations." Although the church was a divine institution, it was also a human institution, and how it organized itself in the latter capacity might vary considerably with time and place. Particular structures, the constitution said, "could never be permanent, invariable, or uniform throughout the world"; instead, these should be adapted to "the circumstances in which the several churches might be found."[19] In the United States, the right structure seemed obvious.

Civil government was founded on the notion of citizenship, and membership was similarly the starting point in this view of the church. The constitution therefore set out the qualifications that a lay person needed to be a voting member of a Catholic parish. Any man aged twenty-one or older who had been baptized, who now lived in one of the three states, and who had "subscribed his assent" to the constitution (just as naturalized citizens swore allegiance to the civil government) was a Catholic in good standing and thus able to participate in church affairs. A modern reader notices first that participation was confined to males only. Women, though members of the church, were unable to vote in parish affairs, but in the 1820s few would have thought this remarkable. American women of the time could not vote in civil elections, and in many places they could not even own property in their own names. Thus the church restriction was less unusual in its own context. More intriguingly, the diocesan constitution did not restrict church membership to white men, a significant omission in these slave-holding states and in a nation in which citizenship itself was reserved to whites. There were no congregations of black Catholics, slave or free, within England's jurisdiction, but the constitution seems not to have foreclosed the possibility that there might one day be. England himself was no opponent of slavery—in later years, he wrote an extended defense of the "peculiar institution," insisting that it was entirely compatible with Christianity—though he also opened a school for free black children in Charleston.[20] Even so, it is a fair speculation to suppose that, had this constitutional structure survived into a later era, its definition of church membership would have evolved, just as notions of citizenship expanded.

The diocesan constitution next outlined the organization of local parishes. Whenever a sufficient number of Catholics was identified in a town or district, the bishop was required to gather them together "at some convenient time and place." Once assembled, the congregation would proceed to elect a board called a vestry, named for the anteroom of a church building where they normally held their meetings. Each vestry was made up of the resident pastor and as many "discreet, well-conducted men, having a regard for religion" as seemed appropriate. These officers were elected in January and served one-year terms; they in turn chose wardens, who had practical jobs: "to preserve in decency and repair the buildings and other property," to "aid the clergyman in preserving order and decency in the church," and, if necessary, "to remove therefrom all disturbers or nuisances." The power to appoint the pastor—the source of so many earlier disputes—was expressly vested in the bishop alone, but if a congregation were unhappy with its priest, the constitution required the bishop to investigate right away and report back to them. Otherwise, all practical affairs were decided by the vestry, strictly according to majority rule; the pastor could not veto a decision if he disagreed with it. There was to be an annual accounting of all funds, and the money given to support one parish could not be drawn off to support another.[21]

Across the diocese, Catholics formed parishes according to these rules. In Charleston itself, the Church of Saint Finbar (named after the cathedral in Bishop England's native city of Cork in Ireland) elected a vestry consisting of the pastor, a secretary, a treasurer, a collector of the general fund, two wardens, and three other lay men. Across town, Saint Peter's Church chose a secretary, a treasurer, a collector, and two wardens. In the Georgetown district of South Carolina, up the coast, a pastor had not yet been appointed, but the Catholics of that place gathered nonetheless at the county courthouse and chose an interim vestry, consisting of two wardens (Michael Calverly and Louis Siau), a secretary-treasurer (Joseph Puche), and a collector of funds (J. M. Leribour). In Georgia, too, parishes took their first steps. At Holy Trinity Church in Augusta, the members stayed behind after Mass on Christmas day to elect their vestry: John McCormick, Joseph Bignon, B. Bonyer, G. Dillon, and L. Rossignol, with Paul Rossignol ("a very respectable, pious man") chosen as secre-

tary.[22] We know virtually nothing of any of these men, but the
care with which their names were recorded on the church books
shows that they were recognized as leaders of their parishes.

Once formed, vestries set about their routine business. At
Saint Finbar's, the board drew up a set of detailed bylaws. The
congregation as a whole approved these after Mass one Sunday in
September 1825 and sent them on to Bishop England "for his
concurrence and sanction"; that "having been given, they were
declared to be constitutionally in force." Next the treasurer, Edward Lynah, presented his report—there was $260 in the build-
ing fund—and an audit committee declared that everything was
in order. The demands of Lynah's own business forced him to
step aside as parish treasurer, however, so the vestry issued a legal
"certificate of the discharge of his responsibility" and passed a resolution of thanks "for his zealous and efficient services." Factional
disputes were still a recent memory in the parish, but now the
mere fact that there were orderly, written, and democratically
adopted procedures dispelled the tension. Decisions could be
made and recognized as "constitutionally in force." The advantage of this kind of arrangement was plain. "The process is clear,
the right defined, the wrong palpable," a newspaper, the *United
States Catholic Miscellany,* editorialized. "Each individual knows
his rights, each officer his power, and all the members of the
community being fully aware of the extent of jurisdiction and
the limits of obedience, there can be no mistake." Parishioners
were partners with the clergy rather than opponents. "We are
gratified," the *Miscellany* said on another occasion, "that the unfortunate divisions which have during the last thirteen years existed in the church of this city, are finally terminated to the full
satisfaction of all the parties." The constitution had done its
work: "thus happily are peace and regular discipline fully established."[23]

The diocesan constitution also provided for an annual convention to which all parishes would send delegates. Initially, each of the three states was to hold its own convention, but in the late 1830s the charter was amended to create one general convention. Every local church was entitled to choose representatives to these gatherings, and the number of delegates each one sent varied: larger congregations could send four, and smaller ones could send two, but even the tiniest was entitled to one. The bishop would open each convention (which was required to last no less than three days, so as to be sure that no important matter was left off the agenda) with a solemn Mass, but then clergy and laity would withdraw to their separate houses and get down to business. In order to become effective, any measure had to be approved by both houses and then presented to the bishop for his approbation, just as civil laws had to be passed by both legislative houses and signed by the governor or president. The diocesan convention had no authority to change church doctrine or the administration of the sacraments, but any practical concern was within its jurisdiction. Bishops and priests elsewhere were wary of "interference" and "insubordination" from lay people, but the Charleston constitution defined these representatives of the laity as "a body of sage, prudent, and religious counselors" who, by "their advice and exertions . . . will be most beneficial."[24]

The first South Carolina convention was held in November 1823 with nine lay representatives: four from Charleston and one each from Beaufort, Camden, Georgetown, Pocotaligo, and Barnwell. The ceremonies began with a high Mass, at which a new priest was ordained. Bishop England made "a few appropriate remarks," and then laity and clergy withdrew to their respective houses, with the laity under the chairmanship of Dr. James McDonald. There are no surviving records of the resolutions adopted over the next two days. These measures may have been largely ceremonial, but even without much substantive business, the convention was "a meeting of brethren"—that word again. Just as important as any resolutions were the personal connections that were forged and the growing unity of purpose. The meeting "brought at once under the eye of the Bishop and of his clergy, and of a respectable portion of the laity, much of the state of this Diocess which could not otherwise be known without labour, delay, and expense."

The conventions subsequently held in Georgia (at Savannah in 1824) and North Carolina (at Fayetteville in 1829) were much the same. That the laity were ready to help govern their own church was demonstrated tangibly at the Georgia convention, which authorized a collection to support Catholic missions in the state. The convention raised eighty dollars—a sum which, a newspaper said, "considering the depressed state of business in this city, was a liberal contribution."[25]

The business of these conventions—there were fifteen for South Carolina, eight for Georgia, two for North Carolina, and then three general diocesan conventions—was hardly earth-shaking. At the first diocesan-wide assembly in 1839, for example, which consisted of thirty-one lay delegates and sixteen priests from all three states, the proceedings seem like nothing so much as ritualized exercises in parliamentary procedure, consisting largely of resolutions of thanks. The meetings did not debate fine points of theology or church discipline. Rather, their tasks were invariably practical. When the convention in South Carolina in 1828 voted that "aid to small or poor congregations or parishes, in the erection of Churches" should "rather be by loan than donation"; when the convention in Georgia in 1826 made Saint Peter the official patron saint of the diocese; when the convention in North Carolina in 1831 resolved that "each member of this Convention will make it his particular duty to inquire . . . where there may exist any Catholics in the State at present, unknown to us"—when lay people, priests, and bishop concurred in all these actions, there were few significant historical turning points. Instead, Catholics simply worked together to meet basic needs. Opening new parishes, finding priests to serve in them, raising funds so that Bishop England could travel around the three states visiting congregations—these were the issues that absorbed their attention. In accomplishing such mundane tasks and, just as important, in laying to rest the turmoil of earlier disputes, the constitutional system was effective. "The utmost harmony subsists between the clergy and the lay delegates," the *Miscellany* observed after one convention. "They perceive that, according as they are enabled to act upon the constitutional provisions, their labours are abridged, their mutual rights protected, and the welfare of the church ensured."[26]

But who were the lay people who took up this work? Sadly, most of the convention participants are now largely unknown. None of them achieved national or even statewide renown, and personal details are few and random. They were obviously prominent in their own local communities and were judged "discreet, well-conducted men" by their fellow parishioners. Several were members of those professions from which leaders in most localities derive. Alexander England (no relation to the bishop), a delegate to several South Carolina conventions, was a merchant; Stevens Perry, secretary of the 1829 convention, was an attorney; and Louis Pitray, president of the 1830 house of the laity, was a principal in a Charleston banking firm. There were planters and land speculators among the delegates. Edward Lynah, the treasurer of Saint Finbar's parish and a delegate to several conventions, was the son of a surgeon who briefly pursued a medical career himself, though he "always preferred the pursuit of agriculture," a descendant wrote.[27] Even those who are now unremembered by history were well enough regarded by their neighbors to be chosen for office repeatedly. Rare was the convention delegate who served only a single term. All had their own affairs to attend to, but they also took on the duties of vestryman or convention delegate because they thought it an important part of their religious responsibility.

Not all observers of this constitutional system were sanguine about it. Bishops elsewhere were still deeply suspicious of anything that smacked of "trusteeism." If the Charleston constitution were to become the model for organizing the church in the United States, Philadelphia's Bishop Henry Conwell told an official in Rome, "it would mean the quick collapse of the American Church." This approach was much too "democratic"—at the time still a scare word that suggested mob rule. "Ecclesiastical liberty" was at stake, in Conwell's view, by which he meant the liberty of bishops to govern their churches as they alone saw fit. Others in the American hierarchy were more open to the idea of church constitutions. Bishop Joseph Rosati in Saint Louis, for example, wrote to John England, predicting that the system would "secure to your flock the deposit of faith; to ecclesiastical jurisdiction, respect and submission; to the clergy, honor and support; and to Religion at large, propagation and stability." Even so, no other bishop ever tried to replicate England's constitution, and after his death in 1842, his successor in Charleston quietly discontinued the conventions.[28] By then, bishops everywhere were consolidating their own authority at the expense of lay "interference" and "abuse."

If purely local control of parishes by trustees was a road not taken for American Catholics, so too was this constitutional system. Something was lost in the process. Defining what role the laity had in their own church was just as important as defining the role they did not have. Political and social conditions in the United States had given American Catholics, no less than their fellow citizens, certain irreducible views about how institutions of all kinds should be organized and run. This was, after all, the age in which Alexis de Tocqueville, a French aristocrat traveling the country in 1831 and 1832, was singing the praises of "democracy in

America." It was critical, Tocqueville wrote, that all religions, "while carefully putting themselves out of the way of the daily movement of affairs, not collide unnecessarily with the generally accepted ideas and permanent interests that reign among" the citizens.[29] That was precisely what the Catholics of the South thought they were doing: taking the "generally accepted ideas" that Americans had concerning authority and applying them to their church. Doing so did not diminish their attachment to their faith; it enhanced it. The constitutional system had been a bold experiment, even if no one else ever tried to repeat it.

Lay convention delegates and local vestrymen devoted their own time and energy to church business, but being Catholic was not about managing parish finances. Rather, it was the religious life of the church that attracted and held their loyalty. In sustaining a commitment to practice their faith, these American Catholics enjoyed advantages that those of an earlier era had not, for the church was an increasingly visible presence in their lives. In contrast to Catholics of the priestless church, parishioners no longer experienced months-long fallow periods of waiting for a missionary to arrive; now they might encounter a priest weekly or even daily. Catholic churches became common features on the local landscape, joining the spires of Protestant churches in piercing the low skylines of towns and cities. For the first time since the establishment of the church in the United States, routine religious practice came to characterize the way lay people expressed their Catholicism.

In these early decades of the nineteenth century, Catholics went through a process that might be called "churchifying." Increasingly, they showed that they were Catholics by attending regularly scheduled services in their local parish church. A Roman prelate traveling the country was happy to observe a near-

obsession with constructing new church buildings, the more impressive the better. "These are vital thoughts for them," he
reported to papal officials. "The majesty, the convenience of external worship, is now a dire necessity." The churches' "majesty"
served the important social purpose of demonstrating that Catholics were respectable citizens, he said, but more important, construction was driven by a desire to provide for "the convenience
of external worship." Church law had always insisted that Catholics attend Mass every Sunday, but this requirement had often
been a practical impossibility. Now Catholics might approach
this ideal. The churches in question, however, were not always
very majestic. A Unitarian minister from New England was de-
cidedly unimpressed by Saint Finbar's in Charleston, for example,
when he visited there in 1827. It was "a new and somewhat
shabby church for a Romish cathedral," he thought, "the whole
with an air of poverty."[30] Still, the prospect that Mass could be
said every week, in public, and for crowds of worshipers—not occasionally, privately, and in someone's home for a few family
members and neighbors—changed the face of American Catholicism. Like other American denominations, this one was now a
faith marked by the regularity of public worship.

Because they were more likely than earlier generations to live
close to a church, lay Catholics could for the first time internalize
the rhythms of week-to-week religious practice, and Sunday was
their focus. The Sabbath was to be observed in two ways, an early
directory of the American church instructed its readers. "The first
is to abstain from all work, from all commerce and manual labor
which is not necessary." The second was "to sanctify one's self by
. . . applying himself to what relates to [God's] worship, and the
duties of piety and religion." Those duties began with the "great
obligation . . . to assist at the Holy Sacrifice of the Mass, the first
and most august of all the acts of religion." What Sunday Mass
should look like for American Catholics had been spelled out

clearly. The local priest presided, and wherever possible, a *missa cantata* (that is, a sung or "high" Mass) was to be performed by "a choir trained to sing the proper parts" and "celebrated with all the dignity of the ceremonial." At the point in the service where the priest read the gospel in Latin, he also turned to the congregation and read it aloud in English. After various announcements of parish activities, "a short sermon was to be given of an exhortatory nature in order that all present should strive for higher Christian perfection." The ceremony then continued, with the chance for those in attendance to receive Communion.[31]

The religious obligations of Sunday, however, did not end with morning Mass. Parishioners were also encouraged to return to church in the afternoon for Vespers, though failure to do so was not seriously sinful, as skipping Mass was. This service was part of the ancient church practice of marking the "hours" of each day with prescribed psalms and prayers, a liturgy performed most completely in monasteries. On Sundays, priests in American parishes conducted this service publicly, and lay people were urged to attend "faithfully and assiduously." Vespers did not last very long, only about half an hour: a few prayers were recited, the choir might render a psalm, then the priest would deliver a short "instruction." The service concluded with Benediction of the Blessed Sacrament, a ceremony in which the priest blessed the congregation using a piece of consecrated Eucharistic bread. Framing the day with morning Mass and afternoon Vespers, church officials said, then allowed the observant Catholic to "take some hours to relax his mind and comfort his body after the labour and fatigue of the week, by an innocent rest, or any lawful recreation."[32]

No attendance records were kept, so we cannot know how closely American Catholics approached these expectations for Sunday observance. All the circumstantial evidence, however, points to steadily rising levels of religious practice. Church schedules indicate that Catholics quickly got into the habit of attending Mass. The growing number of services shows that enough Catholics were filling the pews to justify having them; in effect, supply serves as a rough gauge of demand. In the 1830s, for example, Mass was said at one of the half-dozen churches in Boston at 6, 7, and 10 o'clock in the morning—7, 8, and 10 o'clock during the winter months, when the sun rose later. A church in St. Louis had a similar schedule for white parishioners and a separate Mass at 9 o'clock "for the coloured people." New Orleans had five churches, each with at least two Masses on Sunday, including several at which preaching was done in both French and English. Moreover, priests were routinely given permission to say two Masses on Sunday, even though church law normally permitted them to say only one. Bishops had to allow their priests to "binate" (as the practice was called), simply because not all parishioners could be accommodated at a single service. Vespers, by contrast—in most places offered at three in the afternoon during the summer and at two in the winter—was not nearly so well attended. Repeated exhortations by the clergy that parishioners set aside their "lawful recreation" and come to the afternoon service suggest that Catholics were, in practice, less regular about attendance at Vespers than at Mass. Even so, the expanding schedule of services constituted a kind of "devotional revolution."[33] Catholics were no longer identified by infrequent, ad hoc worship, but by weekly churchgoing.

Concern that the liturgy be conducted with "the dignity of the ceremonial" meant that parishes devoted new attention to acquiring and maintaining the equipment needed for public worship. The priest wore special robes at Mass and used certain "hardware" for Communion. Traveling missionaries generally carried their own equipment around with them, but local parishes bought full sets as soon as they could. A priest visiting a church in Savannah, Georgia, for example, was pleased to discover that the parishioners had on hand two silver chalices (for the wine to be consecrated into Christ's blood in the Eucharist), a ciborium (the cup holding the consecrated bread during the distribution of Communion), and a monstrance, which held the Eucharistic particle used in the blessing during Benediction. This church also had "six suits of Vestments complete," one in each of the colors for the different seasons of the church year. A church in Augusta was not so well equipped: it had only "one suit of poor vestments," though it had three cloths for covering the altar and eight candlesticks.[34] As time went on, churches acquired the liturgical equipment they needed, often through bequests from parishioners in memory of deceased family members or friends.

Some effort in these years also went into helping the laity understand what was happening at Mass. Whereas earlier devotional manuals had been designed to give lay people religious exercises they could conduct on their own, the prayer books of the early nineteenth century offered detailed explanations of public worship. Since the service was now regularly available to lay people, it made sense to explain to them what they were seeing as they sat in church Sunday after Sunday. A *Laity's Directory* of the 1820s, for example, went into considerable detail on the subject, beginning with the color of the priest's robes: white for the major festivals, like Easter; red (symbolizing blood) for the feast days of martyred saints; somber purple for the penitential season of Lent; green during the bulk of the church year; black on Good Friday (commemorating Christ's crucifixion) and for funerals.[35] Earlier generations, attending Mass in a neighbor's living room, had probably seen a priest wearing his street clothes, which would have been indistinguishable from those of any other gentleman. (Distinctive clothing for the Catholic clergy, including the so-called Roman collar, would not become common in the United States until the end of the nineteenth century.) Now, parishioners saw a man whose distinctive garb reinforced the religious significance of what he was doing. For those laity who might well wonder what they were seeing, published guides were an integral part of the churchifying process.

Even more useful were explanations of the ceremony of the Mass itself, which began to proliferate in the 1820s. Most often, these came in the form of a "missal" (from the Latin word for the Mass, *missa*), containing the actual text of the service, which parishioners could use to follow along as the liturgy unfolded.[36] From the perspective of a later period, those attending Mass in the early nineteenth century did not have much to do: they were largely spectators at a ceremony that, in some ways, did not even take account of the fact that they were there. The priest stood with his back to the congregation most of the time: the theological understanding was that he addressed God, as represented on the altar, on behalf of the people arrayed behind him. What is more, he spoke in Latin, the ancient universal language, and usually in a low voice. Only the altar boys who assisted him ever said anything in response, and they too were speaking quietly in the Latin phrases they had managed to memorize, often with difficulty. The congregation could not see or hear much of what was going on, though through dint of repetition they could follow the general rhythm of the Mass. Missals offered more detailed guidance by providing the text of the prayers in Latin and English, printed in parallel columns on the page, together with italicized stage directions explaining the priest's movements.

Few lay people who used a missal probably understood the Latin, but by reading along in English they could see what prayers the priest was saying as he said them. Some parts of the Mass were the same each week, while others (the gospel reading, for example) changed every time, and the missal included all these varying texts. Although intended mostly for use on Sundays, it also contained material for other occasions as well. One missal gave all the readings for daily Mass during Lent, for example, when the especially devout were encouraged to attend, and it translated the texts for the special Mass to be said at weddings. Finally, it included prayers for particular occasions: prayers for rain, for families in distress, for help in various "tribulations," and so on.[37] Earlier devotional manuals, such as those of Richard Challoner, had provided only summaries of the prayers of the Mass, but these newly available missals gave the actual texts. While we cannot know how many ordinary parishioners owned such a book, the expanding number of editions attests to their role in the churchifying of American Catholics.

From the beginning, Bishop John Carroll had hoped to render the entire liturgy into English, though he did not think he had the authority to mandate this innovation on his own. Priests would have to say the words of the Mass in Latin, he and other American bishops agreed in 1810, but "it does not appear to be contrary to the injunctions of the church" to provide English translations for the people in attendance. One bishop who presided at the ordination of a new priest, a rare sight in American Catholic communities in those years, noted that "the form [of the ceremony] was translated into English for [the people's] use and distributed" in the hopes that it would be helpful to both the "strangers" and the Catholics who were there. Taking further advantage of that teaching opportunity, he added, "I also preached upon the subject." Sometimes, translating the Mass into a vernacular language was more complicated. One missionary, traveling among American Indians in Maine in 1827, explained the Mass in English to an assembled group of interested Protestants and then, with the help of a bilingual native, "caused my discourse to be interpreted to the Indians who did not understand English."[38] In this way, the clergy took every chance they could to explain church ceremonies to lay people, particularly those who were just getting used to the idea of regular church attendance.

The hope that a church would have "a choir trained to sing

the proper parts" was also progressively realized during the churchifying of Catholics. Hymn singing by the congregation, long a
staple of Protestant worship, was not generally encouraged, and
in fact would not become a part of Catholic practice until later.
Still, Catholic churches began to appreciate the value of music in
enhancing "the dignity of the ceremonial." An organ, even a
small one, was an expensive piece of equipment, but local congregations set about procuring one as soon as they could. Moreover, they assembled singers from among the parishioners, rang-
ing in ability from the experienced to the merely enthusiastic.
Compared with rural areas, most cities had a larger talent pool
from which to draw, but even in out-of-the-way places the results
could be impressive. In 1843, a discerning visitor to Saint Peter's,
the original Catholic parish in New York City, was not surprised
to find the "music excellent, organ first rate," but a few years earlier he had been no less impressed by the choir at a church in Fall
River, Massachusetts, which he described as "pretty well conducted . . . for a Country Church." This was not always the
case. In an immigrant parish in Lowell, Massachusetts, the music
could only be described as "bad" and the "singing worse"; in yet
another place, the choir was judged "abominable, being com-
posed of a parcel of Individuals who had neither voices nor
knowledge of Music."[39] Critics could always carp, but American
Catholics still came to think of their services as not entirely complete without the proper kinds of accompaniment.

Desire to promote a greater "knowledge of Music" led to the
production of the first choir books for use in American Catholic
parishes. These were not "hymnals" as such, insofar as that term
suggests use by the people in the pews. Rather, they were for organized choirs directed by musicians who themselves had greater
or lesser training. One volume, published in 1841, proclaimed itself "a standard work for the regulation of the Music in the choirs
of all the Catholic churches." It gave the organ and voice parts for

"the Service, both of the forenoon and afternoon"—that is, both Mass and Vespers—"of the Sundays and principal Festivals of the year." By providing this "regulation," the volume hoped to prevent "introducing into the Choirs Music which is neither appropriate to the season, nor adapted to the majesty of the house of God." The contents could be adapted to whatever musical resources a particular church had available. The vocal lines contained soprano, alto, and tenor parts, as well as a bass line, which "with a very few exceptions, agrees with the Organ Bass"; in smaller choirs, the hymns might be performed in two parts only, soprano and bass. The organ lines were complete, but anyone reasonably accomplished on the instrument "need not confine himself to the chords only as they are laid down here" and might feel free to improvise. For beginners, the volume contained a twenty-page overview of "elementary principles of music," including scales, time signatures, and instructions on how to follow a conductor's arm movements. There was music for several complete Masses, various litanies, and almost fifty pages of psalms for use during Vespers. Most of the words were in Latin, a circumstance that virtually precluded congregational singing, though some pieces could also be sung in English.[40]

In the hands of trained musicians, choir books could be used to improve the quality of music in American Catholic churches and thereby make the services seem more "like church." At Holy Cross Cathedral in Boston, for instance, an immigrant violinist named Luigi Ostinelli took over responsibility for the choir shortly after his arrival in 1818. Other parishes in the city asked him to rehearse their singers as well, and by the 1830s several choirs were performing weekly in their own churches and coming together for joint concerts as the "Gregorian Society." In Dover, New Hampshire, at about the same time, a Catholic music teacher enlisted his students, young and old, to perform at services. On one occasion, Mass was said to the accompaniment of an ensemble consisting of a bass violin, a bassoon, a clarinet, and a flute. Harmony, alas, did not always produce harmony. Musicians could be notoriously temperamental, and disagreements sometimes arose. Ostinelli faced a rebellion in his choir in 1832, when some members took a dislike to their organist, who, they thought, was making fun of them. A few quit the group—imagine refusing "to sing the praises of God from a private sniff!" a priest of the parish exclaimed—but they came back after receiving assurances that the organist would be more understanding.[41] Earlier American Catholics had not found many aesthetic rewards in their ad hoc services, but later parishioners came to expect that music would enhance their experience of church.

In addition to increased Mass attendance, American Catholics became both more able and more willing to partake of the other sacraments of their faith, now that they had regular access to a church. For clergy and laity alike, this was a welcome improvement, since it meant that the ceremonies could be conducted with the proper decorum. In a letter to his diocese in 1827, John Dubois, the bishop of New York, was happy to note that Catholics were leaving behind the days when their rituals were "a simple meeting of a few friends, in a private room, where refreshments are prepared," where the people in attendance did not "appear sensible of [the] impropriety" of such informality. Now, the very solemnity of the church itself, "the sacred vestments, the baptismal fonts, and above all, the presence of the adorable victim [that is, Christ], from whose blood all the sacraments derive their virtue, are calculated to excite the gravity" of the congregation.[42]

Changing practice surrounding the baptism of Catholic children shows the new focus on the parish church. Newborns no longer had to wait for months or years until a priest happened through town; children could now be baptized almost immediately after birth, and for Catholic parents this was a positive development. The theology of the time maintained that infants who died before being baptized were excluded from heaven for all eternity. They were not consigned to hell, since they had not committed any sins that would leave them to that terrible fate. Instead, it was thought that their souls went to a neutral place in the afterlife called "limbo," where they suffered none of the torments of hell but also enjoyed none of the glories of heaven. The theological foundations for limbo ranged from shaky to nonexistent, and the church later admitted that it simply did not know the fate of unbaptized babies. Popular belief did not waver, however, and for American Catholic parents, the terrors of high infant mortality rates—even by the end of the century, these still averaged about 165 per 1,000 births—made it imperative that their children be baptized as soon as possible.

The baptismal records of one church—it happens to be Saint Mary's, in the North End section of Boston, but its experience was replicated throughout Catholic America—show both the high number of baptisms and how soon after birth the ceremony usually came. The parish was located in one of the densest neighborhoods of the city, and in 1837, its first full year, it was the scene of 335 baptisms. Of these, just over half were performed within three days of the child's birth; almost 30 percent were done either on the very day of birth or the day after.[43] These parishioners had become accustomed to making the church an intimate part of their lives. Even amid all the household turmoil that came with a newborn, their thoughts turned to fulfilling the demands of church membership.

In these different ways, the Catholic laity in the church of the democratic republic were transformed into what may for the first time be described as a churchgoing people. Many might have wanted to be that in the past, but only with the expanding infrastructure of faith could they become, like so many of their Protestant neighbors, regular churchgoers. Faithful attendance at services in their local parish church was now the way they expressed their identity as Catholics. They had the chance to go to Mass every Sunday; in fact, they had a choice of several on any given Sunday and had only to decide which was most convenient for them. This availability of public worship transformed their ways of religious expression. Priests still devoted no small amount of energy to instructing lay people in correct belief, and they continued to teach the basics of faith through the catechism. All this helped promote orthodoxy (literally, in Greek, "correct opinion"). It was, however, the more unusual but more accurate word *orthopraxy* ("correct practice") that marked these parishioners. They were Catholics because they acted like Catholics. They went to church both regularly and frequently because they were at last able to meet longstanding injunctions that they do so. To be sure, some did not, and the problem of those who had "fallen away" first began to worry priests in these years, just as it was beginning to worry Protestant churchmen. For the majority of Catholics, however, routine religious practice became their way of being members of their church.

At the same time, even as Catholics became more regular they also became in some senses more passive. The responsibility for conducting religious worship had shifted from lay people, aided by devotional manuals prepared for that purpose, to the priest, who said the official prayers to which parishioners might or might not be paying attention. The distinction may be a fine one, but religious worship was now something Catholics attended rather than something they did. We should not push the economic analogy too far, but American Catholics became consumers of religion more than its producers. They were encouraged to follow the prayers of the Mass in their missal (if they had one), but even if they did not their attendance was still sufficient.

Churchgoing made American Catholics more like American Protestants, but many issues still divided the two groups of Christians. Primary among these was the pope, and the question of American Catholics' relationship to the leader of their church took on new urgency in these years. While an earlier generation of Catholics in the United States had been effectively popeless, those in the church of the democratic republic began to pay closer attention to the pontiff. The man who had merited but a single question in John Carroll's catechism of the 1790s now got more extended consideration. Kings came and went, another catechism, published in 1820, maintained, "but the bishops of Rome have never failed; there never was a period," the volume continued (not entirely accurately), "during which the world did not recognize with certainty the lawful successor to St. Peter." For that reason, "each one of the Pontiffs is a link in that great chain, which binds the present members of the Catholic church to the glorious days of the Redeemer and his Apostles." An almanac from 1835 gave visual expression to this chain. It featured a twenty-page "chronological table" of world history, beginning with Adam (the traditional date of 4004 B.C. was given for his creation), proceeding through the figures of the Old and New Testaments, and then listing every pope from Saint Peter (34 A.D., another notional date) until the current one, elected just four years earlier.[44] The chart's unbroken chronology was intended to be reassuring: a succession of popes from antiquity to their own times offered Catholics evidence that their religion could survive any uncertainty.

Expressions of devotion to the papacy were now commonplace. In November 1823, the delegates to the first convention in South Carolina took a morning off from their deliberations to commemorate the life of Pope Pius VII, who had died that summer. The cathedral was draped in black, and a reproduction of the pope's coat of arms was set up before the "large congregation." Bishop England preached for more than an hour "upon the virtues" of the deceased pontiff, taking the occasion "to remark upon the many mistakes which are too often made by the un-

thinking and the ill-informed respecting the doctrines of the
Catholic Church" concerning the pope. "It was our duty as affectionate children," a participant noted, reverting to the language
of childhood, "to moisten the tomb of our father with our tears."
Sentimental language is expected on such occasions, but these
ceremonies reminded Catholics that "the earliest antiquity had
established upon the best authority" the leadership of the pope.
For many Catholics, this authority was central to the pope's appeal, an appeal that might also attract converts to the faith. A
wealthy Philadelphia woman, raised a Unitarian, became a Catholic in the 1840s because she came to accept the authority of the
papacy as something that traced to Christ himself. Jesus, she explained to a skeptical cousin, had committed leadership to Saint
Peter, "whom He declared to be the corner-stone of His church;
this authority to be transmitted by him to his successors to the
end of time, so that these eighteen hundred and forty-eight years
had been bound together by ties as strong as God could make
them."[45]

A representative of the pope, touring the country in 1853, was
pleased to see that American Catholics had come to feel "the
greatest love for the Holy See and for the Holy Father." Everywhere he went, said Archbishop Gaetano Bedini, who had been
dispatched to explore the possibility of establishing diplomatic
relations between the Papal States and the American government,
he was greeted with signs of "love and respect for the reigning
Pontiff." During his seven-month visit, Bedini reported that he
had been the recipient of more than two hundred speeches affirming American Catholics' love of the pope, "in so many languages, always given with great veneration and joy." Young Catholics in particular, he thought, were unlikely to forget "such holy
impressions" and would, in the future, "bind themselves more se-
curely to the Holy Father and to Rome and to the Catholic
Faith."[46] His phrasing betrayed a telling order of value—the pope

came first, then Rome, and only then the faith itself—but none-theless Bedini had reason to assert that "every Catholic was proud of his religion and those who were formerly cool and indifferent did not remain so." The sentiment probably did not apply to "every" Catholic, but the number for whom it did was steadily growing.

Bedini's visit had in fact been more controversial than he let on, both with Catholics and with other Americans. The nation's bishops eyed him warily, fearful that he was spying on them. "I did not ask them many questions," Bedini said afterward, "lest I appear the investigator, which many bishops suspected I was, and of which only a few approved." The bishops did appreciate his help in suppressing the last vestiges of trusteeism, as he was able to do with a lingering lay board at a parish in Buffalo. "I am happy to report that this matter is completely and finally ended," he declared when he got back to Italy, and he could not resist adding: "All the American bishops . . . have highly praised my re-plies to these men."[47] But he had also been a target of popular hostility, with some non-Catholics expressing their own suspi-cions of this agent of the pope on American soil. In several cities he visited there were massive public demonstrations against him, some of them violent. Any increased visibility of the pope had a negative as well as a positive side, because the successor of Saint Peter was once again a figure of contention on the world's stage.

The papacy had managed to survive the turmoil of the French Revolution and the Napoleonic era, but survival had often been a near thing. After Pope Pius VI (1775–1799) died as Napoleon's prisoner, his successor, Pius VII (1800–1823), spent many years similarly confined here and there across Europe. Once the Con-gress of Vienna restored order on the Continent in 1815, however, popes reasserted their power in the Papal States of central Italy and, more broadly, aligned themselves with the forces of reaction. Revolution and democracy were obviously dangerous—look at all the trouble they had caused—and successive popes encouraged new theories of their own powers. In 1799 a Benedictine priest, who would later become Pope Gregory XVI (1831–1846), published a five-hundred-page treatise entitled *The Triumph of the Holy See and the Church over the Assaults of Rejected Innovators*, which was soon translated into several languages. The world was always in turmoil, the argument went, but the church was unchanging and infallible, guided by the pope as its absolute monarch. Twenty years later, a Sardinian diplomat produced a discourse, *Du Pape* ("On the Pope"), which argued that the survival of civilization itself depended on an all-powerful papacy. The logic was simple: "There can be no public morality and no national character without religion; there can be no Christianity without Catholicism; there can be no Catholicism without the Pope."[48]

Armed with such views, popes became newly assertive within the church. John Carroll had rejected the idea that the pope was a "universal administrator," but that was precisely what popes now strove to become. "I leave myself entirely in the hands of the Holy Father," wrote an American priest who was under consideration for appointment as a bishop in 1835.[49] No earlier bishops would have denied the pope's spiritual supremacy, but few would have thought of themselves as being "entirely" in his hands. This priest, however, was "ready to obey what he orders, as obeying Christ." Here was a new rhetoric, and popes took advantage of it by cementing control over the appointment of bishops. The process was fitful in Europe, but in America it proceeded quickly. New dioceses were created, and the pope chose the bishops who would lead them, putting in place men who shared his vision of his authority. There had been only five dioceses in the United States at the time of Carroll's death in 1815, but the number grew to eight by 1825, twelve by 1835, and twenty-one by 1845, a fourfold increase in just thirty years.

Popes were also steadily more enthusiastic in their denunciations of the "rejected innovators" of modern life. Gregory XVI even condemned the new technology of railroads, punning that these *chemins de fer* ("roads of iron"), as they were known in French, were *chemins d'enfer* ("roads to hell"). More seriously, popes adopted a broadly reactionary political and social outlook that seemed at odds with some characteristically American notions. In 1832, Gregory decried the "absurd and erroneous maxim, or rather . . . delirium, that freedom of conscience [in religion] must be assured and guaranteed to everyone." Possibly worse, he thought, was "that deadly freedom that cannot be sufficiently feared, the freedom of the press."[50]

Few Catholics in the United States shared such extreme sentiments. They had profited from the freedom of conscience that was available to them, and they enthusiastically embraced this ideal. But with their pope expressing such blatantly "un-American" ideas, they could well expect their fellow citizens to react with suspicion and hostility. Anti-Catholic feeling in America stretched back at least to the Massachusetts "anti-priest" law of 1647, though by the early nineteenth century this had become a largely rhetorical stance for most non-Catholics. In the face of this newly aggressive papacy, however, fear that Catholics posed a genuine threat to the nation's values gained a new life. In 1831, a person who signed himself simply "A True American" posted a notice on the door of a newly opened Catholic church in Connecticut: "Be it known . . . that all Catholics and all persons in favor of the Catholic religion are a set of vile imposters, liars, villains and cowardly cut-throats . . . I bid defiance to that villain the Pope."[51]

In the summer of 1834, anonymous defiance turned to violence in Charlestown, Massachusetts, a working-class town just across the harbor from Boston. Several evangelical Protestant ministers had passed through on the lecture circuit, detailing the dangers of reinvigorated popery. One of the most enthusiastic was Lyman Beecher of Cincinnati, father of Harriet Beecher Stowe, who later galvanized northern opposition to slavery with her best seller *Uncle Tom's Cabin.* During a hot mid-August week, Beecher delivered a series of inflammatory addresses, exposing a supposed papal plot to seize control of the Mississippi Valley, the first step in a Catholic power-grab whose purpose was to wipe out American freedom. In response, popular anger focused on a convent of Ursuline nuns in Charlestown and the school for girls (most of them the daughters of well-to-do Protestants) that they ran. Perhaps in reaction to the rising tension, perhaps simply from the heat, one of the sisters suffered an epileptic seizure and left the convent, though a day or two later she recovered her senses and returned. The incident prompted rumors that she had attempted to "escape" the clutches of the church and had been dragged back against her will. This was enough to set off a mob, which attacked the convent, drove nuns and pupils alike into the night, and burned the place to the ground; fortunately, no one was killed. The ringleaders, some of whom boasted openly of their part in the riot, were tried but acquitted by a sympathetic jury.[52]

Convents of nuns and what went on inside them suddenly seized the popular imagination. Given contemporary attitudes about women as properly confined to roles as wives and mothers, anti-Catholics saw something unnatural and even subversive in these independent institutions run by and for women. A new literary genre emerged almost overnight: the tale of the "escaped nun." Most successful were two books published immediately after the riot in Massachusetts: *Six Months in a Convent* (1835) by Rebecca Reed, and *Awful Disclosures of the Hotel Dieu Nunnery* (1836), ostensibly by a woman named Maria Monk. Reed was an actual person; Monk, as her too-coincidental name suggests, was not—the book had been written by a team of evangelical ministers—though someone using that name toured the country in the wake of its success. Both volumes compiled lurid tales of the cruelty and other abominations that they "proved" went on behind the cloister walls. Priests regularly slipped in through secret passages to have sex with the sisters, for instance, and the babies born of these illicit passions were first strangled and then buried in the cellar, the graves filled with lime to make their tiny bodies decay faster. Much of this writing was thinly disguised pornography, at least as that term was defined in the 1830s. Monk's book even included what purported to be floor plans of a convent in Montreal, showing trap doors, hidden staircases, "gaming and feasting rooms," and just enough chambers marked "unknown" to make it all seem real. The books sold hundreds of thousands of copies: in the entire period before the Civil War, only *Uncle Tom's Cabin* itself had a better market. No amount of Catholic refutation could entirely shake the notion that these descriptions were accurate, and their role in keeping popular anti-Catholic feeling alive was considerable.[53]

A decade later, Philadelphia was the scene of more destructive rioting. Catholic leaders there had been pressing for a change in the requirement that only the King James Version of the Bible—the so-called Protestant translation, to which Catholics objected—be used daily in the public schools. This effort brought the charge that Catholics were against the Bible altogether, and violence exploded one afternoon in May 1844, when two Catholic churches and nearly three dozen private homes were burned to the ground. Order was restored after a week, but blame was placed squarely on the Catholics. The incident had resulted from "the efforts of a portion of the community to exclude the Bible from our public schools," a grand jury investigating the incident concluded. Violence flared again right after the Fourth of July. This time the cause was a rumor that churches were being used as storehouses for guns; when a cache of weapons was indeed found in one church (most likely kept for defensive purposes), rioting began again. A group even dragged in some cannon from ships in the river and aimed them directly at a church; lacking ammunition, they loaded the cannons with nails and metal scraps and then fired. This had the desired effect: the defending Catholics fled, and the church was ransacked, though not destroyed. Rival militia companies were called in to restore order, but they only added to the confusion. When the incident was over, fourteen people had been killed and another fifty wounded.[54]

As dramatic as they were, episodes of overt violence against Catholics were not sustained in their intensity over long periods: they came and they went quickly. Nor did they characterize the attitudes of most American Protestants. Civic and religious leaders always denounced anti-Catholic violence, partly on account of the bigotry involved, partly because riots presented an unacceptable level of social disorder. The incidents were recurrent enough, however, to have an effect. A lingering suspicion of Catholicism embedded itself as a theme in American history, one that might manifest itself at any time. In 1854, for example, the alarm was raised when Pope Pius IX, following the example of other foreign leaders, contributed an inscribed stone to the Washington Monument, which was just going up in the nation's capital. A vigilante group managed to steal the papal stone, which was either hammered to pieces or thrown into the Potomac River.[55] The episode halted construction for nearly thirty years, and close observers of the monument even today can see that the color of the stones changes about one-third of the way up the famous obelisk, where the project was suspended.

For Catholics, too, the hostility they faced had a lasting effect. They thought of themselves as loyal to their nation and to their church at the same time, but those who rioted against them were convinced that such dual loyalties were impossible to sustain. Would American Catholics always have to answer the charge that they were "liars, villains, and cowardly cut-throats"? How many times would they have to prove that their religion and their patriotism were compatible? They had become faithful citizens and regular, churchgoing people, but to some Americans they still presented a threat.

Neither the rioters in Philadelphia nor the Catholics who were their victims had any idea of how much more complicated the question of American Catholic identity was about to become. Before the decade was over, the number of Catholic immigrants from Ireland and other European countries would suddenly swell to enormous proportions. How (or whether) these newcomers would assimilate themselves into American life became the urgent question, one that would take generations to play out. For American Catholics, the steady stream of new arrivals changed their church forever. The small church of the priestless era and that of the democratic republic were no more. Theirs would now be a large and steadily growing denomination, and the experience of the immigrants would define its character.

3

The Immigrant Church

Anna Hurban was born in 1855 in the village of Egbell in Slovakia, part of the Austro-Hungarian Empire. Had she stayed there, history would probably not have remembered her, but she left for America about thirty years later with her husband and small children, settling in a Slovak neighborhood of Cleveland, Ohio. There, she got to know Father Stephen Furdek, the pastor of Saint Ladislaus Church at the corner of Corwin and Holton Avenues. For the Hurbans and immigrants like them, the parish was not just a place of spiritual solace amid the turmoil of uprooting from the old world and transplanting to the new. It was also the place where they sent their children to school and where they gathered with their neighbors in the many societies that flourished there.

Furdek was by nature an organizer, and so was Mrs. Hurban. He had begun a Saint Joseph Society in 1889 that offered regular devotional exercises and, just as important, affordable insurance policies, something to cushion the blow if a family's breadwinner were injured in the crowded factories where most of them worked. A year later, Father Furdek assembled representatives of similar groups from parishes all over the Midwest to form a coordinating body known as the First Catholic Slovak Union. The union steadily expanded its membership and its programs, eventually publishing a newspaper and offering classes in labor organizing and workers' rights. Anna Hurban watched all this and then outdid her pastor in organizing ability. She and eight neighbors formed the First Catholic Slovak Ladies Union in 1892 and embarked on an ambitious agenda. In less than ten years, the ladies union had 84 local affiliates in half a dozen states. It opened an orphanage, ran schools to preserve language and culture, published its own newspaper, and established a related society for young people. By the time of Hurban's death in 1928, the small club she had started had more than 65,000 members across the nation.[1]

What is most distinctive about Anna Hurban, perhaps, is that she was not particularly distinctive at all. Many other Catholic immigrants, from housewives to factory workers, did what she did. By the beginning of the twentieth century, the American Catholic landscape was crowded with churches, schools, hospitals, orphanages, social welfare agencies, and devotional societies, organized along ethnic lines and sustained by immigrants and their families. Even a casual observer could see this infrastructure just by walking around the Catholic neighborhoods of almost any city. A single intersection might have a church on two or three of its four corners, each serving the needs of a different nationality. Residents identified with these churches, and it was parish as much as place that defined them. If asked, "Where do you live?" they did not reply, "Dorchester" or "Harlem" or "Woodland," but rather, "Saint Brendan's" or "Our Lady's" or "Saint Lad's."[2] This dense network of churches was evidence of a flourishing Catholicism in America that Roger Hanly and James McDonald could hardly have dreamed of. The Mass was available every day of the week and half a dozen times on Sunday. Immigrants could hear sermons and go to confession in their own language. Four or five priests lived in the parish rectory, and they were available at virtually any hour of the day or night. The church itself was an imposing and beautiful building just down the street, where people might stop in to say a quick prayer or light a candle on their way home from work or the grocery store. This is what it was like to be an American Catholic in the immigrant church.

Immigrant life was full of uncertainties: the physical hardship and dangers of industrial labor, the economic ups and downs, sometimes the hostility of better-established groups who resented outsiders. Amid all that, the church was an anchor, stabilizing things otherwise left adrift. The church also offered opportunity. The sons and daughters of immigrants became priests and nuns in numbers previously unimagined, and their vocations gave them and their families advantages in this world as well as the next one. They earned advanced degrees at a time when education was still a luxury, and they achieved a kind of elite status in the community. In the process, they embodied the church's presence for lay Catholics.

Local parishes were busy because there were now cadres of religious men and women to plan and oversee them. Priests and nuns lived among their people, as familiar as the cop on the beat or the shopkeeper around the corner. Most important, they directed the religious activities of the parish. Sunday morning Mass was only the beginning. Other exercises embedded themselves into the routines of immigrant Catholics: novenas, prayers for specified causes conducted over nine successive days; parish missions, a week or two of intense preaching designed, like Protestant revival meetings, to stir the fervor of the faithful; religious processions through the neighborhood streets. Catholics' participation in their religion grew to unprecedented levels in this rich religious culture, wiping out the memory of earlier, more perilous times. The church the immigrants made—in cooperation with the clergy, but also on their own—was distinct from that of both earlier and later eras, and it had an enduring impact on American Catholics.

The general story of immigration to America, like the particular story of Catholic immigration, is often told using metaphors of water. At first there was just a trickle. In the 1820s, when reliable counting began, only about 140,000 foreign passengers debarked in United States ports, and not all of them intended to stay. Given that the total population in 1830 was about 13 million, the arrivals represented a statistically insignificant number, barely 1 percent. Relative peace in Europe thereafter made crossing the Atlantic a reasonably safe endeavor, and as changing economic conditions on the old continent forced some to look for better prospects in the new, the flow grew until it became a wave. By the 1840s, the trickle had become a tidal surge: more than 1.5 million migrants in that decade, more than 2.5 million in the next one. In some cities, this surge became a flood, frightening many with its force and speed. Only about 2,000 immigrants had come into Boston in 1820, but almost 110,000 arrived in 1850, nearly as many people as lived there already. By 1850, 45 percent of the population of New York City had been born abroad, and the numbers only went higher thereafter.[3]

These immigrants came from a short list of countries, and Ireland stood at the head of that list. A persistent and destructive fungus was attacking the potato plants on which the island's agriculture depended, and the failure of successive annual crops brought famine and destitution on a wide scale. British government policy in the crisis, most historians now agree, made matters worse. Getting out was the only sensible course of action for anyone who could scrape together the resources to do so. Almost 800,000 Irish moved to the United States in the 1840s, accounting for almost half of all arrivals. They dwarfed the mere 30,000 from England and the only slightly larger number who came across the border from Canada. Second to the Irish were migrants from the still disunited German states, where times were not so hard though still uncertain. More than 400,000 Germans moved to America in the 1840s, five times as many as came from France and thirty times more than those from all the Scandinavian countries combined. The nation's total population jumped by roughly 35 percent in that decade, about a third of it accounted for by new arrivals from abroad. Immigration had become central to American life.[4]

Understandably, the pace slackened during the Civil War. As soon as the conflict was over, however, immigration resumed, and once again water was the governing metaphor. A new tide rose, as immigrants came in still greater numbers, at a faster rate, and from a wider range of places. The 1880s were typical. Altogether, about 5.2 million people entered the United States in that decade, a figure equal to 10 percent of the existing population. As before, Germany and Ireland led the list: 650,000 from Ireland, 1.5 million from Germany. But now, migrants from other parts of Europe joined the flow: 300,000 from Italy; a comparable number from various parts of the Austro-Hungarian Empire; 265,000 from Russia and its territories, including Poland; more than 600,000 from Norway, Sweden, and Denmark. For the first time ever, noticeable numbers of Chinese (61,000) and other Asians populated the western United States.[5]

In the face of this massive movement of peoples, those who considered themselves native citizens—they were not really natives, of course, but merely the descendants of earlier immigrants—began to wonder about the nation's ability to absorb the newcomers, who were accused of bringing crime, social problems, and political radicalism with them. An emerging "science" of ethnic and racial classification began to distinguish "good" immigrants, who might be encouraged to come, from "bad" ones, who surely should not. Asians, for example, were presumed to be undesirable, and legislation to exclude Chinese from American shores first passed Congress in 1882; it was renewed every ten years thereafter. Other groups, too, were suspect: eleven Italian immigrants were lynched in New Orleans in 1891, a vigilante punishment usually reserved for African Americans. Broad political pressure built to restrict the number of migrants who could enter the nation and the countries from which they could come. These efforts culminated in legislation in the 1920s that effectively closed the spigot on immigration by setting low annual quotas, country by country.[6]

Not all nineteenth-century immigrants were Catholics, of course. Many were not: Lutherans from Sweden, Jews from Russia and Poland, several denominations of Protestants from central Europe, Buddhists and Confucians from Asia. The Irish, by contrast, were overwhelmingly Catholic, and their Catholicism was of a particularly fervid kind. Partly in response to the terrors of the famine, church leaders in Ireland had made a concerted effort to turn previously lukewarm Irish Catholics into devout and regular churchgoers. Mass attendance rose to previously unknown levels on the island, and other pious practices were introduced: communal recitations of the rosary, devotions to various saints, pilgrimages to holy sites. When these Irish immigrants set out for America, they already had deeply ingrained religious habits. Among Germans, Catholics came largely from Bavaria, while those from elsewhere were mostly Protestants. German Catholics had not experienced a revival as intense as that of the Irish, but they had lived through the harsh policies of Bismarck, who had declared *Kulturkampf*—"culture war"—against the church, limiting the public role of the clergy and restricting Catholic schools. Such persecutions made the German Catholics who fled to America all the more likely to hold onto their faith. Levels of devotional intensity varied among the other immigrant groups—it was generally higher among Poles and Lithuanians than among Italians, for example—but Catholicism came in the trunks of immigrants along with their other prized possessions.[7]

"Immigrants" who were not really immigrants at all also attracted notice in the nineteenth century: Native American and Hispanic Catholics in the Southwest. Missionaries had come with Spanish explorers and conquerors from the beginning, and when these territories were absorbed by the United States in the 1840s, chains of missions ran up the Pacific Coast and crisscrossed the inland reaches north of the Rio Grande. These missions were sites for the conversion and "civilizing" of Indians, but the religion that flourished among the people was a hybrid of traditions. Strict Spanish Catholicism blended with ancient folkways to produce a faith that was different from that of the eastern half of the nation. Its practitioners probably had the best claim to the title of "natives," but church officials usually saw them as merely another foreign group to be absorbed, no less than Bohemians or Slovaks. For decades, these Catholics would remain marginal to the power structures of the church in America, but they would nonetheless contribute even greater ethnic variety to the immigrant church.[8]

With such a massive infusion of peoples, the Catholic population of the United States jumped. The federal census rarely gathered data about church membership (the separation of church and state blocked detailed questioning on the subject), and local parishes only occasionally found the time to stop and count their members. Still, the pattern was easy to see. Catholics accounted for only about 3 percent of the nation in 1830, but by 1850 that number was already up to 8 percent. At the outbreak of the Civil War, the Catholic Church had become the largest single religious denomination in the country, though it was still outnumbered if all the distinct Protestant churches were counted together. By the end of the century, Catholics made up 18 percent of the population, and the number rose to almost 21 percent in the 1920s. By then, Catholics numbered 16 million and constituted 38 percent of all self-identified church members, according to one survey. Baptists and Methodists, by comparison, amounted to less than half that number, at about 7 million each. Presbyterians (more than 2 million) and Episcopalians (just over 1 million), members of the churches of the "establishment" in many places, lagged far behind; Jewish congregations could count only about 360,000 members. The Catholic Church in the United States, a Catholic sociologist wrote a decade later, "stands today a living exponent of the parable of the mustard seed . . . this mustard seed has developed into a great tree."[9]

The institutions of the church expanded to meet the needs of these new members. In 1840, there had been seventeen dioceses in the United States, each with its own bishop to supervise local churches; a decade later, as the immigrant wave began to gather, there were thirty of them. The church was following the population west, but the fastest expansion was in the cities of the East and Midwest, which were filling up with immigrants: by 1850, there were new bishops for Buffalo, Pittsburgh, and Cleveland. By 1880, the count would double again to sixty dioceses, needed now in places like Fort Wayne, Indiana; Green Bay, Wisconsin; and Little Rock, Arkansas. Fewer than five hundred priests served the Catholic population in 1840, but by 1890 that number had reached nearly nine thousand. In cities everywhere, Catholics needed new parishes, a demand church leaders tried to satisfy as quickly as they could. Detroit, for instance, had fifteen parishes in 1880, twenty-nine by 1900, and eighty-nine when the floodgates of immigration closed in 1925. In the time it took for a Catholic girl born in Detroit in 1880 to grow to adulthood, the church around her had increased more than fivefold. For a child born in St. Louis, the growth from infancy to middle age was modest by comparison: the number of parish churches there had only—only!—doubled during that time.[10]

Local parishes grew organically, almost genealogically, from one another. A parish was defined by a certain territory: any Catholic living within that district, whose boundaries were precisely drawn, was expected to worship at that church. Pastors guarded their territory as jealously as any feudal baron, and disputes erupted in many places. Just before the First World War, for example, churches in Cincinnati were plagued with persistent arguments over which streets belonged to which parish. As a church's population increased, however, another parish would be needed, perhaps at the opposite end of the neighborhood. The decision to divide a congregation was largely a practical one. Were there enough people to erect a second church building and to support the clergy assigned to it? The priests of a parish received a small salary (diocesan clergy did not take a vow of poverty) which, together with their living expenses, came exclusively from the people of that church rather than from central diocesan funds. Thus a parish might grow very large before it could be divided without imperiling the survival of either the original, "mother" church or the new "daughter" parish. Ethnic differences further complicated the process. Large numbers of non–English-speaking parishioners were likely to press for a church of their own. Only when they could support it would a new parish be created. All Catholics speaking their language could attend that church, regardless of where they lived. Thus there were two overlapping grids of parishes, one based on geography (called "territorial" parishes), the other on language or ethnicity ("national" parishes).[11]

The Bridgeport neighborhood of Chicago offers an example of how this system worked. Bridgeport was only a little more than one square mile bounded by the city's famous stockyards and the Chicago River. The first church there was Saint Bridget's, which opened in 1850 as the parish for the entire district. As the church's name suggests, the congregation consisted mostly of Irish immigrants, who were then flooding into Chicago. Saint Bridget's was in the northwest corner of Bridgeport, however, and could not accommodate the influx of people who settled elsewhere. Thus a second territorial parish, Nativity of Our Lord, was opened in 1868 in the far southeast corner. By then, many Bohemians and Germans were moving to the area. Few of them could understand sermons in English, the vernacular language of Saint Bridget's and Nativity, and the Irish priests could not understand these parishioners when they came to confession. In response, two national parishes were formed: Saint John Nepomucene for Bohemians in 1871, and Saint Anthony of Padua for Germans two years later. A third territorial parish, again with mostly Irish congregants, was added in 1875, but by the early 1880s there were even more non–English-speakers in the neighborhood. Accordingly, in 1883, a second German parish, Immaculate Conception, was added, together with a church for Polish Catholics, Saint Mary of Perpetual Help. By 1910, the process of dividing and dividing again had produced yet one more territorial parish and three new national parishes, for German, Polish, and Lithuanian Catholics, respectively—a total of eleven now, all within walking distance of one another in the square mile that was Bridgeport.[12] Lay people, who experienced Catholicism primarily in these local churches, found it easy to identify the parish that was "theirs."

Catholic institutional expansion in the immigrant church was even more dramatically evident in the rapidly growing number of religious sisters. The earlier, priestless church had also been a sisterless church. Communities of nuns (officially called "women religious") had been common in Europe for centuries, but since most had devoted themselves to cloistered prayer, apart from the world, they had to rely on long-established endowments of land and money for their support. Absent generations of bequests, it was difficult to transfer that model of religious life to America. With time, however, orders of nuns organized themselves and spread widely. Some Carmelite sisters established the first convent in the United States at Port Tobacco, Maryland, in 1790, and in Baltimore in 1808 Elizabeth Seton, a wealthy widow and convert to Catholicism, formed a group calling themselves the Sisters of Charity. Other sisterhoods followed, some through the transplantation of European religious communities, others through the efforts of American women who, like Seton, felt the call to religious life. By the time immigrants began arriving, they found several orders of nuns: Sisters of Notre Dame, Ursuline Sisters, Dominicans, Franciscans, Sisters of the Child Jesus, Sisters of the Holy Family, Sisters of the Good Shepherd, and many more.[13]

With these new communities came an important redefinition of the work that sisters did. No longer confining themselves to prayer, they also assumed responsibility for works of charity and education. In church law, sisters were considered lay people, and it was thus perhaps natural for them to engage in various activities "in the world." Seton's Sisters of Charity, for example, staffed schools and orphanages in several cities. Later, they and other nuns also took on nursing roles. Each community of sisters had its own internal governance procedures. Some were essentially independent, while others maintained ties to European religious orders. However they were structured, the number of sisterhoods and their membership grew in parallel with the American Catholic population: there were about 900 sisters in 15 communities in 1840; nearly 50,000 in 170 orders by 1900; and almost 135,000 nuns in 300 different orders by 1930. Officially, the male clergy were the leaders of the church and exercised all its powers; in practice, female sisters exerted a greater impact on the Catholic laity than did priests, if only because there were more of them. In the mid-1830s, for example, the archbishop of Baltimore had 29 priests working in his parishes compared with 44 Sisters of Charity as well as nuns from other communities. Nationwide by 1820, nuns had come to outnumber priests; by the twentieth century, in many places sisters outnumbered priests by factors of five and six to one.[14] For the ordinary Catholic in the immigrant era, the face of the church was most often a woman's face.

Nowhere was the impact of sisters more apparent than in church-related schools. Many orders focused on teaching, but the Sisters of Saint Joseph may stand for all of them. The Congregation of Saint Joseph (called CSJs, for short), which traced its origins to seventeenth-century France, sent 6 women to the United States in 1836. They settled just outside St. Louis, in a town they named Carondelet after their French motherhouse. They ran a boarding school for young ladies, accepted day students from the parishes of the city, taught special classes for deaf children, and even took in orphans. While most of the young women who passed through their schools chose conventional lives of marriage and family, some were themselves attracted to religious life; more than 3,300 women joined the order between its founding and 1920. By then, the CSJs were among the largest group of teachers in American parish schools. The Catholic bishops of the nation had begun promoting the building of schools shortly after the Civil War. "No parish is complete till it has schools adequate to the needs of its children," they wrote, "and the pastor and people of such a parish should feel that they have not accomplished their entire duty until the want is supplied." This goal was never fully achieved, but the pace at which schools opened was still staggering. Consider Milwaukee. There were 4,000 pupils in the schools of 14 Milwaukee parishes in 1880, but by 1900 that number had tripled to more than 13,000 in 28 schools; by 1920, enrollment had almost doubled again to 25,000 students in 43 schools.[15]

Nuns also addressed the special needs of national parishes. Certain sisterhoods flourished in each ethnic group, drawing membership from immigrants and their daughters, and the schools of national parishes depended on them: Felician Sisters in Polish parishes, Sisters of the Presentation of Mary in French-Canadian churches, and Franciscan Sisters in Italian parishes. Lay teachers, male and female, were sometimes hired to cover specialized subjects, particularly in the higher grades, but this was a rare occurrence: overwhelmingly, women religious were the workforce on which all Catholic schools depended. Three Italian schools in Pittsburgh in 1910, for example, had an enrollment of more than five hundred pupils, who were taught by eleven sisters and one lay person (not identified, but probably a woman). Instruction in such schools was done in both the mother tongue and English. At the Holy Trinity elementary school, attached to a church in Chicago's Polonia on the near northwest side, the catechism was taught in Polish to students in grades one through eight. The sisters also taught Polish reading and grammar to help make religious lessons intelligible to their pupils. They did not neglect English spelling, reading, and grammar, however, and they always taught arithmetic in English. Singing was bilingual so that the children could learn both the folk songs of their old country and the patriotic tunes of their new one.[16]

In that way, children were acculturated to their American surroundings, particularly as one generation gave way to the next. Critics worried that these parish schools perpetuated ethnic distinctions, but defenders were quick to point out that these institutions actually helped the process of Americanization. Precisely because students were instructed in both of the languages they heard every day (one at home, the other in public), a commentator wrote, "the process of assimilation has gone on quietly, smoothly, rapidly." For some, this absorption into an English-speaking world may even have been a little too successful. "Not two boys out of twenty employ Polish in their conversation with one another," a Polish pastor noted shortly after the turn of the century. Girls seemed to hold onto their parents' language a little longer, for reasons he could not explain, but as children grew up, they gradually lost their fluency. After graduation from high school, the priest said, most students, male and female, largely forgot whatever Polish they had learned. "The young man and the young woman of twenty-two or three years do not devote an hour a week to the reading of Polish books or papers, while of writing in Polish there is practically none." This loss of the mother tongue had consequences, large and small. Ease in English undoubtedly helped these second-generation children get ahead, but there was "a growing difficulty to find a young man or young woman equipped with a sufficient knowledge of Polish to assume the duties of recording secretary in our parish and national societies."[17] Minutes of meetings, once entirely in Polish or the language of other parishes, made the transition to English.

Loss of language across the generations was accompanied by fears that faith might be lost as well. Catholics were warned not to be taken in by suggestions that all "true" Americans were Protestants or by other enticements. Boston's Catholic newspaper, *The Pilot,* reported in 1913 that an Episcopal church had opened in the Italian North End neighborhood of the city. It had been decorated deliberately to look as much like a Catholic church as possible, the paper's editors complained, with the intention of tricking unsuspecting immigrants into worshiping there. Even the Unitarian Church, whose members were largely of the educated upper class, was opening a chapel for Italians, a move that evoked a howl of derision: "Is it possible to imagine a Unitarian Italian?"[18]

Some Catholic immigrants did convert to a Protestant church, and they did so for many reasons. The Baptist owner of a shoe factory in a small New England town brought in a preacher to work among his employees, most of them Italians. These men were not regular churchgoers, an observer wrote, and at first they showed little interest in converting. "Since Mr. Evans was the owner of the factory," however, "and it was good to be looked upon favorably by 'the boss,' they decided to attend" his Baptist chapel and to bring their wives and children along with them. Even so, Catholic fears over what bishops called "leakage" were overstated. A priest-sociologist studying the matter in 1925 answered the question, "Has the immigrant kept the faith?" with an unequivocal "yes." There had indeed been some "defections," he said, but these were minimal and attributable only to "the weakness of human nature."[19] Immigrants who came to America with Catholicism in their religious baggage usually held onto it.

An observer of the flourishing immigrant churches and schools might well have wondered how parishioners could afford to support them. "The ordinary parish is not well-to-do," one priest wrote in 1912, stating the obvious. "To keep up the church and its equipment, and to pay off the debt, with the prospect, perhaps, of necessary enlargement of the church in the future, or its replacement by a larger and finer structure"—all this was sufficient "to tax the energies of the ablest and most zealous priest." Most parishioners stood on the lower rungs of society's economic ladder. Early Maryland Catholics were often well off, but the church of the immigrants was a church of the working class. Holy Rosary parish, for example, located just north of downtown Denver, was opened in 1918 for Slovenian Catholics, and its organizers included a butcher, a shoemaker, a driver, three grocers, three laborers, and a bartender.[20]

Even as immigrants strove to improve their lot, personal and family finances were always close to the edge. Sickness or unemployment could bring a sudden change of fortune to virtually any family, and there was a thin line between getting by and disaster. Children, particularly older sons, often had to leave school sooner rather than later, so as to contribute to the welfare of the family. Given such hardships, how had Catholics marshaled the resources to build—literally—the immigrant church?

The secret to success lay in gathering a large number of small donations. Modern fundraising campaigns of all kinds usually take the opposite approach, lining up a few big donors first, and only then making an effort to get smaller contributions from a wider circle of supporters. Catholic finances in the immigrant church, by contrast, took their model from the story of the widow's mite in the Gospel of Saint Mark: the old woman who sacrificed a tiny sum was more blessed than the showy hypocrites who gave greater amounts that they would not miss. Encouraged by the clergy to follow this example, most parishioners could make only a small contribution to their church, but if they gave it regularly, the total added up soon enough. "Who is there," the rector of the cathedral parish in Boston asked his people in 1872, while raising money to put up a new building, "that cannot contribute to the new Cathedral fifty cents a month?" In fact, many of his parishioners probably found that sum too much, but enough of them could spare it that the effort went ahead: within five years, an enormous new church edifice had been completed.[21] Bishops and pastors usually got the credit for marshaling these limited resources, and their leadership was surely essential. In the end, however, the money came from lay people.

Fundraising in American Catholic churches employed several specific methods, and these changed over time. In the earliest years, many parishes followed the pattern of Protestant churches in selling or renting their pews. A parishioner (usually the head of a household) paid a certain amount every year in one lump sum and also pledged to contribute something each week. This entitled the family to occupy a designated pew in the church, and they were given an actual deed, documenting their legal right to the space. Other parishioners had to stay out of that pew, even if the owners were not present, and "trespassers" were regularly warned. This system guaranteed the parish a regular income, but it had its drawbacks. It tended, for example, to reinforce differences of social rank in a way that seemed at odds with the demands of Christian fellowship. In South Carolina, Bishop John

England had denounced the sale of pews as early as 1822, saying that it created "a very painful and galling distinction . . . between the rich and the poor, which causes pride and self-conceit in the one, and mortification and shame in the other." More practically, this system was useless in any parish that lacked enough Catholics who could afford the down payment or a predictable weekly pledge. That, of course, was the case in most parishes. One church in an immigrant neighborhood of Boston, first opened in the 1840s, was even known popularly as "the Free Church," precisely because it did not sell its pews. Although this practice was unusual then, by the end of the century it was the norm.[22]

The sale of pews was replaced by a voluntary collection from parishioners at every Sunday's Mass. Lay ushers took up this collection, most commonly right after the preaching of the sermon. They passed wicker baskets on long poles through each pew successively, row by row. This job was always supposed to be done by lay men, never by the priest himself, apparently to preclude coercion, though some priests did occasionally "pass the basket." No single contributor had to give very much, but collectively the sums might be considerable, given the number of parishioners who packed the pews. A Philadelphia newspaper sent reporters out one Sunday in January 1879 (a typical Sabbath, the paper thought) to conduct an "actual count" of worshipers in the churches of various denominations. Nineteen Catholic parishes in the city had nearly 83,000 people at Mass that day: even if the average donation was small, the total figure was impressive. Better yet for Catholic pride, the paper reported that 130 Protestant churches had had a combined attendance of only 42,000 that day: seven times as many churches for the Protestants, half as many people.[23]

Sometimes two collections were taken at the same service, the first for the regular support of the parish, the second for some special charitable cause. Churches also conducted occasional fundraising fairs, especially as part of building campaigns. Fairs for the cathedral in Boston, for instance, held in the half-completed shell of the new building itself, ran over several weeks in the fall of 1871 and again in 1874. Attendees could take a chance on raffles, attend the concerts of parish choirs, and taste the offerings of food tables, with goodies provided by the women of the parish. The 1871 fair, open nightly from the end of October until the beginning of December, took in close to $100,000 for the construction project.[24] Not every fair at every church was this successful, but the method was widely copied in American Catholic parishes.

By any measure, financial or otherwise, the expansion of the Catholic Church in the United States during the immigrant era was nothing short of remarkable. By the time immigration slowed in the 1920s, the church, its institutions, and its people were virtually everywhere. Clerical and lay Catholics alike took satisfaction from what they had managed to build. "But," the nation's bishops wrote in a general letter to the faithful in 1919, "what we regard as far more important is the growth and manifestation of an active religious spirit" among parishioners.[25] The bishops were right. American Catholics were not interested in buildings and institutions alone; it was the substance of religion that attracted and held their loyalty. The changed historical circumstances in which they practiced their faith meant that they found new ways to embody their "religious spirit." In the process, they articulated new ways of being Catholic in America.

Immigrants and their families lived their religion in the churches they built. Earlier generations of American Catholics had gathered in someone's parlor or in small churches like the one the Yankee visitor to Charleston considered "shabby." Immigrants now came to expect a substantial church building down the block

or around the corner, a place to which they could have recourse
any time they wanted. The churchifying process, begun in the
age of the democratic republic, was completed in the immigrant
generations.

Architectural styles of American Catholic churches varied, but
there were some recurring favorites. Gothic and Romanesque designs were most popular; the occasional Byzantine pile, though
exotic, might be put up; imitations of spare colonial meeting-
houses were rare but not unknown. The choice of one design
over another was usually a matter of local circumstance, and
rarely did a city or region have an artistic master plan. All churches
shared common features in creating the space, both physical and
mental, in which parishioners worshiped. Traditionally, the foot-
print of a church was supposed to be in the form of a cross, so
that the interior had a long aisle down the center, with a shorter
aisle intersecting it near the front, just before the altar. Churches
that were wide enough also had side aisles with seating on either
side of them. Most of the floor space was filled with open pews
that stretched from aisle to aisle. The box pews of some earlier
churches (enclosures with latching doors, designed to keep both
drafts and trespassers out) were abandoned quickly. Each pew
had a long kneeler at its occupants' feet. Sometimes this kneeler
could be folded up and out of the way, but even when that was
possible, it was usually left down, since those attending Mass
spent much of the time on their knees.[26]

In front of all the pews was the area containing the altar,
known as the sanctuary, which stood one or two steps higher
than the main floor of the church. This area was set off by a low
railing about two and a half feet high, which served a double purpose. Practically, parishioners knelt at it when receiving Communion, and it was usually accompanied by a leather pad—"preferably green," one authority suggested—to soften the impact on
the knees. Symbolically, this altar rail formed a barrier between

the priests who were celebrating the Mass and the lay people who were in attendance. The distinction was an important one. "The sanctuary is cut off as a place specially sacred, and reserved to the clergy, between whom and the laity there is a distinction of divine origin," one theologian wrote. Some lay people might temporarily enter the sanctuary (as altar boys or cleaners, for instance), but they were exceptions. Whenever anyone did so, they were admitted "only out of necessity, and [were], for the purpose, temporarily regarded as clerics."[27] Most parishioners spent their entire lives without ever entering this part of the church they attended every week.

Against the back wall of the sanctuary was the main altar, which was raised above the floor by another several steps, in part so that those sitting far away could see it. The surface of the altar was covered with a long linen runner atop which sat candles that were lit only during services. In the middle was a boxlike structure called the tabernacle, usually with a locking door, in which already-consecrated Eucharistic wafers were stored or "reserved." The extra wafers were used when the number of communicants at Mass was larger than usual, or when priests needed to bring Communion to the homebound sick and elderly. Because, according to Catholic theology, these had been transformed into the actual body of Christ, they were treated with particular reverence. As a reminder that Jesus was, in this way, truly present, a special candle, known as a sanctuary lamp, was placed off to one side and kept constantly burning so long as there were hosts in the tabernacle. Sometimes the sanctuary contained two smaller altars, one at the head of each side aisle. These were used when the crowd at a service was small—early-morning Mass on a weekday, for example—or when a priest said Mass privately by himself.[28]

The rest of the interior was filled with objects that became so familiar parishioners stopped noticing them. There were confessional boxes—sometimes two, sometimes four—either standing out from the walls or built into them. These were the places where lay people came anonymously to relate their sins to the priest and to receive God's forgiveness. Some churches had statues in the sanctuary and elsewhere, representing Jesus, Mary, or one of the saints. The windows also depicted saints or biblical scenes in stained glass, usually the product of special fundraising efforts. The side walls contained the fourteen Stations of the Cross, which depicted, either in bas relief or on canvas, scenes from the crucifixion of Jesus. Inside the sanctuary, just behind the altar rail, might be racks of small votive candles, which parishioners could light after making a small donation. These constituted a form of symbolic prayer, kept up as long as the candles burned, for the spiritual intentions of the person who lit them. Over the front door to the church was a choir loft, the usual location for the organ, which in many Protestant churches was placed in the sanctuary. Finally, the entire space might be replicated in the basement of the church, beneath the main floor. Thus many parishes had essentially two churches in which services could be conducted simultaneously. There might be a separate Mass for children downstairs while their parents worshiped upstairs, for instance, or a Mass with preaching in a foreign language at the same time as another one for English speakers. Particularly well off parishes built a separate, adjacent chapel in lieu of a basement church, but this was unusual.[29]

Two examples from literally thousands illustrate these principles of church design. Immaculate Conception in Burlington, Vermont, was finished right after the Civil War. The church, with both Irish and French-Canadian parishioners, was 175 feet long, its crosslike transepts 100 feet wide. A brilliant bronze tabernacle sat atop the marble altar, and on the wall above it were two rows of paintings portraying the life of the Virgin Mary. The stained-glass windows depicted the Ten Commandments on one side and elements of the Christian creed on the other. Halfway across the country, Sacred Heart Church in Stearns County, Minnesota, was built along similar lines. The third church building used by its largely German parishioners, it opened in 1906 and was nearly 200 feet long, easily accommodating the 1,200 members of the parish. It had three marble altars at the front and statues of Saint Francis and of Jesus himself. Carved Stations of the Cross, each about four feet square, flanked the windows, the glass in which depicted scenes from the Old and New Testaments.[30] Not merely impressive architectural objects—though they were that—churches such as these shaped the mental geography of faith for the people sitting in the pews. Those people might not understand all (or even most) of the symbolism around them, but they knew from it that they were part of a religious tradition that was long and deep.

The devotional practices conducted in these buildings grew in number and variety in the immigrant church, but Sunday morning Mass remained at the center of parishioners' worshiping lives. Like the 83,000 Philadelphians who turned out that Sunday in 1879, Catholics nationwide made this the focus of their religious activity. The Mass they attended was the same one that Catholics of earlier eras would have recognized, but there were also some differences. To begin with, the service was much more available than ever before. Whereas churches had once been able to offer only one or two Masses every Sunday, now they routinely held half a dozen or maybe even more. A parish in New York City, visited by a reporter from the *Atlantic Monthly* on a cold Sunday in December 1867, had Masses at 6:00, 7:00, 9:00, and 10:30, with an additional service in the basement chapel at 9:30 for school children. In the 1890s, half the churches in Baltimore had at least four Masses every Sunday. A generation after that, Catholics in Milwaukee in 1920 were faced with an embarrassment of riches. Saint Adalbert's, a Polish parish on the city's near south side, had

eight Masses each Sunday, every hour on the hour from five A.M.
until noon. (Every weekday it had four Masses, at half-hour in-
tervals between 7:00 and 8:30.) Across town, the Gesu church
had four Sunday Masses upstairs and three downstairs. Altogether, Mass was said somewhere in the city of Milwaukee more
than 165 times every Sunday morning.[31]

Scheduling so many Masses was necessary to meet the demands of the exploding population, but it was possible because
the number of priests was rising to unprecedented levels. For the
first time, the typical American parish had more than one priest
in residence. The transition happened quickly. In 1900, for example, Cleveland had 36 parishes, 22 of them (61 percent) staffed by
a pastor who lived and worked alone. Unless he could secure the
help of a visiting clergyman, the parish could offer only the two
Masses the pastor was allowed to say himself. By 1925, however,
the number of parishes in Cleveland had grown to 89 (two and a
half times as many in twenty-five years), and 53 of those (60 percent) were staffed by a pastor who had at least one assistant priest
living and working with him. Now the parish might offer four,
six, or even more Masses every Sunday. Brooklyn in 1925 had an
even greater concentration of clergy. The borough was home to
127 parish churches, 83 of them (65 percent) with two or more
curates in addition to the pastor.[32] No longer priestless, American
Catholicism now had an abundance of priests, and this highlighted the shifting balance between clergy and laity. The priest
conducted religious worship; lay people knelt or sat and watched
him do it.

The appearance of the Mass also changed. "The gradual but
brilliant development of the ritual," a New York priest wrote in
1905, heralded "a new era for divine worship." This priest was a
bit over-enthusiastic, but an important change was under way in
how American Catholics experienced the Mass. "Marble altars of
artistic quality" replaced wooden altars in the "shabby" churches

of an earlier era. "Decorated sanctuaries, well furnished, well-heated churches and comfortable pews" were now the sites of religious practice. The change might even be apparent over the course of a single lifetime. In 1824, Father John Timon had been a young missionary, traveling rural Missouri in search of scattered Catholics. It was he who claimed to have said Mass in "a pretty large hog pen" cleaned out for the occasion. By the 1860s, Timon was the bishop of Buffalo, New York, presiding in a massive new cathedral church in the heart of the city. Timon was presumably struck by the contrast, but his parishioners also had a new relationship to the church. In the past, priests came to them and said Mass in their homes. Now priests had homes of their own, both figurative (the church) and literal (the rectory), and lay people went to them. What went on in church was recognizably different from what went on elsewhere. Formality replaced informality, and ceremonies "calculated to excite devotion and impress the faithful with the awful grandeur of the holy sacrifice" became the norm.[33]

Catholic parishes now paid closer attention to the "rubrics," the precise rules for celebrating Mass. The priest was assisted by one or more altar boys between the ages of ten and sixteen. These young helpers were chosen from among the boys—girls were not permitted—in the parish school, recruited partly in the hope that serving at the Mass would encourage them to think about becoming priests themselves. Their duties were both prayerful and practical. They moved the missal book, from which the priest read the service, from one place on the altar to another, and they rang a little bell at the moment when the priest consecrated the Eucharist. More important, they responded aloud to certain prayers the priest said, speaking on behalf of the congregation, which kept silent throughout. In order to recite these prayers, the boys, who were of course not native speakers of Latin, had to be drilled to memorize the appropriate responses and when to say them. Crib sheets were forbidden, and months of coaching in "the manner of serving a priest at Mass" preceded a boy's debut. Altar boys learned from a kind of script. "When you see the Priest spread his hands over the chalice," the instructions said at one point, "give warning, by the bell, of the Consecration which is about to be made. Then holding the vestment with your left hand, and having the bell in your right, ring during the elevation of the host and of the chalice." When the boys did their jobs well, they enhanced the solemnity of the liturgy, not to mention the pride of their parents. "Make them thoroughly good and pious," a seminary textbook advised in the 1890s, "and you will make their mothers happy and edify the entire congregation."[34]

The presence of these servers—"temporarily regarded" in effect as junior priests, as the expert on church design had noted, and even dressed like the priest in liturgical garments—further reinforced the difference between laity and clergy. Lay Catholics might well conclude that a "distinction of divine origin" existed between them, and it was easy for lay people to assume the role of spectators at a ritual they attended but did not really participate in, conducted in a language they did not understand. Prayer books for the laity underlined this separation, providing prayers and devotions that churchgoers could read instead of those of the Mass. In 1876, in a departure from earlier missals, one volume included a sixty-five-page collection of prayers to be said at Mass but did not contain the text of the liturgy itself. The presumption seemed to be that users would not (or perhaps would not want to try to) keep abreast of what the priest was doing on the altar.

A few years later, the American Catholic bishops authorized a standard prayer book for use throughout the country, and a *Manual of Prayers for the Use of the Catholic Laity*, expressly designated "The Official Prayer Book of the Catholic Church," appeared in 1888. It was reissued, substantially unchanged, in 1916 and remained in print until the 1950s. While this volume did provide the actual prayers of the Mass, they were almost lost amid a host of other spiritual exercises. As the priest was reading the gospel of the day to himself, for example, the manual's users could read a prayer about the Gospels generally: "All that is written of Thee, O Jesus, in Thy Gospel is Truth itself . . . Give me, O God, grace to practise [sic] what Thou commandest, and command what Thou pleasest."[35]

Such prayers furthered the impression that there was a kind of spiritual division of labor at Mass: the priest did what he did, and lay people did what they did, perhaps without much reference to each other. Theological textbooks spoke of "the intimate union which the priest enters into with the Divine Saviour," but lay people only "share[d] in the fruits of the Sacred Mystery," one step removed. It was the priest who "said" the Mass; the laity only "heard" or "assisted" at it. Moreover, since the priest kept his back to the congregation most of the time, it was easy to maintain the separation. Even when they did turn to face the people, priests were warned by their seminary professors not to make eye contact with anyone in the congregation. Once again, the altar rail drew a psychological as well as an architectural line. "It is very common," one priest wrote in the 1920s, "for the laity to take very little active part indeed in the official prayers and ceremonies of the Church. Thus at holy Mass you will commonly find the congregation engaged in all kinds of private devotions—recitation of the Rosary, reading the so-called 'devotions for Mass' provided in popular prayer books."[36]

In this way, the Mass was a curious combination for lay people. It was private prayer done in public, an individual exercise that just happened to be carried out in the presence of other people. The service itself was more widely available than ever before, and yet it remained remote. Parishioners were there, but they were passive, often absorbed in their own thoughts. Altar boys rang a bell at the consecration of the Eucharist partly for this reason: it attracted the attention of the worshipers, however momentarily; after that, they could go back to what they were doing. Some might simply lapse into inattention, of course, but those who tried to be prayerful could do so without actually following the liturgy.

The view that some of these alternative prayers took of the spiritual condition of the laity was a dim one and only widened the distinction between priests and lay people. Unworthiness was a persistent theme. "I adore thee," a prayer from 1876 said, "confessing my own misery and nothingness." Taking a spiritual approach that historians have called a "purgative way," many prayers drove home the idea that sufferings in this life were justly deserved punishments; enduring them without complaint helped cleanse sinful souls, which needed as much help as they could get. Sickness, like health, was a "gift," one prayer said: "Let me burn and be tormented here; spare me not here that thou mayest spare me in eternity." Even at Mass, participants were not allowed to forget their faults. "O Almighty Lord of Heaven and earth," the official prayer manual had its users say at the start of the Mass, "behold I, a wretched sinner, presume to appear before Thee this day . . . I here confess, in the sight of the whole court of heaven and of all Thy faithful, my innumerable treasons against Thy divine majesty."[37] This language was considerably more graphic than that of the prayer of confession the priest was saying in Latin at the same time.

Evidence suggests that the laity absorbed much of this outlook about themselves, and the low rate at which those attending Mass went forward to take Communion is particularly telling. Consecrating and distributing the Eucharist was the whole point of the liturgy, and American Catholics of an earlier age had often hoped in vain for more regular access to the sacrament. This was now possible, but Catholics in the immigrant church did not usually avail themselves of the opportunity, largely because they feared "unworthy" reception. In Boston in May 1899, for example, a priest in a large parish of Irish and German immigrants reported that about seven hundred people were at his 7:45 Mass one Sunday morning, and that exactly forty of them came to Communion. The rest had apparently taken to heart the prayer of one devotional manual, even if they had never read it: "Conscious of my infirmities and sins, I dare not now receive Thee sacramentally . . . Come, therefore, O Lord, to me in spirit, and heal my sinful soul."[38] This sort of "spiritual communion" had often been a necessity for American Catholics in the priestless era. Now, with priests and churches nearly everywhere, lay people maintained this habit by choice.

Even without Communion, lay people were still expected to be in church. "A Catholic who through his own fault misses Mass on a Sunday," a catechism said unequivocally, "commits a mortal sin." Mass attendance was also mandatory on certain other days of the year. These were the so-called holy days of obligation. In medieval times, the calendar had been full of such feasts, and they later became a special target of reformers. In America, there had been considerable variation from place to place. Some American dioceses celebrated as many as ten feast days, while others observed as few as six. In 1884, the nation's bishops settled on six as the official number: Christmas; New Year's Day (observed in commemoration of the circumcision of Jesus); Ascension Thursday (forty days after Easter, when Jesus rose into heaven); August 15 (celebrating the bodily assumption of the Virgin Mary into heaven); November 1 (All Saints' Day); and December 8 (honoring the immaculate conception of Mary). On such days, churches offered several Masses, scheduled for the convenience of working parishioners. "Whenever a holyday [sic] of obligation happens to fall on a week day," an adviser to parish clergy wrote, "one Mass ought to be said early in the morning (five or six o'clock) to give parties that have to work a chance to assist." In the 1920s, Saint

Lawrence's Church in Milwaukee held the first of its four regular
Sunday Masses at 6:00 and 7:30 A.M., but on holy days Masses
began half an hour earlier; Saint John's Cathedral in that city had
a Mass at noon on holy days, presumably so that workers in the
city's downtown could attend on their lunch hour.[39] No statistics
tell us how faithfully Catholics went to Mass on holy days, but
rates of observance were apparently high. The absence of scolding
from priests on the subject seems to indicate that most parishioners were indeed in their pews as expected.

Apart from weekly Mass, the religious practices of American Catholics expanded significantly in the era of the immigrant church. Sunday afternoon Vespers and Benediction were
still conducted in most churches, but as in the earlier period, attendance was often thin, to the consternation of the clergy. "People who habitually stay away from Vespers for apparently no reason," one priest complained in 1897, "understand little what the
divine law demands of them . . . and can hardly lay any claim to
the name of good Catholics." It was discouraging, he thought,
"where at Vespers you meet only the school children and a few
pious women." As with morning Mass, those lay people who
did attend might be following the service or not, depending on
their inclination. "During this holy Rite," the official manual of
prayers remarked, "the devout worshipper may either join in the
chant of the choir, or pour out his soul in aspirations of love, ado-
ration, gratitude, petition, or contrition." Meanwhile, other devotions were proliferating: "occasional offices" (cycles of prayer to
be recited for special purposes); penitential psalms, recited in sorrow for sin; meditations on the "seven words upon the cross" (the
utterances of the dying Jesus as recorded in the Gospels). A service for the so-called churching of women after childbirth, "a pious and praiseworthy custom," was available and included in the
prayer manual among the official sacraments of the church, even
though it was not one of them.[40]

Two particular exercises gained popularity in the immigrant church. The first used the Stations of the Cross on the church's walls. Tracing its origin to the twelfth century, this devotion offered a kind of vicarious pilgrimage to the Holy Land by recreating the *via dolorosa* ("sorrowful way") that Jesus had walked to his crucifixion. There were fourteen scenes or "stations," some of which (such as Jesus' trial before Pontius Pilate) had explicit scriptural warrant, while others (his encounter with a woman who wiped his bloody face) were rooted in popular tradition. A parishioner could say the stations alone, walking the church aisles and stopping to pray before each one. The images were usually arranged with the first seven running down one wall and the remainder coming back up the opposite wall. A larger congregation, assembled in the pews, might say them collectively, with only the priest walking from station to station. Prayers were said in front of each scene, beginning every time with the injunction, "We adore Thee, O Christ, and we bless Thee," to which parishioners responded, "Because by Thy holy cross Thou hast redeemed the world."[41] The devotion could be practiced at any time of the year, but it was especially common during Lent, since it directed participants' attention in a suitably penitential direction; many parishes also offered the stations every Friday, since it was on a Friday that the events commemorated had occurred.

A less formal but more pervasive practice consisted of individual visits to the church, specifically to pray before the consecrated Eucharistic wafers reserved in the tabernacle on the altar. Catholic belief in the "real presence" of Christ in the elements of Communion was the foundation of this custom. Few lay people could probably have given a sophisticated account of the doctrine of transubstantiation, the theological explanation for how the bread and wine were transformed into the body and blood of Christ. Nevertheless, their reverence for what was called, in this context, "the Blessed Sacrament," was constantly reinforced. Little acts of reverence were expected in the church and beyond its walls. "Men and boys, in passing a church," said a manual of Catholic etiquette in the 1920s, "should tip their hat or cap." Jesus was really there at all times—"I believe that thou art present in the blessed Sacrament of the Altar," one prayer began—and lay people were encouraged literally to visit him.[42]

Devotional manuals offered some prayers that parishioners might say, or they could simply engage in their own meditations during these visits, which might last only a few minutes. In either case, the encounter between the believer and God was direct and personal, since, in the words of one prayer, Christ remained "with them, day and night, in this Sacrament, full of mercy and of love, expecting, inviting, and receiving all who come to visit." With so many churches in urban neighborhoods, the devout might stop in at any time. Boston's former mayor John F. Fitzgerald once bragged that his daughter Rose, who married the young Joe Kennedy in 1914 and became the matriarch of one of the nation's premier political families, was particularly fond of this devotion. "She never visits a place," the old pol wrote to a churchman, "that at some time of the day she does not find a church in which to make a visit, and whoever happens to be with her goes right along."[43] Rose Fitzgerald Kennedy was probably not an "ordinary" Catholic in any sense of the term, but her habit of Eucharistic visits was a common one, particularly among lay women of her generation.

Saying the Stations of the Cross and visiting the Blessed Sacrament were, like Sunday Mass, at once public and private activities. They required physical presence in the public space that was the church, but they were also occasions for individual prayer. In saying those prayers, Catholics of the immigrant era found some new spiritual emphases, two of which are especially noteworthy: devotion to the saints in general and devotion to Mary, the mother of Jesus, in particular. Honoring holy men and women was an ancient practice that Catholics had preserved. Whereas Protestants thought that praying to saints shaded the line between true worship and idolatry, Catholics viewed the saints both as figures whose lives might be emulated and as heavenly intercessors who could lend support to prayers directed to God. The saints had occupied a relatively minor place in the religious imagination of earlier generations of American Catholics. Seldom did missionary priests emphasize prayer to the saints as part of lay devotions. The instructions that Father John Cheverus gave the Hanly family of Maine in the 1790s had encouraged Scripture reading, but commemoration of the saints was not important enough for him to mention. Cheverus would not have opposed the idea; it just never occurred to him. By the immigrant era, however, American Catholics were interacting with a large cast of heavenly characters: apostles, martyrs, "doctors of the church" (such as Augustine and Jerome), and many others, male and female, each of whom they invoked in litanies by name, with the request, "Pray for us." Many of these saintly figures were unfamiliar: it seems unlikely that the ordinary Catholic could have said much about the life of Saints Agatha or Sylvester, for example, both of whom were in the litanies. Still, the catechism explanation that "when we pray to the saints we ask them to offer their prayers to God for us" was increasingly persuasive to lay Catholics, and saints assumed a more prominent place in their religious world.[44]

Of all the saints, Mary was particularly powerful as an intercessor with her son, and the immigrant church saw a great flowering of devotion to the Virgin, both in America and worldwide. Beginning in the 1830s, there were periodic reports of her miraculous appearances at various places in Europe, most notably to a group of children at the village of Lourdes in southwestern France in 1858. Here again, many Protestants thought Catholic devotion to Mary approached the idolatrous, but American

Catholic enthusiasm for the Blessed Virgin was everywhere in the immigrant church. Amid the hardships of immigrant life, this comforting mother figure had a powerfully reassuring appeal. Hymnals for lay use promoted devotion to her. A volume from 1865, originally for Sunday school pupils in New York but soon available nationwide, contained no fewer than twenty-two hymns to Mary. Only six hymns in the entire book referred to any other saints. The practice of naming newly established parishes also reflected a burst of devotion to Mary. By 1925, fully one-quarter (32 out of 127) of all the churches in Brooklyn bore a Marian title of some kind: 1 Virgin Mary parish, 3 Saint Mary's, and 20 Our Lady's (of Charity, of Guadalupe, of Perpetual Help, and so on). The ratio was much the same—16 out of 57 parishes—in nearby Queens, which even had a church named for Saints Joachim and Anne, whom tradition (though not the Gospels) identified as Mary's parents. Only four parishes in Brooklyn and Queens commemorated Mary's husband, Saint Joseph.[45] Church names were chosen by the clergy, of course, not the parishioners, but so many parishes invoking the Virgin's patronage reflected the laity's ardor for Mary.

Taken together, all these devotions, public and private, embodied a distinctive religious worldview for immigrants and their families. If the religion of earlier Catholics such as Charles Carroll of Carrollton may be described as a rational, "Enlightenment Catholicism," the immigrant church had a different, more emotional valence. In the saints and in Mary, American Catholics found real people with whom they could identify and to whom they could speak through prayer. In visits to the Blessed Sacrament they had personal access to Christ himself, whom they could approach whenever they wanted, to ask for favors, to express gratitude, or simply to adore. Through the Stations of the Cross, they could recall the sufferings of Jesus to save mankind, to save them. Lay people did not have to figure out the truths of religion for themselves; the church had already done that for them. Catholicism, a sympathetic yet skeptical Protestant wrote shortly after the Civil War, offered "cheerfulness, certainty, and love—especially *certainty!* . . . A Catholic cannot doubt." The task for lay people was simply to give their assent to the defined truths of faith and then to express that assent through regular religious practice. Attending Sunday Mass and saying some prayers—those of the liturgy itself or others, it almost did not matter which—defined one as a Catholic. Sitting amid the splendor of a church, "always open, always in use, always cheering and comforting," was the way to direct one's attention to higher things.[46] In ways that had once been impossible, Catholics confirmed their identity as churchgoers.

Supporting them in their faith was the growing sense that they were part of something much larger than themselves. Immigrants might be living in straitened and uncertain circumstances, but they could be heartened by the large and enduring institution of which they were a part. "Such edifices as St. Peter's [in Rome], the cathedrals of Milan and of Cologne," a condescending Protestant observed, were reassuring to the "lonely" or "insignificant" priest in America who said Mass for "a few railroad laborers," even if none of them had ever seen those places. Knowing that these cultural landmarks were "theirs" was enough. The Catholic popular press reinforced these larger connections, circulating news that showed just how widespread the church was. A list of "Catholic Memoranda" for 1878 and 1879, for example, contained news from far and wide to encourage this sense of connectedness among lay Catholics: a new church was dedicated in Floresville, Texas, in November 1878; a Lutheran minister and his wife in Owatonna, Minnesota, converted to Catholicism a month later; the cornerstone of a new school for Saint Vincent's parish in New Orleans was laid just after the new year; Michael Kelly, a prominent lay man in Baltimore, died; and so on for eleven pages.[47]

Only local Catholics knew anything of these events directly, but by reading about them Catholics nationwide could know that the church they saw around them was prospering everywhere. Even so, it was their own parish church that held their allegiance. In this sense, all religion was local. The parish routines were interwoven with the rest of life, and parishioners turned to their church for all sorts of help, practical as well as spiritual. The clergy were often social workers as much as intermediaries between the human and the divine. A priest in Boston recorded in his diary what he considered a typical day's activity in March 1900. He said early Mass one Thursday morning and worked on his sermon for the following Sunday. Then, a succession of people rang the rectory doorbell, seeking his help: "Mrs. S," who had a "meddlesome married step-daughter"; a young woman "who, with her sister, has been under the evil influence of a married man"; a young man "previously engaged, now engaged to another, with prospect of trouble from #1"; another young man so "excessively annoyed by scruples" that he found it difficult to accept God's forgiveness after confession; a social worker from a state agency whose clients were a "wife with two black eyes, husband in jail, children in want."

Priests might also be called out to parishioners' homes, especially to anoint the dying. At a New York City parish in the 1860s, according to one estimate (perhaps exaggerated), priests were called out for this purpose sixty-five times in one week, and forty-five of those occasions had come between sunset and sunrise. On New Year's Eve 1899 in Boston, a priest was rousted from bed at 1:20 A.M. "in a blustering snow storm, wind very cold." He suspected (accurately, as it turned out) that the sick man in question was merely drunk, but he went anyway. He did not return to his rectory until 2:30 and did not get back to sleep until an hour later. More often, parochial encounters demonstrated a genuine attachment between lay people and their clergy. After the funeral of a parishioner who had lost an arm in an industrial accident years before, this same priest concluded, "Larry's corpus has followed his long-lost arm, and we hope for him the joys of the blessed. He was no saint, but he died well."[48] The assembled relatives of "Larry," like parishioners elsewhere, came to expect the comforts their local church provided in good times and bad.

From any perspective, the Catholic Church of the immigrant era was a rich and many-layered phenomenon—not just religiously but culturally, sociologically, even anthropologically. It offered a regular schedule of devotional services that provided the most ordinary person—someone like "Larry" or "Mrs. S."—with a connection to God. It encouraged believers, through prayer, to visit and talk with heavenly beings as readily as they would with their neighbors. Such encounters were not symbolic; they were real, and the reality of the supernatural for parishioners was palpable. One lay man told his parish priest that he would not take a sip of medicinal whiskey before he died, "as he did not want the smell of it on him in the place where he was going." A woman who had bruised her face in a fall jokingly told the same priest that she did not want to die "because she had always been a respectable woman and it would kill her to go before her judge [that is, God] with that black eye."[49] Such sentiments cannot be dismissed with a condescending smirk. To do so would fail to take account of the powerful hold that these religious ideas and practices had on American Catholics in the immigrant church.

As immigrant Catholic religious life was flourishing in America, significant changes in the church were under way in Europe. The figure of Pope Pius IX hovers over this revival, and not merely because he served as pope from 1846 to 1878, longer than any other man. On his election, Giovanni Mastai-Feretti had seemed the herald of an about-face in papal policy. Openly critical of earlier efforts to align the church with reactionary political forces—even his cats were liberals, another churchman complained—he established a representative legislature for the Papal States and tried to make peace with the gathering forces of Italian nationalism. He even built the railroads his predecessor had so enthusiastically condemned. Both Catholics and non-Catholics in the United States took optimistic note of these developments. A great-grandson of Jonathan Edwards, the stern Puritan divine of the eighteenth century, thought Pius "the man Heaven seemed to have chosen to lead the human race out of the house of bondage," an opinion about any pope that would have horrified his formidable ancestor. "God bless the Pope of Rome," a newspaper in Washington, D.C., proclaimed in verse: "He hath looked forward to the coming light:/ God bless him, ancient champion of the right." The paper's editors knew that their largely Protestant readers "may be startled to see verses to the Pope" in its pages, but they were not alone in hoping that Pius would turn the church in a new direction.[50]

Within two years, events had converted Pio Nono, as he was affectionately called, from a cautious liberal to an unyielding conservative. Forced by mobs to flee Rome (disguised, it was falsely reported, as a woman), he took refuge outside Naples and was restored to power in 1850 only through the intervention of French troops. The experience left him a changed man, determined to resist any movement toward democracy as the first step toward inevitable chaos and irreligion. Reasserting the power of the papacy within the church was part of this program. In 1854, Pius proclaimed the doctrine of the Immaculate Conception of Mary, the assertion that the Virgin, like her son, had been conceived without original sin. Popular belief in the Immaculate Conception was of ancient origin, but it had never been defined as an official Catholic dogma. Just as important as the decree itself was the way Pius issued it: on his own, without endorsement from any other authority. Just by doing it, he proved that he could. Ten years later, he published a "syllabus of errors," a list of eighty propositions that he condemned as heretical. The last of these— that "the Roman Pontiff can and should reconcile himself with progress, liberalism, and recent civilization"—seemed an all-purpose screed against modern life. Finally, in 1869 and 1870 he assembled bishops from around the world at the Vatican to endorse the infallibility of the pope, the dogma that formal statements by a pope on matters of faith or morals were inerrant. That this infallibility was rarely exercised—the only infallible statement since, made in 1950, has been the dogma of the bodily Assumption of Mary into heaven—was less significant than the insistence that popes indeed had this power, given them directly by God.[51]

The high politics of church and state in Europe were far removed from the world of immigrant Catholics in the United States, but the expansive view of the pope and his role in the church had real effects on them. The emergent papalism that Archbishop Bedini had seen in the 1850s continued to grow throughout the immigrant era. The climax came in 1870, when Italian troops made a final, successful assault on Rome, unifying the Italian nation, wiping out the Papal States, and forcing Pius to take refuge in the Vatican, where he was a self-proclaimed "prisoner." American Catholics rallied to his cause. At mass meetings in cities around the country they protested the "usurpation." Five thousand Catholics marched through the streets of Covington, Kentucky, to condemn "the invasion of the Papal Dominions." Defiant speeches were the order of the day. "We have a great and holy duty," an assembly of German Catholics in Louisville resolved, "to defend our Holy Church [and] the visible head of our Church on earth, the suffering Pius IX." The fate of the pope was the fate of the church everywhere. "The Catholics of the world own every inch of ground in Rome," a Catholic newspaper in Rochester, New York, thundered; the rebellious

Italians should give it back.[52] The contest between the popes and the Italian government would not be settled until 1929, when the sovereignty of the Vatican City state was finally confirmed by treaty. In the meantime, American Catholics lost few opportunities to show their solidarity with the papacy.

They supported the pope not merely with their words but also with their money. Having lost his territory on the Italian peninsula and the taxes that came from it, Pius was in a precarious financial position. Accordingly, in 1850 the church revived the medieval practice of collecting the so-called Peter's Pence. Catholics around the world were asked to contribute a small amount to the successor of Saint Peter, even so little as a single "pence." Encouraged by their priests, American Catholics became enthusiastic contributors to this cause, by means of an annual collection taken up in all parish churches every June. In the first year, American parishes raised nearly $26,000 "for the relief of His Holiness." The major Catholic centers led the way—$6,200 from New York City, $2,800 from Philadelphia—but even the parishioners in Galveston, Texas, managed to assemble $123.60. Although it was rare, individual lay people sometimes sent contributions on their own. A man named P. A. Murphy from Oakland, California, described simply as a "merchant," sent $133 in 1874. Sometimes the pope's needs trumped local causes. In the summer of 1875, for instance, the newly appointed bishop of Green Bay received a donation of two thousand French francs from a Catholic group in Paris that was eager to support his missionary work in northern Wisconsin. Rather than use the money himself, he immediately sent a check for the same amount to Rome. The wisdom of such an action aside, it was a tangible measure of commitment to the pope. Pio Nono and his successors came to rely on American contributions to this fund as the decades went on.[53]

More than just a martyr on the international stage, the pope also became a regular presence in the religious lives of American Catholics. The summary treatment accorded the papacy in earlier catechisms was replaced by greater attention to the pope's position within the church. "We must believe," said the official prayer manual of 1888, that "the Church is always One, in all its members professing one faith, in one communion, under one chief pastor, called the Pope." Another catechism, an English-language edition of a French original, published in 1871, seemed to take a still broader view of the pope's status. Even today, this volume taught, Christ continued to be present with the church primarily through "the Holy Sacrament of the Altar," but "He is also present with his Church in the person of His Vicar, the Roman Pontiff." Going so far as to equate the pope with the Eucharist was possibly heretical, but such sentiments found a willing audience among American Catholics. "God Bless Our Pope" was only one of the hymns that parochial school children in New York were taught to sing. Other references to the papacy appeared in their music books, including one song that ended with the couplet: "Then we'll cling to the Priest, and we'll cling to the Pope;/ We'll cling to Christ's Vicar, for Christ is our hope."[54]

The pope's role in Catholic prayer life also expanded, particularly through a new emphasis on indulgences. Church teaching on this subject had been controversial at least since the time of Martin Luther, three hundred years before. The Catholic position, first developed around the ninth century, was that the good works of believers built up a "treasury of merit" on which others could draw, both for their own benefit and for that of deceased relatives and friends. In particular, credit for these good works could be applied to the souls of the dead in purgatory, the place in the afterlife where, Catholics believed, those destined for heaven underwent purification from their sins. The contents of the treasury could also be used by the living to reduce the time they themselves would have to spend in purgatory after they died.

Churchmen of the middle ages had taken this notion and developed an elaborate mathematical system of indulgences, with prayers and actions assigned precise values. Fasting when not required, for instance, might be the equivalent of doing public penance for a year; a fervent prayer might yield the same benefit. It was the apparent exactness of this system, together with the custom of securing a not-entirely-voluntary monetary contribution in exchange for the indulgence, that had outraged Luther and other reformers.[55]

Although indulgences had remained part of Catholic belief, they had never occupied a very prominent place in the religious imagination of American Catholics. Indulgences went unmentioned in early recommendations for lay devotion, and prayer books rarely included them. Richard Challoner's *Garden of the Soul,* so popular with Catholics in the priestless era, included but a single reference to the subject. Moreover, winning that indulgence was a complicated and difficult matter, requiring persistence. In addition to reciting acts of faith, hope, and charity every day for a month—missing a day required starting over— the believer had to go to confession and Communion during that month and then say prayers "for peace and concord among Christian Princes, for the extirpation of heresy, and the exaltation of the Catholic Church." Shorter devout "aspirations and ejaculations" ("Lord, be merciful to me, a sinner," for example) were worth saying, Challoner insisted, but merely for their own sake, not because they carried a specified spiritual credit. John Carroll's catechism of 1798 had explained succinctly what an indulgence was—"a releasing of temporal punishment which often remains due to sin"—but it was silent on whether Catholics could, or should even try to, accumulate these benefits.[56]

In the immigrant church, however, indulgences took on a new importance directly connected to the pope. Pius IX had ordered that all the grants of indulgence that popes had declared over the centuries be codified, and the result was an official compilation called the *Raccoltà* (the word means "collection" in Italian), published in 1877; a year later, it was available in English and other languages. "What a gain," said the Jesuit translators who prepared the American edition at their seminary in Woodstock, Maryland, "if, by making use of the proper prayers, we add to their intrinsic merit the rich treasures of indulgences attached to them by the Sovereign Pontiffs." Although the *Raccoltà* included earlier indulgences, the majority of those listed in its 450 pages came from recent decrees by Pio Nono himself. In 1876, for example, he declared that a visit to a church for prayer before the Blessed Sacrament carried an indulgence of three hundred days: the recipient had done the equivalent of that much penance. Reciting the prayers of any one of twenty different novenas also carried three hundred days of benefit; under certain circumstances, these could merit what was called a plenary indulgence, the total elimination of the punishment for sin. Even making the sign of the cross, one of the most common religious acts of lay Catholics, who began and ended any formal prayer this way, carried an indulgence of fifty days, according to yet another of Pius's decrees.[57]

Few parishioners probably followed the advice of the *Raccoltà*'s editors that they use the volume as a prayer book. Catholics did not say any of these prayers merely because they were indulgenced, and they seldom paused, in effect, to read the footnotes to see which pope had granted which benefit. Still, awareness of indulgences spread because devotional manuals for the laity now listed them exactly. Praying before a crucifix carried a plenary indulgence if it was done after going to confession and receiving Communion; praying for the dead yielded one hundred days of benefit; reciting a litany in honor of Saint Joseph earned three hundred days. Reading the Bible for fifteen minutes also merited three hundred days, "provided that the edition of the Gospel has been approved by legitimate [that is, Catholic] authority." Saying

the rosary had a complicated set of indulgences attached to it. Individuals benefited from saying it alone, but if a group of parishioners said the rosary together, they earned a plenary indulgence
on the last Sunday of every month. They also had to "visit a
church or public oratory, and pray there, for some time, for the
intention of His Holiness."[58] It was easy for this system to become a caricature of itself, and it was also easy for non-Catholics
to dismiss it as rank superstition. Most Catholics came to take
the indulgenced prayers for granted, however, and in so doing
they confirmed the role of the pope in regulating church life. It
was his authority that established these indulgences, and they tac-
itly endorsed that power when they prayed.

The pope's authority was also on public display in parish
churches each week, particularly after 1886, when Pio Nono's successor, Leo XIII (pope from 1878 to 1903), ordered that certain
prayers be said by the congregation after Mass. When the priest
concluded the formal liturgy in Latin, he came to the foot of the
altar steps and led the people in reciting these so-called Leonine
Prayers in the vernacular. They consisted of the Hail Mary (said
three times), the traditional "Hail, Holy Queen" prayer (also addressed to Mary), and then two prayers of Leo's own composi-
tion. One of these implored God "for the conversion of sinners, and for the liberty and exaltation of our holy mother the
Church"; the other asked Michael the Archangel to "defend us
in battle" and to "be our safeguard against the wickedness and
snares of the devil."[59] In the 1930s, another pope ordered that
these prayers be recited specifically for the conversion of communist Russia, and they remained a part of regular Sunday practice
in American Catholic parishes until the 1960s. For lay people, the
prayers became as much a part of the ritual as the Mass itself—
perhaps even more so, since these were the only prayers they
themselves actually said aloud. The laity might not have noticed
how these papally mandated prayers became part of their reli-

gious practice, but this direct involvement of the pope in the prayer life of ordinary American Catholics had been unknown in earlier ages.

Catholics attending their local church might also see a human embodiment of the pope's expanded role in a new category of priest that appeared in the immigrant church: the monsignor. The word, meaning simply "My Lord," had been common in Europe for centuries. By the time of Pius IX and Leo XIII, however, it was an honorific specifically granted by popes to recognize and reward certain parish priests. It was also a means of creating a kind of fictional court around the pope, whose real aristocracy had been dispersed with the collapse of the Papal States. Now, a new papal nobility was constructed imaginatively. A local bishop would petition Rome to have a priest granted the title of monsignor. Priests honored in this way were "elevated" to one of three ranks: a papal chamberlain, a domestic prelate, or a prothonotary apostolic. These titles had meant something in the medieval church, but they now entailed no responsibilities: there were no duties, but there were honors. The priest so distinguished was entitled to sign his name, not with the simple "Reverend," but with "Right Reverend"; he was addressed not merely as "Father" but as "Monsignor." He could also wear distinctive clothing. While most priests wore a simple black cassock—in 1884, American bishops had for the first time mandated that priests wear the cassock and so-called Roman collar—a monsignor could adorn his cassock with crimson buttons and piping; during official ceremonies, he was entitled to wear a cassock that was entirely crimson, top to bottom. The document raising a priest to the rank of monsignor ran in the name of the pope himself: it was a personal honor granted by the leader of the worldwide church.[60]

The creation of a corps of monsignors offered bishops a way to reward priests who had done well. A pastor who had built up a large parish, for example, or opened a successful school deserved some recognition, and petitioning Rome to make this priest a monsignor was a tangible expression of appreciation. Most frequently, local pastors won the honor, though bishops also sought it for their closest administrative aides. Of course, the distinction was valuable only if it was not used too often, and bishops seem to have targeted about 15 percent of their pastors for this reward. By 1925, ten of the eighty-one parishes in Pittsburgh were led by a monsignor, and these were the pastors of the older and larger churches in various neighborhoods. The same rough percentage was apparent in other Catholic centers, too: eleven of seventy-two parishes in Buffalo had monsignors, as did eleven of eighty-nine in Detroit.[61] The honor attached to the clergyman himself, but his parishioners shared in the reflected glory. If their pastor was a monsignor, it meant that the leader of the church worldwide had acknowledged theirs as a particularly noteworthy parish. They could take pride that their pastor—and, by extension, they themselves—had been singled out for recognition that came from the pope himself.

Celebrating their pastor's designation as a monsignor, contributing to Peter's Pence, reciting prayers to which popes had attached special benefits, taking the pontiff's side in his political distress—in all these ways, American Catholics in the immigrant church tightened the bonds of attachment between themselves and the bishop of Rome. They might be on the bottom rungs of society's ladder, but they were connected nonetheless to this significant international figure. An earlier generation of Catholics in the United States had paid little attention to the man at the top of their hierarchy. By the opening of the twentieth century, a reinvigorated papacy was exerting greater influence within the church, and Catholics welcomed it. John Carroll had once speculated on how the church might survive without a pope; now the power of the papacy was no longer in question. John Cheverus had denied that papal infallibility was a part of Catholic doctrine;

now it had been officially declared, a guarantee of the "certainty" that the *Atlantic Monthly* correspondent had recognized. American Catholics became accustomed to following the pope's every lead, making his spiritual emphases their own. Fewer than ten Catholic churches in the country had been named "Immaculate Conception" in 1850, for example; by 1860, just six years after Pio Nono had unilaterally defined that dogma, it was easier to count the cities that did not have a parish with that name than those that did, including the cathedrals in Portland, Maine; Albany, New York; and Mobile, Alabama. "We turn Romeward," an American churchman said in 1901, "as naturally . . . as the needle seeks the North."[62] It had not always been so, but by then his was an accurate gauge of a new enthusiasm.

In addition to gaining a greater sense of themselves as members of the worldwide church, Catholics in the immigrant era also deepened their sense of being Americans. They faced both new challenges and new opportunities to demonstrate their attachment to their country. Nativist anti-Catholicism came and went in cycles, roughly parallel to the successive waves of immigration between the 1840s and the 1920s. Lurid antipopery literature always found some market, and the "escaped-nun" saga never seemed to get old with a portion of the American book-buying public. The pope's temporal misfortunes cheered many. Margaret Fuller, a transcendentalist and friend of Emerson's, wrote simply from Rome in 1850 that "the Roman Catholic religion must go." The spiritual authority of the church was incompatible with contemporary life, she thought: "the influence of the clergy is too perverting, too foreign to every hope of advancement and health." After the destruction of the Papal States twenty years later, a small town newspaper in New Hampshire was exultant. "The great scandal of the ages is wiped out, and the deeds of vio-

lence, blood and shame, enacted by an ecclesiastical prince, are to
be known no more except in history," it editorialized. "That's
something."[63]

Despite its persistence, the high-water mark for nativism came
early, in the 1850s, with spectacular but short-lived political success. A new political party—its members were popularly called
Know Nothings, because they supposedly promised to say that
they "knew nothing" when asked about it—swept state and local
elections in 1854. The party seemed everywhere triumphant, from
Delaware and Maryland to Tennessee and Kentucky, and even to
the new state of California. The Know Nothing platform included such planks as immigration restriction and lengthening
the waiting period before naturalized citizens could vote. A child
born in the United States had to wait twenty-one years before
voting, they argued; why shouldn't a naturalized immigrant, even
if an adult, have to wait that long? The greatest victory came in
Massachusetts, where the governor and all but two of the state's
four hundred legislators were Know Nothings. But the movement burned out quickly, partly because the Know Nothings
overplayed their hand. A "nunnery committee" in Massachusetts,
charged with inspecting Catholic convents, attracted more attention for padding its expense accounts and for its chairman, who
was discovered in a hotel room with a woman who was not his
wife. More important, the deepening crisis of the 1850s over slavery made that issue, rather than immigration, the central concern
for the nation.

By 1856 Know-Nothing-ism as a political movement was dead.
Anti-immigrant hostility reappeared occasionally thereafter, but
without much impact. An American Protective Association was
formed in 1887 to "protect" the country from foreigners, and in
the 1920s a reinvigorated Ku Klux Klan, temporarily more hostile
to Catholics and Jews than to African Americans, achieved brief
political success in Indiana and elsewhere. The Oregon legislature

attempted to outlaw Catholic schools in 1922, but the law was overturned by the U.S. Supreme Court three years later.[64]

In response, American Catholics took every chance to prove that they were loyal citizens. War provided several good opportunities for doing so. Catholics fought on both sides in the Civil War, and there were Catholic heroes for North and South. Thomas Francis Meagher, an immigrant, organized one of several "Irish Regiments" for the Union and served under the irascible William Tecumseh Sherman, a baptized (though nonpracticing) Catholic whose son later became a Jesuit priest. The Confederacy claimed the flamboyant General Pierre G. T. Beauregard from Louisiana and Stephen Mallory from Florida, the rebel secretary of the navy whose sons attended Georgetown College. Several of the co-conspirators of John Wilkes Booth in the plot to assassinate Abraham Lincoln were Catholics, a fact that nativists offered as proof of Catholic treachery but that received little attention in the aftermath of the shocking event. More helpfully, about eight hundred Catholic nuns served as nurses in military hospitals for both armies, and they were celebrated after the war in sentimental poetry as "angels of the battlefield."[65]

The Spanish-American War was an even better occasion for Catholics to show that they were Americans first, since the enemy was a Catholic country. The "splendid little war," as Secretary of State John Hay famously called it, did not last very long (April–August 1898), but some attributed great significance to it. The conflict was, an American priest wrote, a "question of all that is old & vile & mean & rotten & cruel & false in Europe against all [that] is free & noble & open & true & humane in America." Some lay people were wary of the drift toward imperialism—a "folly and danger," the editors of one Catholic newspaper called it—but once the war was under way they climbed aboard the patriotic bandwagon. "The flag is unfurled," another paper editorialized, "the sword is drawn, and every American patriot, whatever his race or his faith, will stand resolutely by the government at Washington." In the same way, Catholics—even German Americans—supported America's cause in the First World War, despite carping from President Woodrow Wilson that "hyphenated Americans" were unreliable. The bilingual newspaper of a German Catholic parish in Boston, for example, proudly listed the names of soldiers and sailors and published letters home from men at the front. The nativist argument had long been that Catholics had divided allegiances and that they would always put fealty to their church ahead of attachment to their country. Heeding the call to serve gave Catholics the opportunity to show that they were as patriotic as anyone else.[66]

In peacetime, too, Catholics wove themselves into the American fabric, and politics proved an effective means of doing so. Steadily growing numbers gave them real voting power, especially in the Democratic Party. In city after city, Catholics were putting "one of their own" into nearly every available office, a development not universally welcomed. "Among the cities led captive by Irishmen and their sons," a dismayed reformer wrote in 1894, equating Irish and Catholics, were the obvious ones (New York, Boston, and Chicago) but also places like Kansas City and Omaha. Why, even in Salt Lake City the chief police detective was a man named Donovan. Virtually every city had its own example of the prototypical Catholic political boss, loved by his supporters and reviled by "good-government" opponents: Richard Croker, the leader of New York's Tammany Hall in the 1880s; James Michael Curley, who held a succession of offices in Boston a generation later; Johnny Powers, whose name accurately described his influence as a Chicago alderman; Edward Butler, head of "the Combine" that controlled St. Louis; and a succession of mayors in San Francisco named Buckley, Phelan, and McCarthy. Hard-nosed politics combined with conventional religiosity in most of these leaders. Frank Hague, the mayor of Jersey City for thirty years after 1917, who had proclaimed, disarmingly, "I am the law," was a conspicuously observant Catholic. He was a regular in his local parish church, at least when he was not at one of the houses that graft had bought him at the shore or in Palm Beach.[67]

Elsewhere, more respectable Catholics demonstrated a commitment to American public life. The labor movement counted large numbers of Catholics among its ranks. These lay people happily greeted an encyclical letter from Pope Leo XIII in 1891 defending the rights of workers to organize and to press for a living wage. Catholic membership steered many unions away from more radical organizers, including the secularized Mary Harris ("Mother") Jones of the Industrial Workers of the World, whose brother was a priest. In culture, Catholic writers began to win recognition beyond their own people. In 1890, John Boyle O'Reilly, an immigrant poet and essayist, delivered an epic poem at the dedication of a new memorial at Plymouth Rock, that quintessential American icon. Some Catholics joined others in pressing for social reforms. Catholic "T.A." (total abstinence) societies made common cause with such unlikely allies as the evangelical Women's Christian Temperance Union in battling a problem many thought especially rife in immigrant neighborhoods. In professional sports, Catholics became heroes to the public at large. James J. ("Gentleman Jim") Corbett, the boxing champion, was a fine Catholic gentleman outside the ring, while Connie Mack (real name: Cornelius McGillicuddy), manager of the Philadelphia Athletics baseball team, was aggressively pious, never missing Sunday Mass himself and often dragging unsuspecting members of the team along with him. George Herman ("Babe") Ruth did not live an entirely edifying adult life, but he had been raised in a Catholic orphanage in Baltimore, and the archbishop of New York presided at his funeral. Among the first genuine celebrities of national culture, these public figures helped make Catholics appear just as American as anybody else.[68]

For all their advances, however, American Catholics still had

reason to conclude that their story had not been an entirely successful one. By 1924, they had lost the battle over immigration restriction when Congress enacted a rigid quota system, capping
the total number of annual immigrants and apportioning them
country by country. Worse, they felt a collective sense of insult
when Governor Al Smith of New York, the son of Irish immigrants and the first Catholic to run as the presidential candidate
of a major political party, was humiliated in the election of 1928.
The campaign had been an ugly one, and while many factors
contributed to Smith's defeat—he was a confirmed "wet" amid
the still widespread support for Prohibition—his religion had
been the unavoidable issue. His decisive loss (60 percent to 40
percent in the popular vote; 444 to 87 in the electoral college)
seemed at the time to foreclose the possibility that a Catholic
could ever attain the nation's highest office.[69]

But American Catholics were not, as one priest wrote in the aftermath of the election, about to "wither up and blow away."[70]
They had achieved too much in the immigrant era, and they
would continue to flourish in the coming years. They would also
find a new rallying cry for their role in both church and society,
one that seemed to emphasize the role of lay people. This was the
cry of "Catholic Action," and it would be the hallmark of the
next age of the Catholic Church in the United States.

4

The Church of Catholic Action

Dorothy Day spent more than her share of time in jail. Drawn from her youth to radical causes, she was caught up in protests and frequently found herself in a cell, either awaiting trial or serving a sentence upon conviction. One of the first of these occasions came in 1917, when she was barely twenty and was arrested while protesting for women's suffrage in front of the White House. Well into old age, she was still at it. Throughout the late 1950s, she was arrested in New York City every summer for refusing to participate in practice air raid drills that were supposed to prepare the populace to survive a nuclear attack. In between, she had undergone a dramatic religious conversion, abandoning socialist politics and a bohemian lifestyle for a deep commitment to the Catholic Church. It had been an improbable choice, but it was one she made wholeheartedly.

Together with a French émigré named Peter Maurin, a mystical self-declared philosopher, Day attracted an informal band of followers who called themselves the Catholic Workers. Taking in deadly earnest the biblical injunction to feed the hungry and tend the sick, they opened "houses of hospitality," first in New York and then around the country, to serve the poor, the homeless, the addicted, the unemployed, and anyone else in need. But their approach was not that of professional social workers who coolly served "clients." Rather, Catholic Workers lived among those they helped as members of the same family. Such work required an unqualified commitment, but Day continued to inspire people, young and old, to make it until her death in 1980—and even afterward.[1]

The Catholic Worker Movement was unusual in its intensity, but it was far from unique in American Catholicism during the first half of the twentieth century. Other groups of lay people, both radical and apolitical, organized themselves so as to make the church's work their own. A Catholic Rural Life Movement promoted back-to-the-land programs and sought to improve farm conditions during the dust-bowl years of the Great Depression. The Association of Catholic Trade Unionists coordinated the work of Catholics in organized labor. The Catholic Youth Organization spread in local parishes, and parents formed their own societies for lay men and lay women. All these groups saw themselves as playing their own particular role in promoting what was called Catholic Action. That phrase had been used in many contexts before, but it took on new life once Pope Pius XI (1922–1939) spoke of it approvingly in 1931 as the "participation of the laity in the apostolate of the hierarchy."

According to the tenets of Catholic Action, the church was best understood not merely as a religious institution concerned with the other-worldly salvation of individual souls; it was also a this-worldly organization whose members had the responsibility to apply its teachings in the social, economic, and political spheres of life. That duty fell to lay people no less than to bishops, priests, and sisters. The laity would be guided by the hierarchy, it was understood, but the church's work had to be theirs, too. That understanding provided the energy for lay people in the church of Catholic Action.[2]

Lay Catholics in America had been organizing themselves into associations almost from the beginning. Most often these had been devotional in character, emphasizing prayer and the spiritual benefits of membership. Such groups, a seminary professor told soon-to-be-ordained priests, encouraged parishioners to be "mindful of their [religious] obligations," and they also served as a "bulwark" against the attractions of secular social clubs.[3] Catholic Action built on these earlier organizational efforts but also differed from them in several important respects. Whereas devotional societies promoted the religious welfare of the individual member, Catholic Action groups were more deliberately collective in their intent. The benefits they sought were societal as much as they were personal. In the process, they encouraged members to look beyond their own parish and neighborhood. Work in the local community was fine, but some problems were too big to be addressed only on the parochial level. Comprehensive solutions were needed to persistent, systemic problems. Moreover, Catholic Action groups drew on the deep American urge for reform. Many Protestant churches were pursuing what they called the Social Gospel, and Catholic Action was an expression of that impulse in the Roman Church. Like their Protestant counterparts, these Catholics were moving away from a stoic acceptance of the way things were to a more deliberate effort to make them better. Individuals were still required to pray, but prayer had to be followed by sustained work in the world. When they came together under the figurative banner of Catholic Action, these Catholics defined a new era for their church.

The work of Catholic Action also began to shift the balance between lay people and the clergy. Even as the immigrant church had successfully reinforced denominational commitment, it had also introduced a new passivity into the laity. Precisely because the institutions and personnel of the church were so readily available in the immigrant era, lay people could rely on them to do the work of the church and to sustain their own faith. The laity need not wrestle personally with the truths of religion or its consequences. The church had already done that for them, and they simply had to give their assent through routine religious practice. What is more, many immigrant Catholics were struggling financially, and they had little time or energy for the luxury of personal theological reflection. Catholic Action called them to a different standard: they were now expected to study the church's teaching and then put it into practice. Attending Mass on Sunday and fulfilling their other religious duties were necessary but not sufficient. The clergy might be the ones to issue this new call, but the laity's own initiative would be no less important. In the process, the active, involved laity of earlier ages would begin to return to American Catholicism.

Broad movements of Catholic Action could not have succeeded absent the tradition of parish-based associations that had proliferated in the immigrant church. American Catholic lay people picked up the organizational habit close to home before applying it on a wider scale.

Women's groups had long been staples of local church life. Since women were presumed to bear the primary responsibility for transmitting the faith to the next generation, priests were eager to see them develop regular devotional practices. Prayers often focused on Mary, particularly through devotion to the rosary. Rosary sodalities attracted large numbers, partly because they gave women otherwise absorbed in the duties of home and family a chance to get out for an evening. The women's group at a parish in Boston at the turn of the twentieth century drew almost 400 members to its Tuesday-night meetings. On one occasion, right after Christmas, a priest of the parish was disappointed when only 314 women turned out, a number that had, he thought, "not recovered from [the] holiday season." The women of a parish might also form an altar society, charged mainly with cleaning and decorating the church sanctuary. The altar society at a parish in Kalamazoo, Michigan, met on the evening of the first Friday of every month, recited the rosary, celebrated Benediction of the Blessed Sacrament, and then collected ten cents from each member to adorn the church. "Flowers of many kinds," the group's membership certificate reminded them, "contribute to the beauty of the church."[4]

Most priests believed that it was relatively easy to organize the women of a parish because, as one said, "the female sex has a natural tendency towards religion and is inclined to works of piety." Men, by contrast, were thought to be both more difficult and more important to organize. "No class of people deserve more attention and care on the part of the parish priest," a seminary textbook advised, "for no class is exposed to greater danger regarding faith and morals." Nearly everywhere, pastors reported persistent but not always successful attempts to form sodalities for their male parishioners. "They prefer, unfortunately, to organize themselves in worldly associations," the long-time pastor of a church in Oswego, New York, lamented. "They are quite ready to form debating clubs, literary societies, lyceums; quite ready to organize brass bands, and drum corps, become firemen or soldiers for dress parade, but are unwilling to become humble, faithful sodalists. They begin with alacrity, but they do not persevere. What a pity!" Some parishes formed mutual benefit societies that offered low-cost disability insurance as an inducement to devotional practice, but membership still waxed and waned unpredictably.[5]

After some experimentation with different approaches, two parish-based organizations for men proved to be particularly popular. The first was the Holy Name Society. Claiming a genealogy back to the thirteenth century, the association was in fact a more recent phenomenon. A group bearing that name had been established at a church in Marion County, Kentucky, as early as 1808, and a larger society was formed at a parish in New York City right after the Civil War. Its steady growth came fifty years later, a product of the energies of a Dominican priest named Charles Hyacinth McKenna, an Irish immigrant to Wisconsin. In 1900 he was given responsibility for promoting the society around the country, and he did so with abandon. By the time of his death in 1917, there were almost 1,800 branches in American Catholic parishes, and the number grew steadily until mid-century. By providing a devotional and social outlet for the men of a parish, the society hoped to ensure that they would be "kept to their religious practices, and the laity associated largely with the clergy in the work of the church."[6]

The society's purpose was to encourage obedience to what was, according to the Catholic numbering, the Second Commandment, which forbade taking the Lord's name in vain. The group campaigned against "blasphemy, profanity, and obscene speech." At every meeting, members recited the Holy Name Pledge, promising to resist their own temptations to curse and "to give good example" by encouraging similar restraint in others. Every member received a small button depicting Jesus as an innocent child, which he was to wear on the lapel of his coat as "a constant reminder of [his] membership in the Society and a challenge to remain faithful and active"; it was also a form of witness to nonmembers. Notions of manliness were never very far beneath the surface of the society, and the not-so-subtle message was that a man could still be a man even if he did not swear or tell dirty jokes. The society also reinforced ideas about respectability. The group was entirely egalitarian, leaders pointed out, "drawing its members from all classes of men," but there was a clear implication that foul language was something a man left behind as he climbed the ladders of economic and social success. "Any com-

munity may measure its spiritual value by the piety of its men,"
said one Holy Name handbook. "The American parish is no exception. It needs spirituality, especially of that masculine type
which the Society has been promoting."[7]

By the 1920s, the Holy Name Society was the most common
organization for lay men in American Catholic parishes. Even
school children were drafted as recruiting agents. One priest had
each student in his school's penmanship classes write a postcard,
addressed to Dad, urging him to attend the next meeting or to
become a member if he was not already. Meetings were held
monthly, always on Sunday mornings. Women could meet during the week, but priests thought it unlikely that men would
come to church on any day other than Sunday. As a practical
matter, a pastor pointed out, meeting on a weeknight would require working men to change into nicer clothes, "which many
dislike to do after a hard day's work." According to a typical
schedule, the men gathered at the parish school and marched
into the church, where they sat together at the 8:00 A.M. Mass. By
9:00 they were back at the school or in the church hall. After an
opening prayer, the president asked everyone to turn to the man
next to him, introduce himself, and exchange hearty handshakes.
Next, a simple breakfast was served: sausages (even, perhaps, hot
dogs!), sweet rolls, coffee cake, "and plenty of good coffee with
cream and sugar [which] will always satisfy a hungry man." After
a short business meeting, a speaker, "to talk only 15 or 20 minutes," was introduced. Suggested topics included family life, the
foreign missions, or recent papal statements. Staging short debates was permissible, so long as the subject matter was not too
controversial. There might be singing or other entertainment: if
the latter was provided, officers were enjoined to "be sure it's
clean." By 10:30 the meeting was over, with the pastor coming in
to offer some concluding words and a blessing.[8]

The group had a slogan—"Every man a Holy Name man!"—

and this goal was very nearly realized in parishes across the country. In and around Cincinnati, for example, the number of chapters grew from zero to more than seventy in less than twenty years. Saint Antoninus's parish, in the Covedale section of the city, even had two thriving societies, one for single men, the other for married men, though this distinction was rare elsewhere. In Detroit in the 1930s, Holy Name membership was counted at 100,000, and officials estimated that at least 75,000 members and their sons had participated one week on "Father and Son Sunday." In some places, the society was active even before the parish church itself was built. At Saint Anthony's parish in Denver right after the Second World War, the Holy Name men met at a local dry cleaner's for nearly a year and a half before they managed to finish construction of their church.[9]

The society had become a mass movement, and members liked to demonstrate this by assembling groups from local parishes for marches through the public streets. The men of Cincinnati were particularly attached to this form of "good example." In 1934, their parade consisted of 35 marching bands and 45,000 men from more than 100 parishes, snaking through the city and concluding with a prayer rally in Crosley Field, home of the Cincinnati Reds baseball team. The society also held national demonstrations, including a massive convention in Washington, D.C., in September 1924. On the Sunday that climaxed the four-day event, Holy Name men from around the country lined up at the foot of Capitol Hill for open-air Masses, which were offered every half hour from 5:30 A.M. until noon. Then, in a steady drizzle, they marched down Pennsylvania Avenue and gathered around the Washington Monument—all 106,284 of them, according to an improbably precise count. Although overtly nonpartisan, the event nevertheless showed off Catholic political strength. The marchers were treated to an uncharacteristically long speech from President Calvin Coolidge—it was only six weeks before election day—and a year later the Ku Klux Klan felt compelled to stage a counterparade of its own in the capital, lest Catholics go unchallenged in the streets.[10]

The second popular organization that attracted men in local parishes was the Saint Vincent de Paul Society. This sodality shared the Holy Name desire to promote individual religious fervor, but it also had more expressly social service goals. Taking its name from a seventeenth-century French priest known for his charitable works, this group was for those who wanted to help the poor. The first local branch (or "conference") had been formed in St. Louis in 1845 by Bryan Mullanphy, mayor of the city and son of the man thought to be Missouri's first millionaire. With a membership of more than one hundred, it relied on "visitors," whose task was to "ascertain the particular cases in the neighborhood of their respective Parishes requiring immediate attention and assistance." This was done through personal contact with the needy; the Saint Vincent de Paul men literally walked around their neighborhoods in search of those in need. "The disbursements by this conference," an early report explained, "are generally made in groceries, clothing, and fuel. In extraordinary cases of sickness, cash is sometimes allowed; and occasionally the burial expenses of poor deceased persons are paid." The society provided aid without regard to the religion of the recipients. "This conference," said another early group, "never makes inquiry either into the birthplace or religious faith of those who apply for assistance. Its members are ever ready to afford instruction and information to those willing to receive them; but they studiously abstain from thrusting either upon anyone." The only criterion for receiving assistance was "that the proposed objects of their charity are really needy."[11]

From its midwestern foundation, the Saint Vincent de Paul Society spread to parishes around the country, and it relied on small financial donations for support. The group at the parish

of the Cathedral of the Madeleine in Salt Lake City, just up
the street from the Mormon temple, installed poor boxes at the
church's front door, a common practice elsewhere as well. Most
members, who were known as "Vincentians," came from the
working class. Some were not far removed from the need for assistance themselves, and this added urgency to their work. The
members of an early St. Louis parish conference included a team-
ster, a drayman, a livery stable attendant, and a "lime-burner";
the first conference formed at Saint Patrick's Cathedral in New
York City had several small shopkeepers, a printer, two tailors,
and at least three students. By 1900, there were more than 700 local conferences nationwide, claiming at least 12,500 members.
The roster of a parish conference overlapped with that of other
groups, but not entirely. Most Vincent de Paul members were
probably members of the Holy Name Society, for example, but
not all Holy Name men were Vincentians. Whereas the one
group required only a monthly meeting, the work of the other
was more intense: weekly meetings, visiting the homes of those in
need, providing assistance when appropriate, and (the harder
task) sometimes refusing it. Not every parishioner was cut out for
this kind of thing.[12]

Vincentians believed, however, that theirs was a religious work
no less than a charitable one. Anyone might help the poor from
purely humanitarian motives, but they were performing what the
catechism called "the corporal and spiritual works of mercy." One
would expect to find priests and nuns engaging in such activity, a
chaplain pointed out, but it was praiseworthy that "laymen living
in the world, men engrossed with mundane affairs, men occupied
with problems of commerce, trade, industry, [and] the rearing of
their own families should embrace a quasi-religious vocation."
Vincentian meetings included prayer and other devotions over-
seen by a priest of the parish, and the men were submissive to his
authority. "We will always remember that we are only laymen," a
1924 guide said, measuring the distance between members and

the clergy with the word "only" and promising to "follow with respect the course which the ecclesiastical superiors think proper."[13] The Saint Vincent de Paul Society thus combined lay initiative with deference to the clergy, always in balance. Later Catholic Action movements would shift more directly toward the former.

Children no less than their parents enlisted in parish organizations supervised by the clergy. Girls could join the Children of Mary, a junior version of the rosary sodalities to which their mothers belonged, and altar boys, while not constituting an association as such, developed their own sense of camaraderie. By far the largest parish group, however, was the Catholic Youth Organization (CYO). The organizing genius behind it was a Chicago priest named Bernard Sheil, who rose through the administrative ranks to the position of auxiliary bishop. In 1930, he began to devote his energies to the "problem of youth" in the hopes of saving young people (at first, mostly boys) from the evil influences around them. Athletics offered the key, he thought: if parish lads could be formed into sports teams, they would be less likely to get into trouble. Sheil thought boxing particularly useful in this regard—he would run a checkers tournament if it attracted more participants, he told a critic—and he promoted citywide boxing matches under the CYO banner. Basketball, baseball, and other teams, for girls as well as boys, soon followed, together with marching bands and drum corps. In the 1940s and 1950s, CYO groups were promoting citizenship education and public-speaking contests, and they were holding strictly supervised dances. While rigorously nonpolitical, the CYO might, like the Holy Name Society, demonstrate the Catholic presence on the public stage. An eight-hour parade of 80,000 CYO members pointedly marched through Boston in October 1948, just a month before voters faced a referendum ballot question to liberalize the birth control laws in Massachusetts; the measure went down to crushing defeat.[14]

Like the Catholic Youth Organization, the Knights of Columbus had both local branches and a national coordinating office. First organized in New Haven, Connecticut, in 1882, the "K of C," as it was familiarly known, grew rapidly. Within twenty years, there were chapters in every state in the Union, several Canadian provinces, and even in the Philippines. The K of C met several needs at once. The American Catholic hierarchy had long worried about what they called "secret societies," like the Masons, and had forbidden Catholics to join them. The all-male knights, together with their affiliates for women (the Daughters of Isabella and the Catholic Daughters of America), offered an alternative, providing the social connections of a fraternal organization with none of the potential dangers to the faith of members. The group placed itself under the patronage of Christopher Columbus, a hero who was both Catholic and American. The K of C thus became a vehicle for Catholics to demonstrate that they could be loyal to church and country at the same time. Local councils chose names associated with the explorer ("Pinta" and "San Salvador," for instance) or names with a patriotic resonance ("Washington" and "Bunker Hill"). Protestant elites might well claim descent from passengers on the *Mayflower* in 1620, but they seemed like parvenus and upstarts in comparison with the Catholics who had come on the *Santa Maria* two centuries before that.[15]

The Knights of Columbus was first and foremost a mutual benefit society that provided life and health insurance to members as an incentive for joining. Very quickly, however, it expanded its scope. By the time of the First World War, with a membership of more than 300,000, it had taken on the role of an antidefamation league for Catholics, ready to challenge slurs against the church. Patrick Henry Callahan, a leader of the knights in Kentucky, chaired a Commission on Religious Prejudices, established "to study the causes, investigate conditions, and suggest remedies for the religious prejudice that has been manifest through press and rostrum." More visibly, the knights worked with Catholics in the armed forces, at first during border skirmishes with Mexico and later with American troops in Europe. K of C "huts" offered refreshment and entertainment to soldiers in the field—"Everyone Welcome, Everything Free," their banners proclaimed—and knights joined with the Salvation Army and other groups in giving soldiers a taste of home. In later decades, they funded scholarships for veterans, evening schools for self-advancement, and employment bureaus, and they became outspoken critics of communism at home and abroad. By the middle of the twentieth century, there were more than a million members of the K of C in close to a thousand local councils, all affiliated with the national office in New Haven.[16]

Other knights also did a kind of symbolic battle for the faith, and they were often organized along ethnic lines. The K of C, though open to men of any background, was dominated by Irish Americans, and this prompted other nationalities to form their own cohorts. The Knights of Saint George was founded at a German parish in Pittsburgh, and members gave special attention to raising money to educate German-speaking seminarians. The Knights of Lithuania, first assembled from immigrants in Lawrence, Massachusetts, promoted traditional music and dance as well as religious practice. The Knights of Saint Mary of Czechstochowa drew members from Polish parishes in Connecticut and elsewhere. For African-American Catholics, never very numerous, the Knights of Saint Peter Claver grew from an organization at a parish in Mobile, Alabama. Claver himself had been a Spanish missionary to Colombia in the seventeenth century, and his humanitarian work with slaves had made him a hero to later black Catholics who were themselves only a generation or two removed from slavery. In many places, North and South, blacks had been effectively blocked from joining groups like the Knights of Columbus: the K of C in Cleveland, for example, was not finally integrated until 1956. The Knights of Saint Peter Claver provided the mutual aid and social benefits denied its members elsewhere.[17] Alexis de Tocqueville had noted long before that Americans were incorrigible "joiners," and Catholic Americans were as enthusiastic in this regard as their fellow citizens.

None of these organizations was, strictly speaking, an expression of Catholic Action as the phrase was popularized in the 1930s. Nevertheless, they were significant precursors to that movement, which could not have taken root without them. Although always supervised by the clergy, they provided the foundation for a broadening view of the responsibilities of lay people, allowing the laity to "participate" in the church's work, as Pius XI had hoped. These societies demonstrated that religion was not merely a Sunday thing; it might also be a Tuesday or a Friday night thing. They encouraged Catholics to connect religious practice to other dimensions of their lives, such as aiding the poor or offering comfort to troops far from home. They even, in some cases, baptized boxing.

Thus accustomed to linking their faith to the rest of life, American Catholic lay people could begin to seek still broader applications. They could, for instance, start to think not only about helping the poor directly but also about reforming the structures of society that seemed to perpetuate poverty and other social ills. Once in the habit of forming groups for purposes of prayer, lay people took the short step to wider involvement. If parish devotional sodalities aimed at getting parishioners to change themselves—to stop cursing, for example, or to pray more devoutly—Catholic Action encouraged them to think about changing society, too.

The poor will always be with us, as Jesus himself had noted, but by the early twentieth century, Americans widely recognized the need to address the nation's problems systematically, in part because the problems had come to seem so formidable. Poverty and crime, the harsh conditions of industrial labor, questions of child welfare, and other issues demanded attention. Personal and local efforts, however commendable, were inadequate to the task. Political Progressives and Protestant Social Gospelers were calling for structural reform, and Catholics began to speak this language, too. "We are determined," a priest from Cleveland told a lay gathering in 1909, "to approach these problems not only in an individual way, but by organization."[18] Catholics, he thought, had special reasons to work for fundamental change. After all, some social problems hit them hardest and first. Many of them lived in the older, decaying city neighborhoods most in need of revitalization. They toiled in unsafe factories, and in many cases their children had to leave school to help support the family. Aiding those in need would always be a religious duty, but efforts such as those of the Saint Vincent de Paul Society were unavoidably piecemeal. Might not more basic reforms, more collective effort and "organization," attack the root causes of all these ills?

Catholics had other reasons for wanting to organize their own reform efforts, including the fear that political and social radicals might capture the reform agenda and woo Catholics away from their church. When the extremist Industrial Workers of the World (known as the IWW or "Wobblies") made headway among the largely Catholic textile laborers of Lawrence, Massachusetts, in the "Bread and Roses" strike of 1912, for example, the need to keep reform within proper bounds seemed obvious to many churchmen. The case of Nicola Sacco and Bartolomeo Vanzetti, a cause célèbre in the 1920s, raised a similar specter. The two Italian anarchists "ought" to have been Catholics, church leaders believed. "There is a very real danger," one priest wrote, "that large masses of our workingmen will, before many years have gone by . . . look upon the Church as indifferent to human rights and careful only about the rights of property." A church-sanctioned reform program would demonstrate that working for change did not require abandoning one's faith. After all, one bishop said, "The poor belong to us."[19]

Desire to join the reform project was growing, and social progress within the Catholic community was helping to make it possible. The American Catholic population held steady at roughly 16 percent of the nation between the two world wars, but more important, Catholics were beginning to take their place in the middle class. Education, particularly higher education, had been crucial to this process. By the 1930s, there were about 70 Catholic colleges and universities in the United States, all preparing graduates for careers that would have been unthinkable for their immigrant parents. At the beginning of the century, less than 5 percent of the graduates of the all-male College of the Holy Cross in Worcester, Massachusetts, run by the Jesuit order, had wound up in management positions; by the 1940s, nearly 30 percent were going into business, and another 25 percent were going into law or medicine. It was the same with the men who graduated from the Jesuits' Loyola College in Baltimore. Among 2,200 living alumni surveyed in 1952 there were 180 doctors, 115 accountants, 80 engineers, and almost 900 businessmen in firms large and small.

Graduates of women's colleges made occupational progress more slowly, in part because of differing societal expectations about women and work. The president of Manhattanville College, directed by Religious of the Sacred Heart, observed in 1942 that most of the alumnae at her school were marrying shortly after graduation, but that "a second group, smaller by far but keen, ambitious, and with wide outlook," were pursuing careers as doctors, lawyers, and teachers.[20] All these "keen" Catholic professionals, with their "wide outlook," were ready to tackle social problems.

As the troop work of the Knights of Columbus had demonstrated, the First World War marked a turning point by showing the impact that coordinated efforts could have. The country's bishops formed the National Catholic War Council "to unify the energies of the whole Catholic body and direct them toward the American purpose." When peace returned, the council was renamed the National Catholic Welfare Conference (NCWC). It had permanent structures to continue the collaboration, with a general secretary and several administrative departments, headquartered in the nation's capital. Two NCWC agencies, those devoted to social action and lay activities, proved especially energetic. John A. Ryan, a priest from Minnesota who taught at Catholic University in Washington, headed the former, and he drafted a detailed plan for "social reconstruction" that the bishops endorsed as their own. The plan supported workers' rights to a living wage, social security insurance, restrictions on child labor, and an expanded program of affordable housing.[21]

The lay department of the NCWC was equally active, particularly in aiding the work of local Catholic organizations for women. Here the spark was Agnes Regan, a retired schoolteacher from California who was appointed in 1920 to oversee formation of the National Council of Catholic Women. The year before, ratification of the Nineteenth Amendment, granting women the right to vote, suggested new, more active roles for women. Under Regan's guidance, the council focused much of its effort on promoting women in social work. It ran an employment agency for social workers and also started a training school of social service, which soon became a professional school affiliated with Catholic University. Perhaps more important was Regan's monitoring of state and federal legislation. She was an active lobbyist for the restriction of child labor, for instance. Across the board, the benefits of expanding the work of women's organizations seemed obvious. "We have no desire to interfere with any existing activities," a speaker said at an early meeting of the women's council. Instead, the goal was "to unify, to coordinate, all these various splendid efforts," giving "national scope to the works which now often languish because they are restricted to this or that particular quarter." Within two years, more than a thousand local groups had affiliated with the National Council of Catholic Women.[22]

Organizations established by the hierarchy were fine, but groups formed by lay people themselves were more significant signs of the emerging spirit of Catholic Action. The Catholic Workers were the most widely recognized example of this lay initiative. Dorothy Day had lived an eventful life before startling her friends in 1926 by becoming a Catholic. A few years later, she and Peter Maurin began publishing a monthly newspaper, *The Catholic Worker*. They chose the title deliberately, taking the name of the Communist Party's *Daily Worker* and transforming it into something else. The paper's first appearance on May 1, 1933—May Day, the great workers' holiday—further underlined the point. Others quickly gathered around the austere but charismatic pair in their houses of hospitality, which combined the features of traditional settlement houses with those of religious communes. Residents maintained an active life of prayer and reflection, guided by Maurin's approach to the philosophy of Christian "personalism." He outlined a plan of self-examination and discussion known as the "clarification of thought," a process that was more or less constant among Catholic Workers. The movement also opened farming communities, grandly titled "agronomic universities," first on Staten Island, New York, then upstate, then elsewhere. These yielded produce for Worker soup kitchens, but, more important, they were attempts to recreate the traditional monastic ideal that fused prayer and manual labor.[23]

Membership in the Catholic Worker Movement was never very large and always somewhat fluid, but its impact was considerable. The newspaper had a nationwide circulation of more than

100,000. Most readers would never visit a house of hospitality themselves, but they were inspired by the intense personal commitment the Workers were making. Many among the clergy were cautious at first, troubled by the radical tone and, during the Second World War, by Day's insistent and absolute pacifism. New York's powerful Cardinal Francis Spellman had a pointed run-in with Day in 1949, when she picketed his residence on behalf of the gravediggers in Catholic cemeteries who were trying to form a union. Catholic prelates were not accustomed to being picketed by their own people, and once again, Day was arrested for her trouble. But her example was hard to ignore; it might even be a "literal interpretation of the Gospels," one supporter thought.[24] Not everyone could make such a radical commitment, but they could recognize it as a kind of ideal to which they might aspire. Most important, the Catholic Workers were lay people. Priests occasionally visited for Mass, prayer, and their own "clarification of thought," but the houses of hospitality were always run by and for lay Catholics. Thus they represented the new model of lay action.

Maurin's agronomic universities were never the success he hoped them to be, but other groups turned their attention to the needs of those who lived on the land. This interest was somewhat unexpected, for Catholics were overwhelmingly concentrated in the nation's cities. Still, the decline of the family farm, together with the problems of soil exhaustion and uncertain markets during the Depression years of the 1930s, led some Catholics to explore the contribution they might make. Spurred by a priest from Granger, Iowa, the National Catholic Rural Life Conference (NCRLC) was formed. Some conference statements sounded considerably more radical than those usually coming from church sources. "The industrialization of agriculture," an early guidebook thundered, "permits machines to plow under the farm families . . . the very culture on which America has grown to greatness. This reckless destruction which our system of unbridled free enterprise has made possible must be stopped." Farmers organized numerous committees in their widely scattered parishes, establishing cooperatives and credit unions. "Cooperation is merely the free operation of the Golden Rule in our economy," one NCRLC brochure said, a nice religious alternative to "unbridled free enterprise." In the 1930s, between 5,000 and 10,000 rural Catholics (mostly lay people, with a few priests) were attending the conference's annual national convention; in the 1940s, attendance hovered between 20,000 and 30,000.[25]

Another rural movement, conducted by and for women, emerged in the 1940s at the Grail community, a farm in Loveland, Ohio, just outside Cincinnati. Modeled after an association in the Netherlands, the Grail attracted well-educated women to a simple life of prayer and work as preparation for their eventual return to "the world." Grail was to be "a countercultural oasis," one founder said, well before that adjective achieved currency. Members did not take the religious vows of nuns, but they followed a daily monastic schedule combining farm labor with study and personal reflection in "the spirit of total dedication to God." Emphasizing "woman's spiritual mission and its practical consequences for her role in the social order," the group insisted on integrating religion with all aspects of one's personality. "Christianity," members said, "is a way of life, not a matter of Mass on Sunday and living like everyone else the rest of the week." In particular, Grail members stressed the arts as an area where women could make a distinctive contribution. Their tastes were eclectic, from learning Gregorian chant to adapting folk music for use in the Mass. Some specialized in weaving and ceramics, making church vestments, banners, and chalices in a style that contrasted with more traditional forms. They designed prayer services that incorporated modern dance. The mere fact that lay women were doing all these things gave the movement a vigor that was infectious. These were all, one participant said, "normal, attractive girls living on principle and being utterly wholehearted about it."[26] Their numbers were always small (only a few dozen in residence at any one time), but the Grail movement proved a significant precursor to later efforts to forge a link between Catholicism and the emerging feminism of the mid-twentieth century.

Most Catholic lay men and women lived and worked in the nation's industrialized cities, and it was thus natural that Catholic Action should find outlets there. Catholics had long formed the core of union membership. As early as 1902, parishioners in Cincinnati took up a collection for the relief of striking workers; a decade later, when the city's streetcar workers (80 percent of whom were Catholics) went out on strike, local pastors helped mediate a settlement. In Detroit, Catholics filled the ranks of the United Auto Workers throughout the 1920s and 1930s. Many parishes opened "labor schools," weeknight programs in which lay people studied *Rerum Novarum,* the papal encyclical of 1891 that had endorsed workers' rights to a fair wage and to collective bargaining. In Pittsburgh, Philip Murray, a near-daily communicant, was the principal force behind the powerful United Steel Workers Union and went on to head the Congress of Industrial Organizations (CIO). He found support among the local clergy. Father James Cox, pastor of a parish in the city's Strip District, organized a march of the unemployed on Washington, and Monsignor Charles Owen Rice, a close friend of Murray's, became an unofficial chaplain to the CIO.

"Labor priests" such as these and the Jesuit John Corridan in New York City were such familiar figures that they were even memorialized on film. Father Pete Barry, played by Karl Malden in *On the Waterfront* (1953), inspired dockworkers, including Marlon Brando's Terry Molloy, to organize to protect their interests. Not everyone approved of such activism. The head of the

Chevrolet division of General Motors told a churchman in Detroit in 1940 that priestly blessings at union meetings helped sustain "the position that Labor has been willfully abused and imposed upon by Management." Such a view was not "constructive," he complained. But John Brophy, yet another Catholic who succeeded Murray as president of the CIO, disagreed. It was not enough, he thought, for union members to say, "I am a Catholic and I know the principles of Catholic social justice"; instead, "we must get into the fight."[27]

The same inclination that was prompting other Catholic Action programs quickly found expression in organized labor with the formation of the Association of Catholic Trade Unionists (ACTU). The name was an accurate description: it was not a Catholic union as such, but an organization for individual Catholics who were also union members. Its founder was John C. Cort, who had converted to Catholicism while an undergraduate at Harvard. In February 1937, he and a dozen friends from the Catholic Worker house on Mott Street in Manhattan resolved "to bring to Catholic workingmen and women a knowledge of the social teaching of the Catholic Church." That spring, they threw their support behind striking saleswomen at Woolworth's department store, and they garnered public attention by picketing the home of the socialite (and Woolworth heiress) Barbara Hutton. Defenders of Hutton pointed to the millions she gave to charity, but Cort and his companions fired back with a quotation from Pope Pius XI: "Workers are not to receive as alms what is their due in justice." By the 1940s, ACTU was running 150 labor schools in parishes around the country, every year graduating more than 5,000 men and women who were determined to apply Catholic principles to the cause of labor.[28] The association gradually fell apart in the 1970s, the victim of dramatic declines in union membership nationwide. While it flourished, however, it mobilized lay Catholics in a movement that combined their working and religious lives.

Proponents of Catholic Action were not so successful when it came to racial injustice. The number of African Americans who were Catholics remained small, far outstripped by white European immigrants and their children. In 1920, blacks numbered only about 200,000 in a Catholic population of 18 million, making them a "minority within a minority." Everywhere across the South, the legal segregation that applied to drinking fountains, hotels, and buses also applied in parish churches and schools. Blacks sat separately in church and usually had to wait until white parishioners had received Communion at Sunday Mass before they could approach the altar. In the North, the de facto segregation of urban housing patterns achieved much the same effect. Some cities had distinct parishes for black Catholics, modeled on the "national" parishes of other ethnic groups, but these were ambiguous institutions. They provided black parishioners with churches of their own, but they also perpetuated separation of the races, which many Catholics were coming to see as inimical to the message of the Gospels.[29]

In response, some Catholics scattered across the country formed groups to confront racial issues. In New York City, the Jesuit writer and editor John LaFarge, son of the painter of the same name, took the lead in establishing the Catholic Interracial Council in 1934. Six hundred lay people, black and white, attended an organizational meeting in Town Hall that spring, vowing "to promote in every practicable way relations between the races based on Christian principles." Biweekly meetings attracted far smaller numbers but sponsored a range of speakers, including representatives of the National Urban League and other civil rights organizations. The group's membership was overwhelmingly white, and ironically, its energy undercut earlier efforts on the part of black Catholics to organize on their own. Still, with personal action rather than public forms of protest marking their approach, such groups helped prepare Catholics for participation in the civil rights movement of the 1950s.

College students were particularly avid supporters of racial tolerance. One group at Manhattanville College resolved "to be courteous and kind to every colored person . . . not to speak slightingly or use nick names which tend to humiliate . . . to recognize that the Negro shares my membership in the Mystical Body of Christ . . . to engage actively in some form of Catholic Action looking to the betterment" of black citizens. Such language seems quaint and even insulting today, but it provided a basis for the previously unthinkable. Students, black and white, from the four Catholic colleges in New Orleans, for instance, held regular interracial gatherings in the late 1940s and early 1950s, to the dismay of many of their parents.[30]

Catholic Action groups working for "social reconstruction" generally clustered on the left side of the political spectrum. It was no coincidence that while Catholic Workers and others were promoting the interests of the poor and the working class, Catholic voters nationwide had assumed a central place in the grand coalition that was the New Deal Democratic Party. But others found their religious ideals taking them in a different political direction, and none was more influential than the Michigan priest Father Charles Coughlin. Canadian by birth, Coughlin (he pronounced it "Cog-lin") was pastor of the Shrine of the Little Flower in Royal Oak, a suburb of Detroit, and he turned in the mid-1920s to the new medium of radio to raise funds for a new church. He had an ideal voice for radio—deep, round, and mellow—and soon his Sunday-afternoon sermons were syndicated to a national audience. It was said that, with every radio tuned in to his program at the same time, one could hear Coughlin's voice in the very air, simply by walking down the street of any Catholic neighborhood. He cited church teachings as the solution to the nation's economic woes, and in 1932 he made no secret of his support for the candidacy of Franklin Roosevelt. Almost immediately after the election, however, Coughlin turned against Roosevelt and the emerging policies of the New Deal. He saw the slowness of recovery in increasingly conspiratorial terms, and he latched onto arcane details of monetary policy as the key to explaining the troubled economy. This led him into a virulent anti-Semitism—"international Jewish bankers" were the real culprits, he concluded—and he formed his own political party, the National Union for Social Justice, hoping to win the White House in 1936.[31]

Coughlin's movement has not generally been seen as an expression of Catholic Action, but it shared many characteristics with the other groups claiming that mantle. The priest cited papal statements regularly, and he added the natural law philosophy of Thomas Aquinas often enough to lend further support. His critics insisted that Coughlin did not really understand the church teachings to which he alluded—"the people clamor for action," the liberal lay magazine *Commonweal* editorialized, but those "who have studied least are listened to most." Nonetheless, his followers saw themselves as engaging in a form of Catholic Action. They, too, were applying religious principles to political and economic life, even if they came to different conclusions about how best to do so. In practical terms, the political platform of Coughlin's union was a hodge-podge, drawing on the "share-our-wealth" demagoguery of Louisiana's flamboyant Huey Long and other bizarre schemes. Coughlin tapped an obscure congressman from North Dakota to run for president on this ticket, and in spite of the radio preacher's vast audience, the Union Party candidate was swamped in the Roosevelt reelection landslide. Catholic listeners tuned in every week, but they still voted for FDR. Thereafter, Coughlin's popularity fell off sharply, and he became increasingly marginalized as a political and religious crank. He was finally forced off the air in 1942.[32]

Clergy and lay people alike applied the cry for Catholic Action to culture no less than to politics. In particular, bringing church principles to bear on the emerging mass media seemed a suddenly urgent task: motion pictures offered what one priest called "Catholic Action's big opportunity." The vividness with which films could portray morally questionable activity—love triangles, suggestive dancing and speech, disrespect for authority—worried many. The movie industry had adopted a self-censoring production code, but church leaders judged this insufficient. Some Catholic newspapers began to rate movies on the basis of their moral content, and soon a more systematic effort was under way. The nation's bishops established a Legion of Decency, and the laity signed on enthusiastically. Fifty thousand Catholics filled a stadium in Cleveland in June 1934 to vow their opposition to "indecent" movies, and that September 70,000 parochial school children marched through Chicago carrying banners with such slogans as "Admission to an indecent film is an admission to hell." By the end of the year, almost 9 million Catholics across the country had taken the legion's pledge, administered annually thereafter in parish churches on one of the Sundays just before Christmas: "I condemn all indecent and immoral motion pictures, and those which glorify crime and criminals . . . I acknowledge my obligation to form a right conscience about pictures that are dangerous to my moral life. I pledge myself to remain away from them. I promise, further, to stay away altogether from places of amusement which show them as a matter of policy."[33]

The threat of Catholic boycotts was a powerful one, and sometimes it was backed up by direct action. A movie house in Sayville, Long Island, was showing *Belle of the Nineties,* starring Mae West, until a priest from the local parish showed up and stood outside, examining the faces of those who bought tickets to see if any of his parishioners were among them. Attendance dropped off immediately, and the manager closed the picture down. In 1935, the legion opened a national office in New York City and oversaw an elaborate system, run mostly by lay women, of rating films. One hundred volunteers from the Federation of Catholic Alumnae, an organization for graduates of Catholic women's colleges, viewed newly released films and assessed their content, assigning letter grades from A ("morally unobjectionable"), through several grades of A-minus ("morally unobjectionable in part"), to C ("condemned"). The legion office trained them and monitored their work: one new volunteer was reprimanded when she rated as unobjectionable a movie in which a man divorced his wife to marry someone else. The ratings were published in diocesan newspapers, and sometimes priests announced the grades of movies playing in local theaters from the pulpit on Sunday mornings.

Some non-Catholics objected to this blunt exercise of Catholic power, but many Protestant churches praised the legion. The Federal Council of Churches, representing the nation's mainline Protestant denominations, thanked Catholics for their "aggressive position" on the subject, even though the council was otherwise wary of Catholic "aggression." For their part, Catholics who were enthusiastic about the effort to clean up the movies had no doubt about what they were doing. One priest called it a "newly-begun fight for the Kingdom of Christ," while a lay man told the editor of *America* magazine that it was "a real bit of Catholic Action."[34]

Catholic Action groups proliferated around particular interests, but the finest expression of the impulse was an effort to organize Catholics literally where they lived: in their own homes. The Christian Family Movement (CFM) was built on the idea that the health of society depended on the happiness of individual families. Catholic families had the duty to improve society, starting in their own immediate surroundings. The movement took its inspiration and its method from Joseph Cardijn, a Belgian priest who promoted Catholic Action in Europe. He had directed a movement called *Jeunesse Ouvriere Chretienne* (Young Christian Workers), and this prompted some recent Catholic college graduates to form a parallel organization in the United

States. This workers' group was never large, but the CFM successfully adopted the "social inquiry" method Cardijn had articulated, encapsulated in the slogan "Observe, Judge, Act." Each "cell" of CFM members—no more than six couples was the recommended number—met regularly in one another's homes and, after reflecting on a passage from the Bible, turned to a pressing issue in daily life. "Members bring in facts about some aspect of their lives, judge these facts in the light of Christian principles, and take some kind of action to bring *what is* more closely in line with *what ought to be*," said one early guide. "This inquiry method—observe, judge, act—produces more than a series of good deeds. More important, it shapes good Christians."[35]

An official handbook, *For Happier Families* (known, from its distinctive cover, as "the little yellow book"), helped CFM cells get started. It suggested topics for the first few meetings: welcoming newcomers to the neighborhood; questions pertaining to children; the role of the family in the life of the parish; the relationship between husband and wife. Once participants had worked their way through these topics, they would have mastered the technique and could then go on to explore their own particular concerns. The yellow book also spelled out precisely how the social inquiry method worked. During the consideration of neighborliness, for instance, the "observe" portion of the discussion asked the group to analyze their own street or block: "Give examples of how you and others became acquainted with neighbors . . . Give examples of recent opportunities you and others have had which you could have used as a way of getting to know a certain neighbor better." Then the focus shifted to "judge": "How well do you have to know people to know their needs? . . . If Christ lived in your neighborhood would He be pleased with the way people know each other?" Finally, it was time to act: "Invite a neighbor to your house or to a parish function . . . Ask one of your neighbors to do something for you. (This has been found an effective way of getting to know people.)"

The CFM approach combined the theological with the resolutely mundane: members were asked to reflect on what Jesus himself might have thought, but the result could be something as ordinary as asking a neighbor to watch the kids during a quick errand. Here was Catholic Action that only lay people could perform, and getting to the "action" was always essential. "If no action is taken," an advisory to CFM leaders pointed out, "the group has become a discussion group." Discussions were fine, "but when a CFM group discusses only, there is something dishonest about the meeting. In effect, they are telling themselves that they have faced up to an un-Christian situation when in actuality they ran for cover."[36]

The CFM was not for either men or women alone but for couples. This in itself was valuable, members thought. One of its "happy by-products" was that, "because they are doing more things together, [couples] draw together in a deeper, more mature love." Two couples in particular were responsible for the movement's early success and rapid expansion: Pat and Patty Crowley of Chicago, and Burnett and Helene Bauer of South Bend, Indiana. Hearing of others who shared their interest, these four convened about sixty participants, together with a dozen priests, at a retreat house outside Chicago in June 1949 and established a national organization. The Crowleys were elected co-chairs, a position they held until 1970. Annual conventions followed, and these grew to impressive proportions, though not without some difficulties. One early meeting was held at a monastery: apparently, no one had realized that men and women were not allowed to stay in the same room at this facility, thereby undercutting the closeness of husband and wife that the movement sought to promote. Growing pains aside, the CFM spread quickly. By 1955, more than 300 cities had at least one cell. San Francisco and Denver had enrolled more than 500 couples each—the group always counted its membership in couples—Toledo had more than 300, Los Angeles about 250. Total membership nationwide stood at

16,000 couples that year, and it was twice that number only two years later.[37]

Although the CFM always had priestly advisers, it was an organization of lay people. Chaplains were warned to speak as little as possible at cell meetings. The movement thus gave clear articulation to the ideal, common to all Catholic Action efforts, of direct lay "participation" in the work of the church. "We seek first of all to have Christian principles dominate every phase of our personal living," a Catholic Action text for college students said in 1935, "and then to bring those principles into all the ramifications of life about us."[38] Whenever couples in the Christian Family Movement, or those who lived in a Catholic Worker house, or Catholics who joined their fellow trade unionists, or farmers who relied on the programs of the Catholic Rural Life Conference—whenever any of these people came back to their groups' programs again and again, they made a tighter connection between their religious and their secular lives. They had become Catholic Action Catholics—Catholics not only when they were in church but also when they were on the picket line or in the field or even cooking the family dinner. Studying church teaching on their own, not just hearing about it in sermons, was their responsibility. Here was a more encompassing way of being a lay Catholic.

Enthusiasts of Catholic Action were thus "reawakening to the fact that laymen are not only *in* the Church but that they, too, *are* the Church." Such thinking had the potential to redefine the relationship between clergy and laity, between a priest and the members of his parish. Priests, one CFM chaplain wrote, "must respect the autonomy of the layman in his proper field of responsibility. And it is the laity who are responsible in the domestic area—the area of the family. The clergy in this context are assistants." If carried to its logical conclusion, language of this kind risked undercutting the traditional patterns of authority in the church. The idea that a pastor might be the "assistant" to members of his congregation was a potentially problematic one: not since the days of parish trustees had such a relationship been suggested. Accordingly, Catholic Action statements often stressed the importance of following the clergy's lead. When a Catholic Action text spoke of "the laity's helping the Hierarchy," perhaps only a keen-eyed reader would have noticed that "Hierarchy" was capitalized and "laity" was not. The subliminal point was made nonetheless, and others were more explicit about it. "The laity," one priest told the board of the National Council of Catholic Women in 1934, "serve, of course, under the Bishops . . . Every diocese is ruled by its own Bishop. The Church is made up of Bishops, of priests—and the priests depend upon the Bishops for the exercise of their priestly power—and the laity." The bishop was "the power through whom all life comes to the diocese." In this view, lower-case laity were "of course" subject to upper-case Bishops, whose position was defined by "rule" and "power."

Catholic Action participants did not overtly challenge such notions, and the deference usually accorded the clergy was observed by lay participants. At the same time, however, the possibility was opened that lay people might sometimes take the lead. "Laymen are not second class members of the Body of Christ," the CFM national newsletter said bluntly in 1957.[39] The full implications of that outlook would become apparent in the 1960s, in the aftermath of the Second Vatican Council, but the rhetoric and programs of Catholic Action helped prepare the way for the return of an active laity.

Even as Catholic Action urged lay people toward an effort to bring the church's message to the world, it also encouraged them to assume greater responsibility for their own spiritual lives. The first half of the twentieth century saw a flowering of religious practice among Catholics. Many, no doubt, were attending to their religious duties without much thought, but others were learning to cultivate a spiritual approach that was markedly personal, even as it conformed to the outward demands of the church. Catholic Action meant lay action in church as well as outside it.

Accurate measures of church attendance by American Catholics have always been hard to come by. Parishes never kept systematic track of those who came to Mass every week or those who were less regular; nor did pastors reliably "count the house" from Sunday to Sunday. Anecdotal observations reported consistently high levels of practice. In 1957, the pastor of Saint Nicholas of Tollentine parish on Chicago's southwest side (known fondly as "Saint Nick's") reported that his church could hold 1,100 worshipers and that all the seats were taken for Sunday Mass "every hour on the hour," from six A.M. until noon. A Philadelphia priest asserted flatly that "the average Catholic of this period attended Mass every Sunday," without feeling the need either to identify who these "average" Catholics were or to bother counting them.[40]

A systematic study of parish Mass attendance was prepared in 1951 by Joseph Fichter, a Jesuit sociologist at Loyola University in New Orleans. Fichter and his students had spent the entire previous year studying Mater Dolorosa ("Mother of Sorrows") parish in the city's Carrollton neighborhood, and they confirmed that faithful Mass attendance was "one of the identifiable characteristics of Catholic behavior." The parish—for whites only in the segregated city—had half a dozen Masses every Sunday, hourly between 6:00 and 10:00 A.M., with a final service at 11:30. Average numbers ranged from about 350 at the first Mass to nearly 900 at the last. Unusual events might affect the count on any given Sunday. Only 140, less than half the normal number, showed up for 6:00 Mass one Sunday in January when the city awoke to find icicles on the trees, a rare and daunting sight in

New Orleans. Attendance also varied according to age group. Those over sixty were most faithful: 91 percent of them attended weekly. Parishioners in their thirties were less regular, but they came at a still-commendable 69 percent. For the year, average weekly attendance at all Masses stood at roughly two-thirds (3,500 of 5,300) of the parishioners over the age of seven, though it might reach as high as 85 percent, as it did on Easter Sunday.

From any perspective, these levels of religious practice were impressive. Nationwide, average attendance for all denominations, including Catholics, in the years after World War II never quite reached half—it hit 49 percent twice, according to Gallup Poll surveys: in 1955 and again in 1958—though in some churches it was considerably lower. Episcopalians, for example, were falling through the 20 percent bracket in this period, and heading lower still. Catholics in the United States were also attending church at a rate far higher than their relatives in Europe, where the percentage was plunging into single digits.[41]

The sacraments were the principal points of contact between American Catholics and their church, and lay religious practice came to center on two of them: Communion and confession. The Eucharist was, in a sense, the whole point of every Catholic Mass. Unlike many Protestant churches, which offered only "morning prayer" on some Sundays of the year, Catholics had Communion every week. At the climax of the liturgy, the priest said over the bread and wine the prescribed prayers that transformed them into the body and blood of Christ, ate and drank himself, and then distributed the bread, placing a small round wafer on the tongue of each recipient. (Catholic lay people had not consumed any of the wine since ancient times, a point of contention during the Reformation, when Protestants began to insist that the sacrament be distributed "under both species.") This was an opportunity for every person to commune with God, for Catholic theology insisted on the Real Presence of Christ in the sacrament. The elements of the Eucharist were not merely symbolic or metaphorical: Christ was really there in them.[42]

As a result of the churchifying process of earlier eras, American Catholics in the first half of the twentieth century had ready access to Communion. At every Sunday Mass, lay people had the opportunity to partake of the Eucharist, though they could do so only once on any single day. Most Catholics in this period, however, were reluctant to come forward to receive Communion at the point in the service when it was distributed to them. The long traditions of "purgative" prayer, emphasizing their unworthiness, served as a brake. Since the gap between the goodness of God and the sinfulness of ordinary men and women was so great, it seemed a bit presumptuous to approach so solemn an event too frequently. Better that they reserve Communion for special occasions, when they could be thoroughly prepared. Purely human considerations reinforced the hesitancy. "The communicant must be humble and modest in his exterior bearing," one priest had written, "avoiding vanity in dress and manner," with hands and face "carefully washed," and maintaining decorum. "The communicant does not rush up from his place to the railing, but he slowly walks up to it, the hands joined and the eyes cast down." Women, another priest warned in 1929, should take their gloves off and avoid "indecent or offensive fashions"; pastors, he said, should not hesitate to refuse the sacrament to those who failed to comply. By the 1950s, still another priest was noting the lifelong practice of his own grandfather. This man walked to his neighborhood church for Mass every week, and yet he received Communion only twice a year: once on Christmas and again on Easter. Taking the sacrament more often than that was thought an act of particular piety, probably best not attempted.[43]

In the church of Catholic Action, however, priests encouraged their parishioners toward more frequent Communion, and these urgings gradually changed lay practice. At the beginning of the century, Pope Pius X had declared that Catholics should receive Communion often, even daily if they could. Getting parishioners to go to Communion once a week seemed a more realistic goal, and pastors in America began to tell their people that they should cultivate this habit. Receiving Communion at Mass was not obligatory, a priest wrote in a national Catholic magazine in 1949, responding to an inquiry sent in by a parishioner from Sayre, Pennsylvania, but "to omit Holy Communion without good reason is indefensible self-deprivation."[44]

Fichter's study of Mater Dolorosa in New Orleans showed that these clerical promptings were having some effect, though rates of Communion fluctuated throughout the year. February was a slack time, for instance—in part, the sociologist thought, because that was the "social season," and parishioners who had been out late on Saturday night tended not to come forward on Sunday morning. Variations aside, the average number of hosts distributed at all the Sunday Masses in the parish was only about 500. Given that average weekly attendance was 3,500, only 14 percent of the people seem to have acquired the habit of Communion every Sunday. For others, monthly reception was the standard, with a more encouraging rate of nearly half. Young adults were most likely to have adopted the monthly routine (41 percent of parishioners in their twenties), while those over age sixty held to a lower frequency: only 25 percent of them were monthly communicants. School children had the highest rate of all (71 percent), perhaps as a result of enforced reception at the hands of parents and the sisters in the parish school.[45]

Those intending to receive Communion faced some obstacles, not least the regulations governing what was called the Eucharistic fast. Anyone approaching the Communion rail was required to abstain from eating or drinking anything, including water, from midnight the night before. This reminder of the solemnity of the act "helps preserve a respectful attitude," said the *Catholic Digest,*

a popular magazine for the laity, in 1945. Thus most people had
to receive the Eucharist early in the morning, simply because few
could put off breakfast until later. The fast was strictly enforced
but, significantly, not through any action of the clergy, who had
no way of knowing who might have broken it. Rather, it was lay
people themselves who internalized the requirement and their responsibility to meet it.

Stories of near misses were legion, often centering on a child
who almost took a drink of water before church. Even in extreme
cases, the law was the law. "Albert," the boy in a 1942 grade
school catechism story, broke his fast one Sunday, though he insisted that he had not done so deliberately. "That is too bad," his
father replied, "but you can not go to Holy Communion today."
This parent, however fictional, and his real-life counterparts were
equally at ease with their role as the religious enforcers in their
families. "Even the smallest morsel of food that reaches the stomach" broke the fast, a guide to Catholic practice had said in 1929,
and this absoluteness prompted some lay people to seek painfully
precise advice from experts about what constituted "food." Medicine was permitted, for example, but at least one authority drew a
distinction between pills taken with water (permissible) and those
taken with a cup of coffee (impermissible). Nurses and night-
shift workers during wartime might receive special dispensations,
but these exceptions only reinforced the more general rule for everyone else.[46] A papal decree of 1957 relaxed the fast—only three
hours before Communion for food and drink, with water permitted anytime—and this helped improve the rate at which people
received the Eucharist.

Attitudes toward reception of the Eucharist by children also
changed, focusing particularly on a child's first experience, "a
landmark in the life of a Catholic," one priest wrote. Church custom had long decreed that children should first receive Communion when they reached the "age of discretion," that is, when

they were able to tell right from wrong. Authorities disagreed, however, on precisely what that age was. American bishops had set a window of no earlier than ten and no later than fourteen, but within that pastors were free to determine the best time in their individual circumstances. As with increased frequency of Communion, change in this matter was initiated at the top. Pope Pius X declared in 1910 that children as young as seven be admitted to the Eucharist, and thereafter it became common for American parishes to schedule First Communion for those in the second grade, usually at a special Sunday Mass in the spring. Lined up according to height, the children were shown how to hold their hands prayerfully, how to march forward at the appropriate time, and what the penalties were for whispering or fooling with their friends. Teachers presided over repeated rehearsals to ensure that everything went as planned on the great day. Parents embraced the whole idea, and by the 1940s and 1950s, they had built an elaborate ritual of childhood around First Communion. Boys were attired in what was probably their first suit of formal clothes, and girls, appearing as "little brides," wore lacy white dresses and veils. Priests and sisters warned against excess in such fashions, but this was often a losing battle.[47] After their First Communion, children could fall into the patterns of their own families when it came to the frequency of Communion.

Reception of the Eucharist was closely tied to the second important sacrament for American Catholics in this era: confession, known officially as the sacrament of penance. Anyone planning to take Communion at Mass was expected to have gone to confession beforehand, and very recently at that. Commonly, those receiving the Eucharist on Sunday morning confessed the day before, and parishes everywhere built their schedules on this presumption, with several hours set aside on Saturday afternoon and evening. At Saint Benedict's, a church in Highland Park, Michigan, in 1949, for example, priests heard confessions every Satur-

day from 3:00 to 6:00 in the afternoon and again from 7:30 to
9:30. The parish even specified an hour (11:00 until noon) on
Saturday morning when children could confess, thereby getting
them out of the way of adults later in the day. Additional hours
were also provided before important feasts, like Christmas or
Easter. A parish in suburban Boston in the 1940s was not alone in
having regular Saturday hours for confession, but during Lent at
least one priest was also available every weekday morning between 8:30 and 9:00. Although it was rare, confessions might
even be heard on Sundays. The parish clergy devoted so much
time to hearing confessions because lay people came in such large
numbers. Fichter calculated that nearly 70 percent of the parishioners at Mater Dolorosa in New Orleans were in the habit of going to confession at least once a month.[48]

Even more clearly than with Communion, lay people made
fully their own the church's teachings on confession, assuming
the task of enforcing its requirements on themselves. The sacrament turned on the detailed Catholic theology of sin, which
could be classified according to several overlapping categories.
There was original sin (the sin of Adam and Eve, passed on to all
their descendants) and actual sin (specific transgressions against
God and neighbor). There were venial sins (such as speaking angrily to one's children or disobeying one's parents) and mortal
sins (grave offenses which, left unforgiven, severed one's connection to God altogether and sent the sinner immediately to hell at
death). There were sins of commission (bad things done deliberately) and sins of omission (good deeds neglected). From their
earliest childhood, lay Catholics became fluent in speaking this
theological language and in applying it to themselves. They knew
how to identify and describe their sins, though they might sometimes have to seek advice from the clergy. Priests were always
ready to provide the right answer to inquiring penitents, either in
the confessional itself or in the pages of Catholic periodicals. In

1942, for example, at a time when Catholics were warned never to attend Protestant religious services, a man who had tuned in to a non-Catholic program on the radio was told that if he had listened only out of curiosity, his sin was venial; if he had intended "to take part in some way in the service," he had committed a mortal sin. Women's use of cosmetics might be a mortal sin if done "for the purpose of enticing or encouraging others to sins of impurity," another priest had ruled in 1935. If worn out of "vanity," makeup was merely a venial sin, and if used "to hide a defect in one's appearance," it was no sin at all.[49]

Catholics applied these concepts in a standardized procedure when they went to confession. First, they were expected to call to mind their sins and the number of times they had committed each one. This was known as the examination of conscience, and it demanded that sinners be honest with themselves in confronting what they had done and why it was wrong. Next, they had to "excite contrition" for these actions—that is, to feel sorry for having done them—but it was crucial that they feel sorry for the right reason. Sorrow motivated merely by fear of God's punishment ("imperfect contrition") was sufficient, but it was better to strive for "perfect" contrition, motivated by recognition that sin offended God, who deserved better from his people. Once this inner conversation had been completed, parishioners one by one entered the confessional box, where the priest sat in darkness behind a screen. They whispered their sins so that those waiting outside could not overhear. The priest might ask a few questions if the nature of the offenses was unclear—priests were routinely admonished to keep any questioning to a minimum—and then he said the prayer of forgiveness and assigned a penance. This usually involved the recitation of a few prayers, which the parishioner could do after leaving the box and before heading home. The penance was understood both as a punishment for the enumerated sins and as a way of expressing sorrow. It might also as-

sist with developing in the sinner what was called the "firm purpose of amendment," an effort to avoid committing the same sins
in the future. The whole business did not take very long—Fichter
calculated that, from start to finish, a penitent might spend as little as fifteen minutes in church for this purpose, depending on
the crowd—but the effect was to wipe clean the sinner's slate. Parishioners were thus purified in anticipation of Communion, but
more generally they were also reassured that God, acting through
the priest, had forgiven them.[50]

For lay people, confession was the most personal of all church
rituals, not least because it was conducted in their own vernacular
language; only the priest's absolution was in Latin. Moreover, the
real work of the sacrament went on inside their own heads, and it
required them to apply the teaching of the church to what they
themselves had done. Sin was everywhere—or, more precisely, it
might be anywhere, and they always had to be on watch for it.
Popular guides to help with the examination of conscience specified just how pervasive it was. One booklet from the 1940s identified 367 common sins (220 were mortal, 147 were venial): failing
to pray when tempted to sin; performing religious duties "in a
distracted, impersonal, halfhearted manner"; being "miserly or
grudging in alms giving"; "taking delight in impure thoughts";
"snubbing people or being sarcastic"; and on and on. Many penitents fell into an unthinking confessional routine, describing the
same sins over and over, but even so, this was a moral world of
the utmost seriousness. Lay Catholics had perhaps dozens of opportunities, every single day, to send themselves to hell for all
eternity, and that would be a frightening prospect indeed without the remedy that the sacrament offered. Confession reminded
them of their own responsibility for what they had done: no
blaming someone else, no claiming mitigating circumstances, no
hoping that secret sins could be kept secret. Confession was like a
court proceeding, sermons and textbooks explained, and the pen-

itent was both the defendant and the prosecutor. The only reason for being there was to plead guilty.[51] The confessional was where they owned up to what they had done wrong and acknowledged their need to do better. If they did that, they had a hope of salvation; if not, they knew the consequences. Either way, they were the ones accountable for their own moral standing.

Personal responsibility was also evident in other aspects of lay prayer life in the church of Catholic Action. Priests could show them the path to prayer, but lay people were the ones who had to walk it. The catalog of standard prayers was both ancient and extensive, and generations of parents had taught them to their children. The "big three" were familiar to most Catholics literally for as long as they could remember: the Our Father—Catholics seldom called this "The Lord's Prayer," which they considered a Protestant designation—the Hail Mary, and the short Glory Be ("Glory be to the Father, and to the Son, and to the Holy Ghost, as it was in the beginning, is now and ever shall be, world without end. Amen."). They also learned the Apostles' Creed, a briefer version of the summary of faith that the priest said at Mass; a second prayer to the Virgin Mary, which began "Hail, Holy Queen"; and a short Act of Contrition ("O my God, I am heartily sorry for having offended Thee . . ."), which they could use in confession and at other times as well. There were Acts of Faith, Hope, and Charity, together with prayers to be said before and after meals and prayers for early in the morning, dedicating the day to God's purposes. Individuals found their own favorites among all these, and saying them quickly became habitual.[52]

To many non-Catholics—and, indeed, to some Catholics themselves—recitation of these prescribed prayers seemed like a mindless rote. The criticism had some validity. So ingrained were the words that Catholics could say their prayers, silently or aloud, with minimal attention. Lay people increasingly heard the church's message, however, that they should attempt to pray in ways that had personal meaning for them. "May we use our own words in praying to God?" asked a child's catechism from the 1940s. The answer was yes: "We may use our own words in praying to God, and it is well to do so."

Catholics with particular concerns could tailor their prayer by appealing to specific saints. As in the immigrant church, the Virgin Mary still led the list, but there were dozens of other holy figures whom one might approach. Saint Anthony helped in finding household items (keys, quite often) that had been lost; Saint Lucy, a martyr said to have been tortured by having her eyes plucked out, now cured eye diseases; Saint Joseph, the earthly father of Jesus, might help with real estate transactions. Most famous of all was Saint Jude, an invented figure who was declared the patron saint of otherwise "hopeless causes." From a shrine in Chicago beginning in the 1920s, priests managed a nationwide network of devotions to Jude, whose aid was sought especially by women facing marital problems, the unemployment of spouses, and other troubles. Nearly every profession had its own patron saint, too: doctors (Saint Luke), lawyers (Thomas More), secretaries (Genesius), and even housewives (Saint Anne, the mother of Mary). Saints provided individualized points of contact between ordinary believers and powerful inhabitants of the heavenly realm, and the relationships were close ones. "Everybody seems to know him," one priest wrote in 1930 of Anthony, "the People's Saint," and this established a personal connection. "Wherever and whenever you find devotion to him in a flourishing condition, you will also find that he is generous in answering the people's prayers."[53]

Whether repeating traditional formulas or expressing their own thoughts in their own words, Catholics were confident that praying had real consequences. Prayers were not just empty words, mumbled unconsciously and sent off into an uncomprehending universe. Rather, they placed the believer in the midst of what one scholar has called "a divine economy which encompassed things visible and invisible, Earth and Heaven, humanity and God." What Catholics said and did in prayer had tangible outcomes. In 1937, one devotee of Mary reported an unexpected pay raise after attending a parish novena in her honor. In 1953, a nurse prayed to Saint Jude after her father had been injured in a car accident and no medical treatment had helped. The man's recovery took more than a year, but his daughter was sure that the turning point had come the moment she talked to Jude.[54]

Personal stories like these filled the Catholic press, but prayers could also be enlisted on behalf of larger causes. Father Patrick Peyton, an Irish immigrant priest in Scranton, Pennsylvania, began a fabulously successful Family Rosary Crusade in 1942, hoping to counteract divorce and juvenile delinquency by insisting that "the family that prays together stays together." Peyton made effective use of the radio, and later of television, in encouraging families to gather regularly in their own homes to recite the rosary. Peyton himself led the prayers over the air, and those who tuned in across the country prayed along with him and with one another. Beyond any personal benefits, these prayers might even play a geopolitical role, especially as a weapon against "godless communism," on the march after the Second World War. With communists poised to win in Italian national elections in 1948, for example, Peyton urged his crusaders to direct their prayers toward preventing that outcome—and it seemed to work: communist gains at the polls fell off sharply in favor of the Christian Democrats, a largely Catholic party. For others, too, prayer was a weapon in the Cold War. In September 1959, when Nikita Khrushchev, the Soviet premier, visited the United Nations, more than 20,000 Catholics in Boston stood around the Bunker Hill Monument, which commemorated a battle of the American Revolution, to pray the rosary, asking God to frustrate the Russian's

wicked schemes.[55] Catholics such as these prayed because they
were convinced that their prayers had real effects. They themselves might just be housewives or office workers, but their ability
to pray gave them an important role in truly cosmic events. The
triumph of good and the defeat of evil depended, to no small degree, on them.

New ways of promoting this personal approach to Catholic
prayer also developed, and few were more popular than the lay
retreat. It had long been customary for priests and sisters to make
an annual retreat, withdrawing from their usual surroundings for
a week or two of reflection and prayer, under the guidance of an
experienced spiritual director. The church of Catholic Action
promoted the idea that lay people, too, might profit from this
kind of exercise. "When soldiers retreat," one lay man wrote in
1953, after returning from his first such experience, "they retire orderly [sic] and intact to stronger positions in order to reorganize
their strength for a new assault. Similarly, when a man makes a
[religious] retreat, he withdraws from the workaday, playaday
world. He 'retires' for a few days in order to recoup his spiritual
powers for a new advance." Few lay people could devote an entire
week to this purpose, however, so retreat masters created a weekend program that typically lasted from the dinner hour on Friday
until Sunday afternoon. "The retreat's success or failure," the enthusiastic first-timer said, "is our own to decide; by attention and
cooperation we can gain immense spiritual grace, by deficiency in
these respects we may forfeit the abundant good available to us."
Throughout, the participants listened to talks (often called "conferences") by the clergy, engaged in such devotional exercises as
praying the rosary or the Stations of the Cross, attended Mass
and went to confession, and also had time for private reflection or
individual consultation with a priest on any matter that might be
troubling them.[56]

The number of retreats increased exponentially. Members of

parish sodalities and Holy Name societies could go off to a retreat house for a "weekend with God," and in many parishes this became an annual event. The broad democracy of it all was part of the appeal. An early account noted that the participants one weekend included "three lawyers, two bricklayers, three carpenters, a school principal, nine business men," and many others. Retreat houses opened in nearly every state, and though they were staffed by the clergy, lay people often took the initiative. In 1922, a Laymen's Weekend Retreat League opened a house in Malvern, Pennsylvania, that was so successful it was soon conducting retreats for two separate groups every weekend.

Retreats for particular clientele also became popular. A Matt Talbot Retreat League, for instance, named for an Irish temperance reformer, was organized in Morristown, New Jersey, in 1943, combining a religious program with the twelve-step recovery method of Alcoholics Anonymous. At about the same time, a convent of sisters in Philadelphia began offering retreats for married couples in the process of adopting children. By the 1960s, there were more than one hundred retreat houses for men and more than seventy-five for women—except for members of the Christian Family Movement, retreats were usually segregated by sex—across the country, most of them filled every weekend. In 1961, a Jesuit even published a manual for a "do-it-yourself" retreat, with guided meditations for those who wanted to make a retreat but could not; those who had attended one and wanted to sustain that level of religious intensity; or "husbands and wives who would like to make a retreat at home, either together or individually."[57]

Regardless of their format, retreats promoted a spiritual approach that theologians called "interiority," and this marked the religious outlook of lay people in the age of Catholic Action. What went on spiritually inside each of them was what mattered. The churchifying process of the previous century had successfully turned them into regular churchgoers, and that was no small accomplishment. They were in the habit of going through the expected motions of religious practice. But now concern arose that too many were *only* going through the motions. Yes, they were attending Mass regularly, but were they really "attending" in the sense of paying attention? The effort to build up interior religious sentiments was a counterweight to the possibility that many lay people were just fulfilling their obligations. Like the retreatant who said that the weekend's success was "our own to decide," lay people were encouraged to nurture their own religious life. "It is not the listening or the reading that does you the most good" on a retreat, another observer said; "the important thing is the *thinking over* what you have heard or read . . . That is the really valuable part of the retreat: the work you do for yourself."[58] To be sure, not every parishioner wanted to make this kind of effort. Increasingly, however, lay people were urged to aspire to that standard. By going on retreat, by talking with individual saints about matters large and small, by examining their consciences and actions in confession, by communing directly with God more frequently—in all these ways, lay people in the church of Catholic Action worked at personalizing their faith. It was work they did for themselves.

When individuals prayed or received the sacraments, they saw themselves as joining their actions to those of other Catholics around the country and around the world. They were part of these larger communities, both real and imagined. They were united to one another and, in a particular way, to the pope. The age of Catholic Action saw a tightening of the bonds between American Catholics and the head of their church in Rome. In contrast to earlier generations, most of them now knew a good deal about the pope, and his authority meant something to them. It was, after all, a pope who had popularized the term "Catholic Action" in the first place, and whenever Americans affiliated themselves with that broad program, they were following his lead. That members of the ACTU could instinctively quote a papal statement in the middle of a labor strike, for instance, signified that the pope had come to occupy a prominent place in the mental universe of American Catholics.

Mass communications made it newly possible for the pope to reach into American Catholic homes over the radio. In February 1931, Pius XI broadcast a message to the world for the first time, joined by the inventor of the wireless, Guglielmo Marconi, now a member of the Italian senate. American Catholics gathered around their sets to hear the pope's words—translated into English, since he spoke in Italian—and they marveled at the immediacy of it all. An observer in Salt Lake City enthusiastically reported the "clear reception in Utah." At the end of the broadcast, when Pius imparted his blessing, many listeners knelt in the street around the stores where those without radios at home had gathered to listen. As with President Roosevelt's fireside chats a few years later, the impact was direct. Imagine: there they were, half a world away in places like Salt Lake City, and the pope was speaking directly to them. Other media attention to the papacy followed, evident in the news coverage given to the visit of Cardinal Eugenio Pacelli to the United States in the fall of 1936. Pacelli was the Vatican secretary of state, the second most powerful position in the church, and he was widely recognized as heir apparent to the current pontiff; indeed, he would be elected pope three years later, taking the name Pius XII. Although later a controversial figure for his actions (or inactions) during the Second World War and the Holocaust, he was greeted as a first-rank celebrity during his American tour. Flying from New York to California and back, he stopped in a dozen cities, lunched with Roosevelt just two days after the president's easy reelection, and was greeted by crowds of Catholics eager to catch a glimpse of him.[59]

The pope (or at least a future pope) not only came to see

Americans; increasingly, they traveled to Rome to see him. Pilgrimages to the Eternal City had once been possible only for the wealthy, but the improving economic position of American Catholics put devotional travel within reach for many. The tourism industry tapped into this market, offering affordable packages, and thousands of Catholics signed up. Nineteen fifty proved an especially busy year. It was a "Holy Year," a jubilee that popes since the middle ages had been declaring every quarter-century, and pilgrims earned special blessings by visiting churches in Rome. Americans avidly participated. One of the largest groups—more than five hundred men and women from thirty-three states—sailed in February, accompanied by New York's Cardinal Francis Spellman, a personal friend of Pius XII. Once in Rome, they took part in official ceremonies and then had a personal audience with the pope. The usually austere Pius seemed particularly happy to see them. He joked with the crowd, and when an eighty-year-old pilgrim asked him to bless a replica of the white papal skull cap the man had bought as a souvenir, the pope took his own cap off and traded it with him: "You take mine and I'll take yours," he said.

Tour groups vied with one another for closeness to the pope. A pilgrim from Los Angeles was proud that his party had had "a favored place to the left of the throne." By the end of the Holy Year, dozens of pilgrimage groups had come from America, their appeal enhanced because they mixed relaxation with piety: the New York party, for instance, stopped on the way home for several days at Nice on the French Riviera. More important, American Catholics took the opportunity to reaffirm their connection to the papacy and its historic role. In seeing the pontiff, one pilgrim exclaimed later, "one sees not one Pope but the last Pope in an unbroken chain of Popes stretching back into the mists of time, beyond the Renaissance into the Middle Ages, and still back into the Dark Ages, to the Catacombs, to Imperial Rome itself—to St. Peter."[60]

That thousands of Catholics could afford such pilgrimages demonstrated that they were cementing their position in the middle class. In that way, as in others, Catholics had become ever more like other Americans—at least other white Americans—and the Second World War marked a turning point. Although Catholics could be found among isolationists and pacifists, most threw themselves ardently behind the war effort in the aftermath of Pearl Harbor. Somewhere between 25 and 35 percent of all members of the armed forces were Catholics, according to one estimate, and more than 3,000 priests signed up to serve as army, navy, and air corps chaplains. Comparing their own service to that of Christ, who, in the words of a special soldier's prayer, wrested "from the hands of the dictator, Hate, Thy Father's pilfered empire on earth," these Catholics shared with their fellow citizens the experience of war and its aftermath. On returning home, they eagerly took advantage of the G. I. Bill, swelling the enrollment of Catholic colleges and securing places in the white-collar workforce. Changing circumstances fueled changing expectations. "These guys whose grandfathers used to want to be captain of the ward," one slightly dismayed Catholic politician told the reporter Theodore H. White, "now all want to be president of the country club."[61]

For many Catholics, figurative movement up the economic ladder was accompanied by literal movement out of crowded city neighborhoods and into the suburbs. Housing construction skyrocketed, and the infrastructure of the church boomed right along with it. Parishes and schools multiplied in the suburban ring of every major Catholic center. Long Island, New York, for example, had just under 300 parishes in 1945, 214 of them in Brooklyn and Queens, the remainder scattered the length of the island. By 1960, a scant fifteen years later, the number of parishes in the two city boroughs remained the same, but the number on the rest of the island had jumped from 81 to 114, and a separate diocese with its own bishop had been created to oversee

them. There were new churches in places that had not even existed at the end of the war. Levittown, one of the developments
that made homeownership possible for returning veterans, sprang
from nothing, and by 1960 it had a parish with five priests in residence; three years later, it opened an elementary school that enrolled 600 children. It was the same on the opposite side of the
country. Anaheim, California, just south of Los Angeles, had one
parish in 1945, but three of them in 1960; Van Nuys, in the San
Fernando Valley, had a single parish in 1945, but four of them in
1960, and three of these had schools with a total of 2,300 pupils.
In 1957, one priest noted, more Catholics moved to the suburbs than had immigrated to America from Ireland in all of the
1890s.[62] That estimate may or may not have been accurate, but
the trend was undeniable.

Suburbanization had many effects on the entire population,
and one of these was a muting of religious differences. Overt
anti-Catholicism generally ceased to be respectable as people of
all faiths mixed together as never before, living next door to one
another, joining the same boy and girl scout troops or the Rotary
Club. The sociologist Will Herberg argued in the mid-1950s that
even as they identified with one of the three major religious traditions (Protestant, Catholic, or Jewish), Americans had come to
think of the "American Way of Life" as their fundamental faith,
one in which commonalities outweighed distinctions. Herberg's
thesis was controversial, at the time and later, but he had nonetheless captured something essential. Those once inclined to stand
on denominational distinctions, he claimed, were now more
likely to mute them, saying, "After all, we're all Americans."[63]

Anti-Catholicism was not entirely dead, as demonstrated by
the meteoric career of Paul Blanshard. A former Congregational
minister who became a lawyer (and an atheist), Blanshard hit
the best-seller list in 1949 with his book *American Freedom and
Catholic Power,* which described an irrepressible "conflict between
Catholic hierarchical power and American institutions." Even

as Catholics were apparently assimilating into American life, he said, their hierarchy remained "fundamentally Roman in its spirit," always looking for ways to extend its "autocratic moral monarchy." By influencing law and public policy in such areas as divorce, censorship, and birth control, the church had nothing less than an all-encompassing "Catholic plan for America." The plot began, Blanshard insisted, with an assault on basic liberties, and it would be capped by repeal of the First Amendment to the Constitution and an outright ban on non-Catholic religious practice.[64] For all the passion of his argument, however, not to mention the success of his book (six printings in as many months), Blanshard's impact was marginal. His ideas touched few who were not already convinced. Most Americans had difficulty picturing those nice Catholics who lived next door, whose kids played with theirs, as crafty fifth columnists, intent on helping the pope conquer America.

In fact, Catholics had come to play larger roles in American public life. On the political stage, a Catholic senator from Wisconsin, Joseph McCarthy, led the fight against supposed communist infiltration. Early in his career, McCarthy had recognized the mileage he could get from making himself the country's most relentless adversary of the "red menace." Before reaction set in against his steadily wilder charges and irresponsible methods, McCarthy was a hero to many, regardless of their faith. The Catholic hierarchy supported him energetically. Since the Soviets had occupied the countries of Eastern Europe, many with traditionally Catholic populations, bishops and priests praised McCarthy for fighting the enemies of God as well as those of the United States. The Catholic laity was cooler toward the senator. To be sure, he seemed to be on the right side of things in opposing the communists. Unlike most of them, however, he was a Republican, and thus he always faced opposition from the solidly Catholic, solidly Democratic labor vote. Still, that a Catholic was leading the charge against America's foe in the Cold War was not lost on observers. Contrary to the old nativist stereotype of Catholics as subverters of American freedom, they now seemed its stoutest defenders. To be a Catholic, the political scientist and future senator Daniel Patrick Moynihan said, was "prima facie evidence of loyalty. Harvard men were to be checked [for tinges of red]; Fordham men would do the checking."[65] Blanshard had tried to insist that the Vatican and the Kremlin were equally totalitarian and equally sinister, but to most Americans, that equation seemed absurd on its face.

In the realm of popular culture, too, Catholics were in the American mainstream. One of their bishops, Fulton Sheen, even emerged as an unlikely television star. Originally from downstate Illinois, Sheen had earned degrees in philosophy and taught at Catholic University in Washington. He first appeared on the weekly *Catholic Hour* radio program in the 1930s, and with the emergence of television after the war it was immediately clear that he and that medium were made for each other. His new program, *Life Is Worth Living,* was broadcast on Tuesday evenings, first on the Dumont Network and then on ABC. Assigned a deadly timeslot opposite Milton Berle's apparently unbeatable *Texaco Comedy Hour,* Sheen quickly triumphed over "Uncle Miltie" in the ratings, earning him the nickname "Uncle Fultie." Not only Catholics tuned in; at one point, his audience was measured at thirty million, and in 1957 he won an Emmy. For half an hour every week, Sheen appeared in his impressive ecclesiastical robes and used his smooth, well-modulated voice to discuss the concerns of modern life: love of God, love of neighbor, finding peace amid the hectic pace of contemporary society. He attracted some celebrity converts to the church—including Clare Booth Luce and Henry Ford II—but unlike Father Peyton, he never prayed or discussed specific Catholic doctrines. Instead, he echoed the nondenominational and agreeably inspirational messages of such Protestant and Jewish preachers as Norman Vincent Peale, whose *Power of Positive Thinking* (1952) sold two million copies, and Joshua Loth Liebman, whose *Peace of Mind* (1946) was nearly as popular. Sheen's point was simple: life was indeed worth living if one turned attention periodically to higher things. For Americans who had put their "faith in faith," Sheen's message did not require adherence to Catholicism.[66]

Proof of the changed climate for American Catholics came in 1960, when, for the first time in thirty years, a Catholic mounted a serious effort to win the presidency. The defeat of Al Smith in 1928 had been interpreted to mean that Catholicism was an iron-clad disqualification from that office, but a young senator from Massachusetts sought the nomination anyway. John Kennedy and his campaign skillfully maneuvered public opinion, slowly reinforcing the idea that excluding Catholics from the White House was unacceptable bigotry. The West Virginia primary in May was a turning point. Kennedy's support was solid, but because the state had a miniscule Catholic population, his campaign presented it as a decisive test. When he handily defeated Minnesota's Hubert Humphrey, the religious issue began to recede. Kennedy himself delivered the final blow in an address to the Greater Houston Ministerial Association, a gathering of three hundred Protestant ministers, in September. "I am not the Catholic candidate for President," Kennedy said; "I am the Democratic Party's candidate for President, who happens also to be a Catholic. I do not speak for my church on public matters—and the church does not speak for me." Should he ever face an issue in which his official duties and his conscience were at odds, he said, he would resign the presidency, and this was enough to satisfy the skeptics. His election two months later settled the matter.[67] When Kennedy was inaugurated on a cold January day in 1961, the opening prayer was delivered for the first time in history by a Catholic prelate, Kennedy family friend Cardinal Richard Cushing of Boston. By then, even that seemed hardly worthy of remark.

One of their own moving into the White House gave American Catholics a sign that they were accepted by a wider culture once disposed toward suspicion of them. That event may also be seen as a fitting capstone to the church of Catholic Action. Kennedy rejected the notion that he had any duty to implement church programs in public policy. In fact, he actively opposed some of them, resisting all efforts to provide public funds to parochial schools, for example. He also, as one of his aides said later, "wore his Catholicism lightly": he attended Sunday Mass regularly but revealed few other signs of religious practice. Even so, he seemed a model of the new kind of active, engaged lay person, embodying the self-confidence of American Catholics at mid-century. They were a people comfortable with both their religion and their country, with their Catholicism and their Americanness. More and more of them had "made it," and they believed that they were in control of their own destinies. In church, they were feeling some of that same confidence. Lay people were warming to the idea that they bore a share of responsibility for their spiritual welfare, just as they were in charge of other aspects of their lives. A previous generation might have had to rely passively on the church and its hierarchy. These confident Catholics did not question the important role the institutional church played; indeed, by demanding so many new parishes and schools, they sought to guarantee that the church would always be readily available to them. But they were also ready to expand their own scope. In Catholic Action, inside and outside the church, they would be the ones who acted.

For American Catholics watching on television as a fellow Catholic was inaugurated as president, it was easy to conclude that the future was bright, but also that it would be more or less a continuation of the past. Their future would be more of the same—better in so many ways, with more of everything, but still fundamentally the same. And then, everything seemed to change.

5

The Church of Vatican II

Patricia Caron Crowley was always called Patty, perhaps so as not to confuse her with her husband, whose name was Pat. The Crowleys, who married in 1937, raised five children of their own and, over the years, cared for nearly fifty foster children in their home outside Chicago. They founded the Christian Family Movement in 1949, and a little more than a decade later they, together with Catholics everywhere, were caught up in the sudden and profound changes of the Second Vatican Council. Pope John XXIII had surprised nearly everyone by calling bishops from around the world to an "ecumenical" council in Rome. This would be the first time in nearly a century that such a gathering had been held, and only the second council since the 1500s. Its work, the pope had said, would be *aggiornamento,* a conveniently vague Italian word usually translated as "updating." The council initiated dramatic changes in Catholic religious practice, most of which were on display at Mass every Sunday morning. It also changed the formulation of some important Catholic doctrines, including the governing metaphor for the church itself. Once defined as the "Mystical Body of Christ," an image many Catholics found difficult to visualize, the church was now better understood as the "People of God." The shift to this fundamentally democratic imagery was full of significance. Catholics like the Crowleys were told insistently that *they* were the church—not (or not only) the pope, the bishops, the priests, and the sisters, but they themselves. More to the point, the Crowleys and other American Catholics actually believed it.[1]

The implications of this new vision became intensely personal for Patty and Pat in 1964, when they were appointed to a special commission chosen by Pope John's successor, Paul VI, to study the controversial subject of birth control and advise the pope on whether the church's position should be changed. Official teaching maintained a distinction between so-called natural means of family planning (such as periodic abstinence), which were permissible for Catholics, and "artificial" means (chemical and physical methods of contraception), which were not. Pressure had been building to modify that view and to join other Christian churches in allowing married couples to decide whether and how to limit the size of their families. The newly available birth control pill only heightened the demand for change. The pope's study group had initially consisted only of priests and theologians, but the Crowleys were made members so as to include the perspective of married couples. The commission met several times over the next two years, and a majority quickly came to favor a revision of the church's stance.

During the deliberations, one incident encapsulated all the changes that had come to the church with the Second Vatican Council. Father Marcelino Zalba, a formidable Spanish Jesuit, was insisting one day that the church's policy simply could not be changed. To do so would call into question the validity of the earlier teaching and thereby undermine all church authority. If the condemnation of artificial contraception had been wrong, he asked, "what, then, with the millions we have sent to hell" for disobeying it? Buoyed by confidence in the new understanding of the church and her role in it, Patty Crowley blurted out: "Father Zalba, do you really believe God has carried out all your orders?"[2] It was apparent in that one moment how much had changed. Fifty years earlier—perhaps even five years earlier—a lay woman would not have dared to speak to a priest in that way. That Patty Crowley felt capable of doing so was a measure of what it was like to be an American Catholic in the church of Vatican II.

The Second Vatican Council had convened in October 1962, and by the time it adjourned in December 1965, the church in the United States, as elsewhere in the world, was a very different institution. At the start, officials of the Roman curia, the bureaucratic agencies of the modern papacy, hoped to limit its scope, but their resistance was overcome, and church leaders headed out in unexpected directions. In four separate sessions, each lasting for two months in the fall of the successive years, the council drafted, debated, and approved a flow of documents. There were statements on the church's responsibility to address contemporary social and economic problems, on the role of the laity, on religious liberty, on relations with non-Catholics and non-Christians, and on a host of other topics. These documents of "Vatican II," as the gathering was commonly called, were translated from their original Latin in the hope, the first American edition said, of prompting widespread discussion. Perhaps just as surprising, for the first time in nearly two thousand years, a church council had ended without condemning anything as heretical; that alone seemed to indicate that something new was happening.

For American Catholics, these changes signaled the opening of a distinct new age. Many lay people came to describe themselves as "Vatican II Catholics," a designation that marked their movement beyond the religious world of their parents and grandparents. Some drew an analogy to growing up. The church of Catholic Action had been their adolescence, but they were adults now. One of the council's documents had addressed what it called "the church in the modern world." That was a church in which American Catholics were ready to live.

When Giovanni Roncalli was elected pope in October 1958 following the death of Pius XII, who had reigned for twenty eventful years, little was expected of him. He was already seventy-seven years old, and most people thought that he would be just another of the many "caretaker" popes the centuries had seen, a man who would fill the office for a time but would leave little mark on it. After a career in the Vatican diplomatic corps, Roncalli had been made the patriarch of Venice as a prelude to retirement, and he was a compromise choice as pope. He had the uncomplicated faith of his peasant parents, and he was easy-going and engaging. Asked on one occasion how many people worked at the Vatican, he is said to have replied, "About half of them." He was the twenty-third pope to take the name John, and he quickly showed that he would not sit quietly on the chair of Saint Peter. Less than three months after his election, he abruptly issued his order for the historic gathering of the world's three thousand bishops. "This holy old boy doesn't realize what a hornet's nest he's stirring up," one cynical Vatican insider remarked. John's reign would be brief. He died five years later in the summer of 1963, after only a single session of his council, but he set in motion some monumental changes.[3]

The council opened amid the splendor of Saint Peter's Basilica on October 11, 1962, and one of its first topics was a remaking of the rituals of the church, particularly the Mass. "Restoration" of the liturgy was essential, the bishops declared, striking a theme that would recur in all their deliberations. Generations of customs had accumulated in worship, and these now obscured as much as they enlightened. The bishops understood the work of reform as a restoration of earlier, presumably purer ways, rather than the invention of new ones. Their goal, in particular, was "full, conscious, and active" participation by lay people in church ceremonies, such as had been practiced in ancient times. The Mass as a spectacle that the laity merely watched was unsatisfactory; a reformed Mass, "distinguished by a noble simplicity . . . unencumbered by useless repetitions" of prayers, and well "within the powers of comprehension" of those in attendance, was to take its place. Latin would remain the universal language of the church, but the translation of some or all of the Mass would undoubtedly be "of great advantage to the people." Other sacraments, too, were to be reformed and translated, so that those participating in them could have a clearer sense of the meaning of these ritual actions.[4]

Since the days of John Carroll and his unrealized hopes for a vernacular translation of the Mass, American Catholics had rarely faced these questions. Sunday worship had always been conducted in Latin and, as far as they knew, always would be. By the early twentieth century, however, a few American priests had been encouraging parishioners to take a more active role. Centered primarily in the Midwest, this liturgical movement promoted what members called a "dialogue Mass," in which the entire congregation said aloud the Latin responses to the priest's prayers. Ordinary Catholics had not been clamoring for such participation, and some lay people were hesitant. "I felt as though we were interfering with the altar boys," said one man in Chicago, attending a dialogue Mass for the first time. "I felt I shouldn't be doing this." The clerical backers of the movement pressed on, however, and they experimented with other modifications as well. A lay commentator might join the priest in the sanctuary, for example, to explain to the congregation what was going on at various points in the service. Members of the liturgical movement also recommended that the people in the pews sing along with the choir, and new hymns, easier to sing than complex Gregorian chants, were introduced. Although it was never very widespread and always remained an elite, "top-down" effort by a small core of committed priests, the liturgical movement nonetheless laid the groundwork for the broader changes mandated by the Vatican Council.[5]

What was widely known as "the new Mass" came to American Catholic parishes in several phases between 1964 and 1969. The most significant step was probably the first one, taken on November 29, 1964, the Sunday after Thanksgiving. Parishioners sitting in their places that morning knew something was different from the moment the Mass began. The week before, the priest and altar boys had entered in silence; now everyone was expected to sing at least two verses of a processional hymn. The scriptural passages for the day were read aloud in the vernacular, either by the priest or by a lay lector. The priest, standing behind a new altar set up in the middle of the sanctuary, still said some prayers in Latin, but the people were encouraged to recite others along with him, again in their own language. A few familiar parts of the service were eliminated altogether: the reading of a second gospel passage at the end of Mass, for example, was done away with. "The Mass is over," one priest explained abruptly, "and the Gospel has already been proclaimed." The prayers for the conversion of Russia also disappeared: "redundant and not very effective," the same priest called them. The distribution of Communion was now different. In the past, the priest had repeated a prayer in Latin as he worked his way along the line of parishioners kneeling at the altar. He now paused in front of each parishioner, in many places standing rather than kneeling, held up the Communion host so they could look at it, and said, "Corpus Christi" ("the Body of Christ"), to which the communicant responded, "Amen." In a few months this, too, would be said in English, and the altar rail itself would be gone.[6]

Other changes followed rapidly over the next several years—so quickly, in fact, that many lay people wondered whether it was worth the effort of trying to keep up. "I would not invest very heavily in a missal at the present time," one priest advised a worried parishioner. In some parts of the service, the priest could choose among several possible prayers rather than saying the same one every week. A passage from the Old Testament was added to the usual New Testament epistle and gospel readings in 1969, "since the Church sees all the aspirations of the ancient Hebrews fulfilled in Christ." Priests were required always to give a short homily—not a traditional sermon (which might address any topic), but rather a reflection on the specific scriptural passages that the people had just heard. Moreover, participation of the laity also required parishioners to move about. An offertory procession was instituted, in which members of the congregation carried the bread and wine from the middle of the church up to the altar before the consecration of these "gifts" as the Eucharist. A "Kiss of Peace" was also introduced: just before Communion, parishioners were asked to turn to one another and exchange "a sign of peace and love, according to local custom." In most American parishes, this amounted to an awkward and sometimes perfunctory handshake. Taken together, all these modifications meant that lay people had more to do at Mass than formerly. "There is no time for idle dreaming," one priest concluded.[7]

When Catholics might go to Mass was also changing. Beyond the traditional Sunday-morning hours, some churches began to experiment with Masses later that afternoon or evening. A more dramatic change came when the church authorized Sunday Mass on Saturday. These "anticipation" or "vigil" masses had originally been approved for use in missionary countries, where a priest could not reliably predict when he might arrive in a given locality to say Mass. Amid the general enthusiasm for reform, the practice spread to the United States as well. The Mass for Sunday might be said as early as the late afternoon (usually defined as 4 P.M. or after) of the preceding Saturday, and Catholics attending at that time fulfilled their weekly obligation. Drawing the parallel to the Jewish Sabbath, theologians explained that the "liturgical day" always began with sundown the day before. Few lay people had ever heard of the notion of a "liturgical day," but they got used to the new schedule. Soon, it was a rare American Catholic parish that did not have at least one Saturday anticipation Mass. The fifty-six churches in Houston, for example, offered Mass about three hundred times every Sunday in 1969, a year before vigils were approved. A decade later, every parish (increased now to sixty-eight in number) had at least one Mass on Saturday as well—a handful had two—bringing the total number of Masses in the city every weekend closer to four hundred. In Pittsburgh, by 1990 fully one-quarter of all Sunday Masses were offered on Saturday.[8]

Not everyone thought this was a good idea. Extending the time when Catholics could go to Mass put too much emphasis on the negative consequences of their not going, one pastor thought, and this encouraged what he called a "get-it-over-with" mentality. Would it not be better for parishioners to attend the weekly liturgy because they wanted to, rather than because they hoped to get their spiritual ticket punched at a more convenient time? He also worried about a slippery slope of "permissiveness," an attitude that said, in effect, "if you can't get people to fulfill an obligation, change the obligation. Make it easier." Some clergymen also worried that offering Mass a day early would lead to a general de-sacralizing of Sunday, reducing the traditional day of rest to just another day. Larger social forces were obviously at work here, but the impact on Catholics was particularly noticeable. "I have some doubts" about Saturday Mass, one bishop said in March 1969, "since it means a real change in the practice of worship among our people." He gave in only two months later and approved the idea: parishes in towns bordering another state where anticipating Sunday was permitted had been losing attendance. Within a short time, most priests were confirming the popularity of these services, especially among older parishioners.[9]

Whether on Saturday afternoon or Sunday morning, priests now said the Mass in a loud, clear voice, facing the congregation, and this practice raised questions that had never come up before. Seminary training had traditionally emphasized attention to the "rubrics" of the service, the gestures and movements of the priest, which had been prescribed in minute detail. When the priest held his hands in a prayerful position, one rubric had specified, "the fingers of each hand are extended against the fingers of the other hand. It is incorrect to interlock the fingers or to cup them together." Suddenly, some gestures seemed curious. In drinking the Eucharistic wine, for example, the priest had held a small plate (called a paten) up to his throat. This was "not a very elegant gesture," a priest from New Jersey pointed out—fine, perhaps, so long as his back was turned, but awkward now because the congregation could see him doing it. "Normally when drinking," he went on, "we do not pick up a plate and hold it under our chin. To do so would be the height of bad manners." There were other problems as well. The altar had always had a cross on it; no matter how small this cross was, it now blocked the people's line of sight and thus "defeated the purpose" of saying Mass facing them. A seminary professor in Denver wondered what to tell his soon-to-be-ordained students about this and other things. What about the size and shape of altar cloths? Was it really all right to use one "which does not extend over the sides and does not reach the floor?" These seemed like "small points," he acknowledged, but since they had once been so precisely regulated it was not immediately apparent how to make adjustments. No wonder some Catholics found the whole thing bewildering. "Will someone please explain the 'why' behind the liturgical changes," an exasperated parishioner asked a priest in Davenport, Iowa. "Why? Why? Why?"[10]

Frustration might have been expected, given that preparation for these changes had been uneven. Some places embraced them enthusiastically. Churches in Superior, Wisconsin, had begun using the new liturgy as early as June 1964, several months ahead of the official starting date. Other dioceses had held training programs for priests and laity alike. Almost seven hundred lay men from parishes surrounding New Ulm, in southwestern Minnesota, went through six training sessions to prepare them to be readers at Mass. In other places, however, the liturgical gears had shifted without much warning. A pastor in New Jersey was curt in letting his people know that a new experience of Mass was on the way. "As some of you are probably aware," he announced from the pulpit, "there will begin next Sunday the implementation of a series of changes in the Mass . . . We realize that this will be difficult for many of you, but realize that this is the will of the Holy Father, the Vatican Council, and his Excellency [that is, the local bishop], and we know we can count on your fine cooperation just as we have so many times in the past." That was that.

Some resistance to change came from the clergy themselves. "The introduction of the new rite is not a matter of choice," the archbishop of Boston sternly reminded his priests; "it is ordered by the Holy See and must be carefully implemented in all the churches and chapels of the archdiocese." The archbishop of St. Paul, Minnesota, sent a gentler letter to the priests in his jurisdiction, but he made it clear that he would not tolerate "endless procrastination and surely not . . . outright obstruction."[11]

In general, Catholics favored the new Mass. "The Latin is prettier," one woman conceded, but "I'd like to see more English used." An eighth-grader agreed: "I wish the whole Mass could be in English." Soon enough, it would be. The church discontinued all Latin by 1969, and for some Catholics that change could not come too quickly. The transition was dragging, a man told an interviewer outside his parish church. "Why don't they do it and get it over with, instead of a little at a time?" he wanted to know. "I think we're intelligent enough to do it. Let's face the changes and make them." A parishioner in Massachusetts thought the new liturgy was "just great, but I do hope we can get together on the kneeling, sitting, Latin and English responses. It seems that all churches do it a little different from one another." He was right, but maybe that was not a bad thing. A guide for parish clergy spoke approvingly of "opening the way for each parish to take on its own character in liturgical expression": what had once been uniform practice could now vary from place to place. Even little things, however, assumed large importance. One man wrote a long letter to his diocesan newspaper, explaining why he found being told to say "ay-men" rather than "ah-men" objectionable. Some were shocked at the conclusion of the service to hear the priest say, in English now, "Go, the Mass is ended," to which they were expected to reply, "Thanks be to God," a statement that might be misinterpreted to imply that they had not been entirely happy about being there in the first place. A reluctant pastor in Minnesota alluded to the common story that John XXIII had described the Vatican Council's work as "opening up the windows" of the church, but, he said, "when a window is open, there is a danger of extremely valuable things being blown away."[12]

Only a few systematic studies of the new Mass were undertaken, and these showed broad support among American lay people. In 1966 *U.S. Catholic,* a magazine designed for a middle-class audience, found some regional variation but widespread approval. A parish in Durand, Wisconsin, reported having so many men volunteer as readers that each was needed only once every five weeks. The parishioners at a church in Chicago favored congregational hymn-singing by 54 to 14 percent, and seven out of eight of them preferred to have the priest face them during Mass.

Churchgoers in Sierra Madre, California, actually took a vote and confirmed their approval of priests who were "distinct and reasonably slow" in leading the service. Standing for Communion was taking hold a little more slowly, with just 21 percent of the nation's parishes adopting the practice, but a priest in Nebraska made a virtue of necessity in this. His parishioners were reluctant to receive Communion standing, but after a broken leg reduced his mobility, they found that they liked the new format. To be sure, problems remained. For one thing, the English translations in use left much to be desired. Many people felt that these had been "done in a hurry," while others criticized them for being either too stilted or too informal. Using eager high school students as lectors was problematic, notably on those occasions when the scriptural passage of the day spoke of lust and other graphic sins. Even so, a priest in Illinois concluded, "whatever the lay people are permitted to do, we not only allow them, but encourage, and they respond wonderfully."[13]

In subtle but important ways, the new structure of weekly worship changed the dynamic in American Catholic parishes, especially that between lay people and their priests. "An exclusive identification of the Church with the clergy is misleading," a priest in Chicago wrote in 1965, and the new Mass conveyed the "true image of the Church, priest and people working together." The man who had insisted that the laity was "intelligent enough" to accept liturgical change was voicing a widely held sentiment, one that was often described as a passage from childhood to adulthood. Mary Perkins Ryan, a veteran of numerous Catholic Action causes, gave succinct expression to this view. In the past, she said, too many Catholics went to church either out of obligation or simply to "feel good." These were essentially "childish motives, not those of mature persons." Now, by contrast, adult Catholics could appreciate the "real reasons for going to Mass." A lay man from New Hampshire expressed a similar sentiment when he wrote to a national magazine in 1968 to say that he and "countless" other "thinking Catholics" approved of the changes already under way and hoped for more.[14]

Many priests reinforced this view that "mature" and "thinking" Catholics were being acknowledged by the church. After "a kind of collective adolescence," one Jesuit said, lay people had to become comfortable with their new "maturity." Like adolescence in general, this might be "a challenging, if not a frightening, experience," but adulthood was preferable to an imagined "golden childhood or the cozy womb." More generally, the mere fact that the Mass, celebrated in the same way for centuries, was now different suggested that other changes were possible or even likely. If traditional worship, formerly "viewed as heaven-sent and absolute," was subject to such drastic remaking in so short a time, a sociologist wrote, what other aspects of belief and practice might be changed as well? That was a prospect to be faced by mature adults, not docile children.[15]

The effect of the changes on American Catholic women was particularly significant, and this impact was apparent from the earliest stages of Vatican II reforms. If lay men could serve as scripture readers at their parish Masses, why could women not assume the same roles? A skeptical pastor in Minnesota reported that the high school girls of his parish wanted to "get into the act." He prohibited them from doing so, citing passages from the New Testament admonishing women not to speak in church. This biblical literalism was uncommon among Catholics, but the girls had to be satisfied with playing the organ and singing. Other questions arose, too. If young lads could act as altar boys, why exactly were their sisters banned from service? "Are we not capable?" one young woman demanded to know. Some priests, armed with common gender stereotypes, dismissed the possibility out of hand. The idea of "female altar-servers wearing surplices" was simply "comical," one clergyman thought, without feeling the need to explain what was so funny. Others, however, were open to the possibility. "Why not start a girls' participators campaign?" a syndicated columnist suggested. Such a campaign would be a long one, with official approval of female altar servers not coming until 1994; many American Catholic parishes had already begun the practice much earlier on their own.[16]

The council coincided with the emergence of new forms of feminism in America—Betty Friedan published *The Feminine Mystique* in 1963, while Vatican II was in session—to permit an unprecedented discussion of women's roles in church. "We believe the position of women in the church should reflect the developments in the condition of women in the modern world," a national gathering of parish liturgy coordinators (male and female, clergy and laity) at Notre Dame University resolved in the summer of 1967. In particular, they thought, lay women, "in virtue of their baptism," should be able to serve as readers and commentators at Mass. Formal sanction for such service was slow in coming. At first, Vatican officials conceded only that "well-known women of adequate years and moral way of life"—preferably nuns—could read when "a suitable male lector" was not available, so long as they did so from outside the church sanctuary. The earlier notion that any lay person entering that sacred space was "temporarily" regarded as a priest was thought to exclude women by definition. By the time full approval was finally given in 1975 for sisters and lay women alike to serve as lectors, most American parishes had been using them for years, thereby rendering the point moot.[17] Across the board, however, the scope and pace of changes proved difficult to confine. Some parishioners wanted to cry out, "Why?" Others asked, "Why not?"

In response to the requirements of the new Mass, alterations also had to be made in the physical space of parish churches. The priest would need a new altar to stand behind as he looked out at the congregation. The original altar remained against the back wall, but this new one, generally smaller, was moved in and used in its place. Church supply houses began to offer these new "tables"—the term long used by many Protestant denominations but now adopted by American Catholics as well—but, one liturgical specialist noted later, "in the rush of things, the atmosphere for worship and the talent of the artist was [sic] not always carefully developed." Only with time were "minimal makeshift modifications" replaced with more suitable altars. Newly constructed churches could take the changed Mass into account from the beginning, and several in and around the Twin Cities of Minnesota show a process that was under way nationwide. In 1963, Saint Joseph's parish in the town of Red Wing built an oval-shaped church, with seats arrayed in a semi-circle around the altar. Saint Leo's Church in St. Paul itself was an octagon, and special attention was paid to its acoustics, since it was newly important for the congregation to hear what was being said. In Cannon Falls, Saint Pius Church had a more conventional exterior shape, but it had pews on three sides of the altar. The new Saint George's in Long Lake also had pews on three sides, and it even had a "mother's room" behind the altar, to which parents with crying children could retreat. Some parishioners found these designs frankly "ugly," and in many cases the criticism was undoubtedly justified. Others defended the new styles. After so many years of staring at baroque altarpieces whose design could be "distracting," one commentator concluded, "the shock of a plain table with its rigid lines may be a good antidote for us."[18]

Beyond aesthetics, sacramental practice also changed significantly in the wake of Vatican II, and standing for Communion was only one of the shifts in the relationship between American Catholics and the Eucharist. The new climate at Mass reinforced the long effort by priests to increase the frequency with which their parishioners came to Communion. On a practical level, the required fast before reception of the sacrament, which had been reduced to three hours in 1957, was shortened again in 1964 to just one hour. This meant that virtually everyone—save perhaps those rare souls who were swallowing their morning coffee on the way in the church door—could satisfy its demands. More important, church officials acknowledged that the earlier emphasis on keeping the fast had often transformed reception of the Eucharist from a happy event into one filled with anxiety. Recalling his own childhood, one priest wrote that "my earliest Communions were concerned more with the integrity of the fast than with the joy of union with my savior." Easing this impediment helped send rates of Communion steadily upward. One national study showed that, in 1963, barely 29 percent of those at any given Mass were going to Communion; by 1976, the rate was already more than 50 percent, and it continued to climb thereafter.[19] Earlier in the century, the overwhelming majority of Catholic churchgoers had stayed in their seats during Communion; by the end of the century, a similarly decisive majority came forward and would have thought it strange not to.

In addition to increased frequency, the manner in which lay people received the sacrament was changing in several distinct but parallel ways. Traditionally, the priest had administered Communion by placing the wafer of bread directly onto the recipient's tongue. "When the priest who is distributing Holy Communion reaches him," a guide to Catholic behavior had explained in the 1920s, "the communicant should slowly open his mouth and stretch out his tongue, so that it projects a little over the lower lip, keeping his eyes half closed. As soon as he feels the sacred Host on his tongue, one ought to draw it in and close his mouth." As with some other liturgical gestures, this one now seemed unnatural. "I find myself hardly able to open my mouth and have the Host shoved in," a woman from Ohio said. Theologically, the Eucharist was understood as a ritual meal, a reenactment of the last supper Jesus had shared with his followers. It was odd to think of a meal in which the participants were fed by someone else, and lay people's objections to this method were of a piece with their insistence that they not be treated like children. "We are adults and as such we feed ourselves," the parishioners of a church in Windsor, Connecticut, resolved; "we are not fed."[20]

Accordingly, many parishes began the practice of "Communion in the hand." As each person came forward, the priest placed the Communion host in the recipient's outstretched palm, cupped by the other hand to receive it; communicants then picked it up and placed it in their own mouths. The practice, which grew up spontaneously in many places, proved controversial, since it had not been officially authorized. A Vatican commission was appointed to study the matter. This change was, they admitted, "not a true innovation," since it had been the practice of the church for centuries in earlier times. Pressure for Communion in the hand, however, was "the work of a small number of priests and laity, who seek to impose their point of view on others and to force the hand of authority." Giving in to this kind of overt challenge might lead to worse: "To approve it would encourage these persons who are never satisfied with the laws of the Church." Deliberation continued, and in 1977 the hierarchy formally approved this option for receiving Communion; by then, it was already common practice in American parishes. The priests at the Connecticut church estimated that 97 percent of their parishioners took the sacrament in this way.[21]

The period of liturgical reform also brought demands that during Communion lay people receive not only the Eucharistic bread but also the sacramental wine. This practice had been strictly forbidden by the Council of Trent in the sixteenth century, but now a case was made for "restoring" it. The words of the Mass quoted Jesus as saying, "Take and eat," but they also repeated his injunction to "take and drink"; barring the laity from the Communion cup seemed a direct disobedience of that command. The clergy generally supported a change, and it spread widely in American parishes. Official decrees were characteristically cautious, suggesting that "communion under both species" be limited to special occasions: the bride and groom at their wedding, for instance. But as one observer noted, the rules were vague enough "to have allowed liberal interpretation." The archbishop of Cincinnati broadly encouraged churches in his jurisdiction to take up the practice, and by March 1968, when a national magazine ran a cover photo of Becky Ruby, a student at Indiana University, drinking from a chalice, few readers thought it unusual.[22]

One more change was in the offing. In 1973, parishes began appointing what were called "extraordinary ministers of the Eucharist." In places where the number of priests was small or the demand for the sacrament was high, lay people were authorized to help with the distribution of Communion during Mass. They might also bring the Eucharist to fellow parishioners in the hospital. The church devised a simple ceremony commissioning parishioners for this task—parishes in Indianapolis did so every year on Holy Thursday, right before Easter—and lay people volunteered in impressive numbers. Some priests voiced concern about women wearing the clergy's liturgical garments, and at least one priest, fearful of worldly distractions, wondered whether particularly attractive women should be enlisted. So many women volunteered, however, that it seemed foolish to turn them away. Once the exclusive province of the clergy, distribution of the Eucharist was now a task that the laity could share. "All those who are baptized are in some sense priests," a theologian said, so there was no reason that lay people could not undertake this priestly duty.[23]

Communion had always been linked to confession, and Vatican II brought even more dramatic changes to the sacrament of penance. Here, however, the effect ran in the opposite direction. Whereas reception of Communion rose steadily, the rate at which American Catholics went to confession plummeted. The monthly standard urged by priests had become common: in 1965, 38 percent of American Catholics were going that often. Almost immediately thereafter, however, the practice fell off precipitously. By 1975, less than half as many American Catholics (only 17 percent) were seeking God's forgiveness monthly in the confessional. Those who responded that they "never" or "practically never" confessed rose in the same period from 18 percent to 38 percent. Yet another decade after that, a survey of "core Catholics" (those most actively involved in parish activities) confirmed the collapse of confession: 26 percent of these Catholics said that they never went at all, 35 percent said that they went at most once a year, and only 6 percent said that they still confessed every month. The decline was evident in local churches everywhere. In 1962, Saint Thomas Aquinas parish in the Jamaica Plain section of Boston made priests available for confession for three and a half hours every Saturday afternoon and evening; in 1969 this was cut back to an hour and a half, and by 1990 it had been reduced again to just half an hour. Parishioners were simply not coming. One pastor told his congregation that he had been growing shrubs in the confessional boxes for months and that no one had yet noticed. He was joking, but he had his finger on the trend nonetheless.[24]

Most Catholics had never really liked going to confession, but in the aftermath of the Vatican Council they felt newly free to act on their dissatisfactions. The enumeration of relatively trivial offenses came to look like an empty ritual. "The priests I encountered seemed so much more concerned with how often I was late for Mass than with my relationships with my children, my husband, or my neighbors," a woman from New York said in 1978, explaining why she had stopped going to confession. Some priests shared her unease about trifles. "The last time I went to confession," a woman from Illinois reported, "I was made to feel I was wasting the priest's time," and still another woman from New Jersey noted that she would confess "sins that have bothered me," only to have the priests "chuckle—like 'you came to confession for this?'" The way the clergy spoke about the sacrament discouraged lay recourse to it. "If we have consciously chosen against the Lord in our life," one guide, published in 1966, said, "we should promptly seek His mercy . . . If there is no question of turning away from God in this way, Confession is not necessary for us, regardless of how long it may be since our last Confession." A year later, a mother in New Hampshire was amazed to hear her pastor tell the children of his First Communion class that they should stay away from confession unless they had committed a mortal sin, of which few of them were capable.[25] That kind of talk was all the added encouragement many lay people needed to abandon their earlier confessional habits.

Faced with this sharp decline, church officials sought ways to revive confession. They began referring to the sacrament as "reconciliation," which had a softer (though probably more theologically accurate) sound than "penance," the traditional name. In the early 1970s, they also instituted a so-called new rite for expressing sorrow for sins. Private confession remained possible, but the church also authorized two new options. One was face-to-face confession, in which priest and penitent sat together and talked, often without the usual ritual formulas. This could seem more like psychological counseling than confession of sins, and as such it was intended to be "more personal, more human." Parish clergy consistently said that they preferred this method, but lay people were cooler to the idea. A survey conducted in 1977 showed that only 20 percent of those Catholics who were still going to confession opted to receive the sacrament face-to-face.

The other option was a wider use of what was called "general absolution." Parishioners could attend a liturgical service that included scripture readings, time for personal reflection, and (only if they wanted) the chance to confess to a priest; after this, the priest said a general prayer of forgiveness. Churches experimented with this approach, and at least one did so on a large scale. On a Sunday in December 1976, twelve thousand Catholics filled an arena in Memphis, Tennessee, for such a service, and a week later an equal number turned out seventy-five miles away in the city of Jackson. Although meaningful to the participants, these services proved controversial. If sinners could be forgiven en masse, why would they ever return to the confessional box? Accordingly, the Vatican chastised the bishop of Memphis for the program and severely restricted the use of this rite in the future. Doing so did not send Catholics back to the confessional: parish priests across the country reported that they were hearing at most about twenty confessions per week.[26] For all practical purposes, the regular confession of sins had ceased to be a part of American Catholic life.

While confession was disappearing, another sacrament was being revived and almost totally reimagined. This was the anointing of the sick and dying, a practice known as Extreme Unction—"unction" in that it involved anointing with blessed oils; "extreme" in that it was administered only at or near the point of death. "To receive the sacrament of Extreme Unction," a child's catechism had explained in the 1940s, "you must be in danger of death." This "last act of the drama of human life," another text said, was the one "on which the success or failure of the whole depends," since Satan might use the attendant distress to tempt the dying into despair. So fully had American Catholics internalized the notion that this sacrament was only for the very end of life that they usually resisted calling a priest until it was unavoidable; to do so earlier, they feared, would alarm the patient by suggesting that the family had given up hope of recovery. Priests argued with little success against this reluctance, urging instead the benefits of recourse to the sacrament in circumstances that were not extreme. "If we are going to die," a catechism from 1964 said more hopefully, it "helps us to die a holy death. But if it is better for us to get well, then [Jesus] makes us better."[27]

The church introduced a new rite of anointing in 1972 and revised it again in 1983. Those who experienced the sacrament this way often found it a powerful ritual. "When done by some priests it looks like magic," said a nurse at a hospital in Texas, who had been present at many anointings, "but when done properly it is very meaningful," particularly if the entire family was involved. Another nurse concurred: "Most patients look on anointing as very helpful to them in accepting the will of God," whatever that might be. Parishes also began to use this rite in communal services as well as individual cases. In some places, such services became a regular part of the parish calendar, with anyone suffering from infirmity, physical or spiritual, encouraged to attend. "A special annual Mass for the sick of the parish who can be brought to Church has been greatly appreciated," one priest observed. As awareness of the AIDS epidemic spread in the 1980s, many parishes instituted special anointing services for those afflicted with the disease.[28]

Taken together, the changes in American Catholic religious practice that came from the Second Vatican Council were remarkable for their scope and their speed. To some degree, the long years of Catholic Action had prepared believers for the innovations, but even so, the experience of going to church was plainly different in 1970 from what it had been in 1960. Many people had an understandably hard time breaking old habits. "The quiet Mass was nice," one parishioner in Chicago said. "I could concentrate on the things that happened to me during the week . . . and I could get the Rosary in." A friend had the same experience, though apparently without much spiritual benefit. "I'd say the rosary and look at somebody's hat and notice who had a new dress and finally I would look at my watch and then I was out. I was through for another week." That kind of inattention was now harder to sustain, and the clergy actively discouraged private prayer at Mass in favor of communal participation. Lay people were "not free to pray each in his own little way," a priest in Minnesota said sharply; rather, collective liturgical prayer was designed to make them realize that "they belong to a people whom God has taught how to pray."[29] The tension between the individual and communal dimensions of prayer remained, however, and just as the council promoted public participation in the church's rites, it also encouraged individual, personalized approaches to spiritual matters. These found a ready audience among American Catholics in the late twentieth century.

The encouragement that lay people make worship and prayer their own always implied the possibility, of course, that some would instead choose to become inactive Catholics. In the past, the laity and clergy alike had strongly stigmatized "falling away." It was the product, a priest wrote in the 1920s, of "an ungenerous and stingy spirit towards God" or, another said, of "bad homes" and "just plain laziness." One lay man who fell away for a time even blamed himself: "My leaving the Church lay in my own weaknesses," he said on returning in the 1950s. Catholics were advised to shun those who had abandoned the church. A woman in Ohio was told that it would be "disedifying or scandalous" to attend the wedding of a Protestant friend to a fallen-away Catholic. She could send a gift, provided that it was for the Protestant bride alone and not for the formerly Catholic groom.[30] Such attitudes meant that instances of Catholics' leaving the church, though never precisely measured, had generally been rare. In the 1960s, however, some lay people not only stopped going to confession;

they stopped going to church altogether. For the first time since the churchifying process had begun a century before, there were many "lapsed" Catholics. Some joined other churches, but most simply enlisted in the ranks of the unchurched.

Because the Catholic population continued to grow in absolute numbers—Catholics held steady at just below one-quarter of the total population, which reached and then surpassed 200 million in these decades—the rate of regular Mass attendance was a better measure of changing practice. A Gallup poll taken in 1958 found that 74 percent of American Catholics said they had gone to church in the previous week. This number was most likely a little high; some people who had not gone to Mass probably thought they should have and so gave pollsters the "right" answer anyway. By 1970, however, just five years after Vatican II had ended, a decline was already apparent. At that time, 60 percent of Catholics attended weekly Mass. This was a sharp decrease, though weekly attendance by Protestants had fallen further, to less than 40 percent. The slide continued, and by the mid-1980s weekly Mass attendance was down to 53 percent, before finally settling in between 30 and 40 percent, where it remained until the end of the century. Reasons for non-attendance were as varied as the individuals in question, but there were now distinct groups within the Catholic populace, based on the regularity of practice. By the early 1990s, one study found, 21 percent of those who had once been Catholics could be considered entirely "dormant," while 23 percent attended Mass weekly and another 56 percent at least monthly.[31] Lay Catholics had obviously made choices. Some gave up religious practice completely; others decided that they could still be Catholics even if they did not attend church quite as regularly as their parents or grandparents had.

At the same time, a number of traditional devotions disappeared from American Catholic practice. Vespers and Benediction, for example, staples in churches on Sunday afternoons since the early nineteenth century, were abandoned nearly everywhere. Some liturgists thought that these services distracted from the Mass itself, and practical factors also steadily eroded their appeal. In largely urban parishes, most parishioners could easily walk the two or three blocks from home to church for a second time on Sundays. In suburban settings, where the church was a car ride away, making the extra effort was a little more complicated. "For better or worse," one lay man noted as early as 1965, "many popular, so-called pious, devotions have been downgraded in recent years. The rosary, visits to the Blessed Sacrament, devotional confessions," and other practices were deemphasized. Statuary and banks of votive lights were relegated to the church storerooms, on the theory that these, too, diverted the attention of worshipers. These changes led some Catholics, who had enjoyed the older forms and found meaning in them, to discern a "piety void." Even those who supported the liturgical changes acknowledged the problem. "It is easy enough," one priest said, to laugh at those who mourned the loss of these longstanding practices, "or to pity them," but he thought that many Catholics, "not just the super pious," were legitimately uneasy about the changes.[32] Whether newer expressions of devotion would ever fully replace the older ones remained uncertain.

The church of Vatican II tried to fill this piety void by urging Catholics to find new ways to pray. Merely going through the motions—like the woman who said a quick rosary, checked her watch, "and then I was out"—was not good enough. Just as she was now expected to participate in Sunday Mass, so she was expected to exert additional effort toward making prayer her own. In earlier ages of the church, the religious obligations of believers had been spelled out in clear and concise terms. The so-called Commandments of the Church, paralleling those of Sinai, neatly summarized every Catholic's obligations. The widely used Baltimore Catechism itemized these six laws for generations of school children: "to assist at Mass on all Sundays and holydays of obligation; to fast and to abstain on the days appointed; to confess our sins at least once a year; to receive Holy Communion during the Easter time; to contribute to the support of the Church; to observe the laws of the Church concerning marriage."[33]

In the 1960s, Catholics began to think that these minimum demands were an insufficient expression of religious commitment, and some of the practices (such as annual confession) were becoming dead letters. Others ceased to have much meaning: the requirement that believers abstain from eating meat on Fridays, for example, was abolished in December 1966, thereby eliminating one of the most familiar public markers of Catholic identity. Instead, parishioners increasingly heard the call, first sounded in the church of Catholic Action, that they make religion personally meaningful. Many took it to heart. The number of lay people who said they prayed every day rose ten points (from 52 to 62 percent) between 1972 and 1984, one survey discovered; in the latter year, fully 31 percent said that they had had "at least one intense religious experience in their life." By the end of the century, 80 percent of practicing Catholics still said that Mass attendance was essential to the faith. But 82 percent of them said that "learning more about Catholic teaching and spirituality" on their own was important, too, and fully 97 percent said that helping those in need was essential to continuing to think of oneself as a Catholic. "Being a devout Catholic was much easier," one man said; "practicing full Christianity is much more difficult."[34] The external demands of church membership had to be matched by a commitment to nurturing interior faith.

American Catholics thus developed some new devotional habits. Study of the Bible, for example, spread rapidly. In contrast to their Protestant neighbors, Catholics had traditionally been encouraged to study the catechism rather than the Bible itself. The faithful had to be guarded, the nation's bishops had said in 1829, "from Bibles spoiled by non-Catholics" (by which they usually meant the King James Version), and later Catholic Bibles included a warning that study of the scriptures should be done only with "the advice and permission of the Pastors and spiritual Guides whom God has appointed to govern his Church." A physician in Philadelphia, who had been at countless bedsides during thirty years of medical practice, noted in 1952 that Catholics were more likely to have a rosary nearby than a Bible, which was "undeviatingly a sign of Protestantism." Now, however, Catholic lay people joined small parish groups to read the Bible and discuss its meaning; individual study was similarly encouraged. Between 1977 and 1986, one survey found, the number of Catholics who regularly read the Bible on their own grew from 23 to 32 percent, while another reported that around 13 percent of them did so with fellow parishioners. These numbers were tiny in comparison to American Protestants, and basic biblical literacy was often spotty: only about one-third of American Catholics could correctly name the four Gospels. Even so, since Catholics now heard passages of scripture read at every Mass, some explored the Bible themselves.[35]

The personalizing of faith was evident in other ways. Lay retreats still offered opportunities for individual reflection, but the popularity of traditional "weekends with God" fell off. In their place, specialized programs attracted those interested in deepening their spirituality. One of the most popular of these was the cursillo, which originated in Spain in the 1940s. Like a traditional retreat, this "little course" in Christianity began with a three-day withdrawal from normal activity in which selected parishioners, chosen by their pastors, reviewed doctrinal basics and were introduced to various methods of prayer. The goal, one description said, was to "help those attending discover their personal calling (or vocation) in order to accomplish it in and for the community." The cursillo drew on the techniques of group dynamics to enhance the experience. At some point in the weekend, for example, the participants were showered with letters, written by previous attendees whom they had never met, assuring them that these strangers were praying for them. The emotional impact could be a powerful one, and it gave the "cursillistas" (those making the retreat) an enthusiasm they were encouraged to spread after the weekend was over. Weekly or monthly gatherings of alumni were held in participants' homes, "an aid to keeping alive in the cursillista the spirit of continuing Christian conversion." Although open to anyone—originally only men, but almost immediately women, too—the cursillo was particularly popular among Hispanic Catholics, in part because all the specialized terminology of the movement was in Spanish. No reliable statistics tell how many lay people participated in the program, but an emerging cadre of lay parish leaders used the experience to shape a spirituality they could call their own.[36]

Retreats for married couples also multiplied, extending the work of the Christian Family Movement. A CFM national meeting in 1967 was the site of the first "Marriage Encounter," a weekend getaway that combined religious and interpersonal exercises. A priest and two or three "previously Encountered couples" led the participants, some of them married for decades, through a reexamination of their lives together. After talks on a range of subjects, each husband and wife wrote a short reflection and then shared it with each other (but not with the larger group). Here again, the emotional power could be considerable. "Masks are put aside and walls are broken down," one participant said. Psychological language, drawn from the wider culture and often reduced to buzzwords, was used overtly. "I've found out how to be more in touch with my feelings," another woman said. Couples might complete an "emotional inventory," rating themselves in such categories as feeling anxious, depressed, or lonely. More important, the goal for husbands and wives was to develop individual and mutual spirituality. "During the weekend I met Don's God and he met mine," one woman said of the experience, and her spouse felt the same way. "We are beginning to build," he said, "our own 'Little Church.'" Earlier generations of Catholics would have thought it peculiar, perhaps even blasphemous, to say that God was somehow "Don's" or that his God was different from anybody else's. Beyond that, though the notion of the family as a "little church" had a long pedigree, it still had a slightly presumptuous tone. By the 1970s, however, the marriage encounter movement had spread throughout the country, claiming to attract 100,000 couples each year; 30,000 people attended one annual convention.[37] Father Patrick Peyton had once insisted that the family that prays together stays together; enthusiasts of the marriage encounter saw themselves as elaborating a particular technique to accomplish that goal.

Even more widespread was the emergence of a distinct Catholic charismatic movement. The phenomenon of speaking in "tongues," thought to parallel the experience of the early church at the feast of Pentecost as described in the New Testament, had appeared among American Protestants at the beginning of the twentieth century, grounded on the conviction that the Holy Spirit touched Christians directly, prompting them to express themselves through various ecstatic "gifts." Beginning with a revival in a storefront on Azusa Street in Los Angeles in 1906, several denominations had institutionalized this experience, including the largely white Assemblies of God and the mostly African American Church of God in Christ. Worship services, described by one scholar as a form of "planned spontaneity," emphasized preaching and testimonials rather than formal sacramental liturgies. In this, they were about as far from even a remade, post–Vatican II Catholic Mass as one could imagine. Moreover, hostility toward the Roman Church was common. In the Protestant Pentecostal catalog, Catholics were responsible for everything from socialism to corruption in Congress, and even to World War I.[38] Such a religious expression seemed unlikely to find a home among American Catholics.

And yet it did. Several cursillo alumni, meeting on the campus of Duquesne University in Pittsburgh in February 1967, gathered in the school's chapel and reported afterward that they had felt a powerful "movement of the Spirit." On returning home, they found they could recreate the experience with others. Assembling in schools and parish halls, usually on weeknights, participants intensified their own reflection and prayer. "From the moment I entered the meeting room," a woman in California said, recalling her first experience, "I was attracted by the spirit of the group. The atmosphere was one of tremendous warmth and friendliness . . . No polemics! No arguments! Just rejoicing in the Lord." Several "gifts of the Holy Spirit" were manifested regularly. Speaking in tongues was the most obvious, often followed by the gift of interpretation, in which another person translated the otherwise indecipherable sounds: "I found that sometimes I could tell what the words of a tongue meant," the Californian reported. A gift of prophecy might appear, "a solemn message in the form of a first-person communication," understood as a message directly from God, such as, "O my children, I love you. Do not fear for the future." Most controversial of all was a gift of healing. "Warmth would flow into my hands in response to the sick and needy," one participant reported. "I would be moved to lay hands on them and pray for them."[39] Such expressions had never been part of American Catholic practice, and many parishioners were wary of their potential for a kind of spiritual anarchy. If even Catholics were going to be encouraged to "do your own thing"—the phrase from pop psychology was just becoming familiar—where would it all end?

Church officials, too, were suspicious, and the nation's bishops combined halting approval of the potential for a deepened prayer life with warnings about the possible abuses. On the local level, however, so many lay people were attracted to this kind of prayer, at least for a time, that pastors found it unwise to discourage it. One group reported in 1971 that between five and six hundred people were coming to its weekly meetings. By the 1980s, charismatics were claiming close to six thousand prayer groups nationwide, attended regularly by a quarter-million people. In at least two places, explicitly charismatic parishes were formed. In Geneva, Illinois, 250 members of a prayer group received permission to form their own parish, to which all nearby charismatics might come, regardless of where they lived. Members had to sign a "covenant agreement," and "baptism in the Holy Spirit is the normal expectation of members." In Rhode Island, another group received "a very, very strong prophecy about God's raising up a new Moses to lead his people in Providence," and a Word of God Community was given jurisdiction over a parish in the inner city, with the pastor its designated Moses.[40] Such intensity might burn brightly for a while and then flicker out, particularly as enthusiastic pastors or parishioners moved away. Still, there were enough Catholic charismatics that bishops established coordinating offices for local groups, and national meetings attracted varying, but still significant, attendance.

To many Catholic ears, the language of the charismatic movement had a distinctly Protestant sound. Those involved preferred the term "charismatic" precisely to distinguish themselves from non-Catholic Pentecostal churches, but they drew on deeper American Protestant impulses nonetheless. The idea that prospective members had to sign a covenant before joining a parish, for example, seemed more akin to the Puritan churches of early New England than to traditional Catholic parish organization. The hope that "lukewarm Catholics can be awakened to the way of the Lord" sounded more like something Jonathan Edwards might have said than a Catholic preacher. One of the original

Duquesne group insisted that "a personal relationship with God" was his goal, letting "Christ become fully the Lord of his life," while another described feeling "God's personal love for me in the depth of my soul." This way of describing religious experience was more like that of a tent revival meeting, with its emphasis on accepting Jesus as "personal savior," than the usual homily in a parish church. These denominational distinctions were less important to Catholic charismatics than was the quality of their "concrete religious experience." True, a shift toward the "affective and emotional" in religion, a belief that "prayer has to be from the depth of the heart as well as from the head," carried the risks of excess, but charismatics often felt a gentle condescension toward those who had not been awakened. The pastor of the Rhode Island parish prayed that God would "increase our compassion for those who simply wish for the 'good old days'": parishioners who were not charismatics deserved "compassion" and maybe pity.[41] Even without this temptation to religious superiority, the charismatic emphasis on personal spirituality shows just how widespread the idea had become in the church of Vatican II.

There were tamer ways of approaching the same goal, including individual spiritual direction. Traditionally, this practice had been undertaken by the clergy and members of religious orders. In regular one-on-one sessions, priests or nuns discussed their experiences of prayer, beyond the mere recitation of prescribed formulas. Jesuits, for example, were guided through the Spiritual Exercises of their founder, Ignatius Loyola, which encouraged such methods as visualizing themselves in conversation with Jesus. For the first time in the years after Vatican II, lay Catholics began to express an interest in adopting similar forms of self-conscious prayer. A Catholic college chaplain from Tennessee noted that "everywhere" he went he found "individuals asking for some plan of deep, longterm spiritual formation." They wanted, he continued, not to turn themselves into pale imitations of cloistered nuns or monks, but rather to define a "secular spirituality, a spirituality lived, not in spite of, but *through* involvement in the secular world of business and politics, family and social life." Lay people seeking direction needed "help with a relationship," two experienced directors wrote; "they want to find a center that holds, a relationship to life and life's mysterious center that will not buckle under the strain of modern conditions." They wanted to be able to "speak about the most profound experiences they have, their experiences of 'the mystery we call God.'" The spiritual director's job was "helping another person to become more aware of God's personal communication to him or her [and] to respond personally to God."[42]

In the process of direction, the two individuals simply conversed, as in psychological counseling. Indeed, many directors drew consciously on the work of psychologists such as Erik Erikson and Carl Rogers, whose writings on human development were achieving wide currency. But "the talk will not be casual and aimless," one director said; it was more than mere "advice-giving." Rather, it was purposeful, since "the person who seeks direction is going somewhere." Most often, people took up the practice because they found "the ways of prayer taught them as children and carried with them into adolescence and young adulthood are no longer satisfying." They wanted something more. Here again was talk of the passage from religious childhood to adulthood. By committing themselves to a regimen of daily prayer and then analyzing their experiences in regular weekly meetings, the director and the directee gradually worked out a plan for spiritual progress. Finding and keeping to a consistent time of day for prayer was important, for example: "morning people" and "night people" were urged to keep an eye on their respective biological clocks. Even when prayer seemed a waste of time, a common problem for "pragmatic, production-oriented Americans," directees were urged to press on, allowing themselves "to waste time gracefully with God." If they persevered, they usually found their self-awareness enhanced. "I'm amazed at how much I can say about what's happened when I've prayed," one person told a director. "When I come, I think I have practically nothing to say. But look how much I've said this morning."[43] The number of people who committed to such sustained efforts at spiritual growth was small, and they were always self-selected. That American lay people sought to do it at all, however, was a sign that they were looking for what the cursillo participant had called "continuing Christian conversion."

Among those most likely to try any of these methods was the core group of lay ministers who emerged in American Catholic parishes in the years after Vatican II. The personnel of the local church no longer consisted exclusively of the priests who lived in the rectory or the sisters in the convent next door. The documents of Vatican II had stressed lay people's involvement in the work of the church and, without removing the theological wall between clergy and laity, had expressed a hope that the laity would be allowed "to exercise certain church functions for a spiritual purpose . . . according to their abilities and the needs of the times." This meant something more than membership in a Catholic Action organization or service on the parish advisory councils that appeared in many places. Lay Eucharistic ministers and readers at Mass were only the beginning of the story. More significant indicators of change were those who undertook careers as lay ministers in the church, including directors of the parish religious instruction program, youth and elderly ministers, and directors of music and liturgy.[44]

At first, the appearance of such people as members of the paid parish staff went unnoticed. Soon, however, the numbers were hard to ignore, and they got steadily larger. By the late 1990s, American Catholic parishes employed almost 30,000 lay ministers who worked at least twenty hours per week. The trend was evident nearly everywhere. In 1970, for example, the diocese of St. Cloud, consisting of 150 parishes spread across the rural stretches of central Minnesota, had only fifteen lay religious education directors and not a single youth minister or "pastoral associate," the title often given to those who performed general duties. By 1990, St. Cloud had more than ninety education directors, seventeen youth ministers, and about twenty pastoral associates. The story in Pittsburgh was much the same. The seventy-five parishes there in 1990 were staffed by 112 active priests whose duties were exclusively those of the parish. But those parishes also had 144 lay ministers—166 if one counted the religious sisters (technically lay people in church law). By the end of the century, 20 percent of all Catholic parish personnel nationwide were lay people. These were overwhelmingly (about 80 percent) women, though there was some specialization by gender. Women were more likely to lead religious education programs, for example, while more men served as musicians or youth ministers. Whatever their job description, they did many things formerly associated with the clergy: 70 percent said that they regularly led members of the parish in prayer; 58 percent had a role in the preparation of Sunday Mass; and 41 percent visited sick parishioners, either at home or in the hospital.[45] On the ground, Catholic parish leadership was clearly becoming a matter of collaboration between clergy and laity.

Lay ministers generally described their work as a "vocation," a familiar term in the Catholic lexicon. Serving their parish was not just a job; it was a response to a "call" from God. Salaries were low, and many lay ministers found that their income was merely supplemental to that of their spouse. One parish education director explained that she took the job out of "a sense of call and commitment" that came from a "deeper part" of her where God spoke. Priests had traditionally described their decision to enter the seminary in this way, and in practice there were many similarities in what clerical and lay ministers actually did. One woman was hired to work with the elderly and sick in her parish. She visited local hospitals and nursing homes, brought Communion to those who could not get to church, and notified her pastor when patients were ill enough to warrant a visit from him for anointing. But she also oversaw scheduling of the lay Eucharistic ministers to ensure adequate coverage at each weekend Mass, trained them, and even led midweek prayer services when the pastor was not available. In another parish, a family life minister found "intense joy," she said, "in helping children grieve when they need to, in helping single-again persons [that is, the separated, divorced, or widowed] find new life, in helping stepparents give the lie to the Cinderella story, in helping couples increase communication and freshen love." Priests could and did perform all these tasks, but lay people added "a different set of perspectives." Their participation "broadened the reach of ministry beyond the more institutional frameworks of yesterday's ministry—the sacraments and schools—to meet the new needs of today's parishioners."[46]

In one sense, lay ministers were merely the logical extensions of an earlier corps of parish volunteers, but a genuinely new category of church worker appeared in the aftermath of Vatican II, and that was the deacon. Most Protestant churches had deacons of one kind or another, but the office had been more restricted among Catholics. Seminarians were made deacons shortly before their ordination to the priesthood, and it was seen as a transitional office. After years of studying theology, they spent a few months learning the practicalities of saying Mass and performing the other sacraments. At the prompting of some European churchmen, the council had "restored" the office of deacon as it was thought to have been practiced in the ancient church. Lay men could apply for ordination as deacons without any intention of ever becoming priests. They kept their regular jobs, but they also assumed liturgical and other functions in their parishes.

They could baptize and officiate at weddings, for example, and they could preach homilies, conduct adult education classes, and visit the sick; they could not say Mass, hear confessions, or anoint the dying, all of which were still reserved to priests. Moreover, a "permanent" deacon could be married, though if his wife died he could not remarry. Beginning in 1968, programs for the preparation of deacons multiplied around the country.[47]

Small but steady numbers of lay men signed up: from 7 the first year, their number grew by the end of the century to more than 12,000. At that time, one in three American Catholic parishes had at least 1 active deacon. The deacons in Boston were typical. In 1973, the first year of the program there, almost 180 men applied for training, which was conducted on weekends; 40 of them were accepted, and 37 were finally ordained in 1976. Their ranks included a policeman, a postal worker, an electrician, a lawyer, and several men who ran their own businesses. They were well into middle age, and most reported that they saw the diaconate as a way to broaden the work they were already doing for the church. Most deacons served in their own parishes and were made to feel a part of the "team," though difficulties sometimes arose. A deacon from Cleveland noted that his pastor always scheduled him to help out at the Christmas and Easter Masses, though he tried not to complain: "While I am honored to share in this liturgical role, I wish that he would realize that my wife and I often want to visit our children and grandchildren around the holidays." Such problems notwithstanding, parishioners generally accepted the deacons, and their role quickly came to seem normal. Saint James's Church in Petaluma, California, for example, self-described as "a rather average American parish," had 1 priest and 3 deacons serving 2,200 families. Beyond helping out with regular Sunday Mass, the deacons ran programs for couples preparing to marry, made visits to the sick, baptized infants, and presided at graveside burials when there was no funeral Mass.

"Not everyone is a theologian," a Boston deacon (a firefighter by trade) said, "but together we make up the church community.[48]

Given the emphasis that Vatican II had placed on the "People of God," lay ministries would probably have expanded in any case, but the need for them was made more urgent by the rapidly declining number of priests. The cadre of priests in America reached its historic high at the time of the council and then fell off, in some years precipitously. At one time, becoming a priest had held many attractions. Foremost among these were the priesthood's spiritual dimensions, but the office had something to offer in this world, too. Their brothers might still be working at physically demanding and dangerous jobs, but priests were professional men, white-collar workers who actually wore white collars. They were respected community leaders. To be sure, they made sacrifices, the most obvious of which was forgoing marriage and a family of their own, and they often spent long years of apprenticeship under older pastors. In Detroit, for example, a priest in the 1950s waited on average close to twenty years after his ordination before becoming a pastor himself. This meant that, well into middle age, these priests were still what their historian has called "dependent men, living for the most part under the direction and scrutiny of their elders." Nevertheless, Catholic parents valued the priesthood and encouraged at least one son to heed the call. Even the mother of Studs Lonigan, the drinking, brawling, and not very pious youth in James T. Farrell's novels of 1930s Chicago, had urged her son to think about such a career. The vision of the priesthood on the movie screen further underlined its appeal. A young man did not have to have the suave coolness of Bing Crosby (*Going My Way,* 1944), the kindly tough love of Spencer Tracy (*Boys' Town,* 1938), the stoic adherence to principle of Montgomery Clift (*I Confess,* 1952), or the passion for justice of Karl Malden (*On the Waterfront,* 1954) to find the life of a priest, in its own way, romantic.[49]

In response to this combination of motives, the number of priests in the United States had risen steadily during the first two-thirds of the twentieth century. In 1965, the final year of the council, the church in America was served by 58,000 priests, with about 1,600 new ones ordained annually. This number was comfortably above the replacement rate for the 850 who died or left the ministry every year. The ratio of priests to Catholics was low: in 1960, it was 1:649 in New York, 1:881 in Cleveland, and 1:578 in Seattle. Trouble quickly became apparent, however, as large numbers of priests resigned their positions—some to marry, others simply to join the lay workforce—in the years after Vatican II. In 1971, for the first time those who left the priesthood almost equaled the newly ordained (667 and 692, respectively), and thereafter those leaving consistently outnumbered those coming in. The total number of priests in the country was down to 46,000 by the end of the century, and the situation was even worse than it appeared: fully one-quarter of the total were retired from active ministry by then.[50]

Those who remained were rapidly "graying." In the year 2000, the average age of an American priest was fifty-nine and rising; only 19 percent of priests were younger than forty-five, and just 5 percent were under thirty-five. Enrollment in seminaries plummeted: there were more than 8,000 students in the 1967–68 academic year, and about half that number ten years later. These numbers eventually stabilized, but they remained well below the replacement rate. The two decades after the council brought 15,000 new priests in America but the departure, from one cause or another (including death), of 22,000. Not since its earliest years, two centuries before, had the American Catholic Church faced the prospect of widespread priestlessness. The number of parishes without a resident pastor rose to measurable proportions. By the century's end, about one-third of the parishes in the Northern Plains states had no priest, and one-quarter of those in the Pacific Northwest were similarly vacant. Areas of the country where matters were not quite so dire only underlined the more general trend.[51] A church that had long relied on its clergymen had fewer and fewer of them.

What to do about this "priest shortage" became the subject of considerable debate. Some people hoped to recreate the conditions that had produced large numbers of clerical vocations in the past. About one-third of American Catholics polled in the mid-1980s said that "we must first of all recruit many more priests." More than half thought that promoting "new ways to structure parish leadership, to include more deacons, sisters, and lay persons" was the better approach. This debate continues today, but discussion of the problem in the years after Vatican II demonstrated two things. First, it highlighted the degree to which lay people had already assumed important roles in the life of their church; and second, it showed that there were issues on which they disagreed with the official positions of the church and its leaders. Fully two-thirds of American Catholics believed that priests should be allowed to marry, for example, and the percentage of those who thought that women should be eligible for the priesthood climbed steadily: by 1985, equal numbers (47 percent) of Catholics approved and disapproved the ordaining of women.[52] Both ideas were firmly rejected by church authorities. In that way, the relationship between American Catholics and the hierarchy—and particularly the pope—grew more complicated in the church of Vatican II.

On the face of things, Catholics retained their enthusiasm for the pope, and it was visibly on display in the fall of 1965, when, for the first time in history, a reigning pope visited the United States. Popes had seldom ventured forth into the world, but Pope Paul VI, who had succeeded John XXIII two years before, resolved to change that. A skilled diplomat before his election to the papacy, Paul determined to visit every continent (save Antarctica) at least once as a way to bring the church's message to the modern world. On October 4, 1965, he came to New York to address a session of the General Assembly of the United Nations, concluding his remarks with an impassioned plea for peace: "No more war, war never again" ("Jamais plus la guerre," in the French in which he spoke). Over the course of a single whirlwind day, he also visited a local parish church, stopped to view Michelangelo's Pietà on display in the Vatican pavilion at the World's Fair site in Queens, and said an open-air Mass for 90,000 worshipers in Yankee Stadium. Even skeptical journalists were impressed. "It was an occasion that suspended the normal life of the city," gushed Homer Bigart in the *New York Times,* "and affected the emotions of millions of persons of all faiths."[53] Papal travel became more common under one of Paul's successors, John Paul II, but this first visit was genuinely a landmark event.

Just three years later, American Catholics were rethinking their exuberance for the pope, and the issue prompting the shift was contraception. At least since the 1930s, church teaching on the subject had been clear. One after another, mainline Protestant churches were abandoning their earlier condemnations, but the Catholic position held. Any attempt to prevent conception in the sexual act was inherently sinful because it frustrated God's plans for procreation and the family; only periodic abstinence was acceptable as a way for couples to space or limit the number of children they had. Development of the so-called rhythm method, with sexual activity confined to the woman's infertile periods, moderated the church's position slightly. Now, a distinction was made between "artificial" contraception (the use of various devices and, later, of the birth control pill), which remained sinful, and "natural" methods, which were not. Many lay people sincerely tried to observe this differentiation, but as contraception became more acceptable in society as a whole, Catholics began to question the prohibition on the more effective means of birth control. "All of a sudden," one man from San Francisco told a nationally recognized theologian, "I see no sin involved in this practice." By the 1960s, American Catholic couples were questioning both the implications of the church's stance and the logic behind it. "Does it bring a pleasant picture to your mind," a woman from Michigan asked, "to think of a mother of four or more feeding an infant in arms while a year-old baby sits at her feet begging to be held?" Another mother expressed similar frustration. "I have had seven children within eight years," she said, "despite frantic and distressing efforts to follow rhythm . . . It seems unjust that we who have accepted the responsibilities of marriage should have to practice continence."[54]

Theologians, most of them priests, were often unmoved by such entreaties. A husband and wife might think they had legitimate economic or emotional reasons to use contraceptives, one seminary professor said coolly, but "it will be more advisable and more praiseworthy for a couple to continue to build a family, placing their trust in Divine Providence." Parish priests were more sympathetic, since they were the ones who actually encountered lay people, troubled by the whole question, in the confessional. Bishops sometimes urged the clergy to be strict—in the 1930s, the archbishop of Chicago had told his priests to question married penitents on the subject, even if they did not mention it themselves—and to deny forgiveness to those who were violating the church's precepts. Few parish priests had any taste for that sort of thing, and often they were openly sympathetic with their parishioners. "I have been told explicitly by a priest that it is permissible," one woman wrote to a Catholic magazine in 1960, "one year after the birth of a child to space children for reasons of a mother's health." A woman from the Bronx reported that she had "received permission from my confessor to use contraceptive pills"; the year in which she had done so was, she said, "very relaxed and wonderful" for her marriage. Many priests told their people simply to follow their own "informed conscience." It seems clear, a comprehensive history of the subject concludes, that a majority of American Catholic priests were "less than wholly committed" to the church's official stance. Moreover, informal networks of women exchanged information on which priests in which parishes were sympathetic, and before the practice of confession declined, these networks allowed those who were practicing birth control to find an understanding ear.[55]

Pressure to review the church's position could not be resisted in the face of this widespread dissatisfaction. In 1966, Pope Paul expanded the commission that John XXIII had appointed to study the matter, adding three married couples, including Patty and Pat Crowley from the United States. Two issues dominated the discussion. One was the morality specifically of the birth control pill, which had been approved for sale in 1960 and quickly became the most common form of contraception. Was this an "artificial" method of birth control? And even if it was, was it not acceptable anyway because it was a form of medicine? The other was the potentially thornier problem of changing church teaching so dramatically. This was the dilemma that troubled the commission's Father Zalba: how could something that was sinful last week not be sinful this week?

The Crowleys argued for the change, and they were supported by many of the experts whom the commission consulted. These included another American, John Noonan, a distinguished law professor and historian who had published a book, *Contraception: A History of Its Treatment by the Catholic Theologians and Canonists,* demonstrating that the church's position had already changed over the centuries. A majority report recommended modifying the church's stance, relying in part on the experience of lay Catholics. Taking account of the "sense of the faithful," it said, "condemnation of a couple to a long and often heroic abstinence as a means to regulate conception cannot be founded on the truth." The pope seemed inclined toward this view, but a powerfully argued minority report urged restatement of the distinction between natural and artificial methods. The church "could not have so wrongly erred" in stating its position; if it had, the authority of its teaching on any topic was suspect.[56]

In the end, Paul VI was persuaded by this argument, and in July 1968 he issued an encyclical, *Humanae Vitae* ("Of Human Life"), reaffirming the condemnation of artificial contraception. The language of his letter was subtle, but reaction to it was swift and overwhelmingly negative among American lay people. "How can persons of integrity confess as a sin something which their consciences tell them is not an offense?" one couple asked in an open letter to the nation's bishops. "Many Catholic married people," a parish priest in Baltimore told his archbishop, "not just the lax and indifferent, but also the most conscientious and most enlightened, have time after time told me in confession that they find the approved methods of rhythm and periodic continence unworkable." Polling data confirmed that Catholics were disregarding the papal statement. In 1970, a survey found that more than three-quarters of married Catholic women in their twenties were using a form of birth control that the encyclical had condemned. More tellingly, 62 percent of American Catholics told pollsters in the 1980s that individuals, rather than church leaders, should make the determination about the morality of contraception. The very undermining of authority that some church officials hoped to prevent had become a reality. Just 13 percent of those polled said that the teaching on birth control had reinforced their faith, while 35 percent said that it had weakened their faith; perhaps worst of all, 43 percent said that it had had no effect whatever.[57] Simply ignoring what the leaders of their church had to say was something new for American Catholics.

This easy disregard for clearly stated church teaching opened the door to other signs of independence among American lay people, and it helped solidify a growing polarization of factions, self-consciously identified as liberal or conservative. What was once thought a monolithic body of believers was now visibly divided. Some lay people, for instance, recoiled at changes in religious practice, and they responded with a Catholic Traditionalist Movement. Spearheaded by Father Gommar DePauw, originally from Belgium, this group decried what they saw as the "Protestantizing" of the church. About 150 of them picketed Saint Patrick's Cathedral in New York City one Sunday in 1968, carrying placards that read, "Restore Our Latin Mass" and "Altar Yes, Table No." Unease with the broader cultural changes of the 1960s fueled their passion. The new Mass had been forced on an unwilling church by "liturgical beatniks" and "hippies," DePauw said. Another group, Catholics United for the Faith, was organized expressly to defend the papal position on contraception. They were a rallying point, their founding statement said, "for the multitude of Catholics who have felt bewildered and blown about by the 1,000 winds of false doctrine being constantly puffed out by . . . 1,000 counterfeit teachers." Others saw conspiracy behind the changes in the church. Starting in 1970, Veronica Lueken, a housewife from Queens, New York, reported seeing visions of the Virgin Mary, and a few years later she announced that Mary had revealed to her the plot that was behind it all. The real Pope Paul VI had been drugged and kidnapped, she said, and a look-alike, the product of skillful plastic surgery, had taken his place. Only that could explain the ongoing triumph of "the forces of evil" in the church.[58]

At the opposite end of the spectrum, liberal groups coalesced around the notion that the reforms of Vatican II had not gone far enough, and some of these organizations were no less extreme than their conservative counterparts. Catholics held a "Call to

Action" meeting in Detroit in 1976 as an official vehicle for Catholic participation in that year's observance of the bicentennial of the American Revolution. A splinter group subsequently adopted the Call to Action name and began holding annual conventions. Although the group endorsed some traditional Catholic positions (economic fairness in the workplace, for instance, and opposition to the death penalty), its larger agenda was increasingly at odds with the church. Call to Action issued resolutions supporting a change in the teaching on contraception and other sexual matters (including homosexuality) and an end to mandatory celibacy for priests. Liturgies at the meetings might kindly be described as free-form, and they were thus easy to caricature as the product of latter-day "beatniks." Even more explicitly in opposition to the church were Catholics for a Free Choice (CFFC), a lobbying group founded in 1970 in support of the legalization of abortion. Although it was an organization largely without members—critics said it was nothing more than "a well-funded letterhead" and a fax machine churning out press releases—CFFC was skillful at gaining publicity. Since one of its first official acts had been to stage the mock coronation of a female pope, however, dispassionate observers had reason to think that the first word of the group's title was being applied a bit loosely.[59]

Groups right and left generated a good deal of passion, but the majority of American Catholics refused to identify with either extreme. Most held a mixed collection of views on the issues that so enflamed the partisans of one side or the other. Press reports emphasized the divisions, however, and this led eventually to an effort at reconciliation. In the summer of 1996, Cardinal Joseph Bernardin, the archbishop of Chicago, took the lead in organizing a Common Ground Project. With the support of a number of prominent lay Catholics—Robert Casey, the former governor of Pennsylvania; John Sweeney, the head of the AFL-CIO; Mary Ann Glendon, a professor at Harvard Law School—the initiative was intended to counter "an increasing polarization within the church and, at times, a mean-spiritedness" that "hindered the kind of dialogue that helps us to address our mission and concerns." Not everyone was ready for dialogue. From the left, the head of CFFC denounced the effort, while from the right, four other American prelates complained that the program did not "place sufficient importance on the teachings of the church, through the pope and the bishops, as the basis for common ground." Bernardin's painful death from cancer a few months later undercut the effort, though the group continued to meet in hopes of drawing attention to the middle position on issues, which most Catholic lay people favored.[60]

One persistent point of disagreement between lay people and their church was the question of whether women could be priests. Most Protestant denominations had approved the ordination of women over the course of the twentieth century. The Episcopal Church was one of the last to do so, after the unauthorized ordination of several women in 1974 forced the issue. Some Jewish congregations were ordaining female rabbis: Reform Jews approved the practice in 1972, followed a decade later by Conservative Jews. When the question first came up among Catholics, the answer seemed unequivocal: women priests were simply out of the question. "Females are completely barred from the priestly office," the Jesuits' *America* magazine had said bluntly in 1960, a prohibition based on "divine positive law . . . If it were lawful to have female priests, Mary, Mother of God, would surely have been the first." As new forms of feminism spread throughout American society, however, and as female lay ministers assumed visible positions in Catholic parishes, the law seemed less positive and possibly no longer divine. If women could be lectors and (perhaps especially) Eucharistic ministers, priesthood seemed merely the next logical step. By 1973, *America* had changed its mind. "The total embargo against an ordained female ministry,"

a writer in its pages said, "looks more and more like the preserva-
tion of an aging cultural tradition and the expression of sexist
prejudice." Why, even the Harvard Club was now admitting
women, the writer pointed out, as if that were sufficient to clinch
the case.[61]

The question had not been discussed during the Vatican
Council, and a survey taken in 1965 showed that a clear majority
of American Catholics opposed the idea. As early as 1970, however, opinion was shifting. About half of those polled said that
they would accept women in priestly roles, while one-quarter said
they would not, and another quarter were unsure. Competing
biblical texts—on the one hand, Saint Paul's insistence that women
keep silent in church (I Corinthians 14:34); on the other, his assertion that in Christ there was no distinction between male and
female (Galatians 3:28)—apparently argued the case to a draw.
More important for lay people were the practicalities of women
performing the many tasks in a priest's job description. "How often it takes a woman's heart, thinking, and understanding to solve
a problem," one woman from New Jersey said. "I have been disappointed more than once when I have gone to a priest with a
problem, only to find that he didn't understand my feelings or
thinking and was at a loss to be of much help to me." A man
from California agreed. He had not been to confession in some
time, he admitted, but "if we must continue having private confession, please, please, please let women be ordained so I could
confess to a more sensitive, feeling person!" Those on the other
side had equally pragmatic concerns. "A lady priest going on a
sick call in the 'evil houses,'" a woman from Michigan wondered,
"is this safe?" A woman from Maine had other concerns: "I can't
honestly see a woman priest living peacefully in a rectory, now or
ever." But still another was prepared for the long haul. "I don't
believe this idea would find real acceptance in this generation,"
she said. "However, I am confident that if women were ordained

now, the next generation would completely accept them," just as they had come to accept women doctors and judges.[62]

The debate went public in November 1975, when twelve hundred people, most of them women, gathered in Detroit to support the ordination of women as Catholic priests; another five hundred were turned away for lack of space. Those present represented forty-four states, the District of Columbia, Puerto Rico, and half a dozen foreign countries. Most did not want ordination for themselves, but they thought it should be possible. Speakers acknowledged that they were advocating a thoroughgoing "reinterpretation of the priesthood." Awareness of the declining numbers of priests was by then widespread, and ordaining women was seen as one way of addressing the problem. Participants had assessed the cultural and historical roots of the all-male, celibate priesthood and found them wanting. The argument that Jesus had chosen only men as disciples, for instance, while true, was unconvincing. By that logic, only Jews from Palestine could be ordained as Catholic priests, and in any case Jesus had never actually ordained anybody, as the term was now understood. Conference participants used language that had become common by then in discussions of gender, speaking of "liberation," "empowerment," and "sexism." Several women who did feel called to the priesthood described their experience. "We want to be ordained, not because we want to exercise power," said Rosalie Muschal-Reinhardt, a mother of four from Rochester, New York, "but because we are motivated by love and a concern for the church." Many like her were already filling ministerial roles in their parishes, she pointed out, but they were barred from presiding at the sacraments.[63]

Although they sought radical change, participants rejected the idea of disobeying church law and simply ordaining a few women. This method was working in the Episcopal Church, but it was not one that these Catholics would adopt. Indeed, speaker after

speaker stressed the importance of maintaining "fidelity to the
tradition of the church." Discussion and persuasion were the best
approach, and to this end, a Women's Ordination Conference
opened an office soon afterward in Washington, D.C. Even so,
fidelity rather than rebellion was the watchword. "We come together," Sister Nadine Foley, a college chaplain, said, "not to confront the Church, not to act in defiance of the Church, but to be
the Church." A more insurgent gathering would have ended with
the ad hoc ordination of several of the women present; this one
ended with Sunday Mass, presided over by a male priest. The
officiant began by apologizing for the "inadequacy" of his role in
this context, and the Mass did bend church rules slightly in that a
lay woman delivered the homily, something only a priest was supposed to do. But even her tone was moderate: waiting—to be
sure, "*active,* not passive waiting . . . until the whole Church rec-
ognizes his [that is, Christ's] priesthood in us"—was the way to
address the issue.[64] By historical analogy, the meeting had been
more like the First Continental Congress of 1774 than the Second
Congress of 1776. The former had protested British infringement
of the colonists' "rights as Englishmen"; the latter had declared
American independence. Two hundred years later, there were no
Catholic declarations of independence in Detroit.

Official reaction was nevertheless swift. The nation's bishops
had already issued a preemptive statement, asserting that the reasons for barring women from ordination were serious theological
ones and not grounded merely in sexist cultural tradition. The
Vatican position was also clear, summarized later in a ruling from
the Congregation for the Doctrine of the Faith, the department
charged with oversight of official teaching. After his election to
the papacy in 1978, Pope John Paul II also rejected the idea several times. John Paul, the former Karol Wojtyla, archbishop of
Krakow in Poland and the first non-Italian pope in four centuries, produced many statements on the equality of women, in

church and society, throughout his tenure. Even so, in the pope's view, there were still differences in what men and women could do in the church, and he felt strongly on the subject. One American bishop, lunching with the pope during a visit to Rome, reported that John Paul had "pounded on the table for emphasis" when the subject came up. The church was not "authorized" by God, the pope said, "to admit women to priestly ordination." Hoping to end discussion of the matter once and for all, he declared in 1994 that this view was to be "definitively held" by all Catholics. Any change was out of the question, now or ever; not even some future pope could alter the church's position.[65]

This was an entirely new category of papal teaching, an assertion of the powers of the papacy unmatched since the days of Pius IX a century before. John Paul's statement did not conform to the theological requirements for infallibility, but some lay people were prepared to accept it as such. To continue pressing for the ordination of women "after the pope has already made his statement" was wrong, a woman from Kentucky said. A woman from California concurred, noting that the "first and paramount task" of all Catholics "is to be obedient." Others felt that discussion should not end. "I do not believe that silence is appropriate if we recognize an injustice," another woman from California said. A woman from Pennsylvania thought about her children. "My daughters have to struggle enough in the real world for equality," she said. "The one place they should be welcomed and treated completely equal is in their church." Notwithstanding the pope's desire to end debate, by the close of the twentieth century, two-thirds of American Catholics supported the ordination of women, and Catholics under the age of thirty-five favored it by a margin of four to one. There the matter remains today. Most Catholics saw the "irregular" ordination of several women—including the wife of a former governor of Ohio—by a schismatic bishop in Germany in 2002 as a fringe activity; subsequent ad hoc ordinations have similarly failed to gain much support.[66] American lay Catholics wanted women priests, but they were content to wait until the church authorized them.

Lay people disagreed with John Paul II on this and other questions—he firmly restated the ban on contraception, for example—thus tempering the ardent papalism of previous generations. Nonetheless, American Catholics found the pope a compelling personality. Even as they rejected or ignored some of his teachings, their enthusiasm for the leader of their church seemed to grow. The pope's several visits to America provided occasions to demonstrate this affection. If Paul VI had ventured cautiously outside the Vatican, John Paul made papal travel routine. He was an unquestionably impressive figure, a poet and philosopher, and his long resistance to the communist regime of his native Poland was legendary. Indeed, when he helped bring about the collapse of the Soviet empire in Eastern Europe in the late 1980s and early 1990s, he was apparently fulfilling his historic destiny. He remained physically vigorous well into his seventies, even after an assassination attempt in 1981. All these traits drew people to him as an individual, and newspapers regularly compared him to a rock star in his appeal. Movement on the world stage reinforced this public persona. In the course of his nearly twenty-seven-year papacy, he seemed to visit virtually every spot on the globe, including four separate trips to the United States. The first came in October 1979, barely a year after his election, when he stopped in Boston, New York, Philadelphia, Des Moines, and Chicago before landing in Washington, D.C., where he said Mass on the mall between the Lincoln Memorial and the Washington Monument. Huge crowds turned out to see him, some of them standing in drenching rain for hours just to have that chance.[67]

The pope's appearance at an event called World Youth Day, in a park outside Denver in August 1993, proved his appeal. John

Paul himself had created these biennial gatherings, held in loca-
tions around the world as occasions for young people to renew
their ardor for the church. Frequently compared to the 1960s
Woodstock music festival, they had a serious religious purpose,
one that was enhanced by the adventure of being part of such a
large crowd. The Denver event attracted more than 400,000
young people, most of them from the United States. Under a
blazing summer sun, they prayed, chanted the pope's name, and
participated in a Mass, many wearing t-shirts embossed with such
slogans as "Life is Short, Pray Hard." The excitement was infectious. "Oh, man," said a fourteen-year-old girl from New Orleans, "this is overwhelming." A fifteen-year-old from Virginia
thought so, too. "I'll be honest with you, I was really getting
bored with church," she told a reporter. "I would like to see the
energy and enthusiasm that was here spread around." The celebration, the pope said, "has been a stop along the way, a moment
of prayer and refreshment, but our journey must lead us on."
Later, when John Paul died in the spring of 2005, the expressions
of grief from young American Catholics, most of whom had
never known any other pope, further demonstrated the particular
appeal he had had for them.[68]

These experiences were no doubt genuine, but Catholics
young and old, while drawn to the pope personally, did not hesitate to disagree with him. They could be inspired by the pope,
but they would not always do what he told them. The rate at
which Catholics used the condemned forms of contraception, for
example, was indistinguishable from that of the rest of the American population. Catholics had become comfortable with looking
to their own experience as much as to church teaching in decid-
ing questions of moral and religious behavior. The language of
adulthood and the autonomy it implied had penetrated deeply. A
man from New Hampshire had said as early as 1969 that he and
his fellow Catholics needed "an answer we can believe in" on con-

traception and other issues. Not just any answers would do. Church teachings had to make sense; if they did not, he could dissent from them and still be a Catholic. Critics censured this view, denouncing "cafeteria Catholics" who chose to take the church positions they liked and to pass up those they did not.[69] The criticism was not unfounded, but the Vatican Council's description of the church as the "People of God" had seized the American Catholic imagination. The imagery meant that lay people were defining their identification with the church, sometimes on their own terms.

Catholics faced similar challenges in their identity as Americans in the years after Vatican II. These challenges came at a time when many of them had climbed to the top of the American ladder, and the election of a Catholic president two years before the council opened was only part of the story. Earlier social distinctions had lost their force in the suburban, generally prosperous United States of the late twentieth century. In education and income level, Catholics equaled or exceeded people in other churches: a survey in the mid-1980s showed that only Episcopalians and Presbyterians had a higher percentage of members in the upper income brackets. By the end of the century, nearly one-third of all adult Catholics in America had graduated from college, and another 13 percent had also attended graduate or professional school. Residential patterns confirmed how fully they had blended into the rest of society. Families along one side of the dog-leg street in the central Massachusetts city in which I grew up at the time of the council had the following religious affiliations: Congregationalist, Catholic, Episcopalian, Catholic, Jewish, Catholic (us), Jewish, Catholic; down the other side of the street, it was Greek Orthodox, unchurched, Episcopalian, Catholic, Episcopalian, unchurched, Unitarian, Unitarian, Catholic,

Jewish, Catholic. No single place is entirely representative, but the religious mixture of that neighborhood mirrored the integration that was happening elsewhere.[70]

At the same time, when Vatican II opened, churches were still more likely to emphasize the things that divided them than those they had in common. The legacy of the Reformation was a long one, and though outright hostility was now rare in America, interfaith efforts had made little headway in bridging the gaps. Persistent suspicion ran in both directions. Many Protestants thought Catholics incapable of thinking for themselves, and they considered Catholic worship, beginning with the Mass itself, essentially idolatrous. For their part, Catholics found Protestant services thin and meaningless. Some Protestant denominations haltingly explored common territory—a Federal Council of Churches was formed in 1908 and renamed the National Council of Churches in 1950—but Catholics kept their distance, joining neither one. Papal statements had set the tone. An encyclical of 1928 warned of "false Christianity" and insisted that the union of Christians could be accomplished only by "the return to the one true Church of Christ of those who are separated from it."[71]

On the local level, there were clear lines that Catholics could not cross. Sometimes, one priest explained to a parishioner in North Carolina, a Catholic might find it necessary, for social reasons, to attend a Protestant church service, but such occasions were "fraught with religious danger." Any participation must be done "passively": a Catholic could not be the godparent at a non-Catholic christening, for example. Similarly, a priest told a young man in Chicago in 1955 that it was inadvisable for a Catholic to join the YMCA, even if he only wanted to use the gym or the swimming pool; the Y was not, the priest said, "nonsectarian or neutral." For anyone who asked, there were clear answers about just what was wrong with Protestant churches. Episcopalians did not have valid ordinations, a Catholic priest told a woman from

Ohio; therefore, their Communion services, which looked more
or less like those in a Catholic church, were entirely invalid. Non-
Catholic translations of the Bible, "so garbled" as to be riddled
with "thousands of serious errors," were the product of "muti-
neers" like Luther. The Orthodox churches of Greece and Russia
operated under a "misnomer," a Catholic in Pennsylvania was
told: "no one can be orthodox—that is, sound in doctrine—and
at the same time persist in schism and heresy," which the Orthodox did by rejecting the authority of the pope.[72] Cooperation
among churches could go only so far in such an atmosphere.

One particularly contentious episode demonstrated how far
apart American faiths were. Immediately after the Second World
War, Father Leonard Feeney, a Jesuit priest, was the chaplain of
an informal gathering spot in Cambridge, Massachusetts, for
Catholic students attending Harvard and Radcliffe colleges. His
dynamic personality attracted many converts to Catholicism, including Avery Dulles, son of the future secretary of state in the
Eisenhower administration. By 1949, however, Feeney was giving a rigorist reading to an ancient church maxim, first articulated in the contest with paganism in the third century: "outside the church, there is no salvation" (in Latin, *extra ecclesiam
nulla salus*). Feeney interpreted this literally to mean that all non-
Catholics—Protestants, Jews, Muslims, and everybody else—were
simply going to hell. Serious theologians had moved away from
this absolutist view, but the Feeney group insisted on it, often in
open-air rallies, at which they harangued (and frequently ha-
rassed) passers-by. Local church officials sought to silence Feeney
and his followers; when they refused to recant, several of them
were fired from teaching positions in Catholic schools. Feeney
was dismissed from the Jesuit order and, together with some of
his inner circle, even excommunicated: it was, at the least, ironic
for those who preached damnation outside the Catholic Church
to find themselves outside it. They withdrew to the far Boston

suburbs, where they established their own religious order on a farm commune. Their numbers were always very small, and some, including Feeney himself, eventually reconciled with the Catholic Church, but the vigor with which they insisted on an unbridgeable gulf between Catholics and Protestants showed how potent such divisions could still be.[73]

Barely a decade later, deliberations at the Vatican Council provided a basis for Catholics to begin reaching across these divides. "Without doubt," the council said in a decree of November 1964, discord among Christian churches "openly contradicts the will of Christ." Statements on the Orthodox churches and on non-Christians struck the same themes, and another specifically rejected the centuries-old accusation that Jews were responsible for the death of Jesus. Moreover, largely at the prompting of John Courtney Murray, another American Jesuit, the council endorsed the principle of religious freedom. Earlier popes and councils had rejected any such idea: "error has no rights," the saying went. Freedom to choose one's religion implied accepting the possibility that someone might make the "wrong" choice, and that led only to indifference. Now, the official position of the church was that the inherent dignity of all people gave them the right to choose their own faith: "in matters religious no one is to be forced to act in a manner contrary to his own beliefs."[74] Catholics had once defined the interreligious agenda as a matter of Protestants recognizing that they had been wrong for all those centuries and "returning" to Rome; now, there was a basis for discussion on more equal terms.

With this encouragement, American Catholics cautiously explored common religious ground with their neighbors. It was absurd, one lay group said in 1966, "to pretend that there are no serious differences between religions," but it was no less absurd "to assume that there are nothing *but* differences." Programs of "living room dialogues" began, with people from different churches

meeting to learn about one another's faith. "The principle behind
the discussion," one guidebook said, "is to explore and express
your own values, not to convince the other person." Joint prayer
services were encouraged, provided that they stayed within limits.
Catholics attending them did not thereby satisfy their Sunday
Mass obligation, for instance, and the line was always drawn at
common reception of the Eucharist, which remained a theologically thorny issue. The first steps in such dialogues were usually the hardest. Priests in Boston were urged to take the lead
in approaching local Protestant clergy, perhaps by inviting them
to lunch, but they nonetheless had to observe unspoken rules.
"Protestants, at least in the New England area," the archbishop's
office explained in 1965, almost like an anthropologist describing
an exotic remote tribe, "do not expect a lavish spread; [they]
may even misunderstand or resent 'all-out' hospitality." It was
therefore a good idea to charge them for lunch—"usually $1.00
or $1.50"—as this made "reciprocal hospitality a lesser burden."
Venturing into this uncertain territory, Catholics began to have
religious contact with non-Catholics, and the experience could
be powerful. It was "strange and marvelous," said a parishioner in
Cleveland, New York, near Syracuse, after attending a prayer service in the local Episcopal church, "the first [event] of its kind
since the founding of the village of Cleveland."[75]

Some lay men and women already had personal experience
with a non-Catholic: those who had married one. The church
had long discouraged "mixed marriages," and it did so, a college
theology textbook explained as late as 1960, "for reasons only too
fully justified by sad experience." Not only did such marriages
"imply a communication in things divine with a heretic," but
they also posed a "great danger to the faith of the Catholic party
and often to that of the children as well." In an effort to check
this "evil"—the section in the theology text discussing the subject
was twenty-three lines long, and it used the word "evil" eight

times—the church had several ways of discouraging marriage across religious lines. Such marriages could not be celebrated in the parish church, for example: most often, they were conducted in the rectory parlor, and no Mass could be said. The non-Catholic party had to swear not to interfere with the Catholic's religious practice and to vow that any children born of the marriage would be raised as Catholics. Looking further down the road of life, non-Catholic spouses were also informed that they would have to be buried apart from their husband or wife, since "heretics" could not be admitted to the consecrated ground of a Catholic cemetery. We will never know how many interreligious courtships foundered on these rocks, but the rate of intermarriage was always low. In one large Boston parish in the 1860s and 1870s, for example, only 6 percent of the marriages united a Catholic with a member of another church.[76]

A century later, mixed marriages became more common. Like Boston, Detroit had had a low rate of intermarriage in the nineteenth century, but it rose steadily in the twentieth: about 22 percent in the 1930s, and 34 percent by the 1960s. As Catholics left their tightly bound urban neighborhoods and moved to the suburbs, they increased their likelihood of meeting and marrying someone of a different faith. External circumstances also threw people together as never before: the number of mixed marriages went up during the Second World War. The rate varied by region, depending on the ratio of Catholics to other religious groups: more than half the marriages in the Deep South united Catholics and non-Catholics during the 1940s and 1950s, while only one-quarter of those in the mid-Atlantic states did so. By the 1980s, however, nearly 40 percent of all Catholic marriages nationwide were "mixed," and the church faced this reality by moderating its earlier condemnations. Insisting on "rigid rules," one priest said, "just won't do." The mandatory promises by the non-Catholic were eliminated in 1971; the wedding ceremony could be performed with a Mass in the church; and a clergyman from the non-Catholic tradition could participate. Just as important, the laity's attitude toward the subject had changed. More than three-quarters of Catholics, surveyed in 1958, agreed that, "as a general rule," it was better to marry someone of their own faith; by 1971, only a bare majority felt that way, and thereafter opinion on the subject gradually slipped into indifference.[77]

Cooperation between Catholics and non-Catholics was more publicly apparent when it was directed toward larger problems in American society. The years of Vatican II coincided with dramatic social change in the United States, including the civil rights movement, opposition to American participation in the war in Vietnam, and changing roles for women. Increasingly, Catholics made common cause with non-Catholic churches and church people in addressing these issues. After the somewhat hesitant start made by local Catholic Interracial Councils, for example, Catholics joined the campaign for civil rights, much of it organized by black Protestant ministers. Catholics even offered their own martyr to the cause. Viola Liuzzo, a convert from Michigan, was murdered by three members of the Alabama Ku Klux Klan in March 1965, as she was driving along a country road with fellow demonstrators from the galvanizing march from Selma to Montgomery. Civil rights leaders, including Martin Luther King, Jr., and Roy Wilkins of the NAACP, joined labor union officials Walter Reuther and Jimmy Hoffa—Liuzzo's husband was an officer of the Teamsters union—at her funeral Mass in Immaculate Heart of Mary Church in Detroit. The outpouring of interreligious grief on this occasion matched that shown just two weeks earlier, when forty thousand mourners (most of them Catholics) had crowded the Boston Common to express outrage over the death of James Reeb, a Unitarian minister from that city who had also been gunned down near Selma.[78]

Catholics' efforts to promote racial equality were complicated, however, by the changing demographics of northern cities. In many places, an influx of African Americans into previously all-white Catholic neighborhoods created tensions and even sparked violence. The moral clarity of the civil rights movement blurred when focus shifted from the South onto problems closer to home. In many places, the clergy moved significantly ahead of their parishioners in calling for an end to discrimination in housing and employment. In 1964, priests in Cleveland's Murray Hill neighborhood, trying to reason with a crowd protesting school integration, were greeted with shouts from their own people of "Mind your own business, Father." A year later, Father James Groppi, a white priest in Milwaukee, led an integrated march into one of the city's Polish neighborhoods. He was met by five thousand residents chanting, "Eee-yi-eee-yi-ee-yi oh, Father Groppi's got to go." In cities across the North, many white Catholics, heedless of sermons urging acceptance of integration, fled their traditional ethnic enclaves. Saint Agnes parish in Flint, Michigan, was only one example among many. In a single year (1970–1971), the parish lost two hundred of its twelve hundred families as African Americans bought houses on the city's northwest side, aided by a new open housing law. The decline continued thereafter; by 1980, there were only about two hundred families left in the parish. "They try and force integration on us and we'll rebel," an Italian-American parishioner in Cicero, Illinois, had said in similar circumstances in 1967. He spoke for many.[79]

Lay Catholics' opposition to social activism on the part of their priests ironically drew some of its energy from the changed relationship between clergy and laity that had come with Vatican II. The priests in Cleveland were not the only ones to be told by their parishioners to "mind your own business." Lay people who felt this way could justify their stance in part by all the talk they had heard about how they themselves were the church. When Chicago's Cardinal John Cody expressed his support for integration in the Cicero case, the same angry parishioner abruptly responded, "Cody wasn't elected by us." Ten years earlier, few Catholic laymen would have expressed such sentiments aloud, even if they had thought them. During one demonstration by a largely Irish-American Catholic crowd opposing school busing in Boston in 1974, a parade of women marched past their local parish church. They were loudly praying the rosary, imploring the Virgin Mary's help to reverse a court order that the city's public schools be desegregated. When one of the priests, gathered on the church steps, told them they should not be praying for such a thing, they taunted him. "See," they shouted back, "we don't need you anymore. We deal with God directly."[80] This was not the kind of "dealing with God directly" that the bishops of the council had had in mind, but the door once opened proved hard to shut.

Catholic opinion about the war in Vietnam generally mirrored that of the rest of the population. Several priests were known for opposing the war, including the Berrigan brothers, Daniel and Philip, who broke into a draft board outside Baltimore, took some of the files, and set them ablaze with homemade napalm. Lay Catholics, too, joined the antiwar cause. At a rally in New York in October 1965, David Miller, a twenty-two-year-old from the Catholic Worker house in Manhattan, became one of the first young men to burn his draft card, and four more Catholic Workers did the same two weeks later. Yet another Catholic Worker tore his card in half and mailed it to the attorney general, while still another went so far as to set himself on fire in front of the United Nations building, imitating the Buddhist monks who protested in that way in Saigon. Congress had only recently increased the penalties for draft-card burning, and Miller and the others were picked up by the police, tried, and convicted. Miller's sentence was suspended, provided that he get a new draft card and carry it at all times; this was something, he told the judge, he would not do, and so he was arrested again.

Not all Catholics thought this form of activism was wise. Although *America* magazine called it "stupid" for the courts to send him to jail for his victimless crime, the Catholic periodical thought it was "equally stupid" for Miller to expend so much energy in trying to get the government to do exactly that. Others protested the protests. Egged on by a local state legislator, a crowd of seventy-five high school boys in the Irish Catholic neighborhood of South Boston, Massachusetts, "pinned down and pummeled" seven draft-card burners.[81] The war divided all Americans, and Catholics felt those divisions no less than their fellow citizens.

The far more fractious issue complicating Catholics' relationship to American public life came with the ruling of the U.S. Supreme Court in January 1973 in the case of *Roe v. Wade.* The court's action, invalidating most restrictions on abortion, surprised nearly everyone and short-circuited legislative debates then under way in New York, New Jersey, and elsewhere that were progressively modifying restrictive statutes. Catholics were quick to denounce the decision. Within a week of *Roe,* Lawrence Hogan, a Catholic congressman from Maryland, introduced a constitutional amendment to overturn the ruling, and Senator James Buckley from New York, another Catholic, announced that he would push a similar measure. Senator Edward Kennedy of Massachusetts, head of what was probably the nation's most prominent Catholic political family, decried abortion as "not in accordance with the value which our civilization places on human life." As late as 1979, he was still proudly pointing to his votes against abortion, "whether it is to be paid for by private or public funds—whether the woman is rich or poor." Support for the court's decision grew, however, especially among Democrats such as Kennedy, who came to describe his position as "evolving." By the time of his 1994 reelection campaign, he was proclaiming, "I am pro-choice," while, in a swipe at his rival (who had a fundamentally similar position), "my opponent is multiple choice."[82] It was a clever line, but it showed just how tricky the political terrain of abortion could be.

The nation's Catholic bishops hoped to lead a "pro-life" charge, but their position had been weakened by the opposition of lay people to the church's teaching on birth control, spelled out in *Humanae Vitae* just five years before. John Deedy, an editor of *Commonweal* magazine, noted the "wide and in some quarters deeply felt" Catholic desire to protect the unborn, but he predicted that "quiet disregard for the bishops' moral counsel" on the one issue would spread to the other. He was right on both counts. Catholics remained uneasy about unrestricted access to abortion. A Gallup poll taken immediately after the *Roe* decision showed that only 36 percent of Catholics agreed with it, as opposed to 45 percent of Protestants. At the same time, however, 56 percent of Catholics were willing to leave the decision about abortion to the woman in question and her doctor. A decade later, two-thirds of American Catholics still declared their opposition to abortion on demand, but by then an even wider majority of them had come to think that the procedure should be legal in at least some circumstances. A September 2000 poll indicated that 46 percent of Catholics defined themselves as basically pro-life, with a slightly higher number (49 percent) describing themselves as pro-choice. Many insisted that they were personally opposed to abortion but thought it should nonetheless remain legal; at the same time, Catholics were more likely than other Americans to be uncomfortable with resort to abortion simply because a child was declared "unwanted."[83]

The debate on abortion continues today, but its impact for Catholics was most evident at the polls. The two major political parties moved toward contrasting positions on the issue, with Democrats more supportive of access to abortion and Republicans more likely to support restrictions or even an outright ban. This division helped put Catholic voters in play as they had not been for some time. Catholics had long been overwhelmingly Democratic, but many now found themselves more comfortable in the Republican ranks. In the 1980s, Ronald Reagan was particularly successful at tapping this fluidity, attracting large numbers of formerly Democratic voters with his strong pro-life stance as well as his economic and social policies. On the other side of the aisle, Mario Cuomo, the Catholic governor of New York who was perennially on the list of possible Democratic presidential candidates (though he never ran), tried to articulate a stance on abortion that could be summarized as "personally opposed, but legal." In a widely reported speech at Notre Dame University in 1984, Cuomo advanced this view. Although it mirrored the opinion of many Catholics, they still voted for the other party. Reagan was reelected in a landslide that year, swamping a Democratic ticket that included Geraldine Ferraro, a Catholic congresswoman whose pro-choice stance had been denounced by several bishops. Thereafter, Catholics shifted back and forth between the parties, making them, at least for a time, the quintessential "swing voters."[84]

The abortion debate attracted the most public notice, but it was only one of many issues affecting Catholic Americans in the 1960s and after. For them, the upheaval of those decades seemed more comprehensive than it was for other Americans, for it touched not just politics but their religious identity as well. They had originally been surprised by the "People of God" theology of Vatican II, but they embraced it, in part because it reinforced their new understanding of themselves as thinking adults who engaged with the world on their terms. They quickly became accustomed to active participation in the Mass and the sacraments because that was what autonomous, "thinking" adults did. No more passive watching of a ritual they did not understand. They made the effort at personalizing their faith, too: if they were going to stay in the church, it would mean something to them. Increasingly, American Catholics accepted the responsibility to think about their faith and to act on it, not just to go through the motions.

This new attitude changed the relationship between lay people and their church, as loyalty and dissent, adherence and disaffection, now coexisted. The faithful remained faithful, but they had also, to some degree, "lapsed." On the one hand, there were many signs of continued loyalty. The rapidity with which they accepted the near-total overhaul of weekly Mass showed that they wanted to make more of an effort to understand their religion. The skyrocketing rate at which they went to Communion showed that they were eager for the most intimate connection to the mysteries of their faith. The impulse to find a personal spiritual director or to express their beliefs in the charismatic movement evinced a desire to be a part of the church as they explored new expressions of it. Even their unorthodox position on the ordination of women demonstrated their loyalty. Most American Catholics wanted women to be ordained, and they remained unpersuaded by the church's arguments against the idea. But they were unwilling to take matters into their own hands by ordaining women in defiance of church regulations. They would wait for some future day when that could happen within the rules of their own church.

On the other hand, the links between Catholics and the institutional church were weakened. A sense of religious self-confidence opened the possibility that lay people might not follow the church's lead if such a course made no sense to them. They would point out that they had not elected their archbishop if he was telling them to do something they did not want to do. Dissent from the church's position on contraception offered the clearest case. The man who rejected the teaching on birth control because, "all of a sudden," it made no sense to him was not the only one to have such an epiphany. The collapse of the practice of confession was the religious expression of that seismic shift.

Confession was no longer meaningful, and so Catholics simply stopped going, even as the church tried—unsuccessfully, it was clear—to breathe new life into the sacrament. Catholics flocked in large numbers to cheer the pope, but they did not always think or do what he commanded once they went back home. Lay people who could say to their priests, "We don't need you anymore" had doubtless misinterpreted the theologians who asserted that people were, in a way, priests too. Still, they had reason to think that they had absorbed a broader spirit of council.

Thus the clarity of the American Catholic world in the years before Vatican II was replaced with both a new vitality and a new volatility. Some people succeeded at forging a new relationship to their faith, while others did not. Some found ways to challenge the positions of the church while still thinking of themselves as Catholics. Sometimes they agreed with their leaders, acting and voting accordingly; sometimes they disagreed, acting and voting accordingly. The sense of autonomy, of "Catholic adulthood," was pervasive, and once the centrality of the laity in the church had been endorsed, there was no predicting where it might lead. Only those on the fringes hoped for a simple return to the world before the council, to the silent Mass in which most participants spent their time looking around and checking their watches. Given the extent of cultural change in American society in the second half of the twentieth century, that well-ordered world probably could not have survived in any case. Once it was gone, there was no bringing it back. These were, without doubt, exciting times to be a Catholic, but they were also times of uncertainty. The institution of the church was challenged, and the consequences of its weakened position became only too apparent as a new century opened.

6

The Church in the Twenty-first Century

The sixth American Catholic in our historical gathering will have to be known only as Maria. Not much more can be said of her, because she has not yet been born. Maria will come into the world in Los Angeles early in the second decade of the new century—2012, let's say—and she will die in her middle eighties in the century's final years. She will be an American Catholic in the church of the twenty-first century.

The church that Maria knows will be different from that of our earlier Catholics, and the differences will be both positive and negative, both welcome and not. When she is born, the Catholic Church will still be the largest single religious denomination in the United States. American Catholics will number more than sixty-five million (between 20 and 25 percent of the entire population), and their ranks will continue to grow. This will be an increasingly diverse population. Hispanic Catholics from various places in Central and South America, as well as the Caribbean—Mexico, El Salvador, Guatemala, the Dominican Republic—will rival the descendants of Europeans from earlier eras. There will be French speakers from Haiti. Catholics from Asia (Vietnam, the Philippines, India) and from Africa (Nigeria,

Ghana) will come, too. These people will bring with them differing styles of devotion and worship, and accommodating these to American Catholic practice will not be without its tensions. Immigrants will also highlight widening social divisions within the Catholic community. Even as white "Anglo" Catholics solidify their place in the middle and upper classes, these "Catholics of color" will reconnect the church to its roots among the poor and the working class.

The institution of the church will also be very different for Maria, her family, and her friends. She will be born in an era when, for the first time in its history, the infrastructure of American Catholicism will be shrinking rather than expanding. The number of priests in the country peaked around 1975 at just under 60,000; by the first years of the twenty-first century, the number had dipped below 30,000 and continued steadily downward. The clergy who remained were "graying" rapidly, the average age rising toward 70. A few young men continued to study for the priesthood, but their number—less than 400 ordained every year—was never sufficient to replace those who died, retired, or left the ministry. The decline among religious sisters was more precipitous. There were almost 180,000 women religious at the close of the Vatican Council, but less than 70,000 by the time of Maria's birth, and they were clustered like the priests in the higher age brackets. Nor was it only church personnel who were disappearing. All across the historic Catholic heartland of the Northeast and Midwest, old parishes closed faster than new ones opened. The great-grandchildren of earlier immigrants now lived in the suburbs, having left behind city churches that were now largely empty on Sunday mornings. In many places this process was painful, as Catholics tried to balance the emotional pull of personal ties to ancestral parishes with the hard-headed realities of keeping the buildings open and in good repair. New parishes started up as the population shifted around the country, especially in the Sun Belt, but the total number of churches was declining even as the population was growing.

More serious than all this, the church into which Maria was born was still feeling the after-effects of a public scandal that was shameful, heart-breaking, maddening, and disastrous, all at the same time. Scattered newspaper reports had described cases of Catholic priests sexually molesting children and adolescents, most of them boys. A report here, a conviction there, these cases were thought at first to be tragic anomalies, but by 2002 the floodgates had opened. Suddenly these crimes were everywhere. The news media relentlessly brought the stories to light, and for a time many Catholics felt as though they were getting punched in the stomach each day as they picked up the morning paper. Worse, the bishops who supervised these priests seemed like accomplices, transferring abusers from church to church without warning their new pastors or parishioners; all too often, the offenses simply began again. The resulting public outcry forced American bishops to adopt new policies for the protection of children, but many Catholics remained skeptical, and women were particularly angry. Would abusive priests have been serially reassigned, they wondered, if there had been any mothers at the table as decisions were made? In the meantime, the church paid millions of dollars in legal settlements to victims and their families, payments that could not undo the harm.

What began as rage over the mishandling of these horrific cases grew quickly into a broader crisis of confidence in the leadership of the institutional church. Many Catholics wondered how they could trust their bishops after such a demonstration that their "shepherds" seemed to care so little for their flocks. If lay people, those who had been told for a generation that they were the church, could expect so little regard for themselves and their children, how could they trust church officials with anything? Financial contributions fell, in some places sharply, and lifelong Catholics began to wonder how to sustain their affiliation with the church. Ad hoc groups of angry parishioners came together to talk about what to do, and virtually overnight they formed a national organization of lay people to press for change. The initial intensity of this movement had passed by the time Maria was born, but the days of unquestioning lay deference to the hierarchy were over. Encouraged in part by the example of the growing ranks of lay people with official roles in parish churches—the number of lay ministers had surpassed the number of priests in the country by the mid-1990s—the laity seemed determined to make real the assertion that they were the church.

When reports of sexual abuse by priests first appeared, the incidents seemed unconnected to one another. Something—partly willful, no doubt, but not entirely so—prevented those touched by such cases from seeing them as part of a larger pattern. Starting about 1985, cases began coming to public attention. A priest in the towns of Esther and Henry, in southwestern Louisiana, admitted to abusing thirty-seven teenagers, some of them during his time as the supervisor of church Boy Scout troops. A year later, two priests in Rhode Island entered pleas of no contest to sexual assault charges and were sentenced to jail. Next came cases in New Jersey, Texas, Washington State, and Pennsylvania. In 1990 Father Bruce Ritter, the highly visible founder of Covenant House, an organization that rescued runaway teenagers from drugs and the pornography industry in New York City, stepped down when accused of sexual misconduct with boys in his care. That these incidents were so widely scattered apparently confirmed their exceptional nature. "We don't want to give the impression that it's a rampant problem for the church, because it's not," a spokesman for the nation's bishops said at the time of the Louisiana case, with apparent sincerity. "But," he added, "even one case is too many."[1]

Soon it was clear that the problem was more serious than the bishops and others allowed, or perhaps knew. The career of Father James Porter showed just how wide and destructive a path abusers might cut. Porter was a priest in Fall River, Massachusetts, an old industrial city, and he had apparently started molesting children from the very beginning of his parish work. Complaints had been handled quietly by the local bishop, who repeatedly transferred him to new assignments. Porter left the priesthood in 1974, married, and moved to Minnesota, where, it was subsequently revealed, he continued to molest children, including his own. Asked later how many victims he might have had, he replied with a chillingly casual, "Oh, jeez, I don't know," finally estimating the number at perhaps one hundred. Lawyers and television reporters in Massachusetts, working with some of his victims, unraveled the painful story in 1992. By then, Porter's crimes were outside the scope of the statute of limitations. Since he had left the jurisdiction for another state, however, the "clock" (as legal experts explained it) had "stopped ticking," and he was still liable to prosecution. He was arrested and returned to Massachusetts, where he pled guilty and was sentenced to a prison psychiatric facility. Failing in health, he was released pending civil commitment in 2004 and died a year later. Meanwhile, an attorney representing some of his victims, now grown to middle age, won an agreement from the Fall River diocese to pay each of them about $100,000 for the pain and suffering Porter had inflicted.[2]

A decade later, a case in Boston made headlines nationwide. In January 2002, the *Boston Globe* began a series of reports detailing both the behavior of Father John Geoghan and church officials' response to it. Geoghan's crimes had involved pre-adolescent boys, often from troubled families, who were susceptible to what had seemed his genuine concern for them. Whenever complaints were registered, Geoghan was removed from his parish and sent to one of several treatment centers that claimed to specialize in such cases. Assured after a long or short stay that he had his problem under control, church officials then assigned him to another parish. These letters of reassignment contained boilerplate language about "dedicated priestly service," phrases that were meaningless in themselves but that later came to seem ironic and sinister. After his exposure, Geoghan was convicted of a relatively minor offense, with more serious charges pending, and sent to jail. In August 2003, he was strangled in his cell by another inmate in what many people saw as a fittingly sordid end to a sordid story. In the meantime, attorneys representing his victims became the public face of the scandal, pressing for the release of diocesan personnel files. A month after Geoghan's murder, church officials agreed to pay nearly $85 million to his victims and those of several other abusive priests; $28 million of that went to the lawyers themselves. Even then, there were more cases still to be heard.[3]

Almost immediately, another Bostonian, Father Paul Shanley, supplanted Geoghan as the most egregious example of priestly abuse. In the 1980s Shanley had been famous as a "street priest," working with runaways, drug addicts, and other troubled youths. Press coverage of his work was uniformly positive, even glowing. The *Boston Globe* praised his attention to what it called "sexual minorities"; the liberal newspaper *National Catholic Reporter* commended his "pioneering ministry" and quoted a mother who thanked "this beautiful man" for helping her reconcile with her estranged son. The *New York Times* quoted another woman as saying that "it hurt thousands of people" when Shanley was reassigned to parish work. Now it was clear that beneath this "pioneering" exterior, he had been an omnivorous sexual predator; he had even been recorded speaking publicly in favor of sex between men and boys. The tolerance that his superiors had had for his unusual ministry, once extolled, was suddenly unforgivable. Shanley was tracked to California, extradited to Massachusetts for trial, convicted, and sent to prison. By then, nearly every dio-

cese in every part of the country had admitted to similar cases in
its jurisdiction. The phrase "cover-up" was applied, and even
though victims usually wanted anonymity as much as church
leaders did, the charge nonetheless rang true.[4]

In defending themselves, church officials insisted that the inci-
dence of sexual abuse by Catholic priests was no higher than in
the population at large. A comprehensive study conducted later
by the John Jay College of Criminal Justice in New York put the
figure at 4 percent of the 110,000 priests who had been in active
ministry in the United States at any time between 1950 and 2002.
No equivalent studies of other populations (school teachers or
psychoanalysts, for example) had ever been done, so there were
no benchmarks against which to compare this rate. Still, a few
smaller-scale studies suggested that the percentage of priest offenders was below average. Incidents of priestly abuse had been
concentrated in the 1970s, falling sharply thereafter, even though
press reports made it seem that they were still occurring. The
worst offenders were clergymen whose seminary formation had
come in the 1950s. In this, Porter (ordained 1960), Shanley (also
1960), and Geoghan (1962) were typical. Conservative commentators blamed the church's failure to squelch dissent over
Humanae Vitae: the "organized and public defiance" of the birth
control encyclical of 1968, one writer insisted, ushered in "a period of 'wink and nudge' . . . with respect to sexuality." If only the
hierarchy had not abandoned the certainties of the past, the argument went, none of this would have happened. That explanation
was too facile, and in any event, both the abusers and the bishops
who mishandled their cases were largely products of the pre–
Vatican II church. Liberal commentators, by contrast, identified
priestly celibacy as the root cause: if priests were allowed to
marry, they maintained, the problem would have been avoided.
This explanation, too, was simplistic, since police statistics indicated that sexual abusers were usually married men. The impact

of the sexual revolution in America in the 1960s was hard to discount, but it was also hard to specify.[5]

The victims of abuse by priests were overwhelmingly (81 percent) boys. Even so, the connection between priestly abuse and homosexuality was unclear. The high rate of male victims stood in sharp contrast to the national pattern, in which abused children were more likely to be girls, many of them (like Porter's daughters) molested by their own fathers. "Pedophilia," a sexual attraction to prepubescent children, became the common way of describing the problem, but psychologists pointed out that the cases most often fell under the rubric of a more unusual term: "ephebophilia," a sexual attraction toward postpubescent and late adolescents. In retrospect, it was painfully obvious how little all the "experts" knew. Alfred Kinsey, for example, the noted sex researcher of the 1950s, had concluded coolly that sexual encounters with an adult were "not likely to do the child any appreciable harm." A more recent study from the 1970s had concurred, declaring the lasting effects of sexual abuse to be "quite mild." How wrong these widely respected judgments were now shown to be. Instead, it was clear how little any of this had been studied and understood by the medical or psychological professionals who had treated offenders, the very people on whom bishops had relied for advice.[6] Still, the public at large concluded that a more fundamental moral failing was involved. Should not clergymen be held to a stricter standard of behavior? As the earlier commentator had noted, even one case was too many.

Catholic lay people responded to these revelations with deep sorrow and white-hot anger. Coming just a few months after the terrorist attacks of September 11, 2001, all this news seemed to confirm the shattering of a once-safe world. Details of the actual sexual abuse were harrowing enough, but worse were the responses of church leaders, whose treatment of the offenders seemed only to have encouraged them to continue. In Boston, outrage focused on Cardinal Bernard Law, the archbishop there since 1984. His Masses were dogged by protestors. One young woman outside his cathedral carried a handmade sign that read: "Law"—parishioners did not usually address their archbishop abruptly by his last name—"*You* are as *guilty* as the priests that did it!" Pressure built on Law throughout the Geoghan case, and he finally resigned. Other prelates were also implicated. Two successive bishops of Palm Beach, Florida, resigned (one in 1998, the next in 2002) after revelations that they themselves had abused seminarians earlier in their careers. The bishop of Springfield, in western Massachusetts, stepped down for the same reason in 2004; he was later indicted but not prosecuted (the statute of limitations having expired), and he subsequently disappeared. The settlements paid to victims around the country mounted to the hundreds of millions of dollars: $12 million for the diocese of Bridgeport, Connecticut; $25 million in Louisville, Kentucky; $5 million in Orange County, California; and on and on. The church in Los Angeles set the record in July 2007, paying 500 victims $660 million on top of the $114 million it had previously paid. In Tucson, Arizona ($75 million), Portland, Oregon ($75 million), and Spokane, Washington ($48 million), the judgments led dioceses to seek the protection of the bankruptcy court, and other dioceses considered doing the same.[7] At one point, the scandal seemed unlikely ever to stop spreading.

In the face of growing lay anger, the nation's Catholic bishops met in Dallas, Texas, in June 2002 to draft a new policy for handling cases of sexual abuse by priests. Their usually routine annual meeting was highly charged. It began with a day-long session in which four victims (three men and one woman) told their stories, focusing on the long train of psychological and other problems their abuse had initiated. Next, the bishops were addressed by Margaret O'Brien Steinfels, the editor of *Commonweal* magazine, and Scott Appleby, a history professor from the University of Notre Dame. Neither one minced any words. The scandal, Steinfels said pointedly, showed lay people "how essentially powerless they are," but it had also altered the relationship between the hierarchy and the laity, perhaps forever. "The dam has broken," she went on; "a reservoir of trust has run dry." Appleby took the discussion beyond the familiar liberal-conservative divide. "Catholics on the right, and the left, and in the 'deep middle,'" he said, "all are in basic agreement as to the causes of this scandal: a betrayal of fidelity enabled by the arrogance that comes with unchecked power." Bishops were not used to being talked to this way, and it had some effect. "We've never heard anything like this before," the bishop of Paterson, New Jersey, told a reporter after the session. "It's very strong." The meeting produced a "Charter for the Protection of Children and Young People," which established a so-called zero-tolerance policy. One credible accusation against a priest (past, present, or future) was sufficient to suspend him from his duties pending investigation; one proved allegation was sufficient to remove him permanently from the priesthood.[8] Some commentators criticized the charter on various grounds—did it come too late? did it deflect responsibility from bishops to priests?—but the hierarchy at least recognized that things had to change.

Across the country, lay people tried to make sense of the crisis, which became the topic of conversation whenever Catholics met one another at parish school functions or informal gatherings over coffee after Sunday Mass. Catholics in the greater Boston area, close to the epicenter of the scandal, took more concerted action. A group of parishioners in Saint John the Evangelist parish in Wellesley, a prosperous Boston suburb, began meeting on Monday evenings to commiserate over the state of their church. "We started as a group of heartbroken people who needed to talk," one participant said, but these were people who were prepared to do more than talk. Many were distinguished in their own professional fields, the kind of "thinking" and "adult" Catholics the Vatican II church had produced. One organizer was a university management professor; another was a doctor who had shared the Nobel Prize in 1985 for his work with an organization called International Physicians for the Prevention of Nuclear War. The Monday meetings attracted a handful of parishioners at first, but soon there were hundreds crowding the church basement every week. Their pastor sometimes attended, but the meetings were entirely theirs. Hymn-singing and prayer were followed by wide-ranging discussion, in which people first expressed their sorrow and anger and then proposed various courses of action. "We are trying to save the hierarchy from itself," one woman said. Early on, the group adopted the name Voice of the Faithful (VOTF), and it hit upon a simple slogan: "Keep the Faith; Change the Church."[9]

Members of VOTF also sought a more visible way to express their concerns and to work for change. Accordingly, they organized a national convention to respond to the crisis. They secured a convention center in Boston and issued a call for participants from around the country. On a Saturday in July 2002, four thousand Catholics from around the country gathered in Boston for a day-long meeting. Most were active in their own parishes, the sort of people churches relied on for volunteers and lay ministries. There was prayer, followed by wrenching personal accounts from abuse victims. Panel discussions explored various dimensions of the crisis. As an organization, VOTF committed itself to three goals: to support victims of abuse; to support "priests of integrity" (non-abusers, sometimes judged guilty by association, simply because they were priests); and to "shape structural change within the Catholic Church" so as to prevent such a scandal in the future. Speakers alluded to their location, noting that it had been the site of an earlier revolution. "The people of Boston know what to do about absolute power," one speaker said; "they showed the world 200 years ago." Most, however, were not rebellious. "I'm a moderate," one participant, a housewife, said. "I'm not extreme. I think our power is in the fact that our voices are from the parishes . . . They will have to listen to us," she concluded.[10]

VOTF grew to impressive proportions, eventually claiming a national membership of 30,000 and spawning several local chapters around the country. Even so, it quickly hit its limits as a unifying organization for the laity. The Boston meeting, one newspaper columnist observed, had been full of "the gray-haired and sensibly shod, of middle-aged and older white, suburban, bred-in-the-bone Catholics from well-heeled parishes." It remained virtually impossible to attract recent immigrants or younger Catholics, whose institutional connections to the church were looser than those of their parents. Moreover, most participants recognized how difficult it would be to achieve "structural change" in the church. The majority probably favored, for example, the ordination of women—that and similar issues were deliberately kept off the agenda for fear of losing focus—but they knew that decisions on such questions would come from Rome, and they also knew that change was unlikely. Lay people were thus left with little practical recourse. They pledged to direct their charitable contributions to a separate fund rather than to diocesan fundraising campaigns, thereby setting off an unseemly squabble with church officials, who announced that they would not accept any donations unless they came through official channels. This form of protest, too, proved difficult to sustain. One speaker at the July assembly wrote two weeks later that, on reflection, he was not sure whether he had been at a baptism or a wake, whether the convention had represented the beginning of something or the end.[11]

Perhaps most striking, however, was the decision that most Catholics made not to abandon the church in the aftermath of the scandal. There was little latter-day "leakage." In fact, many Catholics strengthened their ties to their own local parish. In one survey taken in 2004, 78 percent of active Catholics said that the scandal had had no effect on their church attendance, and another 7 percent said that they were actually going to Mass more than they once had. Parishioners may have come to distrust their bishop, but they liked their local pastor. They were deeply angry at the hierarchy, but they still wanted the sacraments in their own parish church. More than 80 percent of them said that being Catholic remained important to them, and almost as many insisted that they could not imagine being anything else. The woman who wanted to "save the hierarchy from itself" was not alone in distinguishing between the church and its leaders. "We love our church and want to do what is right for it," said another VOTF participant, identifying herself as one of the many people "who are faithfully in those pews every week." Still another agreed: lay people might be uncertain about exactly what to do next, but "there is a desire . . . to remain Catholic," he said.[12] The dynamic that held them in tension with the institutional church, a dynamic that had shifted significantly in the aftermath of Vatican II, kept them in the church. In spite of everything, it was their church.

More structural problems compounded the crisis. In many cities, the Catholic infrastructure of local parishes and schools, inherited from earlier eras, no longer fit the demographics of church membership. Older ethnic enclaves broke down and dispersed, and new ethnic populations moved into different city neighborhoods. The facilities and services of the church were not always available where they were most needed. The decline in personnel made matters worse. In Boston in 2002, for example, the year the Geoghan case broke, eighteen diocesan priests retired from active ministry and another twenty-five died; only five new priests were ordained to take their places. Two years later, there were thirty-six retirements or deaths and only seven ordinations.

In some dioceses there were years with no new priests at all. Such net losses (which did not include those suspended for suspected sexual abuse) could not be sustained for very much longer without reconsidering how to deploy limited resources. Everywhere, there were churches and schools in places where they were not needed, fewer of them where they were needed, and not enough priests and sisters to go around.[13] For the first time in American Catholic history, contraction rather than expansion was the watchword.

Churches in Pittsburgh offer a case study of this process. The seventy-five parishes in the city in 1990 had been reduced to forty-one by 2000, a drop of nearly half. Some churches were closed outright, while others were combined into an entirely new parish. In the East End, for example, Holy Rosary (established 1893), Corpus Christi (1903), and Mother of Good Counsel (1908) were joined to form Saint Charles Lwanga parish. Mass was said in each of the three church buildings, requiring the pastor and two assistants to travel among them, though they all lived in the rectory at Holy Rosary. The choice of the new name was significant. Instead of retaining one of the three original names, the parish was now placed under the patronage of a nineteenth-century Christian convert in Uganda who had been martyred for his faith, an acknowledgment of the African immigrants who were moving into Pittsburgh. Other boundary lines, once considered impermeable, were also blurred. In the Strip District, a formerly Irish parish (the oldest one in the city, dating from 1808) and a formerly Polish parish from the 1870s were brought together, and the parish was named Saint Patrick–Saint Stanislaus Kostka, the two ethnicities separated only by a hyphen. Consolidations of this kind meant that Mass was still available, but less readily than before. The parishes in Pittsburgh had offered Mass 278 times every Saturday and Sunday in 1990, but only 164 times each weekend in 2000, a reduction of 40 percent.[14]

However necessary it might have been, the closing of churches with which parishioners and their families had been associated, sometimes for generations, was easier to do on paper than in reality. Lay Catholics had strong bonds to the physical spaces in which their religious lives had been lived, and parishioners often reacted sharply when told that they would have to find a new spiritual home. The emptying of the "reservoir of trust" that came with the sexual abuse scandal made lay people suspicious of their bishops' motives. Were churches being closed and sold, many wondered, to raise money to pay the financial settlements for sexual abuse cases? Diocesan officials insisted that this was not the case, but their assurances were not always convincing. That the official term in canon law for closing a parish was "suppression" exacerbated the tension. By using that word, bishops seemed once again to demonstrate a cold disregard for the feelings of lay people mourning the loss of the church where Grandma had been married.

Sometimes lay people responded with organized resistance, and once again Boston offered the most dramatic cases. Cardinal Law's successor as archbishop, Cardinal Sean O'Malley, won praise in 2003 for agreeing to a financial settlement with abuse victims, but public opinion turned against him a year later when he announced a plan to close as many as 70 of the 350 parishes in the city and surrounding suburbs. Catholics whose churches were on the list reacted angrily, both at the decision itself and at the brusque speed with which it had come. Parishioners at Saint Albert the Great parish in Weymouth, a working-class town south of Boston, took drastic action by occupying their church, changing the locks, and staging a round-the-clock vigil while they appealed its closing. "My Parish, My Faith, My Family," said a hand-lettered banner strung over the door. "Let me keep them all!" Soon, the people in 7 other parishes in the metropolitan area had organized sit-ins in their churches. They conducted daily, priestless prayer services, and sympathetic priests periodically brought them Communion, though they were prohibited from saying Mass for the protestors. Saint Albert's eventually won a reprieve and remained open, but some of the other take-overs are still under way at this writing, three years later.[15]

There were other signs of the broken dam of trust. In tony Oyster Bay, New York, parishioners were indignant at the appointment of a new pastor for Saint Dominic's Church in the spring of 2004. Their previous pastor had been removed following charges of sexual contact with students as a high school chaplain thirty years before. (This was the "zero-tolerance" policy in action.) The new pastor, Father John Alesandro, had been an official in the bishop's office, where his responsibilities had included investigating such charges. He had seemed lenient on abusers, however, so four hundred people from the parish assembled in a nearby Presbyterian church—they had been denied use of both their own church hall and the local town hall—to express their lack of confidence in him. "The moral authority of our pastor has been severely compromised," Geoffrey Boisi, an investment banker and philanthropist, told his fellow parishioners. After questioning Alesandro and other officials about the matter, Boisi and others concluded that "their answers were simply not credible . . . The trust and moral authority of our ecclesial chain of command was irreparably broken." Alesandro kept his position, but the parish remained deeply divided between his opponents and his defenders.

In another case, fifty seniors at a Catholic high school for girls in Manchester, New Hampshire, signed a petition asking the local bishop not to attend their graduation ceremony. He had been an official in Boston at the time of the Geoghan case and had not, the students believed, taken sufficiently decisive action. He came to graduation anyway, but the point had been made. When even high school students were signing petitions—"I feel like I can't look up to him as a leader," one of them said—the extent of the estrangement between bishops and laity was clear.[16]

Disaffection of this kind was fueled by a growing sense among the laity that the clergy, especially bishops, too often thought of themselves as separate from, and even above, ordinary believers. Scott Appleby had sounded this note at the Dallas meeting. "The root of the problem," he told the assembled hierarchs, "is the lack of accountability on the part of the bishops . . . The lack of accountability, in turn, was fostered by a closed clerical culture that infects the priesthood." It was this "closed clerical culture" that had apparently encouraged church administrators to be more solicitous toward an abusive fellow priest than toward his victims. An arrogant, even if unconscious, clericalism, another writer said, was "the original sin" of the sexual abuse and attendant dramas. Church leaders denied that such attitudes existed, but there was evidence for them nonetheless. One seminary director, recalling his own student days, told of attending an ordination ceremony in the late 1960s. As each newly ordained priest came forward, the presiding bishop greeted him heartily with the words "Welcome to the club!" The very existence of that club now seemed to be the problem. Women were particularly sensitive about this issue, since they had only recently been told yet again that they were not members of the club and never could be. More generally, when priests like Porter and Geoghan were stripped of their priestly role, the church's own language betrayed it. The process was popularly known as "defrocking," but in church law it was called being "reduced to the lay state." Only by rejecting the idea that lay people were somehow "reduced" could real progress be made.[17]

The laity demanded greater accountability in order to overcome this clericalism. Many dioceses published annual financial reports, and this practice was fine as far as it went. The demand now, however, was for a broader kind of accountability. "Well-governed institutions ensure full disclosure of information," wrote Mary Jo Bane, a professor at Harvard's Kennedy School of Government and a self-described "lector, parish council member, and regular contributor" at her local church. Such organizations "institutionalize checks and balances on the exercise of power, and establish independent boards to actively advise and participate in choosing the chief executive officer." The Catholic Church in America, she concluded, had none of these safeguards, and one of them (lay participation in choosing leadership) was probably out of the question. But "the culture of secrecy and of excessive deference to clerical and episcopal privilege" could not continue. Other groups joined VOTF in demanding "structural change." One organization calling itself simply "Bishop-Accountability" created a website on which it posted copies of documents from diocesan files showing how abusive priests had been treated. "When there is no genuine effort to build accountability and transparency into diocesan and parish governance," Margaret Steinfels had told the bishops in Dallas, "what conclusion can be drawn except that you don't trust us?"[18] That situation had to change.

Not since the trustee disputes of the early nineteenth century had there been such open antagonism between lay Catholics and church officials. But whereas the trustee fights had been localized, these early twenty-first-century disputes were widespread. The sexual abuse scandal had been traumatic enough on its own terms, and had it occurred amid relative stability for the church, its impact would still have been far-reaching. Coming as it did, however, at the end of nearly half a century of social and religious change, the scandal only served to widen the rift between the laity and the church leadership. Lay Catholics considered themselves thinking adults, but they thought the church was not treating them as such. That an abusive priest could be reassigned to their parish was bad enough; that this might happen without their being told of the danger seemed condescending, insulting, contemptuous, or all three. Once again, women felt especially betrayed. They were told to accept a limited role in the church, but how could that make sense when men had so clearly, and perhaps so callously, failed to protect the church's most vulnerable members? The laity would not leave the church: "it's ours as much as theirs," many insisted. But the very clarity of the division into "us" and "them" only underlined how deep the discontent ran. Structural change might be long in coming or it might never come, but the laity, traditionally deferential to the clergy, would never be quite so docile again.

In Maria's church in the twenty-first century, the ongoing diversification of lay people will present a subtler but more pervasive challenge than that of the sexual abuse crisis. Once, it had been possible to think of the "immigration chapter" in American history as closed, but a new chapter had begun with adoption of the Immigration Reform Act of 1965, which opened the gates once again. Many immigrants from countries outside Europe brought a strong Catholic identity with them. This identity, like that of earlier Catholic groups, was inevitably inflected by ethnicity. New ethnic groups replaced older ones on the ships—now, more likely, the airplanes—of passage. Religion was intimately connected to their other sources of identity: family, food, and culture. If it had ever ceased to be one, the Catholic Church in the twenty-first century had become an immigrant church once again.

The bonds of language were particularly strong for newer immigrants. The church was sympathetic to their desire to retain their mother tongue and even provided language training for non–native-speaking priests. This was especially important because weekly Mass and the other sacraments now had to be offered, not in Latin, but in a language the congregation could understand; not to do so risked driving them to other churches. As a result, many Catholic parishes became polyglot. In Boston in the first years of the new century, for example, the overwhelming majority (80 percent) of the weekend liturgies were said in English, but in some churches the service was conducted in Mandarin, Cantonese, Creole, Portuguese, Spanish, or African languages. In Houston the pattern was even more visible. While English remained the predominant language, almost one-quarter of the 378 Masses in the city every weekend were in Spanish, and another 23 of them were in Vietnamese. Several parishes offered all three languages: Saint Christopher's, in the southeast corner of the city, had five Masses in English, two in Spanish, one in Vietnamese, and some bilingual services as well.[19] By meeting new linguistic demands, parishes hoped to reinforce the connections between Catholic immigrants and their church.

Hispanics were the largest and most visible group amid the renewed ethnic variety. "Hispanic" is a catch-all category, used loosely to designate those whose first language is Spanish, and it can obscure as much as it enlightens. Hispanics are multiform: Mexicans in California, Texas, and the Southwest, with significant numbers also in midwestern cities such as Chicago; Cubans in Florida; Puerto Ricans and Dominicans in New York; Central Americans, particularly Guatemalans, in the Northeast and elsewhere. Their collective impact on the church is beyond question. In the year 2000, the percentage of the American Catholic population identifying itself as Hispanic was variously reported at between 16 and 20 percent, and all observers agreed that it had been rising for decades. Although some Hispanics were converting to various forms of evangelical Protestantism, the Hispanic presence within Catholicism remained undiminished. In three-quarters of all American parishes where at least one weekly Mass was celebrated in a language other than English, that language was Spanish. Lay Hispanics went to Mass at about the same rate as Anglos, and nearly one-quarter of all enrollments in lay ministry training programs came from the Spanish-speaking

community. Moreover, this population was growing rapidly. Hispanic parishes nationwide reported an average of four baptisms
for every funeral: those parishes were getting bigger, and they
were getting younger.[20]

The experience of Hispanic Catholicism was diverse. Mexicans, for example, had a long historic presence in Texas, with immigration depending largely on political and economic developments in Mexico itself. In the past, these Catholics had often
been disparaged by the Anglo priests who served them. "Everyone has the idea that when it comes to deep faith, nobody can
beat the Mexican people," a priest in McAllen, Texas, had written
in the 1940s, "but it's not true . . . Most of these people don't even
begin to measure up to my idea of what faith should be." National agencies supporting Catholic missionaries had similar attitudes. In the half century before 1950, they consistently gave
greater support to English-speaking parishes than to those where
Spanish was the common tongue: English-language churches in
and around Galveston got four times as much financial backing
as Spanish-language parishes. Only slowly did things improve. A
later pastor in McAllen recorded a catalog of parishioners that included many poor farm workers, but there was also a prominent
businessman who was an elected city official, a woman whose
philanthropy was unparalleled, and others on whom the church
depended.[21]

In California, the Mexican Catholic presence was of equally
long standing, its growth quickening in the decades after the Second World War. Itinerant farm workers followed annual crop cycles from the Imperial Valley in the winter up to Fresno in the
fall. The needs, religious and otherwise, of this migrant population were many, and clergy and laity responded. One lay man in
particular helped bring the plight of such workers to national attention. Cesar Chavez had been born in Arizona and moved as a
child with his family to California to work in the fields. In 1962

he founded a union, eventually called the United Farm Workers (UFW), and he led the effort to secure better wages and the right to collective bargaining. Consciously drawing on Catholic social teachings, Chavez embraced nonviolence as a tactic, and many of his marches and demonstrations were overtly religious, resembling devotional processions as much as labor rallies. On one occasion, after violence had disrupted a UFW event, he went on a month-long fast as a public act of penance, concluding it with a Mass outside the town of Delano. "What do we want the church to do?" Chavez had asked at one rally. "We don't ask for bigger churches or fine gifts. We ask for its presence with us, beside [us], as Christ among us." Though he faced opposition from growers and their allies, he won broad support. A nationwide boycott of nonunion grapes, led by the UFW, was encouraged by parishes in California and around the country, and his marches were joined by priests, nuns, and lay people, following models they had learned in the civil rights movement. Until ill health slowed him in the 1980s, Chavez, who died in 1993, almost single-handedly brought a new awareness of the Hispanic presence to Catholics nationwide.[22]

Hispanic groups in other parts of the country usually represented smaller proportions of the local population, but they, too, affected the structure of American Catholicism. The church had traditionally been weak on the island of Cuba, for example, but after Fidel Castro came to power in 1959, tens of thousands of Cubans fled the short distance to Florida. The Cuban population of Dade County, surrounding Miami, grew more than eighteenfold in the three decades after Castro's takeover. Precisely because these refugees were so vigorously anti-communist, they tended to be identified with the church more than earlier Cuban immigrants were: there was, one study concluded, a "virtual evacuation" of active Catholics from the island. Church-related institutions came with them. Belen Jesuit Prep, an old secondary school (the most famous graduate of which was Castro himself), moved to Miami as early as 1961. Cubans also established new institutions in their new home, most notably an enormous shrine to Our Lady of Charity, who was taken as a special patron during what they hoped would be a temporary exile. They held their first Spanish-speaking cursillo in 1962, well before that movement took hold among other American Catholics. In subsequent decades, Guatemalans, Nicaraguans, and Salvadorans replayed the Cuban experience, leaving behind civil strife and economic hardship for relative security in the United States. Puerto Ricans had a sizable presence in New York City by the end of the Second World War; though they, as U.S. citizens, were more likely than others to travel back and forth from the city to their home island, they carried their religious sensibilities with them as they moved.[23]

Hispanic devotional practice added variety to American Catholicism. Elements of folk religion shot through the Hispanic spiritual imagination, expressed, for example, in the maintenance of home altars in honor of particular saints. "In nearly all Catholic homes, of whatever economic class," a Mexican-American woman recalled of her childhood, there was "the tiny shrine in a corner of the bedroom." In a small town in South Texas, a woman found the fragment of a mosaic depiction of Mary, left over from a long-abandoned church, brought it home, and surrounded it with candles and flowers. Her neighbors came in regularly to pray before the shrine, to leave written prayer requests or photographs of sons in the armed forces. In the 1980s, a woman in Phoenix, Arizona, reported seeing apparitions of the Virgin and set up a shrine in her backyard. This attracted weekly rosary devotions and prayer meetings, and the shrine eventually grew into a free-standing chapel with its own community action agency to address issues of housing and crime. Puerto Rican street festivals in honor of San Juan, the patron saint of the island, became annual public events in New York City, while in Chicago, beginning in the 1970s, Mexican-American Catholics staged a recreation of the Way of the Cross, reenacting Jesus' sufferings on his way to crucifixion and death. These graphic presentations, held every year on Good Friday, made their way through the streets of the Pilsen neighborhood of the city, once a bastion of the Polish Catholic community. Thus had one ethnic group supplanted another.[24]

By far the most widespread Hispanic devotion was that of Mexican-Americans to Our Lady of Guadalupe. The tradition derived from the reported appearance of the Virgin Mary to an Indian named Juan Diego, in a village near Mexico City in 1531. She performed miracles and left behind an image of herself, imprinted on the inside of the young man's cloak. That she spoke to him in Nahuatl, the native language, and had the dark features of a Mestiza made her a special defender of the *dignidad* (dignity) of the native and mixed population. When Pope John Paul II formally canonized Juan Diego as a saint in July 2002, his action was seen as a validation of Mexicans' historical and spiritual experience. Images of Our Lady of Guadalupe and shrines to her were kept in homes, and public celebrations began everywhere a small immigrant population was established. At San Fernando Cathedral in San Antonio, Texas, for example, the annual December celebration begins with an evening "serenade" by the thousands jamming the cathedral, after which young people in Aztec costumes dance before her image. Devotees stream forward to kneel, light candles, and say their own prayers. The next morning brings a procession with more singing, followed by a Mass; at another Mass that evening children reenact the original appearance to Juan Diego. Even in private, Guadalupe images are kept in homes, carried as medals, and imprinted on everything from candles to small statues on car dashboards for protection on the road.[25]

Devotions such as this one are reviving the kinds of religious practices that had characterized earlier immigrant groups. The particulars of the devotions and their forms of expression are different in the church of the twentieth century, but the intimate connection they encourage between Catholics and the larger spiritual world of their faith is much the same. A festival may honor the Latin American Lady of Guadalupe rather than the Italian Lady of Mount Carmel, whose festa was once celebrated in New York's Harlem, but the two have much in common. Both linked ordinary believers to heavenly beings, whose powers were brought to bear on immediate concerns in this world. Earlier generations of Irish, Italian, and Polish Catholics sought the help of Saint Jude in curing disease or protecting soldier-sons in battle; millions of Hispanic Catholics seek the Mestiza Virgin's aid with equally broad and no less compelling concerns. "I identify with her as a mother who always believes her children can do it," said one woman in San Antonio, herself of Puerto Rican descent but a "convert" to Guadalupe's powerful love for people who were "hers."[26]

Just as important, at a time when many of these vivid practices have died out among the descendants of earlier immigrants, Hispanics are sustaining them as part of the American Catholic devotional universe. White, suburbanized Catholics may have experienced a "piety void" in the aftermath of Vatican II, and many of them welcomed the abandonment of old ways. "Thank goodness we've outgrown all that nonsense," one woman had written sharply in 1965. For the most part, Catholics like her stopped saying the rosary, setting up home shrines, or marching through the streets in honor of the saints. In the same way, Father Peyton's Family Rosary Crusade declined rapidly in the aftermath of the Vatican Council, and it had all but disappeared by the 1970s, though Peyton himself lived until 1992. Saying the rosary remained significant to many Hispanic Catholics, however, and the devotion was not confined merely to the elderly: one study found that 70 percent of Hispanic women in their twenties and thirties and 58 percent of Hispanic men in the same age range said the rosary regularly. In some places, women wore the rosary as a necklace, and young Hispanic men (39 percent of them) had had their cars blessed before using them. Both actions would probably have been unthinkable to those who had attended the VOTF convention in 2002.[27] White Catholics, their immigrant ancestors now remote, may have moved on from such practices, but Hispanic Catholics demonstrated that these devotions still had the power to speak to individual spiritual needs.

Thus the face of the American Catholic people continues to change—literally so. Hispanic, Asian, and African faces have given the church of the twenty-first century a new social complexity. The American Catholic Church has become a church of the middle class, even the upper-middle class, and a church of the poor and the working class, all at the same time. In its earlier immigrant eras, it was a church mostly of the "bottom," without much representation at the "top" of society. During its present era, it is both. There is danger in this. Catholicism in America may move toward becoming two churches, or perhaps three: one for the well-off and largely white; one for working-class "white ethnics"; and a third for poorer people of color. Such an outcome, however, can be avoided. Catholicism has always been, in the often-cited words of James Joyce, a matter of "here comes everybody." The parishioners at Saint Christopher's in Houston who attend the Sunday 10:30 English Mass, or the noon Spanish Mass, or the 4:00 Vietnamese Mass may all worship separately, but they nonetheless encounter one another at many church functions. Some of them are more openly critical of church leadership, others more deferential, but they are learning to accommodate and value one another. The parishioners of Saint Dominic's in Oyster Bay will have to remember that they are part of the same church as the Guadalupan devotees at San Fernando in San Antonio. Participants in the Way of the Cross processions in Chicago will have to find ways to sustain faith commitments as they themselves—and surely their children and grandchildren—move up the ladders of success and out of the Pilsen neighborhood, just as earlier generations of Polish Catholics had done. Sustaining their Catholic identity is the task ahead for all of them.

The twenty-first century will see American Catholics continue their ambivalent relationship to the papacy. The pattern of lay people as simultaneously loyal and independent was firmly in place by the time of the sexual abuse scandal, and it was further exaggerated by the events of that crisis. As with their insistence on staying in the church despite all that had happened, they would give up neither their attachment to the pope nor their willingness sometimes to chart a course different from his. The enduring tension was particularly evident in three areas: the accountability of the hierarchy, expressed in the way the bishops involved in the scandal had been chosen for office; the nature of Catholic colleges and universities; and the emergence of a group of younger priests who were often more conservative than their parishioners.

When the sexual abuse scandal hit, Pope John Paul II was at first a largely absent player. He was already eighty-two years old, having by then served as pope longer than only a handful of his predecessors, and he was visibly slowed by age and Parkinson's disease. Nothing comparable to the American scandal had ever come before him, and officials in Rome were limited in what they could do in response. Each bishop had charge of his own diocese, with only general direction from the church's center. In April 2002, however, the pope summoned the twelve American cardinals to the Vatican, even as some of them were embroiled in the crisis. The pontiff opened the meeting with strong words. "There is no place in the priesthood and religious life for those who would harm the young," he said, calling abuse "by every standard wrong" and "rightly considered a crime by society." It was also, he added, pointing out a dimension often overlooked amid the lurid details and court proceedings, "an appalling sin." John Paul recognized the broader damage the scandal was causing: "because of the great harm done by some priests," he noted, "the church herself is viewed with distrust, and many are offended at the way in which the church's leaders are perceived to have acted." In follow-up meetings with other officials, the Americans hammered out the details of the zero-tolerance policy that would be adopted at their meeting in Dallas two months later. For his part, John Paul apologized to the victims of abuse, both then and again at a World Youth Day in Toronto, Canada, that July.[28]

The pope was right that the scandal had undercut the confidence of the laity in their bishops, but the distance between lay people and the hierarchy had already been widened during John Paul's tenure by the way bishops were selected. The problem was not so much the lack of direct lay involvement in the process; not since ancient times had lay people had an explicit voice in choosing bishops. Saint Ambrose was famously made the bishop of Milan in 374 by popular acclamation—he had not even been baptized yet—but more recently the power of appointment had been concentrated increasingly in the Vatican. Even so, in the nineteenth century, diocesan bishops in America were mostly priests who had risen up through the ranks of the clergy in the locality they were designated to lead. Once a given diocese was sufficiently well established as something more than an uncertain missionary endeavor, a priest who had served as pastor of one of its larger parishes usually became its bishop. Virtually every diocese had its own succession of "local boys" who "made good" by assuming leadership, one after another, of the Catholics in their jurisdiction.[29]

By the end of the twentieth century, however, these local connections had been progressively severed. During the papacy of John Paul II, bishops were selected for their undeviating loyalty to Roman policy (often with special regard to contraception), and a new bishop might know little or nothing of the people he was supposed to lead. Moreover, bishops were moved repeatedly from one place to another and were often dropped into situations where they had little local knowledge. Just as quickly, they might be reassigned somewhere else. Bernard Law, for example, had been a bishop in rural southern Missouri before he was made archbishop of Boston in 1984. Sean O'Malley, his successor there, had had an even more peripatetic career: he had previously served stints as the bishop of St. Thomas in the Virgin Islands, then of Fall River, Massachusetts, and then of Palm Beach, Florida, all in less than two decades. Parishioners might see a succession of bishops come and go before they ever got to know any of them, and the Catholics of Palm Beach were perhaps the best (or worst) example. The diocese there had been established in 1984, and by the time of the scandal eighteen years later it had had five bishops, not one of them a native. Catholics in Memphis had the same experience. Their diocese had been founded in 1971, and they had four bishops between then and the end of the century. The first one had come from Richmond, Virginia; the next came from Baltimore and eventually moved on to Denver and then to a position at the Vatican; the next came from a monastery in Indiana and soon went back to Indianapolis; the last was at least a nearer neighbor (from Natchez) and had come by way of St. Louis.[30]

The inevitable effect of this transience was to disconnect leaders from the very places where they were expected to be effective. It virtually guaranteed that bishops would have few friends, whether clergy or laity, on whom they could rely for advice, assistance, or frank talk in times of trouble. If there were any lay people in their dioceses who had known them or their families, any local priests who had served in parishes with them, it was purely accidental. The system encouraged careerism and the formation of its own "club," with bishops in smaller dioceses looking to advance to supposedly more important places. To be sure, organizations of all sorts sometimes need a leader from the outside. Here, however, was a system with nothing but outsiders, and the result was a subversion of the bishops' own effectiveness; they were left adrift, uncertain of where to turn for help. It was a system that isolated lay people from their bishops by design: the two were largely strangers to each other. Bad enough under normal circumstances, this inherent alienation only worsened under the pressure of public scandal.[31] Lingering unease at this structural problem—a kind of constitutional crisis—further attenuated the connection between lay people and the institutional church.

Another source of tension between the American laity and the papacy was a lingering conflict over Catholic colleges and universities. American Catholics had built the largest and most successful system of private higher education anywhere in the world, enrolling three-quarters of a million students. Not all those students were Catholics, but the colleges were nonetheless imbued with religious values from the Catholic tradition. Critics worried, however, that the Catholic identity of these institutions was being eroded or, worse, actively squandered. Most of the colleges had been founded by religious orders of men and women, and as the numbers of priests, brothers, and sisters declined, their recognizably Catholic dimensions were at risk. Georgetown University in Washington, D.C., the oldest Catholic college in the country, dating from 1789 and always headed by a priest of the Jesuit order, appointed a lay man as its president in 2001. Other schools already had lay presidents, and almost all were governed by independent boards of trustees with mostly lay membership. This was not in itself a bad thing, but the specter of secularization, a process that had come relentlessly to such formerly Protestant universities as Harvard and Princeton, was nonetheless haunting. Would Catholic universities follow the same path?[32]

In an attempt to reinforce the Catholic dimension of these

schools, Pope John Paul had published a document in 1990 known
by its opening Latin phrase, *"Ex Corde Ecclesiae"*—the work of
Catholic universities ought to proceed "from the heart of the
church." Special attention was focused on theology and religious
studies departments (the name varied from school to school).
Too many colleges, one angry critic chided, had "abandon[ed]
their calling to be ministries of the Catholic Church" in favor of
"a viewpoint that accorded no authority to Catholic doctrine." A
form of "truth in advertising" was at stake, others said: a class in
Catholic theology ought to study official Catholic theology, not
something else. American bishops had proposed general guidelines that addressed these concerns, but the Vatican insisted on
something more "juridical," an unfamiliar word to most Catholics. Accordingly, in 1999 the nation's bishops drafted and Rome
approved a system whereby Catholic faculty members who
taught Catholic theology would have to apply for and receive a
"mandate" from the local bishop in order to continue doing so.
Bishops were the principal teachers in the church, the reasoning
went, and they should thus be in a position to certify, by means
of this license, the orthodoxy of Catholic colleges in their dioceses. Individual faculty members were required to apply for their
mandate, though no data were ever compiled to indicate how
many of them actually did so.[33]

Faculty and school administrators reacted sharply to this idea.
It represented a grave challenge to "two fundamental characteristics of U.S. Catholic universities, autonomy and academic freedom," according to a statement written jointly by the president of the University of Notre Dame and the former president
of Boston College. Most Catholic colleges, they pointed out,
were independent corporate entities, chartered by their respective
states and unconnected to the local diocese; thus bishops had no
legal authority to intervene in their management. Furthermore,
the prospect that faculty members might have to submit their

credentials or their course outlines to the bishop's office for scrutiny seemed too much like a "loyalty oath." At least one bishop agreed, worrying that the system would "destroy the productive dialogue between bishops and university officials" already under way. Universities were not seminaries, a lay theologian on the faculty of Fairfield University, a Jesuit school in Connecticut, pointed out. As such, they had responsibility not for the doctrinal instruction of the catechism class but rather for the development in students of "habits of critical thinking" that took place "with an expressed commitment to the Catholic vision." Worse yet, another lay man said, the controversy itself suggested that "no issue was too small for the Vatican to pronounce on" and that American bishops were too willing to be the mere agents of a policy made in Rome.[34]

Public debate continued, often along the lines of the now-familiar liberal-conservative divide in the church. In the end, however, the sexual abuse scandal, which came to light just after the *Ex Corde* procedures were put into place, rendered the whole question moot. As a practical matter, bishops were too preoccupied by the crisis to worry about what a professor might be saying in a classroom down the street. Responsibility for acquiring the mandate rested with the theologians themselves, and the document spelled out no consequences if they neglected to do so. Thus a bishop had to go looking for trouble to pressure those who had not applied, and bishops were in enough trouble as it was. At the same time, the moral failings of the hierarchy in not removing abusive priests seemed to undermine their right to examine or approve the teaching of others. Criticized for their actions and inactions in dealing with sexual abuse, bishops were seen as unlikely sources of moral authority. What had been intended as an effort to shore up the hierarchy's oversight of Catholic life became instead yet another example of estrangement between the laity and their leadership.

Finally, the emergence of a group of what were often called "John Paul II priests" threatened further strains between American Catholics and the institution of their church. John Paul was unquestionably popular throughout his tenure. His early vigor and his role in bringing an end to the Soviet domination of Eastern Europe had endeared him to Americans, both Catholic and non-Catholic. He was the first pope to publish commercially available books, and each new title became an instant best seller in the United States. His meditation on faith, *Crossing the Threshold of Hope,* published in 1994, sold millions of copies, and a CD recording of his singing and saying the rosary was almost equally popular.[35] Later, his long physical decline, carried out visibly in public appearances on television, and his death in the spring of 2005 offered a poignant and edifying example of how individuals might face the prospect of their own deaths. That some young men wanted to emulate his example by entering the priesthood was not, therefore, surprising, even though their numbers might be small.

John Paul's vivid personality appealed to many prospective seminarians. Some pointed to the experience of seeing him at a World Youth Day rally as the key to their decision to become a priest, and a few had had closer contact. A college quarterback from Buffalo, traveling in Rome with his pastor during an unusual spring break, decided to give up his girlfriend and enter the seminary after attending a small private Mass with the pope. "You could feel his holiness," the football star said. "When he made eye contact with me, I literally had to keep my legs straight and keep myself from falling over." More important was what the pope stood for and, indeed, that he stood so clearly for something. "He didn't compromise ever," a young priest from Milwaukee said. A seminarian from Syracuse responded to the pope's appeal to "the service of something so much bigger" than himself; another from LaCrosse, Wisconsin, described his desire "to embrace an institution with values so different from those of the popular culture." Even the sexual abuse scandal itself rallied some to the pope's side. A young man from Pittsburgh, part of an "unusually large" class of seminarians (there were nine of them), compared his decision to the response to the terrorist attacks of September 11, 2001. "You know how everyone wanted to sign up for the Army right away?" he said. "This is like signing up for God's army." The chance to join the uncompromising leader of that army was appealing. "Their Catholicism is quite focused on John Paul II," said one lay theologian, and a seminary rector agreed. His students were "most influenced," he said, by "the Holy Father and his witness."[36]

The apparent clarity of John Paul's vision inclined some seminarians and younger priests to revive devotional practices that had become uncommon. Some wore the long black cassocks that most older priests had abandoned forty years before. At one time these robes had set the clergy off as distinct from the laity; after Vatican II, that had seemed precisely the problem with them. With the exception of these young seminarians, "you don't see too many cassocks out there anymore," one skeptical fellow seminarian said. "They probably do the liturgy in Latin, too." Few went that far, but other traditional practices were revived. A newly ordained priest, for instance, told an interviewer at some length how important he thought it was to ring bells at various points in the Mass, a custom that had been discontinued in most places. Eucharistic devotions, which emphasized looking at and adoring the host from afar rather than actually consuming it in Communion, were also reinvigorated. An earlier generation of "Vatican II priests" had deemphasized such practices, but now they found new adherents. The Milwaukee priest who had praised the pope's refusal to "compromise ever" said he was sick of the "low-church craziness" that had infected Catholic worship since Vatican II. Individual devotional styles varied, of course, and one of the strengths of Catholicism had always been the variety of its spiritual approaches. By seeming to return to many of the pre–Vatican II practices, however, these younger priests risked becoming, as one older colleague called them, "young fogeys."[37]

A generational split thus opened in the ranks of the clergy. "We were the first orthodox class," one seminarian said flatly, in what may actually have been a slander of his predecessors, but he was not alone in contrasting himself with his elders. "It's disheartening," a thirty-year-old said, "to see older priests not following the rules." Still another agreed: "One of the principal differences between priests who came of age during Vatican II and those of my generation," he said, "is in how we regard church teaching." A priest in Lincoln, Nebraska, concurred: "We follow the Pope," he told a reporter, thereby suggesting that others did not. "A whole string of Popes have said that artificial birth control is seriously sinful, so that's what we tell people . . . Missing Mass is sinful, so that's what we tell people." It was as simple as that. Holding the line on other matters was no less important. In 2003, for instance, 150 priests in Milwaukee and another 100 in St. Paul and Minneapolis published open letters asking for a reconsideration of mandatory celibacy for the clergy. In response, more than twice as many seminarians from around the country published their own letter, insisting on celibacy and pleading for no change. Their attitude, one survey concluded, was that the "exclusive relationship" of marriage was "a distraction from [the] intimacy with Christ" that came with the priesthood. This put them at odds with the vast majority of lay people, who had long since come to favor a married clergy.[38]

This difference of opinion was only one sign of a widening gap between lay people and many of the new priests serving in their churches. The attitudes inculcated in seminaries had emphasized what was called the "clerical difference": priests were fundamentally different sorts of creatures from lay people. A study conducted in 2002 found that one-third of priests who had been in the ministry for five years or less thought that lay people should be more willing "to respect the authority of the priest's word" in such matters as contraception. The priest in Nebraska said of his congregation matter-of-factly, "I'm their father . . . That's what a pastor is." Even though many of his parishioners were much older than he, their role was subordinate. "As in any good Catholic family," he went on, "parents love their children and still control them. They need to be told what's right and wrong with the love and care of a father."[39] Here was a vision of the church in which lay people were children again, and the priest was always in "control." This priest was plainly not ready to be "reduced to the lay state." For their part, lay people were obviously cool to such formulations. They had become accustomed to sharing in the spiritual work of their parishes, not diminishing the work of the clergy but cooperating with it. Worse, such attitudes seemed renewed expressions of the clerical "club," shown in the sexual abuse scandal to have had such deleterious effects. In the future, this reinvigorated clericalism will inevitably remain on a collision course with the outlook of many lay Catholics.

Thus the ways in which American Catholics define themselves as part of the institutional church remain complex. A return to the simpler days when "Father" was in control seems impossible. More than thirty years of lay people's involvement in the ministries of the church—as deacons, Eucharistic ministers, lectors, and dedicated volunteers—will not permit restriction of those activities once again to the ever-shrinking cadre of ordained priests. A new pope, Benedict XVI, took his predecessor's place in 2005, and the themes of his papacy are still unfolding. Despite some early fears that he would prove even more authoritarian than John Paul II, Benedict has also given Catholics encouragement: his first encyclical letter, issued less than a year after he assumed office, was an extended treatise on the virtue of Christian love, apparently signaling a more pastoral approach to the papal office. American Catholics remain connected to the pope amid their disagreements.

The continuing tension between American Catholics and their church finds its parallel in the laity's role in the larger society of which they are a part. In many ways, they are virtually indistinguishable from their fellow Americans, different only in the detail of which church they attend on Sunday mornings. In earlier, nativist eyes, membership in the Roman Church constituted—or ought to have constituted—a disqualification from public office, but now religion is generally a matter of indifference. In the 110th Congress, elected in 2006, 119 (27 percent) of the members of the House of Representatives and 22 of the 100 Senators were Catholics: the latter figure is almost exactly the Catholic percentage of the general population. In the 1950s, Paul Blanshard would have been horrified at such numbers, sure that they portended a Vatican takeover of the nation, but now they are unworthy of remark. Five members of the U.S. Supreme Court are Catholics, a majority that would have sparked wary notice in the past. Nominations to the court are routinely controversial, but the religious affiliation of a nominee is not accepted as a legitimate reason to oppose an appointment.

More broadly, Catholics have joined the general shift of the population to the Sunbelt and to what are called the "exurbs." It is there that the church is expanding. Between 1970 and 2000, the number of parishes in Houston, for instance, grew by about one-third (from fifty-three to seventy-eight). Compare this growth with contraction in other, older cities: Toledo, Ohio, was shrinking in the same period from forty-two parishes to thirty. But the Houston suburbs saw even more steady Catholic expansion. The town of Katy, due west of the metropolis, now has three parishes (opened in 1965, 1981, and 1999, respectively) with a membership of 6,000 families. In the town of Spring, north of the city, there are four parishes, the oldest of them dating only to 1969, with almost 10,000 families. It is much the same in and around Atlanta. There are thirteen parishes within the city limits, all but one of them established before 1964. In the booming suburbs northeast of Atlanta, there are nine parishes, the oldest of them opened in 1970; in the near northwest suburbs, there are ten parishes, all but one of them begun since 1973.[40] The wit who observed that the geography of American Catholicism could be overlaid on the map of major league baseball was still correct, but the important centers now were places that had not fielded teams a century before.

Catholics remain an identifiable voting bloc, and the ongoing definition of their American-ness will continue in this contested political context. The effort to tap the rising Hispanic Catholic vote has become particularly crucial for both political parties. Like many earlier immigrants, Hispanics have usually leaned toward the Democrats. In the presidential election of 2000, for example, Hispanic voters nationwide favored Al Gore over George W. Bush by almost two to one. In the crucial state of Florida, however, with its significant population of staunchly anti-communist Cuban immigrants, Bush won a narrow victory. The success with which Republicans are able to tap the Hispanic vote may well be a measure of their party's future success. The presidential election of 2004 saw, in John Kerry, the first Catholic since John Kennedy to be nominated by a major party, but Kerry faced a different problem from that of the earlier Massachusetts candidate. Conservative groups questioned his standing as a Catholic, citing his pro-choice stance on abortion and insisting that priests should deny him Communion because of it. Some American bishops were sympathetic to this idea, and a Nigerian cardinal at the Vatican also voiced his approval. Cooler heads prevailed among the American hierarchy, however, and the prospect of what one newspaper columnist sarcastically called a "wafer watch"—would Kerry be given the sacrament at Sunday Mass or not?—put off many voters. Kerry lost the election, and he even lost the Catholic vote to Bush, who took 52 percent of it, including a slightly higher percentage of Hispanic Catholics.[41]

Catholic citizens will continue to stake out positions on public issues, but they will not adhere to any single position simply because they are Catholics. Questions surrounding the nature of marriage, for example, as both a civil and a religious institution, were increasingly contested in the first decade of the new century. In 2003, the Supreme Judicial Court of Massachusetts legalized same-sex marriage in that state by a four-to-three vote. Reaction to the case was strong on both sides, in part because, like the earlier *Roe* decision by the U.S. Supreme Court, it removed a contentious issue from the normal political and legislative processes. The state's bishops tried to rally support for a referendum to undo the ruling, but because it came so soon after the sexual abuse scandal, their influence was weakened. The issue remains an open one, in Massachusetts and other states, and how Catholics vote on such referenda remains contested. More than likely, they will express the same variety of opinions as their fellow citizens. Other issues, too, are still very much subject to debate among people of all religious affiliations, including war and peace, immigration policy, and capital punishment. American Catholics will face these issues more broadly as Americans than narrowly as Catholics.

Historians are always more comfortable in the past than in the future or (sometimes) in the present. They are thus unqualified, after recounting events that have brought them to their own times, to say much about what will happen next. But the past is a guide nonetheless, if only because it shows the range of possibilities for the future. For American Catholic lay people, the church of the twenty-first century will, in significant ways, recapitulate the historical experience of its earlier ages. The men and women we have met would recognize many of the challenges ahead, and their experience may suggest ways to face those trials. The church of our lay people from the past will be the church of lay people in the future.

The church that Roger Hanly knew at the time of the American Revolution was largely a priestless one, and that is once again becoming the case. The number of ordained clergy is simply inadequate to serve the growing population to an extent that would once have been considered normal. Stop-gap measures, such as the importation of priests from abroad, may mitigate the impact of this decline temporarily, but they cannot alter the fundamental trajectory. When nine seminarians—some of them will not be ordained; others will leave the priesthood within a few years—constitute an "unusually large" class, the ranks of the clergy will not recover. Parishes have already closed, and a single priest may have responsibility for three or four local congregations, traveling among them like an early circuit rider. In the churches he leaves behind will be a pastoral associate—a religious sister or, more likely, a lay man or woman—who does everything a priest can do except say Mass, hear confessions, and anoint the dying. Faced with that institutional contraction, lay people will, like Hanly and his neighbors, have to find personal and family-based ways to maintain their religious identity. Maria's Catholicism in this century will be expressed at home as much as in church.

The church that Doctor James McDonald knew in the early years of the American republic was one in which the active participation of the laity was essential to the institution's survival and growth. This, too, will mark the church of the twenty-first century. Lay groups such as Voice of the Faithful, formed out of disillusionment with the church's leadership, will probably survive, though their size and impact will be limited. Even so, the hierarchy ignores such committed lay Catholics at its peril. They are the same people on whom the work of local parishes depends: parish council members and the leaders in ministries of education, social service, and devotion. Demands for broader lay participation in decision-making are unlikely to be successful in the near term: too often, bishops still compare such participation to the "abuse" of trusteeism. But the regularity of lay involvement in church affairs is setting a new standard that will have a cumulative effect. Maria's church will be one in which lay people do many of the things that priests used to do to sustain the faith community.

Anna Hurban lived in a church of immigrants, and now a new generation of Anna Hurbans make up the lay Catholics of America. They come to the United States, not from Slovakia or other places in Europe, but from all over the globe. At first, they are sometimes viewed warily by those already here. Anti-immigrant nativism seems never to disappear entirely from American public life. On the whole, however, the church's response to them has been a good one, with priests and lay people learning the languages and customs of their new neighbors and helping them find jobs and housing. As the process of assimilation and economic advancement proceeds across the generations, these new immigrants will join those of the past in determining how to sustain their religious traditions. By the middle of the twenty-first century, sociologists predict, no single racial or ethnic group in America will constitute a majority of the population. Maria's Catholicism will be lived in that diversity.

The church of Dorothy Day was one that was committed to action in this world as well as to prayers and hopes for the next one, and this, too, remains the task for the American Catholic laity. The precise needs of the times may be different—but then again perhaps they are not: housing, employment, education, human dignity. The need to put the message of the Gospels into action continues to fire many, young and old alike. Every year at the Catholic university where I teach, more than seven hundred students spend an "alternative spring break" in poor areas of this and other countries, building homes, digging irrigation ditches, planting and harvesting; students at other Catholic colleges do the same. Some graduates of those schools, most of them the products of well-off, suburban families, sign up for a year or two of service in church-related programs. Even lay people's involvement in political causes—controversial, as most political activity is—derives in important ways from this ongoing commitment to Catholic Action. Whether the cause is the pro-life movement or the anti–death penalty crusade, twenty-first-century Catholics seek to make the church's work their own. Maria's Catholicism will be one that remains committed to both church and world.

Patty and Pat Crowley lived in a church that had been shaped decisively by the Second Vatican Council and its reforms of religious life. The council itself is just now passing out of personal memory for most Catholics, but the impact is still felt. American lay people have fully absorbed the idea that they are "People of God" and that the church is best understood in this fundamentally participatory way. They reject implicitly the idea that they are in any way "reduced." They may still address their priests as "Father," but they do so now in the way that adult children speak to their parents, not as elementary school kids do. They have become comfortable with dissenting from church teachings that they find unpersuasive. At the same time, they remain committed to the church and their membership in it: they refuse to be pushed out of it, even when they are actively at odds with, or scandalized by, the hierarchy. More important, they continue to explore ways to make their faith their own, personalizing prayers and sacraments as a way of addressing their own spiritual needs.

Maria's church will continue to be one in which lay people walk the path laid out at Vatican II.

Had some miracle of time travel permitted our six American Catholics to sit together and talk, they would have found that they had much in common. They would have recognized the same basic elements in the practice of their religion, including the Mass, the sacraments, and the way they prayed. At the same time, they would have noticed differences in their experiences, the products of their own particular times and circumstances. Still, they would have known that together they embodied the American Catholic laity. As these experiences continue to change, understanding them in the past helps us understand the future.

NOTES

ACKNOWLEDGMENTS

INDEX

Notes

1. The Priestless Church

1. Cheverus to Hanly, August 4, 1797, Archives, Archdiocese of Boston (hereafter AABo). On Cheverus and his friends in Puritan Boston, see Walter Muir Whitehill, *A Memorial to Bishop Cheverus* (Boston: Boston Athenaeum, 1951). On the early Catholic settlers around Bristol and Damariscotta, see also William L. Lucey, *The Catholic Church in Maine* (Francestown, N.H.: Marshall Jones, 1957), 28–36. A prayer book belonging to Mary Hanly (who was either Roger's daughter or his niece) is now preserved in the Burns Library, Boston College, Chestnut Hill, Massachusetts.

2. Carroll to Antonelli, March 1, 1785, *John Carroll Papers,* ed. Thomas O'Brien Hanley (Notre Dame, Ind.: University of Notre Dame Press, 1976), 1:179–181; Carroll to Plowden, June 29, 1785, ibid., 1:192; Carroll to Plowden, February 28, 1779, ibid., 1:53; and Carroll to Plowden, June 4, 1787, ibid., 1:253.

3. Benedict J. Fenwick, *Memoirs to Serve for the Future Ecclesiastical History of the Diocess of Boston,* ed. Joseph M. McCarthy (Yonkers, N.Y.: U.S. Catholic Historical Society, 1978), 169; Annabelle M. Melville, *Jean Lefebvre de Cheverus, 1768–1836* (Milwaukee: Bruce, 1958), 43–58; Carroll to Plowden, June 11, 1791, *Carroll Papers,* 1:505.

4. *Diurnal of the Right Rev. John England* (Philadelphia: American Catholic Historical Society, 1895), 8–13.

5. Carroll to Molyneux, April 7, 1807, *Carroll Papers,* 3:14–15; *The*

United States Catholic Almanac, or Laity's Directory for the Year 1833 (Baltimore: James Myres, 1833), 51–53.

6. John Timon, "Barrens Memoir," ed. John E. Rybolt, *Vincentian Heritage* 22 (2001): 55, 63–64; *United States Catholic Miscellany,* October 14, 1826, and February 3, 1827.

7. Stories of itinerant missionaries among Protestant denominations, particularly Baptists and Methodists, are staples of American religious history. See, for example, Jon Butler, *Awash in a Sea of Faith: Christianizing the American People* (Cambridge, Mass.: Harvard University Press, 1990); Christine Leigh Heyrman, *Southern Cross: The Beginnings of the Bible Belt* (Chapel Hill: University of North Carolina Press, 1997); and Nathan O. Hatch, *The Democratization of American Christianity* (New Haven: Yale University Press, 1989).

8. Carroll's distress over the illiterate priest is discussed in his letter to Grassi, July 24, 1815, *Carroll Papers,* 3:349. For problems with the early American Catholic clergy, see James Hennesey, *American Catholics: A History of the Roman Catholic Community in the United States* (New York: Oxford University Press, 1981), 74–85.

9. Albany Catholics, February 1823, quoted in Patrick W. Carey, *People, Priests, and Prelates: Ecclesiastical Democracy and the Tensions of Trusteeism* (Notre Dame, Ind.: University of Notre Dame Press, 1987), 57–58.

10. "Memorandum on Western Territory," December 22, 1790, *Carroll Papers,* 1:479; *United States Catholic Miscellany,* April 21, 1824, and March 17, 1824. See also Beatriz Betancourt Hardy, "Roman Catholics, Not Papists: Catholic Identity in Maryland, 1689–1776," *Maryland Historical Magazine* 92 (Summer 1997): 139–161.

11. "Memorandum on Bohemia Manor, 1812," *Carroll Papers,* 3:168–169; *United States Catholic Miscellany,* September 23, 1826.

12. Carroll to Plowden, September 26, 1783, *Carroll Papers,* 1:77; Carroll to Fenwick, April 14, 1807, ibid., 3:17; Carroll to Antonelli, March 1, 1785, ibid., 1:182.

13. Carroll to Plowden, February 12, 1803, *Carroll Papers,* 2:408; Carroll to Antonelli, September 20, 1793, ibid., 2:102; John Carroll to Charles Carroll, July 15, 1800, ibid., 2:310. On the large and fascinating Carroll family, see Ronald Hoffman, *Princes of Ireland, Planters of Maryland: A Carroll Saga, 1500–1782* (Chapel Hill: University of North Carolina Press, 2000).

14. Carroll to unidentified priest, August 18, 1785, *Carroll Papers*, 1:195; Lenten Pastoral Letter, February 1792, ibid., 2:12–13. On these topics generally, see Tricia T. Pyne, "The Maryland Catholic Community, 1690–1775: A Study in Culture, Region, and Church" (Ph.D. diss.: Catholic University of America, 1995), 77–78; and Maura J. Farrelly, "Papist Patriots: Catholic Identity and Revolutionary Ideology in Maryland" (Ph.D. diss.: Emory University, 2002), 172–180.

15. See John Bossy, *The English Catholic Community* (Oxford: Oxford University Press, 1976).

16. On religious practice in colonial Maryland, see Pyne, "Maryland Catholic Community," esp. 21–23 and 72–78. On the lending libraries, see ibid., 42–43. For the inventory of "church stuff," see Beatriz Betancourt Hardy, "Women and the Catholic Church in Maryland, 1689–1776," *Maryland Historical Magazine* 94 (Winter 1999): 400. See also Carroll, "The Establishment of the Catholic Religion in the United States," *Carroll Papers*, 1:405.

17. The St. Inigoes records are reproduced in Edwin W. Beitzell, *The Jesuit Missions of St. Mary's County, Maryland* (Abell, Md.: privately printed, 1976), 67–70, 74–96.

18. Beitzel, *Jesuit Missions*, 74–96; for the Jarboe baptism, see ibid., 85. On the dynamics of slave conversion, see Albert J. Raboteau, *Slave Religion: The "Invisible Institution" in the Antebellum South* (New York: Oxford University Press, 1978); and Janet Duitsman Cornelius, *Slave Missions and the Black Church in the Antebellum South* (Columbia: University of South Carolina Press, 1999). For a comparison between different churches and their approaches to slave conversion, see Beatriz Betancourt Hardy, "'The Papists . . . have shewn a laudable Care and Concern': Catholicism, Anglicanism, and Slave Religion in Colonial Maryland," *Maryland Historical Magazine* 98 (Spring 2003): 4–33. On later conversions to Catholicism in Maryland, see also Farrelly, "Papist Patriots," 216–221.

19. On the Catholic population of Boston in these years, see *Boston Pilot*, January 16, 1830; on the enduring anti-Catholicism of the city, see Carroll to Plowden, June 11, 1791, *Carroll Papers*, 1:505. On early Catholicism in New York, see Anne Hartfield, "Profile of a Pluralistic Parish: Saint Peter's Roman Catholic Church, New York City, 1785–1815," *Journal of American Ethnic History* 12, no. 3 (Spring 1993): 30–59. On early Catholic Cincinnati, see

United States Catholic Miscellany, February 24, 1827; and Roger Fortin, *Faith and Action: A History of the Archdiocese of Cincinnati, 1821–1996* (Columbus: Ohio State University Press, 2002), 13–17.

20. Richard Challoner, *The Garden of the Soul; or, A Manual of Spiritual Exercises and Instructions for Christians, Who Living in the World Aspire to Devotion* (Dublin: Richard Cross, 1798), 113. More is known about Challoner and Gother than about Baker. See Eamon Duffy, "Richard Challoner, 1691–1781: A Memoir," in Eamon Duffy, ed., *Challoner and His Church: A Catholic Bishop in Georgian England* (London: Darton, Longman, and Todd, 1981), 1–26; and Richard Luckett, "Bishop Challoner: The Devotionary Writer," ibid., 71–89. On Gother, see Marion Norman, "John Gother and the English Way of Spirituality," *Recusant History* 11 (October 1972): 306–319; and J. D. Crichton, "Recusant Writers on the Priesthood of the Laity," *Clergy Review* 71 (December 1986): 455–457.

21. These manuals went through many editions, all more or less identical but produced by different printers. For representative examples, see *Gother's Prayers for Sundays & Festivals, Adapted to the Use of Private Families and Congregations* (Wolverhampton: J. Smart, 1800), and three volumes by Baker: *The Christian Advent, or Entertainments for That Holy Season* (London: J. Coghlan, 1782); *A Lenten Monitor to Christians, In Pious Thoughts, Moral Reflections, and Devout Aspirations* (London: J. Marmaduke, 1755); and *Sundays Kept Holy, In Moral Reflections, Pious Thoughts, and Devout Aspirations* (London: J. Coghlan, 1772). The quotations are from *Gother's Prayers,* iv and vi.

22. Challoner, *Garden of the Soul,* 97–98; *Manual of Catholic Prayers* (Philadelphia: Robert Bell, 1774), 93; Pacificus Baker, *The Devout Communicant: or, Spiritual Entertainments Before and After Communion* (London: J. P. Coghlan, 1779), x.

23. "A Form of Confession," *Manual of Catholic Prayers,* 106–110; Timon, "Barrens Memoir," 64.

24. Cheverus to Hanly, no date, Cheverus Papers, AABo 1:12; *A Short Abridgment of Christian Doctrine: Newly Revised for the Use of the Catholic Church in the United States of America* (Philadelphia: Michael Duffey, 1798). For an example of another kind of catechism, see the later edition of *The Complete Historical Catechism; or Fleury's Short Historical Catechism* (London: Burns and Oates, 1871).

25. Cheverus to Hanly, January 18, 1815, Cheverus Papers, AABo 1:12; Cheverus to Cottrill, April 2, 1816, ibid., 1:4; framed copy of Cheverus to Fitzgerald, September 19, 1799, ibid., 1:20a; *Diurnal of John England,* 8, 62; Challoner, *Garden of the Soul,* 113–114.

26. The output of these early publishers of Catholic materials may be traced in the two pioneering works of American Catholic bibliography: Joseph M. Finotti, *Bibliographia Catholica Americana: A List of Works Written by Catholic Authors and Published in the United States* (New York: Catholic Publication House, 1872); and Wilfrid Parsons, *Early Catholic Americana: A List of Books and Other Works by Catholic Authors in the United States, 1729–1830* (New York: Macmillan, 1939). Also useful as background is J. A. Leo Lemay, *Men of Letters in Colonial Maryland* (Knoxville: University of Tennessee Press, 1972). For an example of Haly's output, see his advertisement in *United States Catholic Miscellany,* April 13, 1825. The John J. Burns Library of Boston College now holds an Irish edition of *The Catholic Christian's Daily Companion* (Dublin: R. Cross, 1810) which was originally owned by a member of the Hanly family; its flyleaf is inscribed "Mary Hanly S[enio]r. Bristol [Maine]. Decr. 12, 1816."

27. Mathew Carey, *Autobiography* (New York: Eugene Schwaab, 1942), 41. See also James N. Green, *Mathew Carey: Publisher and Patriot* (Philadelphia: Library Company of Philadelphia, 1980); David Daniell, *The Bible in English: Its History and Influence* (New Haven: Yale University Press, 2003), ch. 35; and Paul C. Gutjahr, *An American Bible: A History of the Good Book in the United States, 1777–1880* (Stanford, Calif.: Stanford University Press, 1999).

28. Several catalogs of titles available from Carey have survived. See, for example, the list from September 1792, *Mathew Carey's Catalogue of Books* (Philadelphia: Mathew Carey, 1792), a copy of which is included in the microfilmed Early American Imprints series of the American Antiquarian Society, Worcester, Massachusetts, no. 46403.

29. Charity Sermon, undated, *Carroll Papers,* 3:438. For the theological emphases of Catholicism in this period, see Chinnici, *Living Stones,* ch. 4; and E. Brooks Holifield, *Theology in America: Christian Thought from the Age of the Puritans to the Civil War* (New Haven: Yale University Press, 2003), ch. 20.

30. Charles Carroll of Carrollton to Charles Carroll of Annapolis,

January 17, 1759, *Dear Papa, Dear Charly: The Peregrinations of a Revolutionary Aristocrat* (Chapel Hill: University of North Carolina Press, 2001), 1:90.

31. *Practical Reflections for Every Day Throughout the Year* (New York: Bernard Dornin, 1808); *Manual of Catholic Prayers,* 168–214; and *The Catholic Christian's Daily Companion* (Dublin: R. Cross, 1810) 44–49.

32. See, for example, the devotions in *Manual of Catholic Prayers* and *Catholic Christian's Daily Companion;* see also *Short Abridgment of Christian Doctrine,* 21. For a discussion of the devotional emphases of these early works, see Chinnici, *Living Stones,* esp. chs. 2–4.

33. The texts of the two laws are reproduced in John Tracy Ellis, ed., *Documents in American Catholic History* (Chicago: Regnery, 1967), 111–112, 118–120. See the discussion of these in Hennesey, *American Catholics,* 37–38. On the first Catholic Mass in Boston, see Robert Howard Lord et al., *History of the Archdiocese of Boston in the Various Stages of Its Development, 1604–1943* (Boston: Pilot Publishing, 1944), 1:301–309.

34. On the early religious history of Maryland, see Sydney Ahlstrom, *A Religious History of the American People* (New Haven: Yale University Press, 1972), 331–340; see also Hennesey, *American Catholics,* 36–45; Thomas W. Spalding, *The Premier See: A History of the Archdiocese of Baltimore, 1789–1989* (Baltimore: Johns Hopkins University Press, 1989), 3–5; and James J. Hennesey, "Roman Catholicism: The Maryland Tradition," *Thought* 51 (1976): 282–295.

35. On Rhode Island's unusual approach to religious questions, see Ahlstrom, *Religious History of the American People,* 166–170. See also Robert W. Hayman, *Catholicism in Rhode Island and the Diocese of Providence, 1780–1886* (Providence: Diocese of Providence, 1982), ch. 1.

36. The fullest study of the Virginia law and its implications is Merrill D. Peterson and Robert C. Vaughan, eds., *The Virginia Statute for Religious Freedom: Its Evolution and Consequences in American History* (New York: Cambridge University Press, 1988). See also Anson Phelps Stokes, *Church and State in the United States* (New York: Harper and Brothers, 1950), 1:358–446.

37. For a complete discussion of the movement for state "disestablishment," see Stokes, *Church and State,* 1:358–446; Jay's New York bill of 1777 is quoted on 405. See also Patrick J. Dignan, *A History of the Legal Incorpo-*

ration of Catholic Church Property in the United States (1784–1932) (New York: P. J. Kenedy and Sons, 1935), 27.

38. John Adams to Abigail Adams, October 9, 1774, *The Book of Abigail and John: Selected Letters of the Adams Family, 1762–1784,* ed. L. H. Butterfield et al. (Cambridge, Mass.: Harvard University Press, 1975), 78–79. The subscribers' list, with Adams's contribution, is in the Holy Cross Cathedral building subscription account book, 1802–1827, AABo.

39. Carroll to Jennings, October 14, 1766, *Dear Papa, Dear Charly,* 1:419; Carroll to Graves, August 15, 1774, ibid., 2:725–726; Carroll to Charles Carroll of Annapolis, January 1, 1761, ibid., 1:193; and Carroll to Jennings, August 13, 1767, ibid., 1:432.

40. Measuring the Catholic population in these years is a very tricky business. I have relied on the figures, compiled from several sources, in Michael Glazier and Thomas J. Shelley, eds., *The Encyclopedia of American Catholic History* (Collegeville, Minn.: Liturgical Press, 1997), 287–289.

41. On the declining fortunes of the papacy throughout this period, see Eamon Duffy, *Saints and Sinners: A History of the Popes* (New Haven: Yale University Press, 1997), ch. 4.

42. Duffy, *Saints and Sinners,* 186–191.

43. Carroll to Plowden, April 10, 1784, *Carroll Papers,* 1:146; Carroll to Berington, July 10, 1784, ibid., 1:148; Carroll to Farmer, December 1784, ibid., 1:156; Carroll to Coghlan, June 13, 1787, ibid., 1:254–255; Carroll to Ashton, April 18, 1790, ibid., 1:435–437; Cheverus to *The Telegraph,* May 20, 1800, Cheverus Papers, AABo, 1:20.

44. Carroll to Plowden, February 27, 1785, *Carroll Papers,* 1:166; Carroll to Doria Pamphili, November 26, 1784, ibid., 1:153; Carroll to Plowden, September 23, 1783, ibid., 1:78.

45. Carroll to Ashton, April 18, 1790, ibid., 1:437; Carroll to Pope Pius VII, 1813, ibid., 3:207. On the impact of the French Revolution and its aftermath, see Duffy, *Saints and Sinners,* 195–204; and Alec R. Vidler, *The Church in an Age of Revolution, 1789 to the Present* (New York: Penguin, 1971), esp. ch. 1.

46. Carroll's *Short Abridgment of Christian Doctrine,* 13. It is now possible to search the contents of many of the devotional manuals electronically. Word searches, conducted in August 2004, for "pope," "papacy," and the names of the popes of this period produced no results.

2. The Church in the Democratic Republic

1. *United States Catholic Miscellany,* March 24, 1824. The work of these conventions is described in Peter Guilday, *The Life and Times of John England, First Bishop of Charleston, 1762–1842,* 2 vols. (New York: America Press, 1927), 1:377.

2. The fullest study is Patrick W. Carey, *People, Priests, and Prelates: Ecclesiastical Democracy and the Tensions of Trusteeism* (Notre Dame, Ind.: University of Notre Dame Press, 1987). On the dispute in Philadelphia, see Dale B. Light, *Rome and the New Republic: Conflict and Community in Philadelphia Catholicism between the Revolution and the Civil War* (Notre Dame, Ind.: University of Notre Dame Press, 1996).

3. *The United States Catholic Almanac; or, Laity's Directory, for the Year 1833* (Baltimore: James Myres, 1833) is one of the earliest descriptive and statistical compilations of the church in America. The figure of nine new parishes every year between 1815 and 1830 is in Carey, *People, Priests, and Prelates,* 108.

4. The most complete study of the law governing Catholic parishes remains Patrick J. Dignan, *A History of the Legal Incorporation of Catholic Church Property in the United States (1784–1932)* (New York: Kenedy, 1935); the New York incorporation law is quoted on 52–54.

5. Carey, *People, Priests, and Prelates,* 60–74, characterizes several different types of trustee arrangements. The rules of the Boston church are described in an account book for Holy Cross parish, now in AABo.

6. See the bibliography in Carey, *People, Priests, and Prelates,* esp. 342–347, for the fullest listing of the published output of trustee disputes. Excellent surveys of disputes in a number of local parishes are found in Robert F. McNamara, "Trusteeism in the Atlantic States, 1785–1863," *Catholic Historical Review* 30 (July 1944): 135–154; and Alfred G. Strich, "Trusteeism in the Old Northwest, 1800–1850," *Catholic Historical Review* 30 (July 1944): 155–164. On the growth of the American publishing industry and the demand for printed materials, see Isabelle Lehuu, *Carnival on the Page: Popular Print Media in Antebellum America* (Chapel Hill: University of North Carolina Press, 2000); and David M. Henkin, *City Reading: Written Words and Public*

Spaces in Antebellum New York (Ithaca, N.Y.: Cornell University Press, 1998).

7. Philadelphia layman, quoted in Carey, *People, Priests, and Prelates,* 112–113; Cincinnati trustees quoted in ibid., 149; Carroll to de la Poterie, April 3, 1787, *John Carroll Papers,* ed. Thomas O'Brien Hanley (Notre Dame, Ind.: University of Notre Dame Press, 1976), 1:354.

8. On Fernandez, see Patrick W. Carey, "John F. O. Fernandez: Enlightened Lay Catholic Reformer, 1815–1821," *Review of Politics* 43 (January 1981): 112–129; and Peter Guilday, *The Catholic Church in Virginia (1815–1822)* (New York: United States Catholic Historical Society, 1924), esp. ch. 2. On the trustees in Buffalo, see David A. Gerber, "Modernity in the Service of Tradition: Catholic Lay Trustees at Buffalo's St. Louis Church and the Transformation of European Communal Traditions, 1829–1855," *Journal of Social History* 15 (Summer 1982): 655–684, esp. Table IV.

9. Lynch to Neale, October 7, 1815, Archives, Archdiocese of Baltimore; Jay P. Dolan, *The Immigrant Church: New York's Irish and German Catholics, 1815–1865* (Baltimore: Johns Hopkins University Press, 1975), 89–90; Thomas Donohue, *History of the Diocese of Buffalo* (Buffalo: Buffalo Catholic Publication Co., 1929), 132. For another example of intraethnic conflict, see Light, *Rome and the New Republic,* 46–52.

10. The full story of the Norfolk dispute is told in Gerald P. Fogarty, *Commonwealth Catholicism: A History of the Catholic Church in Virginia* (Notre Dame, Ind.: University of Notre Dame Press, 2001), 33–55.

11. There is a substantial literature on the relationship of American Protestant clergymen with their parishes; see, for example, David D. Hall, *The Faithful Shepherd: A History of the New England Ministry in the Seventeenth Century* (Chapel Hill: University of North Carolina Press, 1972). The impact of these traditions on American Catholics is described in Carey, *People, Priests, and Prelates,* ch. 3; and in Patrick W. Carey, "The Laity's Understanding of the Trustee System, 1785–1860," *Catholic Historical Review* 64 (July 1978): 357–377. That American political principles were misapplied to the Catholic Church is argued in a report to Rome by Archbishop Ambrose Marechal, 1818, quoted in Dignan, *Legal Incorporation of Catholic Church Property,* 108.

12. Carey, *People, Priests, and Prelates,* 166 and 188.

13. Carroll to Lynch and Stoughton, January 24, 1784, *Carroll Papers,* 1:204; trustee pamphlet quoted in Carey, *People, Priests, and Prelates,* 184. For the general arguments of trustees, see ibid., ch. 9.

14. Carroll to Trustees of Saint Mary's, Philadelphia, April 16, 1814, *Carroll Papers,* 3:290; see also "Constitution of the Roman Catholic Churches of North Carolina, South Carolina, and Georgia," in John England, *The Works of the Right Rev. John England, First Bishop of Charleston,* ed. Ignatius Reynolds (Baltimore: John Murphy, 1849), 5:92. The denunciation of lay appointments as too Protestant is also evident in a letter from the bishops to the American Catholic people in 1829; for this see Peter Guilday, ed., *The National Pastorals of the American Hierarchy (1792–1919)* (Washington, D.C.: National Catholic Welfare Council, 1923), 33.

15. On the meeting generally, see Peter Guilday, *A History of the Councils of Baltimore (1791–1884)* (New York: Macmillan, 1932), 81–99. The text of the public letter of the bishops to the Catholic people is given in Guilday, *National Pastorals,* 17–38; the quotations are at 31 and 33. The statement of Pope Leo XII on the New Orleans case is given, in translation, in Dignan, *Legal Incorporation of Catholic Church Property,* 138.

16. The 1829 letter to the priests is in Guilday, *National Pastorals,* 39–59; the quotations are at 50 and 51. See also a similar letter from 1837, ibid., 80–119.

17. On the spread of the corporation sole model, see Dignan, *Legal Incorporation,* 240. For examples of the historical characterization of trustees, see ibid., 74–76; Guilday, *Councils of Baltimore,* 87–88; Guilday, *Catholic Church in Virginia,* 5; and McNamara, "Trusteeism in the Atlantic States," 139.

18. "Pastoral Letter of the Right Rev. Dr. England, Roman Catholic Bishop of Charleston," January 21, 1821, in England, *Works,* 2:232–235. See also the opening salutations of England's other letters, ibid., 2:235–270. England has been well served by biographers: see Guilday, *Life and Times of John England;* and Patrick W. Carey, *An Immigrant Bishop: John England's Adaptation of Irish Catholicism to American Republicanism* (Yonkers, N.Y.: U.S. Catholic Historical Society, 1982).

19. Constitution, Preface, in England, *Works,* 5:91–92.

20. Constitution, Title IV, Section I, ibid., 5:101. See the discussion of

church membership in Peter Clarke, *A Free Church in a Free Society: The Ecclesiology of John England, Bishop of Charleston, 1820–1842* (Hartsville, S.C.: Center for John England Studies, 1982), 257–259. For England's views on slavery, see Cyprian Davis, *The History of Black Catholics in the United States* (New York: Crossroad, 1995), 46–48.

21. Constitution, Title V, in England, *Works*, 5:102–104.

22. *United States Catholic Miscellany*, January 7, January 21, and February 4, 1824. See also the entry of February 3, 1823, *Diurnal of the Right Rev. John England* (Philadelphia: American Catholic Historical Society, 1895), 56.

23. *United States Catholic Miscellany*, March 17, 1824, and September 14, 1825.

24. Constitution, Title VI, England, *Works*, 5:104–106.

25. *United States Catholic Miscellany*, January 28, 1824, March 24, 1824, March 28, 1829, and April 18, 1829.

26. Ibid., November 17, 1827. For examples of routine convention business, see ibid., July 29, 1826, December 6, 1828, April 18, 1829, and November 23 and 30, 1839.

27. "Dr. James Lynah, a Surgeon of the Revolution," *South Carolina Historical and Genealogical Magazine* 40 (July 1939): 87–90. Biographical details of other convention delegates have been gleaned from some of the original documents edited and reproduced in the *Magazine* since it began publishing in 1900.

28. Conwell's letters to Propaganda, January 1 and 17, 1825, are quoted in Guilday, *Life and Times of England*, 1:362–363; Rosati to England, December 7, 1826, is quoted in ibid., 1:378. See also the pastoral letter of 1852 from the American bishops in Guilday, *National Pastorals*, 184–185.

29. Alexis de Tocqueville, *Democracy in America*, trans. and ed. Harvey C. Mansfield and Delba Winthrop (Chicago: University of Chicago Press, 2000), 422–423. Interestingly, Tocqueville thought Catholicism particularly well suited to the United States and likely to flourish there; see ibid., 423–425. Still useful in understanding this entire period is John William Ward, *Andrew Jackson: Symbol for an Age* (New York: Oxford University Press, 1955).

30. A translation of the July 1854 report of Gaetano Bedini is included as an appendix to James F. Connelly, *The Visit of Archbishop Gaetano Bedini*

to the United States of America (Rome: Libreria Editrice dell'Università Gregoriana, 1960), 189–287; the quotation is at 213. The observation about Saint Finbar's is in John Hammond Moore, "The Abiel Abbot Journals: A Yankee Preacher in Charleston Society, 1818–1827," *South Carolina Historical Magazine* 68 (October 1967): 232–254.

31. *Laity's Directory, 1822,* 34–35. Sunday regulations from a 1791 synod of priests are included in *Carroll Papers,* 67–68. Although it has little to say specifically about Catholic practice, for general background see Alexis McCrossen, *Holy Day, Holiday: The American Sunday* (Ithaca, N.Y.: Cornell University Press, 2000).

32. *Laity's Directory, 1822,* 36.

33. See examples of the schedule of parish churches (not listed in every case) in *Catholic Almanac, 1833,* 40–54. Other evidence on the number of Masses may be seen in John Timon, "Barrens Memoir," ed. John E. Rybolt, *Vincentian Heritage* 22 (2001): 68–69; and Benedict J. Fenwick, *Memoirs to Serve for the Future Ecclesiastical History of the Diocese of Boston,* ed. Joseph M. McCarthy (Yonkers, N.Y.: U.S. Catholic Historical Society, 1978), 215–216. On permission for priests to binate, see the entry of January 19, 1823, in *Diurnal of John England,* 54. For parallel developments elsewhere in a slightly later period, see Emmett Larkin, "The Devotional Revolution in Ireland, 1850–1875," *American Historical Review* 77 (June 1972): 625–652.

34. Entries of January 18 and 28, 1821, in *Diurnal of John England,* 6, 8.

35. *Laity's Directory, 1822,* 1.

36. One of the earliest is John England, *The Roman Missal, Translated into the English Language for the Use of the Laity* (Philadelphia: Eugene Cummiskey, 1843), iii–iv, 9, 10–26. England also produced an *Explanation of the Construction, Furniture and Ornaments of a Church, of the Vestments of the Clergy, and of the Nature and Ceremonies of the Mass* (Baltimore: F. Lucas, 1834).

37. The full explanation of the movements of the Mass occupies pp. 26–103 of England, *Roman Missal;* the texts of the prayers are on pp. 103–702; the wedding Mass, for example, is on pp. 704–708.

38. "Provincial Council Resolutions," November 15, 1810, *Carroll Papers,* 3:133; *Diurnal of John England,* December 22, 1822, and January 5, 1823, 52–53; Fenwick, *Memoirs to Serve for the Future,* 199.

39. Benedict Fenwick, Bishop's Journal, AABo: entries of August 30,

1840; August 1, 1841; July 16 and December 12, 1843. For general background, see Robert R. Grimes, *How Shall We Sing in a Foreign Land?: Music of Irish Catholic Immigrants in the Antebellum United States* (Notre Dame, Ind.: University of Notre Dame Press, 1996); Stephen A. Marini, *Sacred Song in America: Religion, Music, and Public Culture* (Urbana: University of Illinois Press, 2003); and David W. Stowe, *How Sweet the Sound: Music in the Spiritual Lives of Americans* (Cambridge, Mass.: Harvard University Press, 2004). I have also profited from David McCowin, "A Medley of Meanings: Musical Culture and the Nuances of Bishop Fenwick's Catholic Boston, 1825–1840" (unpublished paper, in author's possession).

40. R. Garbett, *The Morning and Evening Service of the Catholic Church* (Boston: Kidder and Wright, 1841), iii–iv.

41. Fenwick, Bishop's Journal, AABo, entries of September 15, 1830, and November 25–December 3, 1832. See also McCowin, "Medley of Meanings."

42. Dubois's pastoral letter for Lent 1827 is excerpted in Joseph P. Chinnici and Angelyn Dries, *Prayer and Practice in the American Catholic Community* (Maryknoll, N.Y.: Orbis, 2000), 19.

43. The baptismal registers, noting in each case the date of birth and the date of baptism, for Saint Mary's parish, Boston, are now in AABo. The infant mortality rate is charted in Theodore Caplow et al., *The First Measured Century: An Illustrated Guide to Trends in America, 1900–2000* (Washington, D.C.: American Enterprise Institute, 2001), 134–135.

44. Roger Baxter, *The Most Important Tenets of the Roman Catholic Church Fairly Explained* (Washington, D.C.: Davis and Force, 1820), 74; *Laity's Directory, 1835,* 9–31.

45. *United States Catholic Miscellany,* March 24, 1824; letter of Eliza Allen Starr, in Chinnici and Dries, *Prayer and Practice,* 27.

46. Quotations from his report are in Connolly, *Visit of Bedini,* 227, 228, and 229.

47. Ibid., 217 and 239. On the Buffalo dispute, see Gerber, "Modernity in the Service of Tradition."

48. See Eamon Duffy, *Saints and Sinners: A History of the Popes* (New Haven: Yale University Press, 1997), 214–221, for developments in this period. For the emerging theories of papal power, see also Gerald A. McCool, *Catholic Theology in the Nineteenth Century: The Quest for a Unitary Method* (New York: Seabury Press, 1977), esp. ch. 1.

49. Kenrick to Dubuisson, July 25, 1836, quoted in James F. Connelly, ed., *History of the Archdiocese of Philadelphia* (Philadelphia: Archdiocese of Philadelphia, 1976), 148.

50. For a good summary of papal conservatism, see Philippe Levillain, ed., *The Papacy: An Encyclopedia* (New York: Routledge, 2002), s.v. "Gregory XVI."

51. Quoted in Ray Allen Billington, *The Protestant Crusade, 1800–1860: A Study of the Origins of American Nativism* (New York: Macmillan, 1938), 82, n. 99.

52. The fullest recent history of this incident, though not without its flaws, is Nancy Lusignan Schultz, *Fire and Roses: The Burning of the Charlestown Convent, 1834* (New York: Free Press, 2000). See also the older but still reliable account in Billington, *Protestant Crusade,* 53–84.

53. There are many studies of these polemical works and their enduring impact; the best is Jenny Franchot, *Roads to Rome: The Antebellum Protestant Encounter with Catholicism* (Berkeley: University of California Press, 1994), 135–161.

54. For a full description and analysis, see Michael Feldburg, *The Philadelphia Riots of 1844: A Study of Ethnic Conflict* (Westport, Conn.: Greenwood Press, 1975). For a briefer account, see James Hennesey, *American Catholics: A History of the Roman Catholic Community in the United States* (New York: Oxford University Press, 1981), 122–123.

55. This incident is recounted in Charles R. Morris, *American Catholic: The Saints and Sinners Who Built America's Most Powerful Church* (New York: Times Books, 1997), 62–63. For a general study of Catholicism and Americanism as "two traditions in motion," see John McGreevy's masterful book *Catholicism and American Freedom: A History* (New York: Norton, 2003).

3. The Immigrant Church

1. See "The Slovak Community of Cleveland," in Michael S. Pap, ed., *Ethnic Communities of Cleveland: A Reference Work* (Cleveland: Institute for Soviet and East European Studies, John Carroll University, 1973), 261–279.

2. On this identification of parish with place, see John T. McGreevy,

Parish Boundaries: The Catholic Encounter with Race in the Twentieth-Century Urban North (Chicago: University of Chicago Press, 1996).

3. *Statistical Abstract of the United States, 1925* (Washington, D.C.: Department of Commerce, 1926), Table 87 ("Immigration: 1821 to 1925"); Oscar Handlin, *Boston's Immigrants: A Study in Acculturation,* rev. ed. (Cambridge, Mass.: Harvard University Press, 1941), Table V; Ira Rosenwaike, *Population History of New York City* (Syracuse, N.Y.: Syracuse University Press, 1972), Table 9.

4. *Statistical Abstract of the United States, 1925,* Table 92 ("Immigration, by Country of Last Permanent Residence, 1831 to 1920"). The literature on all the various immigrant populations is, of course, enormous. For reliable overviews, see the entries in the *Harvard Encyclopedia of Ethnic Groups* (Cambridge, Mass.: Belknap Press of Harvard University Press, 1980).

5. Immigration statistics are once again taken from *Statistical Abstract of the United States, 1925,* Table 92.

6. For the rise of the movement to restrict immigration, see John Higham, *Strangers in the Land: Patterns of American Nativism, 1860–1925* (New Brunswick, N.J.: Rutgers University Press, 1955). For for the racial dimensions of this movement, see Matthew Frye Jacobson, *Whiteness of a Different Color: European Immigrants and the Alchemy of Race* (Cambridge, Mass.: Harvard University Press, 1998), esp. ch. 2.

7. Once again, the histories of these immigrant groups are substantial; for a useful summary of the principal Catholic groups, see Jay P. Dolan, *The American Catholic Experience: A History from Colonial Times to the Present* (Garden City, N.Y.: Doubleday, 1985), ch. 5. The classic study of the remaking of Catholic Ireland is Emmet Larkin, "The Devotional Revolution in Ireland, 1850–1875," *American Historical Review* 77 (June 1972): 625–652. See also T. G. McGrath, "The Tridentine Evolution of Modern Irish Catholicism, 1563–1962: A Re-examination of the 'Devotional Revolution' Thesis," in Reamonn O'Muiri, ed., *Irish Church History Today* (Armagh: Cumann Seancha Ard Mhacha, 1991).

8. No single-volume history of Hispanic Catholics is available, but this part of the American Catholic story is told in overview form in James Hennesey, *American Catholics: A History of the Roman Catholic Community in the United States* (New York: Oxford University Press, 1981), 9–22; and

Dolan, *American Catholic Experience,* 15–31, 43–68. For specialized studies of religious practice, see Timothy Matovina and Gary Riebe-Estrella, eds., *Horizons of the Sacred: Mexican Traditions in U.S. Catholicism* (Ithaca, N.Y.: Cornell University Press, 2002).

9. Gerald Shaughnessy, *Has the Immigrant Kept the Faith? A Study of Catholic Immigration and Catholic Growth in the United States, 1790–1920* (New York: Macmillan, 1925), 267. The figures for the Catholic percentage of the population are given ibid., Tables 19–36. For comparative data on American church membership in 1916, see *Statistical Abstract of the United States, 1920* (Washington, D.C.: Department of Commerce, 1921), Table 46 ("Religious Organizations Reported").

10. These comparisons have been assembled by comparing the annual directories for the American Catholic Church in selected years. See *Metropolitan Catholic Almanac and Laity's Directory for the Year of Our Lord 1840* (Baltimore: Fielding Lucas, 1840); *Metropolitan Catholic Almanac and Laity's Directory for the Year of Our Lord 1850* (Baltimore: Fielding Lucas, 1850); *Sadlier's Catholic Directory, Almanac, and Ordo, for the Year of Our Lord 1880* (New York: D. and J. Sadlier, 1880); *Hoffmann's Catholic Directory, Almanac, and Clergy List* (Milwaukee: Hoffmann Brothers, 1891); *Catholic Directory, Almanac, and Clergy List-Quarterly, for the Year of Our Lord 1900* (Milwaukee: Wiltzius, 1900); and *Official Catholic Directory for the Year of Our Lord 1925* (New York: P. J. Kenedy and Sons, 1925). Catholic directories were produced by various publishers until the early twentieth century, when the Kenedy company of New York became the "official" listing for the church in the United States. The data of these directories must be used carefully. The Catholic population figures for dioceses and the nation as a whole are extremely unreliable, for example, and should be used only for comparative purposes. The listing of churches and institutions is more accurate.

11. The theory and canon law of parish churches is explained in Charles Augustine Bachofen, *The Canonical and Civil Status of Catholic Parishes in the United States* (St. Louis: Herder, 1926); and Joseph E. Ciesluk, *National Parishes in the United States* (Washington, D.C.: Catholic University of America, 1944). On the boundary troubles in Cincinnati, see Roger Fortin, *Faith and Action: A History of the Archdiocese of Cincinnati, 1821–1996* (Columbus: Ohio State University Press, 2002), 184–185.

12. On the growth of the parishes of Bridgeport, see Ellen Skerrett et al., *Catholicism, Chicago Style* (Chicago: Loyola University Press, 1993), 8–11. See also the capsule history of each of these churches in Harry C. Koenig, ed., *A History of the Parishes of the Archdiocese of Chicago*, 2 vols. (Chicago: Archdiocese of Chicago, 1980). Exactly why the German Saint Anthony's parish was named for an Italian saint is unclear.

13. In the last few decades, Catholic religious women have finally been receiving the historical attention they deserve. For useful overviews, see Mary Ewens, *The Role of the Nun in Nineteenth Century America* (New York: Arno, 1978); Barbara Misner, *Highly Respected and Accomplished Ladies: Catholic Women Religious in America* (New York: Garland, 1988); Karen Kennelly, ed., *American Catholic Women: A Historical Exploration* (New York: Macmillan, 1989); and George C. Stewart, Jr., *Marvels of Charity: History of American Sisters and Nuns* (Huntington, Ind.: Our Sunday Visitor, 1994).

14. A useful table of the total number of religious communities and sisters, 1830–1995, is given in *Encyclopedia of American Catholic History* (Collegeville, Minn.: Liturgical Press, 1997), 1496. Unfortunately, Catholic directories (see note 10, above) are not as informative about sisters as they are about priests. Individual sisters have never been listed in these volumes by name, as priests have been, and reporting dioceses did not count the number of nuns until the early twentieth century, even as they began to gather other statistics about Catholicism in America. For an early example of the outnumbering of priests by nuns, see *United States Catholic Almanac, or Laity's Directory, for the Year 1834* (Baltimore: James Myres, 1834), 48–50, 122–123.

15. For the Sisters of Saint Joseph, see Carol K. Coburn and Martha Smith, *Spirited Lives: How Nuns Shaped Catholic Culture and American Life, 1836–1920* (Chapel Hill: University of North Carolina Press, 1999). For the hierarchy's statements about schools, see "Pastoral Letter of 1866," in Peter Guilday, ed., *The National Pastorals of the American Hierarchy (1792–1919)* (Washington, D.C.: National Catholic Welfare Conference, 1923), 215–216, and "Pastoral Letter of 1884," ibid., 246–247. School enrollment statistics for Milwaukee have been compiled from the 1880, 1900, and 1924 editions of the Catholic directories. A good general overview is Timothy Walch, *Par-

ish School: American Catholic Parochial Education from Colonial Times to the Present (Washington, D.C.: National Catholic Educational Association, 2001).

16. For these examples from the schools of national parishes, see James A. Burns, *The Growth and Development of the Catholic School System in the United States* (New York: Benziger Brothers, 1912), 310, 324.

17. Ibid., 295, 327–328.

18. *Boston Pilot*, November 15, 1913, and July 22, 1916; Shaugnessy, *Has the Immigrant Kept the Faith?*, 221.

19. For the Baptist shoe manufacturer and his workers, see Kristen A. Petersen, "Contested Bodies and Souls: Immigrant Converts in Boston, 1890–1940," in James M. O'Toole and David Quigley, ed., *Boston's Histories: Essays in Honor of Thomas H. O'Connor* (Boston: Northeastern University Press, 2004), 159–160.

20. Burns, *Catholic School System*, 274; Thomas J. Noel, *Colorado Catholicism and the Archdiocese of Denver, 1857–1989* (Denver: Archdiocese of Denver, 1989), 327–328.

21. On this subject generally, see Mary J. Oates, *The Catholic Philanthropic Tradition in America* (Bloomington: Indiana University Press, 1995), especially ch. 2 ("Resource Mobilization in a Working-Class Church"). On the fundraising campaign in Boston, see James M. O'Toole, "Portrait of a Parish: Race, Ethnicity, and Class in Boston's Cathedral of the Holy Cross, 1865–1880," in O'Toole and Quigley, *Boston's Histories*, 105–106.

22. Entry of March 24, 1822, in *Diurnal of the Right Rev. John England* (Philadelphia: American Catholic Historical Society, 1895), 46; Robert Howard Lord et al., *History of the Archdiocese of Boston in the Various Stages of Its Development, 1604–1943* (Boston: Pilot Publishing, 1944), 2:268–269.

23. *Sadlier's Catholic Directory, 1880*, 17.

24. For the origin of special second collections in parishes, see Guilday, *National Pastorals*, 175. The cathedral fairs in Boston are described in James M. O'Toole, *Passing for White: Race, Religion, and the Healy Family, 1820–1920* (Amherst: University of Massachusetts Press, 2002), 119–120.

25. Guilday, *National Pastorals*, 271.

26. For a comprehensive treatment of church design and function, see J. B. O'Connell, *Church Building and Furnishing: The Church's Way; a Study*

in Liturgical Law (Notre Dame, Ind.: University of Notre Dame Press, 1955). See Edward R. Kantowicz, "The Ethnic Church," in Skerrett et al., *Catholicism, Chicago Style,* 17–23, for variations of architectural styles in Chicago.

27. O'Connell, *Church Building and Furnishing,* 12, 14.

28. Ibid., 133–168.

29. A useful source for visualizing the many possible variations on common themes in church design in this period is *Recent Catholic Architecture: A Few Examples from Designs by Maginnis, Walsh, and Sullivan, Boston, Massachusetts* (Boston: Everett Press, 1900), a copy of which is in the Burns Library of Boston College, Chestnut Hill, Massachusetts. For an example of a church designed with a separate chapel (never, in fact, built) instead of a basement church, see the description of Saint Leo's Church, Leominster, Massachusetts, ibid., 19–21.

30. On Immaculate Conception in Vermont, which was destroyed by fire in 1972, see Kevin F. Decker, "Grand and Godly Proportions: Roman Catholic Cathedral Churches of the Northeast, 1840–1900" (Ph.D. diss.: State University of New York at Albany, 2000), 103–118. On Sacred Heart in Minnesota, see Alan K. Lathrop, *Churches of Minnesota: An Illustrated Guide* (Minneapolis: University of Minnesota Press, 2003), 55–57.

31. James Parton, "Our Roman Catholic Brethren," *Atlantic Monthly* 21 (April 1868): 432–435; *Baltimore Catholic Mirror,* March 5, 1898. Sunday Mass schedules for 1920, parish by parish, are given in the "Status Animarum" Reports in the Archives of the Archdiocese of Milwaukee (AAM); two of the city's forty-five parishes did not report their Mass times that year, so the total number of Masses is actually higher.

32. Parishes, pastors, and assistants are all listed by name, diocese by diocese, in the *Official Catholic Directory* (New York: P. J. Kenedy and Sons) for 1900 and 1925. Leslie Woodcock Tentler, "'God's Representative in Our Midst': Toward a History of the Catholic Diocesan Clergy in the United States," *Church History* 67 (June 1998): 338–339, makes the same point about increasing numbers of multipriest parishes in Detroit.

33. John Talbot Smith, *The Catholic Church in New York: A History of the New York Diocese from Its Establishment in 1808 to the Present Time* (New York: Hall and Locke, 1905), 1:315–316; William Stang, *Pastoral Theology*

(New York: Benziger Brothers, 1897), 144. For Timon's Mass in the hog pen, see Chapter 1, above. Tentler, "'God's Representative in Our Midst,'" 334–335 and 339–340, notes the important psychological shift in the balance between clergy and laity.

34. "The Manner of Serving a Priest at Mass," *Manual of Prayers for the Use of the Catholic Laity* (Baltimore: John Murphy, 1916; orig. pub. 1888), 106–108; Stang, *Pastoral Theology,* 154.

35. *Daily Devotions: A Select Manual of Prayers Compiled from Approved Sources* (New York: Sadlier, 1887; orig. pub. 1876), 61–125; "Devotions for Mass," *Manual of Prayers,* 90–105. For another example, see "Prayers at Mass: A Devout Method of Hearing Mass," *Manual of Catholic Devotions, Compiled from Approved Sources* (New York: Catholic Publications Press, 1925), 29–62. On the effort to establish a standardized manual of prayers, see Peter Guilday, *A History of the Councils of Baltimore (1791–1884)* (New York: Macmillan, 1932), 239–240.

36. Frederic Schultze, *Manual of Pastoral Theology* (Milwaukee: Wiltzius, 1899), 81, 91; Stang, *Pastoral Theology,* 145; K. F. McMurtrie, "Liturgy and the Laity," *Orate Fratres* 3 (October 6, 1929): 414.

37. *Daily Devotions,* 604–605, 670–671; *Manual of Prayers,* 90–91; *Manual of Catholic Devotions,* 54. The "purgative way" is described in Joseph P. Chinnici, *Living Stones: The History and Structure of Catholic Spiritual Life in the United States* (New York: Macmillan, 1989), esp. ch. 9.

38. James A. Walsh Diary, AABo, May 21, 1899. On the low rates of Communion in the immigrant era, see Margaret M. McGuinness, "Let Us Go to the Altar: American Catholics and the Eucharist, 1926–1976," in James M. O'Toole, ed., *Habits of Devotion: Catholic Religious Practice in Twentieth Century America* (Ithaca, N.Y.: Cornell University Press, 2004), 187–235.

39. *Father McGuire's New Baltimore Catechism* (New York: Benziger Brothers, 1942), Question 128; Schultze, *Manual of Pastoral Theology,* 93. For a longer list of holy days, see, for example, *Sadlier's Catholic Directory* (New York: Sadlier, 1880), xiii. Parish schedules from Milwaukee are included in the "Status Animarum" Reports, AAM.

40. Schultze, *Manual of Pastoral* Theology, 105; "Benediction of the Blessed Sacrament," *Manual of Prayers,* 220–224; "The Blessing of Women

after Childbirth," ibid., 454–458. The best introduction to these varied practices remains Ann Taves, *The Household of Faith: Roman Catholic Devotions in Mid-Nineteenth Century America* (Notre Dame, Ind.: University of Notre Dame Press, 1986).

41. "The Stations of the Cross," *Manual of Prayers*, 348–360; O'Connell, *Church Building and Furnishing*, 112–115.

42. J. H. Schutz, *A Little Book of Church Etiquette* (Saint Louis: Herder, 1929), 33–34.

43. "Devotions to the Most Holy Sacrament," *Daily Devotions*, 604–605; *Manual of Prayers*, 108, 342. On Rose Kennedy's habit of "visits," see John Fitzgerald to William O'Connell, October 20, 1939, O'Connell Papers, 5:3, AABo.

44. "Litany of the Saints," *Manual of Prayers*, 256–270; *Baltimore Catechism*, Question 95. Compare the devotions to saints in these volumes with those in *The Catholic Christian's Daily Companion* (Dublin: R. Cross, 1810), and Cheverus to Hanly family, Cheverus Papers 1:12, AABo.

45. *Cantica Sacra; or, Hymns for the Children of the Catholic Church* (Boston: Thomas Noonan, 1865), 52–76. The parishes for Brooklyn and Queens are listed by name in the *Official Catholic Directory for 1925*, 258–266. On the role of Lourdes and other apparitions in promoting Marian devotion, see Thomas A. Kselman, *Miracles and Prophecies in Nineteenth-Century France* (New Brunswick, N.J.: Rutgers University Press, 1983).

46. Parton, "Our Roman Catholic Brethren," 439. On the enduring power of the interpersonal nature of prayer to the saints, see Robert A. Orsi, *Thank You, St. Jude: Women's Devotion to the Patron Saint of Hopeless Causes* (New Haven: Yale University Press, 1996).

47. Parton, "Our Roman Catholic Brethren," 435; "Catholic Memoranda of 1878–9," *Sadlier's Catholic Directory for 1880* (New York: Sadlier, 1880), 15–26.

48. Parton, "Our Roman Catholic Brethren," 440; James A. Walsh Diary, January 1 and February 24, 1899, and March 15, 1900, AABo. Priests' diaries are unfortunately very rare; this one is extremely useful in examining the routines of parish life. See also Robert E. Sullivan, "Beneficial Relations: Toward a Social History of the Diocesan Priests of Boston, 1870–1940," *Catholic Boston: Studies in Religion and Community, 1870–1970* (Boston:

Archdiocese of Boston, 1985), 201–238; and Tentler, "'God's Representative in Our Midst.'"

49. Walsh Diary, January 2, 1900, AABo.

50. The papacy of Pius IX is succinctly summarized in Eamon Duffy, *Saints and Sinners: A History of the Popes* (New Haven: Yale University Press, 1997), 222–235. The older biography of E. E. Y. Hales, *Pio Nono: A Study in European Politics and Religion in the Nineteenth Century* (New York: P. J. Kenedy, 1954), is still the best available in English. For the opinion of Charles Edwards Lester, see Peter R. D'Agostino, *Rome in America: Transnational Catholic Ideology from the Risorgimento to Fascism* (Chapel Hill: University of North Carolina Press, 2004), 26; *National Era,* December 23, 1847.

51. Duffy, *Saints and Sinners,* 222–235. For the definition of the Immaculate Conception and the Syllabus of Errors, see *The Papal Encyclicals, 1740–1878,* ed. Claudia Carlen (Raleigh, N.C.: McGrath, 1981), 291–293, 381–386.

52. *Catholic Mirror,* December 17 and 24, 1870; statement of Louisville Catholics, October 5, 1870, quoted in D'Agostino, *Rome in America,* 47; *Catholic Times,* September 3, 1881, quoted ibid., 53. I have profited from Scott O'Leary, "Sympathy and Cynicism: American Reactions to the Roman Question" (Honors thesis: Boston College, 2005), in author's possession.

53. See *Laity's Directory, 1850,* 236. Many letters conveying sums to Peter's Pence appear in *United States Documents in the Propaganda Fide Archives: A Calendar,* comp. Anton Debevec (Washington, D.C.: Academy of American Franciscan History, 1987), vol. 11, nos. 226 and 660. This whole subject is treated comprehensively in John F. Pollard, *Money and the Rise of the Modern Papacy: Financing the Vatican, 1850–1950* (Cambridge: Cambridge University Press, 2005).

54. "A Summary of Christian Faith and Practice," *Manual of Prayers,* 25–36; *The Complete Historical Catechism; or, Fleury's Historical Catechism* (London: Burns and Oates, 1871), Lesson 80; "God Bless Our Pope" and "The Holy Roman Church," *Cantica Sacra,* 99–101.

55. For a complete discussion of this controversial and complicated subject, see Alexius M. Lepicier, *Indulgences: Their Origin, Nature, and Development* (New York: Benziger Brothers, 1906). A useful summary is contained

in Richard P. McBrien, ed., *The Harper Collins Encyclopedia of Catholicism* (New York: Harper Collins, 1995), 662.

56. Richard Challoner, *The Garden of the Soul* (London: J. P. Coghlan, 1798), 353; *A Short Abridgment of Christian Doctrine; Newly Revised for the Use of the Catholic Church in the United States* (Baltimore: Michael Duffey, 1798), 36.

57. *The Raccoltà; or, Collection of Prayers and Good Works, to which the Sovereign Pontiffs Have Attached Holy Indulgences* (Woodstock, Md.: Woodstock College, 1878), iii, 84, 297–298, 4–5.

58. "Prayer Before a Crucifix," *Manual of Catholic Devotions,* 190; "Prayers for the Dying," holy card in *Daily Devotions* (BX2110.D35 1887), Liturgy and Life Collection, Burns Library, Boston College; "New, Approved Litany of the [sic] St. Joseph," *Manual of Catholic Devotions,* 145–146; "Indulgences for Scripture Reading," *New York Freeman's Journal,* February 18, 1899; "The Holy Rosary," *Manual of Catholic Devotions,* 214–218. An earlier prayer book, published before the *Raccoltà,* had specified a different indulgence for saying the rosary; see *Daily Devotions,* 370–375.

59. "Prayers after Mass," *Manual of Prayers,* 106–107. These prayers were themselves indulgenced; see *Manual of Catholic Devotions,* 60–62.

60. For a contemporary account of the arcane rules governing the creation and rights of these "prelates of honor," see *Catholic Encyclopedia* (New York: Appleton, 1911), s.v. "Monsignor." On the mandating of the Roman collar for priests, see Guilday, *History of the Councils of Baltimore,* 233.

61. Compare the listings for clergy in the *Official Catholic Directory* for 1900 and 1925; monsignors are identifiable by the use of "Rt. Rev." (Right Reverend) before their names.

62. William O'Connell, quoted in *Boston Pilot,* July 13, 1901. The number of churches named Immaculate Conception may be counted in the Catholic directories for 1850 and 1860.

63. Fuller quoted in D'Agostino, *Rome in America,* 30; *The Farmer's Cabinet* (Amherst, New Hampshire), November 10, 1870.

64. The historical literature on nativism, and particularly on its political manifestations, is large and still growing. Two classic surveys remain useful: Ray Allen Billington, *The Protestant Crusade, 1800–1860: A Study of the Origins of American Nativism* (New York: Macmillan, 1938); and Higham,

Strangers in the Land. For a good case study, see John R. Mulkern, *The Know-Nothing Party in Massachusetts: The Rise and Fall of a People's Movement* (Boston: Northeastern University Press, 1990).

65. No general survey has yet replaced Benjamin Blied, *Catholics and the Civil War* (Milwaukee: privately published, 1945), but see Hennesey, *American Catholics,* chs. 12–13. See also George Barton, *Angels of the Battlefield: A History of the Labors of the Catholic Sisterhoods in the Late Civil War* (Philadelphia: Catholic Art Publishing Company, 1898).

66. Denis O'Connell to John Ireland, May 24, 1898, quoted in Gerald P. Fogarty, *The Vatican and the American Hierarchy from 1870 to 1965* (Wilmington, Del.: Michael Glazier, 1985), 163; untitled editorial, *New York Freeman's Journal,* March 4, 1899; "Patriotism Forbids Sectarian War Cries," *Baltimore Catholic Mirror,* April 30, 1898; "Catholic Loyalty," ibid., May 7, 1898. See the accounts of German-American soldiers in the *Monatsbote,* March 1918–February 1919, copies of which are in AABo.

67. The political history of nearly every major American city describes the impact of Catholic voters. For useful case studies of a number of them, see Timothy J. Meagher, ed., *From Paddy to Studs: Irish-American Communities in the Turn of the Century Era, 1880–1920* (Westport, Conn.: Greenwood Press, 1986). For the fear of Irish "captivity," see John Paul Bocock, "The Irish Conquest of Our Cities," *The Forum* 17 (April 1894): 186–195. On the now largely forgotten Hague, see Richard J. Connors, *A Cycle of Power: The Career of Jersey City Mayor Frank Hague* (Metuchen, N.J.: Scarecrow Press, 1971).

68. Not only are the people profiled in the multivolume *American National Biography* (New York: Oxford University Press, 1999) more broadly inclusive than those of the earlier *Dictionary of American Biography* (New York: Scribner's, 1928–1959), but the entries also pay greater attention to the religion of their subjects.

69. Higham, *Strangers in the Land,* ch. 11, describes the process of "closing the gates." For Catholic population figures in this period, see Glazier and Shelley, *Encyclopedia of American Catholic History,* 288. Smith and his 1928 campaign have been generally well served by biographers; see especially Christopher M. Finan, *Alfred E. Smith: The Happy Warrior* (New York: Hill and Wang, 2002); Robert A. Slayton, *Empire Statesman: The Rise and Re-*

demption of Al Smith (New York: Free Press, 2001); and Donn C. Neal, *The World beyond the Hudson: Alfred E. Smith and National Politics, 1918–1928* (New York: Garland, 1983).

70. "Editorial Comment: Doing Very Well, Thank You," *Catholic World* 128 (December 1928): 357.

4. The Church of Catholic Action

1. Day's own account of her conversion, *The Long Loneliness* (Garden City, N.Y.: Image Books, 1959), provides the basic outlines of her story but, like most autobiographies, should not be taken as the last word. The best scholarly treatment of her remains William Miller, *Dorothy Day: A Biography* (New York: Harper and Row, 1982).

2. There is no comprehensive history of the Catholic Action movement in the United States, but see David J. O'Brien, *Public Catholicism* (New York: Macmillan, 1989); and Dennis M. Robb, "Specialized Catholic Action in the United States, 1936–1949: Ideology, Leadership, and Organization" (Ph.D. diss.: University of Minnesota, 1972). Pius XI's statement on Catholic Action, *Quadragesimo Anno,* is in Claudia Carlen, *The Papal Encyclicals, 1903–1939* (Raleigh: McGrath, 1981), pp. 445–458.

3. Frederic Schultze, *Manual of Pastoral Theology* (Milwaukee: Wiltzius, 1899), 319.

4. James A. Walsh Diary, AABo, entries of December 20 and 27, 1898; William Stang, *Pastoral Theology* (New York: Benziger Brothers, 1897), 303. Stang reproduces the certificate of the Michigan society, ibid., 302.

5. Schultze, *Pastoral Theology,* 323, 325; Father John Lowery, Oswego, quoted in David O'Brien, *Faith and Friendship: Catholicism in the Diocese of Syracuse, 1886–1986* (Syracuse, N.Y.: Diocese of Syracuse, 1987), 86. See also Leslie Woodcock Tentler, *Seasons of Grace: A History of the Catholic Archdiocese of Detroit* (Detroit: Wayne State University Press, 1990), 204.

6. *In His Name: Official Holy Name Manual* (New York: National Headquarters of the Holy Name Society, 1941), 25. This manual for members went through many editions. For a somewhat pious narrative of the origins of the group, see Peter Biasiotto, *History and Development of Devotion to the Holy Name* (St. Bonaventure, N.Y.: St. Bonaventure College, 1943).

7. "Holy Name Pledge," *In His Name,* inside front cover. For other expressions of the society's program and purpose, see ibid., 26, 28, 139–140, 185; and *Holy Name Spiritual Director's Handbook* (New York: National Headquarters of the Holy Name Society, 1944), 28.

8. The agenda for a typical meeting is given in *Official Handbook for Holy Name Officers,* rev. ed. (New York: National Headquarters of the Holy Name Society, 1951), 65–69; the use of penmanship students to encourage attendance is suggested in *Spiritual Director's Handbook,* 29–30. See also Stang, *Pastoral Theology,* 298–300.

9. Roger Fortin, *Faith and Action: A History of the Archdiocese of Cincinnati, 1821–1996* (Columbus: Ohio State University Press, 2002), 234–235, 267; Tentler, *Seasons of Grace,* 427–428; Thomas J. Noel, *Colorado Catholicism and the Archdiocese of Denver, 1857–1989* (Denver: Archdiocese of Denver, 1989), 343.

10. See Michael J. Ripple, *The Holy Name Society and Its Great National Convention* (New York: National Holy Name Headquarters, 1925).

11. On the origins of the society in Saint Louis, see Daniel T. McColgan, *A Century of Charity: The First One Hundred Years of the Society of St. Vincent de Paul in the United States* (Milwaukee: Bruce, 1951); copies of some of the early records are reproduced in 1: 79 and 113. See also the celebratory but useful pamphlet, Mark K. Carroll, *Ten Decades of Charity* (St. Louis: Archdiocese of Saint Louis, 1945), no pagination.

12. McColgan, *Century of Charity,* 1: 113 and 117–118; Carroll, *Ten Decades,* no pagination; Mary J. Oates, *The Catholic Philanthropic Tradition in America* (Bloomington: University of Indiana Press, 1995), 78. On the Vincentians in Salt Lake, see Bernice M. Mooney, *Salt of the Earth: The History of the Catholic Diocese of Salt Lake City, 1776–1987* (Salt Lake City, Utah: Diocese of Salt Lake City, 1987), 328–329.

13. *Rules of the Society of St. Vincent de Paul* (New York: The Superior Council, 1918), 24, 43–44, 45; *Rules of the Society of St. Vincent de Paul* (New York: The Superior Council, 1924), 41.

14. On Sheil and the CYO, see Steven M. Avella, "The Rise and Fall of Bernard Sheil," *Catholicism, Chicago Style,* ed. Ellen Skerrett et al. (Chicago: Loyola University Press, 1993), 95–108; and Edward R. Kantowicz, *Corporation Sole: Cardinal Mundelein and Chicago Catholicism* (Notre Dame, Ind.:

University of Notre Dame Press, 1983), 173–188. On the anti–birth control campaign in Boston, see James M. O'Toole, "Prelates and Politicos: Catholics and Politics in Massachusetts, 1900–1970," *Catholic Boston: Studies in Religion and Community,* 1870–1970 ed. Robert E. Sullivan and James M. O'Toole (Boston: Archdiocese of Boston, 1985), 49–56.

15. Christopher J. Kauffman, *Faith and Fraternalism: The History of the Knights of Columbus,* rev. ed. (New York: Simon and Schuster, 1992), is a comprehensive history of the knights; see also the useful overview in *The Encyclopedia of American Catholic History,* ed. Michael Glazier and Thomas J. Shelley (Collegeville, Minn.: Liturgical Press, 1997), 768–771. In *Parish Priest: Father Michael McGivney and American Catholicism* (New York: Harper Collins, 2006), Douglas Brinkley and Juliet M. Fenster present a popular account of the knights' founder. On the bishops' fear of "secret societies," see the Pastoral Letter of 1884, Peter K. Guilday, ed., *National Pastorals of the American Hierarchy (1792–1919)* (Washington, D.C.: National Catholic Welfare Conference, 1923), 256–260.

16. On Callahan, see William E. Ellis, "Catholicism and the Southern Ethos: The Role of Patrick Henry Callahan," *Catholic Historical Review* 69 (January 1983): 41–50.

17. For some of these groups, see William Wolkovich, *Lithuanian Fraternalism: Seventy-Five Years of the U.S. Knights of Lithuania* (Brooklyn: Knights of Lithuania, 1988); Dolores Liptak, *European Immigrants and the Catholic Church in Connecticut, 1870–1920* (New York: Center for Migration Studies, 1987), 89–90; Cyprian Davis, *The History of Black Catholics in the United States* (New York: Crossroad, 1990), 235–237; Dorothy Ann Blatnica, *"At the Altar of Their God": African American Catholics in Cleveland, 1922–1961* (New York: Garland, 1995), 176–182; and Morris J. MacGregor, *The Emergence of a Black Catholic Community: St. Augustine's in Washington* (Washington, D.C.: Catholic University of America Press, 1999), 292–293.

18. Peter Dietz, "The Metamorphosis," quoted in Aaron I. Abell, ed., *American Catholic Thought on Social Questions* (Indianapolis: Bobbs-Merrill, 1968), 257–258.

19. John A. Ryan, "The Church and the Workingman," *Catholic World,* 89 (1909), quoted in Patrick W. Carey, ed., *American Catholic Religious Thought* (New York: Paulist Press, 1987), 249. See also Paul Avrich, *Sacco*

and Vanzetti: The Anarchist Background (Princeton: Princeton University Press, 1991); William Cahn, *Lawrence, 1912: The Bread and Roses Strike* (New York: Pilgrim Press, 1980); and Dorothy M. Brown and Elizabeth McKeown, *The Poor Belong to Us: Catholic Charities and American Welfare* (Cambridge, Mass.: Harvard University Press, 1997).

20. For Catholic population numbers and percentages in this period see, for example, the annual *Statistical Abstract of the United States* (Washington, D.C.: Government Printing Office) for 1940, 1951, and 1961. For studies of Catholic colleges, see Edward J. Power, *Catholic Higher Education in America: A History* (New York: Appleton Century-Crofts, 1972); and Philip J. Gleason, *Contending with Modernity: Catholic Higher Education in the Twentieth Century* (New York: Oxford University Press, 1995). Analyses of alumni careers are given in Anthony J. Kuzniewski, *Thy Honored Name: A History of the College of the Holy Cross, 1843–1994* (Washington, D.C.: Catholic University of America Press, 1999), 341; and Nicholas Varga, *Baltimore's Loyola, Loyola's Baltimore, 1851–1986* (Baltimore: Maryland Historical Society, 1990), 362. See also Mother Grace Dammann, "The American Catholic College for Women" (1942), quoted in Mary J. Oates, ed., *Higher Education for Catholic Women: An Historical Anthology* (New York: Garland, 1987), 168–169. A pioneering study of Catholics in academic life is John D. Donovan, *The Academic Man in the Catholic College* (New York: Sheed and Ward, 1964).

21. Douglas J. Slawson, *The Foundation and First Decade of the National Catholic Welfare Council* (Washington, D.C.: Catholic University of America Press, 1992), is a comprehensive history of the organization. See also Elizabeth McKeown, "War and Welfare: A Study of American Catholic Leadership" (Ph.D. diss.: University of Chicago, 1972); and "Pastoral Letter of 1919," in Guilday, ed., *National Pastorals,* 265–340. On Ryan, see Francis L. Broderick, *Right Reverend New Dealer: John A. Ryan* (New York: Macmillan, 1963).

22. The fullest treatment is Ruth Libbey O'Halloran, "Organized Catholic Laywomen: The National Council of Catholic Women, 1920–1995" (Ph.D. diss.: Catholic University of America, 1995); the quotation is at 24. See also Slawson, *National Catholic Welfare Conference,* 76–80. On Regan, see *Notable American Women,* ed. Edward T. James et al. (Cambridge, Mass.: Belknap Press of Harvard University Press, 1971), 3: 128–130.

23. There is an extensive literature on Day, Maurin, and their movement. In addition to their own writings, see Marc Ellis, *Peter Maurin: Prophet in the Twentieth Century* (New York: Paulist Press, 1981); Miller, *Dorothy Day;* Mel Piehl, *Breaking Bread: The Catholic Worker and the Origin of Catholic Radicalism in America* (Philadelphia: Temple University Press, 1982); and James T. Fisher, *The Catholic Counterculture in America, 1933–1962* (Chapel Hill: University of North Carolina Press, 1989).

24. Ed Willock, "Catholic Radicalism in America," quoted in David J. O'Brien, *Public Catholicism* (New York: Macmillan, 1989), 211. Day's picketing of her archbishop is described, in slightly overwrought terms, in John Cooney, *The American Pope: The Life and Times of Francis Cardinal Spellman* (New York: Times Books, 1984), 190.

25. The fullest histories of this movement are Raymond P. Witte, *Twenty-Five Years of Crusading: A History of the National Catholic Rural Life Conference* (Des Moines, Iowa: National Catholic Rural Life Conference, 1948); David S. Bovee, "The Church and the Land: The National Catholic Rural Life Conference and American Society, 1923–1985" (Ph.D. diss.: University of Chicago, 1986); and Jeffrey D. Marlett, *Saving the Heartland: Catholic Missionaries in Rural America, 1920–1960* (DeKalb: Northern Illinois University Press, 2002). See also Thomas E. Howard, *Agricultural Handbook for Rural Pastors and Laymen: Religious, Economic, Social, and Cultural Implications of Rural Life* (Des Moines, Iowa: National Catholic Rural Life Conference, 1946); the quotations are at 4, 28, and 31.

26. Alden V. Brown, *The Grail Movement and American Catholicism, 1940–1975* (Notre Dame, Ind.: University of Notre Dame Press, 1989), 52, 54, 59, 98. For a personal account of a longtime Grail leader, see Janet Kalven, *Women Breaking Boundaries: A Grail Journey, 1940–1995* (Albany: State University of New York Press, 1999), esp. 79–80.

27. Fortin, *Faith and Action,* 247; Tentler, *Seasons of Grace,* 342–347 (quotation at page 343); Kenneth J. Heineman, *A Catholic New Deal: Religion and Reform in Depression Pittsburgh* (University Park: Pennsylvania State University Press, 1999), esp. ch. 4–6 (quotation at page 167).

28. Cort describes the early years and programs of the ACTU in his memoir, *Dreadful Conversions: The Making of a Catholic Socialist* (New York: Fordham University Press, 2003), 82–88. See also the memoirs of another activist, George G. Higgins (with William Bole), *Organized Labor*

and the Church: Reflections of a "Labor Priest" (New York: Paulist Press, 1993). For a less sympathetic view, see Douglas P. Seaton, *Catholics and Radicals: The Association of Catholic Trade Unionists and the American Labor Movement, from Depression to Cold War* (East Brunswick, N.J.: Associated University Presses, 1981).

29. See Davis, *History of Black Catholics,* esp. ch. 7. For studies of individual black parishes, see MacGregor, *Emergence of a Black Catholic Community;* and Blatnica, *"At the Altar of Their God."*

30. See David W. Southern, *John LaFarge and the Limits of Catholic Interracialism, 1911–1963* (Baton Rouge: Louisiana State University Press, 1996); the quotations are at 183 and 203. See also John LaFarge, *No Postponement: U.S. Moral Leadership and the Problem of Racial Minorities* (New York: Longmans, Green, 1950), 152–162. For a detailed study of the college students in New Orleans, see R. Bentley Anderson, *Black, White, and Catholic: New Orleans Interracialism, 1947–1956* (Nashville, Tenn.: Vanderbilt University Press, 2005).

31. There is a substantial body of historical literature on Coughlin; see especially Charles J. Tull, *Father Coughlin and the New Deal* (Syracuse, N.Y.: Syracuse University Press, 1965), and Alan Brinkley, *Voices of Protest: Huey Long, Father Coughlin, and the Great Depression* (New York: Vintage Books, 1983). There is also a very useful summary of his career in Tentler, *Seasons of Grace,* 319–329, 332–342.

32. See Cort's comments on Coughlin's programs in *Dreadful Conversions,* 97, 103–104. See also "Dangers of Demagogy," *Commonweal,* December 8, 1933, 144.

33. For a general history of the origins of the Legion, see Frank Walsh, *Sin and Censorship: The Catholic Church and the Motion Picture Industry* (New Haven: Yale University Press, 1996), 111–113. See also two books by Gregory D. Black: *Hollywood Censored: Morality Codes, Catholics, and the Movies* (Cambridge: Cambridge University Press, 1994), and *The Catholic Crusade against the Movies, 1940–1975* (Cambridge: Cambridge University Press, 1995). For a useful contemporary study see Paul W. Facey, "The Legion of Decency: A Sociological Analysis of the Emergence and Development of a Social Pressure Group" (Ph.D. diss.: Fordham University, 1945). See also McGrath, "Catholic Action's Big Opportunity," *Ecclesiastical Review* 91 (September 1934): 280–287.

34. Walsh, *Sin and Censorship*, 112, 135–136, 146–147; "Federal Council Joins Movie Fight," *New York Times*, June 23, 1934.

35. Bob Senser, *Specialized Apostolates in Action* (Chicago: Christian Family Movement, 1959), 7. For a comprehensive history of the movement, see Jeffrey M. Burns, *Disturbing the Peace: A History of the Christian Family Movement, 1949–1974* (Notre Dame, Ind.: University of Notre Dame Press, 1999).

36. *For Happier Families: An Introduction to C.F.M.*, 4th rev. ed. (Chicago: Coordinating Committee of the CFM, 1955), 28–29; Dennis J. Geaney, *CFM and the Priest* (Chicago: Christian Family Movement, 1960), 36.

37. Burns, *Disturbing the Peace*, 34–35, 39.

38. Burton Confrey, *Catholic Action: A Textbook for College Students and Study Clubs* (New York: Benziger Brothers, 1935), 39–40.

39. Senser, *Specialized Apostolates*, 4; Geaney, *CFM and the Priest*, 16–17; Confrey, *Catholic Action*, 39; statement of Father John J. Burke, Board of Directors Minutes, October 4, 1934, National Council of Catholic Women Records, Box 6, American Catholic Archives and Research Center, Catholic University of America, Washington, D.C.; CFM newsletter, quoted in Burns, *Disturbing the Peace*, 114.

40. The estimate of 90 percent is given in Morris, *American Catholic*, 163, 174, and elsewhere. For particular reports of this level of practice, see Alan Ehrenhalt, *The Lost City: The Forgotten Years of Community in America* (New York: Basic Books, 1995), 112–113; and Hugh J. Nolan, "The Native Son," *History of the Archdiocese of Philadelphia*, ed. James F. Connelly (Philadelphia: Archdiocese of Philadelphia, 1976), 410.

41. Joseph H. Fichter, *Dynamics of a City Church* (Chicago: University of Chicago Press, 1951), ch. 12; see also Joseph H. Fichter, "The Profile of Catholic Religious Life," *American Journal of Sociology* 58 (September 1952): 146. For a broader study that does not look at individual parishes, see George A. Kelly, *Catholics and the Practice of the Faith: A Census Study of the Diocese of Saint Augustine* (Washington, D.C.: Catholic University of America Press, 1946). For rates of church attendance elsewhere in America in this period, see Gallup Opinion Index, *Special Report on Religion, 1967* (Princeton: Gallup International, 1967), 5–10; and Gallup Opinion Index, *Religion in America, 1971* (Princeton: Gallup International, 1971), 43–44. See also Robert Wuthnow, *The Restructuring of American Religion: Society and Faith Since World War II* (Princeton: Princeton University Press, 1988), 15–17.

42. I am indebted throughout this discussion to Margaret M. McGuinness, "Let Us Go to the Altar: American Catholics and the Eucharist, 1926–1976," *Habits of Devotion: Catholic Religious Practice in Twentieth Century America,* ed. James M. O'Toole (Ithaca, N.Y.: Cornell University Press, 2004), 187–235.

43. Stang, *Pastoral Theology,* 129; J. H. Schutz, *A Little Book of Church Etiquette; or, How to Behave before Our Lord in the Blessed Sacrament and at Devotional Exercises in General* (St. Louis: B. Herder, 1929), 60–61; William Leonard, *The Letter Carrier* (Kansas City, Mo.: Sheed and Ward, 1993), 9.

44. "Sign Post," *Sign Magazine* 29, no. 2 (September 1949): 19.

45. Joseph H. Fichter, *Southern Parish* (Chicago: University of Chicago Press, 1951), 57–69; Fichter, "Catholic Religious Life," 146. In his study of white Catholics in Florida, George Kelly found similar rates of monthly Communion; see Kelly, *Catholics and the Practice of the Faith,* 63. On this subject generally, see Joseph N. Stadler, *Frequent Holy Communion: A Historical Synopsis and Commentary* (Washington, D.C.: Catholic University of America Press, 1947).

46. *Catholic Digest* quoted in McGuinness, "Let Us Go to the Altar," 200; *Father McGuire's New Baltimore Catechism* (New York: Benziger Brothers, 1942), 100; Schutz, *Catholic Etiquette,* 58.

47. Schultze, *Pastoral Theology,* 67; Peter Guilday, *A History of the Councils of Baltimore (1791–1884)* (New York: Macmillan, 1932), 209. On this subject generally, see Carrie T. Schultz, "Do This in Memory of Me: American Catholicism and First Communion Customs in the Era of *Quam Singulari,*" *American Catholic Studies* 115, no. 2 (Summer 2004): 45–66.

48. "Saint Benedict's Weekly," December 18, 1949, in Birney Family Papers, Bentley Historical Library, University of Michigan, Box 4; pulpit announcement books, Sacred Heart parish, Newton Centre, Massachusetts, February 11, 1940, Archives, Archdiocese of Boston; Fichter, *Southern Parish,* table 6, p. 55. My fuller treatment of this entire subject is "In the Court of Conscience: American Catholics and Confession, 1900–1975," *Habits of Devotion,* ed. O'Toole, 131–185.

49. "Our Question Box," *Messenger of the Sacred Heart* 77, no. 2 (July 1942), 77; "Our Question Box," *Messenger of the Sacred Heart* 70, no. 5 (May 1935), 79.

50. For a more detailed discussion of the procedure of confession and the thinking behind it, see O'Toole, "In the Court of Conscience," 144–162. Fichter's research on confession, complicated by the fact that it was conducted entirely in secret, is in *Southern Parish,* ch. 5.

51. Donald F. Miller, *Examination of Conscience for Adults: A Comprehensive Examination of Conscience Based on Twelve Virtues for the Twelve Months of the Year* (Liguori, Mo.: Liguorian Pamphlets, 1942); Father Dooley, *I Accuse Myself: A Modern Examination of Conscience* (Techny, Ill.: Mission Press, 1939).

52. For these prayers, see *Father McGuire's New Baltimore Catechism,* 3–7. For an important overview and interpretation, see Joseph P. Chinnici, "The Catholic Community at Prayer, 1926–1976," *Habits of Devotion,* ed. O'Toole, 9–87.

53. For a summation of the Catholic theology of saints, see Christopher O'Donnell, *Ecclesia: A Theological Encyclopedia of the Church* (Collegeville, Minn.: Liturgical Press, 1996), 416–418; on Jude, see Robert A. Orsi, *Thank You, St. Jude: Women's Devotions to the Patron Saint of Hopeless Causes* (New Haven: Yale University Press, 1996). See also *Father McGuire's New Baltimore Catechism,* 127; and "Novena to Saint Anthony," quoted in Chinnici and Dries, eds., *Prayer and Practice in the American Catholic Community,* 141.

54. This discussion relies heavily on James P. McCartin, "The Love of Things Unseen: Catholic Prayer and the Moral Imagination in the Twentieth-Century United States" (Ph.D. diss.: University of Notre Dame, 2003). See especially his discussion of Peyton in chapter 2; the quotes are at 9 and 21. See also Orsi, *Thank You, St. Jude,* 168.

55. McCartin, "Love of Things Unseen," ch. 2; the quotations are at 9 and 21. On the Boston rosary rally, see *Boston Pilot,* September 19, 1959.

56. Hugh Morley and John Jewell, *Week End with God* (New York: D. McKay, 1953), 9, 24. On the retreat movement generally, see Joseph P. Chinnici, *Living Stones: The History and Structure of Catholic Spiritual Life in the United States* (New York: Macmillan, 1989), ch. 14.

57. A useful summary of these developments is given in Jude Mead, "Historical Background of the Lay-Retreat Movement in the United States," in Thomas C. Hennessy, ed., *The Inner Crusade: The Closed Retreat*

in the United States (Chicago: Loyola University Press, 1965), 133–160. See also Joseph F. Hogan, *A Do-It-Yourself Retreat: How to Bring Out the Real Good in You* (Chicago: Loyola University Press, 1961), iii; Gerald C. Treacy, *Father Shealy—A Tribute* (Fort Wadsworth, N.Y.: Mount Manresa, 1927), 119; and Cassian Yuhaus, *Compelled to Speak: The Passionists in America* (Westminster, Md.: Newman Press, 1967), ch. 13.

58. Charles Plater, *A Week-End Retreat* (St. Louis: B. Herder, 1921), 12–13.

59. "Pope Speaks to World in Greatest Broadcast," *New York Times,* February 13, 1931; "Cardinal Rejoices upon Hearing Pope," ibid.; "Cardinal Pacelli, Papal Envoy, Here," ibid., October 9, 1936; "Pacelli Lunches with Roosevelt," ibid., November 6, 1936; "Cardinal Pacelli Sails for Home," ibid., November 8, 1936.

60. "Holy Year Pilgrims Led by the Cardinal," *New York Times,* February 19, 1950; "Pope Gives His Skull Cap to a New York Pilgrim," ibid., March 7, 1950; "Spellman Party on Riviera," ibid., March 10, 1950; "New Pilgrimages Set Up," ibid., March 29, 1950. Other accounts are given in William E. North, *Holy Year Pilgrimage: Archdiocese of Los Angeles, 1950* (Los Angeles: The Tidings, 1950), 22; and H. V. Morton, *This Is Rome: A Pilgrimage in Words and Pictures* (New York: Hawthorn Books, 1960), 119–120. On Americans and earlier jubilees, see Robert Trisco, "The First Jubilees Celebrated in the United States," *Catholic Historical Review* 86 (January 2000): 85–94.

61. Theodore H. White, *The Making of the President, 1960* (New York: Atheneum, 1961), 240; soldier's prayer card, found in a prayerbook (no. 04–19913) in the Liturgy and Life Collection, Burns Library, Boston College. On Catholic participation in the war effort, see James Hennesey, *American Catholics: A History of the Roman Catholic Community in the United States* (New York: Oxford University Press, 1981), 278–282.

62. Compare the entries for the dioceses of Brooklyn, Rockville Center (established 1957), and Los Angeles, 1945 and 1960, in the *Official Catholic Directory* (New York: P. J. Kenedy, 1945 and 1960). On the effects of suburbanization, see John T. McGreevy, *Parish Boundaries: The Catholic Encounter with Race in the Twentieth-Century Urban North* (Chicago: University of Chicago Press, 1996), 83–84.

63. Will Herberg, *Protestant, Catholic, Jew: An Essay in American Religious Sociology* (New York: Doubleday, 1955).

64. Paul Blanshard, *American Freedom and Catholic Power,* 2nd ed. (Boston: Beacon Press, 1958), viii, 14, 303. Blanshard is now a largely forgotten figure; see his obituary, *New York Times,* January 30, 1980.

65. Nathan Glazer and Daniel P. Moynihan, *Beyond the Melting Pot: The Negroes, Puerto Ricans, Jews, Italians, and Irish of New York City* 2nd ed. (Cambridge, Mass.: M.I.T. Press, 1970), 271. The fullest study of this aspect of McCarthy's career remains Donald F. Crosby, *God, Church, and Flag: Senator Joseph McCarthy and the Catholic Church, 1950–1957* (Chapel Hill: University of North Carolina Press, 1978).

66. Sheen has been much studied, but he still lacks an adequate scholarly biography. See the somewhat pious biography by Thomas C. Reeves, *America's Bishop: The Life and Times of Fulton J. Sheen* (San Francisco: Encounter Books, 2001); on his public persona, see Christopher Owen Lynch, *Selling Catholicism: Bishop Sheen and the Power of Television* (Lexington: University Press of Kentucky, 1998). Sheen's own *Treasure in Clay: The Autobiography of Fulton J. Sheen* (Garden City, N.Y.: Doubleday, 1980) tells his own story in his own words. On Sheen and his position in twentieth-century American religion generally, see Morris, *American Catholic,* 225–227; and Sidney E. Ahlstrom, *A Religious History of the American People* (New Haven: Yale University Press, 1972), 955–956, 1009–1011, 1033–1034.

67. The "religious issue" and other dimensions of the Kennedy campaign are treated fully in White, *Making of the President, 1960.* See also the more detailed analysis in Thomas J. Carty, *A Catholic in the White House? Religion, Politics, and John F. Kennedy's Presidential Campaign* (New York: Palgrave-Macmillan, 2004).

5. The Church of Vatican II

1. Historians are just now beginning to put Vatican II into historical context. The work of the council itself is available in *The Documents of Vatican II,* ed. Walter M. Abbott (New York: Guild Press, 1966). The ways in which Catholics worldwide understood and implemented the work of the council (often called its "reception") are described in Giuseppe Alberigo et al., eds., *The Reception of Vatican II,* trans. Matthew J. O'Connell (Washington, D.C.: Catholic University of American Press, 1987).

2. Conversation recorded in Robert McClory, *Turning Point: The Inside Story of the Papal Birth Control Commission* (New York: Crossroad, 1997). The history of American Catholics and birth control is described fully in Leslie Woodcock Tentler, *Catholics and Contraception: An American History* (Ithaca, N.Y.: Cornell University Press, 2004).

3. The standard biography of Roncalli is Peter Hebblethwaite, *John XXIII: Pope of the Council* (London: Chapman, 1984); see also the pope's own *Journal of a Soul,* trans. Dorothy White (New York: McGraw Hill, 1965). As usual, the best summary of John's pontificate is Eamon Duffy, *Saints and Sinners: A History of the Popes* (New Haven: Yale University Press, 1997), 268–275.

4. "Constitution on the Sacred Liturgy," *Documents of Vatican II,* ed. Abbott, nos. 14, 21, 34, and 36. For a comprehensive history of the process of change told from the perspective of a Vatican official who was heavily involved, see Annabile Bugnini, *The Reform of the Liturgy, 1948–1975,* trans. Matthew J. O'Connell (Collegeville, Minn.: Liturgical Press, 1990).

5. A full history of the liturgical movement has yet to be written; most work to date has focused on its leadership. See R. W. Franklin and Robert L. Spaeth, *Virgil Michel: American Catholic* (Collegeville, Minn.: Liturgical Press, 1988); and Robert L. Tuzik, ed., *How Firm a Foundation: Leaders of the Liturgical Movement* (Chicago: Liturgy Training Publications, 1990). For the experience of the Chicago Catholic, see John J. Jankauskas, *Our Tongues Were Loosed: Parish Experiences in the Liturgical Renewal* (Westminster, Md.: Newman Press, 1965), 44. The elite nature of the movement is analyzed in William D. Dinges, "Resistance to Liturgical Change," *Liturgy: Journal of the Liturgical Conference* 6, no. 2 (Fall 1986): 67–73.

6. For a summary of the changes, see *St. Paul Catholic Bulletin,* February 12, 1965; and C. J. McNaspy, *Our Changing Liturgy* (New York: Hawthorn Books, 1966), 91–92. For later assessments, see Joseph P. Chinnici, "The Reception of Vatican II in the United States," *Theological Studies* 64 (September 2003): 461–494; and John W. O'Malley, "Vatican II: Did Anything Happen?" ibid., 67 (March 2006): 3–33.

7. The phasing in of the successive changes in the Mass may be seen by comparing missals published during this period: *Saint Joseph Daily Missal* (New York: Catholic Book Publishing, 1964); *New Saint Joseph Daily Mis-*

sal and Hymnal (New York: Catholic Book Publishing, 1966); *New Saint Joseph Sunday Missal and Hymnal* (New York: Catholic Book Publishing, 1970); and *New Saint Joseph Sunday Missal and Hymnal* (New York: Catholic Book Publishing, 1974). On the difficulty of keeping up with these changes, see "Question Box: Missal Bought Now Outdated Soon," *St. Paul Catholic Bulletin,* December 31, 1965.

8. See the parish schedules given in *Galveston-Houston Catholic Directory, 1968–69* (Galveston, Tex.: Catholic Herald, 1968), 31–38; and *Diocese of Galveston-Houston 1980 Directory* (Galveston, Tex.: Catholic Herald, 1980), 20–36. See also Bugnini, *Reform of the Liturgy,* 324–326; and "Anticipating Sunday," *Herder Correspondence* 5 (July 1968): 217–219.

9. Reaction to the practice may be seen in George W. Casey, "Keep Holy the Sabbath," *Boston Pilot,* May 31, 1969; "Cardinal Polls Clergy on 'Saturday' Masses," ibid., March 22, 1969; and "Saturday Masses Fill Obligations for Sunday Here," ibid., June 21, 1969. For general background, see Alexis McCrossen, *Holy Day, Holiday: The American Sunday* (Ithaca, N.Y.: Cornell University Press, 2000).

10. Nardone to McManus, November 4, 1967, and Martin to McManus, both in Frederick J. McManus Papers, Box 1, Folder 5, Archives, Catholic University of America; "Question Box: Liturgical Changes Queried," *St. Paul Catholic Bulletin,* August 13, 1965. For the traditional rubrics, see Walter J. Schmitz, *Learning the Mass: The New Liturgy Handbook for Priests and Seminarians* (Milwaukee: Bruce, 1965).

11. The New Jersey priest is quoted in Mark J. Massa, *Catholics and American Culture: Fulton Sheen, Dorothy Day, and the Notre Dame Football Team* (New York: Crossroad, 1999), 163. The Boston archbishop's letter, February 4, 1965, is in Chancery Circulars 9:9, AABo. For the implementation of changes in Minnesota, see "Two Sees Prepare for Liturgy Changes," *St. Paul Catholic Bulletin,* November 20, 1964; and "Liturgy Changes Difficult for All," ibid., February 12, 1965.

12. "Impact of English in Mass Welcomed by Parishioners," *St. Paul Catholic Bulletin,* December 4, 1964; "Laity Not Spectators," ibid., August 14, 1964; letter to the editor from Stephen Vuono, *Boston Pilot,* February 22, 1964; "Spotlight on the Liturgy," *Homiletic and Pastoral Review* 65, no. 5 (February 1965): 415.

13. "Liturgy U.S.A.: A Status Report," *U.S. Catholic* 32, no. 3 (July 1966): 6–17; see also the *Bishops' Commission on the Liturgical Apostolate Newsletter* 2 (October 1966): 53–54. For surveys of individual congregations, see "Liturgical Updating Liked by 2 to 1 at Ascension," *St. Paul Catholic Bulletin,* August 13, 1965; and "New Liturgy Finds Favor in Burnsville," ibid., January 28, 1966. For comparative purposes, see a similar study of a British parish: John Fitzsimmons, "The New Liturgy: A Parish Survey," *Clergy Review* 55 (November 1970): 834–840.

14. Jankauskas, *Our Tongues Were Loosed,* 26–27; Mary Perkins Ryan, *Has the New Liturgy Changed You?* (New York: Paulist Press, 1967), 6–7; "Sign Post," *Sign Magazine* 48, no. 6 (January 1969): 33.

15. McNaspy, *Our Changing Liturgy,* 158–159; Dinges, "Resistance to Liturgical Change," 69–70. On the ambiguities of the adulthood metaphor, see Robert A. Orsi, *Between Heaven and Earth: The Religious Worlds People Make and the Scholars Who Study Them* (Princeton: Princeton University Press, 2005), 152–158.

16. "Children to Take Lead Roles at Mass," *St. Paul Catholic Bulletin,* January 8, 1965; "Question Box: Would-Be 'Altar-Girls' Participate," ibid., February 9, 1965. For the dismissal of the notion as "comical," see Bugnini, *Reform of the Liturgy,* 211.

17. "Resolutions of Conference of Diocesan Liturgical Commissions," June 8–10, 1967, McManus Papers, Box 1, Folder 12, Archives, Catholic University of America; see also Adam to McManus, December 30, 1967, ibid., Box 1, Folder 15. On the Vatican approval of altar girls, see Bugnini, *Reform of the Liturgy,* 211, n. 15. See also "Women Lectors Authorized at Mass," a wireservice story in *Boston Pilot,* February 1, 1969.

18. See the reports in the *St. Paul Catholic Bulletin:* "Contracts Let for New St. Joseph's," February 8, 1963; "St. Leo's Has Ground Blessing," April 30, 1965; "Church Design Based on Liturgy," April 16, 1965; and "St. George Cornerstone Rites Sunday," July 12, 1963. See also "New Altars Will Need Artistic Taste," ibid., August 5, 1965. The wary assessment of artistic talent in the redesign of churches was expressed in "Areas of Concern" listed in "Parish Liturgy, American Style," the program book for the 1975 annual meeting of diocesan liturgical commissions, a copy of which is in the Burns Library, Boston College. For a general (if opinionated) treatment of this subject, see Steven J. Schloeder, *Architecture in Communion: Implementing*

the Second Vatican Council through Liturgy and Architecture (San Francisco: Ignatius Press, 1998).

19. As before, the best guide through these issues is Margaret McGuinness, "Let Us Go to the Altar: American Catholics and the Eucharist, 1926–1976," *Habits of Devotion: Catholic Religious Practice in Twentieth Century America,* ed. James M. O'Toole (Ithaca, N.Y.: Cornell University Press, 2004), 187–235; the quotations here are at p. 221.

20. The description of the traditional method is in J. H. Schutz, *A Little Book of Church Etiquette, or How to Behave Before Our Lord in the Blessed Sacrament and at Devotional Exercises in General* (St. Louis: Herder, 1929), 62. The lay woman's objections to it are in a letter to the editor of *U.S. Catholic* 39, no. 7 (July 1974): 45.

21. For a summary of this controversy, see McGuinness, "Let Us Go to the Altar," 225–227. See also Chinnici, "Reception of Vatican II," 475–476; Joseph P. Chinnici, "Changing Religious Practice and the End of Christendom in the United States, 1965–1986," *U.S. Catholic Historian* 23, no. 4 (Fall 2005): 78–81; and Bugnini, *Reform of the Liturgy,* 640–661. Bishops in Canada had approved the practice as early as 1972; see *Homiletic and Pastoral Review* 73, no. 2 (November 1972): 4.

22. Hugh H. Connell, *Putting Vatican II into Practice* (Liguori, Mo.: Liguorian Pamphlets, 1966), 92; "Communion under Both Kinds Now Common," *U.S. Catholic* (October 1967): 44–45. See also McGuinness, "Let Us Go to the Altar," 224–225; and Bugnini, *Reform of the Liturgy,* 626–634, 636–640. The young woman drinking from the chalice appeared on the cover of the March 1968 issue of *U.S. Catholic.*

23. For priests' concerns about the use of women as Eucharistic ministers, see "Questions Answered," *Homiletic and Pastoral Review* 74, no. 9 (June 1974): 74–76. The commissioning ceremony in Indianapolis is described in *Origins* 3 (April 11, 1974): 650.

24. The confession schedules for Saint Thomas Aquinas parish are given in its parish bulletins, a collection of which is in AABo; for the joke about reusing confessionals for other purposes, see Brian T. Joyce, *Penance: Parent and Child* (New York: Sadlier, 1974), 39. On this subject generally, see James M. O'Toole, "In the Court of Conscience: American Catholics and Confession, 1925–1975," *Habits of Devotion,* ed. O'Toole, 168–171.

25. The anonymous comments from lay people are included in the sur-

veys conducted by *U.S. Catholic* magazine, now in the Archives of the University of Notre Dame, case numbers 3/08, 9/15, and 24/16. The discouragement of frequent confession is in *New Saint Joseph Daily Missal and Hymnal,* 1384, and in "Sign Post," *Sign* 47, no. 1 (August 1967): 48.

26. "Is the New Confession Working?" *U.S. Catholic* 42, no. 11 (November 1977): 27–33; Charles E. Miller, *Love in the Language of Penance: A Simple Guide to the New Rite of Penance* (New York: Alba House, 1976), 14; Carroll T. Dozier, *A Call to Reconciliation* (Memphis, Tenn.: Diocese of Memphis, 1976). See also O'Toole, "In the Court of Conscience," 182–185.

27. *Father McGuire's New Baltimore Catechism, No. 1* (New York: Benziger Brothers 1942), 119; *New Saint Joseph Daily Missal,* 1397; *New Saint Joseph Baltimore Catechism* (New York: Catholic Book Publishing, 1964), 134. See also John E. Corrigan, "Pastoral Renewal: The Rites of the Sacraments," *Homiletic and Pastoral Review* 65, no. 1 (October 1964): 39.

28. The reactions of the Texas nurses are included in Kieran Nolan, "The Sacrament of Anointing and Total Patient Care," *Homiletic and Pastoral Review* 74, no. 9 (June 1974): 57–58; special services for AIDS sufferers are described in "Further Development of AIDS Ministry," *Origins* 18 (November 17, 1988): 378–380. For the larger context of these changes, see Bugnini, *Reform of the Liturgy,* 684–695.

29. Compare the parishioners' comments in Jankauskas, xiv and 37, with the comments of James Moudry in *St. Paul Catholic Bulletin,* May 10, 1963.

30. Schutz, *Little Book of Catholic Etiquette,* 7; "Why Do Catholics Leave the Church?" *Ave Maria* 87 (January 11, 1958): 8; Anonymous, "Why Did I Leave the Church?" *Integrity* 9 (September 1955): 15; "Sign Post," *Sign* 33, no. 4 (November 1953): 32.

31. As before, measures of regular Mass attendance are not as precise as one would want them, and they vary significantly depending on how survey questions are phrased. Even so, see George Gallup, Jr., and Jim Castelli, *The American Catholic People: Their Beliefs, Practices, and Values* (New York: Doubleday, 1987), 26–28; William V. D'Antonio et al., *Laity, American and Catholic: Transforming the Church* (Kansas City, Mo.: Sheed and Ward, 1996), 131–133; and Bryan T. Froehle and Mary L. Gautier, *Catholicism U.S.A.: A Portrait of the Catholic Church in the United States* (Maryknoll, N.Y.: Orbis Books, 2000), 22–24.

32. For two contemporary views of the "piety void," see Chinnici and Dries, eds., *Prayer and Practice in the American Catholic Community,* 250–258; see also the discussion in Chinnici, "Catholic Community at Prayer," *Habits of Devotion,* ed. O'Toole, 82–85. For a reflection on what was gained and lost, see William F. Buckley, Jr., *Nearer My God: An Autobiography of Faith* (New York: Doubleday, 1997), ch. 6.

33. *Father McGuire's New Baltimore Catechism,* no. 127.

34. Froehle and Gautier, *Catholicism U.S.A.,* 28; Andrew M. Greeley, *American Catholics since the Council: An Unauthorized Report* (Chicago: Thomas More Press, 1985), 51; Hugh J. O'Connell, *Putting Vatican II into Practice* (Liguori, Mo.: Liguorian Pamphlets, 1966), 70.

35. For the earlier warnings against Catholic Bible reading, see the bishops' statement of 1829, in Joseph Chinnici and Angelyn Dries, eds., *Prayer and Practice in the American Catholic Community* (New York: Orbis, 2000), 22; and Paul C. Gutjahr, *An American Bible: A History of the Good Book in the United States, 1777–1880* (Stanford, Calif.: Stanford University Press, 1999), 132. The doctor's observations are in Chinnici and Dries, *Prayer and Practice,* 218. For the post–Vatican II surveys, see Gallup and Castelli, *American Catholic People,* 30, 34–35; and Jim Castelli and Joseph Gremillion, *The Emerging Parish: The Notre Dame Study of Catholic Life since Vatican II* (San Francisco: Harper and Row, 1987), 149.

36. National Cursillo Center, *The Fundamental Ideas of the Cursillo Movement* (Dallas: National Ultreya Publications, 1974), 56–57; on the role of this and other movements in the development of lay parish leadership, see Charles R. Morris, *American Catholic: The Saints and Sinners Who Built America's Most Powerful Church* (New York: Times Books, 1997), 397.

37. Don Demarest, *Marriage Encounter: A Guide to Sharing* (St. Paul, Minn.: Carillon Books, 1977), 3, 17, 189; see also Antoinette Bosco, *Marriage Encounter: The Rediscovery of Love* (St. Meinrad, Ind.: Abbey Press, 1976).

38. See Grant Wacker, *Heaven Below: Early Pentecostals and American Culture* (Cambridge, Mass.: Harvard University Press, 2001). The notion of "planned spontaneity" is considered in chapter 6; Pentecostal views of Catholics are discussed on pp. 179–182.

39. For a description of a prayer meeting, see Ronda Chervin, *Why I Am*

a Charismatic: A Catholic Explains (Liguori, Mo.: Liguori Publications, 1978), 23, 26, 69; see also James E. Byrne, *Living in the Spirit: A Handbook on Catholic Charismatic Christianity* (New York: Paulist Press, 1975), 164–169. For historical studies, see James T. Connolly, "Neo-Pentecostalism: The Charismatic Revival in the Mainline Protestant and Roman Catholic Churches in the United States, 1960–1971" (Ph.D. diss.: University of Chicago, 1977); and Randy McGuire, "Catholic Charismatic Renewal: The Struggle for Affirmation, 1967–1975" (Ph.D. diss.: St. Louis University, 1998).

40. John Randall, *In God's Providence: The Birth of a Catholic Charismatic Parish* (Locust Valley, Calif.: Living Flame Press, 1973), 41–42, 53; "Questions Answered," *Homiletic and Pastoral Review* 73, no. 2 (January 1973): 67–69. The estimates of the number of groups and participants are in Jay P. Dolan, *The American Catholic Experience: A History from Colonial Times to the Present* (New York: Doubleday, 1985), 432; see also James Hennesey, *American Catholics: A History of the Roman Catholic Community in the United States* (New York: Oxford University Press, 1981), 317–318.

41. Chervin, *Why I Am a Charismatic*, 87, 72; Patrick L. Bourgeois, *Can Catholics Be Charismatic? Fundamentals of the Full Christian Life* (Hicksville, N.Y.: Expositions Press, 1976), 7, 14–15, 22, 95–96, 98; and Randall, *In God's Providence*, 4. For a more recent, dispassionate assessment of the charismatic movement, see Morris, *American Catholics*, 394–401. For a contemporary critique of this movement (and others), see James Hitchcock, *The New Enthusiasts, and What They Are Doing to the Catholic Church* (Chicago: Thomas More Press, 1982).

42. David M. Knight, "A Practical Plan for Lay Spiritual Formation," *Studies in Formative Spirituality* 9 (February 1988): 7–8; William A. Barry and Mary Guy, "The Practice of Supervision in Spiritual Direction," *Review for Religious* 37 (November 1978): 834–835.

43. Madeleine Birmingham and William J. Connolly, *Witnessing to the Fire: Spiritual Direction and the Development of Directors, One Center's Experience* (Kansas City, Mo.: Sheed and Ward, 1994), 210; and William A. Barry and William J. Connolly, *The Practice of Spiritual Direction* (San Francisco: Harper and Row, 1982), 11. See also Paul Wachdorf, "Leading People into

Prayer," *Review for Religious* 47 (May–June 1988): 334–341; and C. Kevin Gillespie, *Psychology and American Catholicism: From Confession to Therapy?* (New York: Crossroad, 2001), 153–154.

44. The key council statements regarding the laity are in "Dogmatic Constitution on the Church," nos. 30–38, and all of the "Decree on the Apostolate of the Laity," both in *Documents of Vatican II*, ed. Abbott.

45. Several studies have documented these trends: see Philip J. Murnion, *New Parish Ministers: Laity and Religious on Parish Staffs* (New York: National Pastoral Life Center, 1992), esp. v–vii, 35, 46; Philip J. Murnion and David DeLambo, *Parishes and Parish Ministers: A Study of Lay Parish Ministry* (New York: National Pastoral Life Center, 1999); and David E. DeLambo, "The New Parish Ministers: A Sociological Study of Lay Ecclesial Ministry in the Catholic Church" (Ph.D. diss.: Fordham University, 2000), esp. p. 120. The Pittsburgh statistics are compiled from the *Diocese of Pittsburgh Catholic Directory* (Pittsburgh: Pittsburgh Catholic Newspaper, 1991). More than 112 priests were living in the city's parishes in those years, but the larger number included those who were retired from active ministry or were assigned to other duties.

46. Douglas Fisher, ed., *Why We Serve: Personal Stories of Catholic Lay Ministers* (New York: Paulist Press, 1984), 6, 9, 109; Murnion, *New Parish Ministers,* 10, 43.

47. See Patrick McCaslin and Michael G. Lawler, *Sacrament of Service: A Vision of the Permanent Diaconate Today* (New York: Paulist Press, 1986); and Owen F. Cummings, *Deacons and the Church* (New York: Paulist Press, 2004). Strictly speaking, once they were ordained these permanent deacons ceased to be lay people and joined the category of "clerics" in church law.

48. The fullest survey is *A National Study on the Permanent Diaconate of the Catholic Church in the United States, 1994–1995* (Washington, D.C.: United States Catholic Conference, 1995); see also Froehle and Gautier, *Catholicism U.S.A.,* ch. 8. For particular experiences, see Ray R. Noll, "The Sacramental Ministry of the Deacon in Parish Life," *The Deacon Reader,* ed. James Keating (New York: Paulist Press, 2006), 198–209; and Mark A. Latcovich, "The Diaconate and Marriage: A Sociological Reflection," ibid., 213–231. The Boston example is treated fully in Matthew Kraycinovich, "A

Servant Sign Unseen: The Restoration Experience of the First Class of Permanent Deacons in the Roman Catholic Archdiocese of Boston" (seminar paper, Boston College, 2004), in the author's possession.

49. Nearly everything remains to be done in writing the social history of the American Catholic priesthood. For two examples, see Robert E. Sullivan, "Beneficial Relations: Toward a Social History of the Diocesan Priests of Boston, 1875–1944," *Catholic Boston,* ed. Sullivan and O'Toole, 201–238; and Leslie Woodcock Tentler, "'God's Representative in Our Midst': Toward a History of the Catholic Diocesan Clergy in the United States," *Church History* 67 (June 1998): 326–349, quotation at 345. Studs's mother pushes him unsuccessfully toward the priesthood in chapter 2 of *Young Lonigan: A Boyhood in the Chicago Streets* (New York: Vanguard, 1932), the first volume of the Lonigan trilogy. For the portrayal of priests in the movies, see Morris, *American Catholic,* 196–200.

50. Froehle and Gautier, *Catholicism U.S.A.,* 109–123; and Morris, *American Catholic,* 477. The comparative priest-parishioner ratios are in Castelli and Gremillion, *Emerging Parish,* 29.

51. The most comprehensive study of this phenomenon is Richard A. Schoenherr and Lawrence A. Young, *Full Pews and Empty Altars: Demographics of the Priest Shortage in United States Catholic Dioceses* (Madison: University of Wisconsin Press, 1993); see especially ch. 2 ("National Trends") and Tables 9.1 and 12.1.

52. See the survey results outlined in Gallup and Castelli, *American Catholic People,* 53–56.

53. News reports of the day's events were subsequently assembled in book form: A. M. Rosenthal and Arthur Gelb, ed., *The Pope's Journey to the United States* (New York: Herder and Herder, 1965); see also Edward T. Fleming, ed., *An Instrument of Your Peace: The Mission for Peace by Pope Paul VI and His Momentous Visit to America* (New York: Commemorative Publications, 1965).

54. This whole subject is treated comprehensively and skillfully in Tentler, *Catholics and Contraception,* quotations at 201 and 202; the comments from the man from San Francisco are in "Sign Post," *Sign* 48, no. 6 (January 1969): 32.

55. Tentler, *Catholics and Contraception,* 81, 183, 243. The woman from

the Bronx who "received permission" described her experience in "Sign Post," *Sign* 48, no. 3 (October 1968): 22. In the course of my own research on confession, I have heard several accounts of women's networks that transferred information on where one might find an understanding confessor.

56. The commission met privately, but its deliberations are described fully in McClory, *Turning Point,* which is based largely on the diaries, papers, and recollections of Patty Crowley; quotations from the majority and minority reports are at 110–113. On Noonan and his influence, see John T. McGreevy, *Catholicism and American Freedom: A History* (New York: W. W. Norton, 2003), 241–243.

57. For reactions to the encyclical, see Mr. and Mrs. W. F. Jones to Shehan, November 4, 1968, and Rev. William Collins to Shehan, August 8, 1968, both in Cardinal Lawrence Shehan Papers ("Humanae Vitae File"), Archives, Archdiocese of Baltimore. For polling data, see William V. D'Antonio et al., *American Catholic Laity in a Changing Church* (Kansas City, Mo.: Sheed and Ward, 1989), Tables 4.1 and 6.3. On the American reaction generally, see Tentler, *Catholics and Contraception,* 264–268; McGreevy, *Catholicism and American Freedom,* 245–248; and McClory, *Turning Point,* 147–159.

58. The fullest treatment of these movements is Michael W. Cuneo, *The Smoke of Satan: Conservative and Traditionalist Dissent in Contemporary American Catholicism* (New York: Oxford University Press, 1997); see esp. 152–162 on Lueken. See also Mary Jo Weaver and R. Scott Appleby, eds., *Being Right: Conservative American Catholics* (Bloomington: Indiana University Press, 1995). For DePauw and his movement, see "St. Patrick's Cathedral Picketed by Traditionalist Catholic Unit," *New York Times,* March 3, 1968. A balanced assessment of Catholics United for the Faith is presented in M. Timothy Iglesias, "CUF and Dissent: A Case Study in Religious Conservatism," *America* 156 (April 11, 1987): 303–301.

59. See the largely sympathetic treatments in Mary Jo Weaver, "Resisting Traditional Catholic Sexual Teaching: Pro-Choice Advocacy and Homosexual Support Groups," 88–108, and Bernard J. Cooke, "Call to Action: Engine of Lay Ministry," 147–154, both in Mary Jo Weaver, ed., *What's Left? Liberal American Catholics* (Bloomington: Indiana University Press, 1999).

More critical assessments are given in Richard Doerflinger, "Who Are Catholics for a Free Choice?" *America* 153 (November 16, 1985): 312–317; and Kathryn Jean Lopez, "Aborting the Church: Frances Kissling and Catholics for a Free Choice," *Crisis* 20, no. 2 (April 2002): 20–26. See also David Gibson, *The Coming Catholic Church: How the Faithful Are Shaping a New American Catholicism* (San Francisco: Harper San Francisco, 2003), 120–122.

60. "Cardinal Aims for New Unity for Catholics," *New York Times,* August 13, 1996; "Cardinal Defends Plan to Promote Discussions," ibid., September 1, 1996. See also Gibson, *Coming Catholic Church,* 288–289; and Peter Steinfels, *A People Adrift: The Crisis of the Roman Catholic Church in America* (New York: Simon and Schuster, 2003), ch. 1.

61. "Current Comment: Women in the Sanctuary?" *America* 103 (June 18, 1960): 367; Gerald O'Collins, "An Argument for Women Priests," ibid., 129 (September 1, 1973): 122–123. For the experience of other denominations, see Carl J. Schneider and Dorothy Schneider, *In Their Own Right: The History of American Clergywomen* (New York: Crossroad, 1997); Virginia Lieson Brereton and Christa Ressmeyer Klein, "American Women in Ministry: A History of Protestant Beginning Points," *Women in American Religion,* ed. Janet Wilson James (Philadelphia: University of Pennsylvania Press, 1980), 171–190; and Jonathan D. Sarna, *American Judaism: A History* (New Haven: Yale University Press, 2004), 340–343.

62. Agnes Cunningham, "Sounding Board: Why Not Women Priests?" *U.S. Catholic* 35, no. 6 (June 1970): 10–14; see also *U.S. Catholic* surveys, 24/16, Archives, University of Notre Dame.

63. The presentations and other materials at the sessions are compiled in *Women and Catholic Priesthood: An Expanded Vision; Proceedings of the Detroit Ordination Conference,* ed. Anne Marie Gardiner (New York: Paulist Press, 1976); quotations are at 136 and 187. See also the report in *New York Times,* December 1, 1975.

64. *Women and Catholic Priesthood,* ed. Gardiner, gives transcripts of the talks at the Mass, 155–158; see also 162.

65. The U.S. bishops' statement and related materials are given in *Women and Catholic Priesthood,* ed. Gardiner, 193–198. A complete history of the Vatican's position, together with translations of the relevant documents, is in Deborah Halter, *The Papal "No": A Comprehensive Guide to the*

Vatican's Rejection of Women's Ordination (New York: Crossroad, 2004); see esp. 211–213. The pope's vehemence on the subject is noted in Thomas J. Reese, *Inside the Vatican: The Politics and Organization of the Catholic Church* (Cambridge, Mass.: Harvard University Press, 1996), 243.

66. For reactions to the statement, see, for example, the letters to the editor column of *U.S. Catholic* magazine, November and December 1994. Also informative is "Women's Ordination: Six Responses," *Commonweal* 121, no. 13 (July 15, 1994): 10–13. On the assertion of papal power, see Francis A. Sullivan, "New Claims for the Pope," *The Tablet*, 248 (June 18, 1994): 767–769. American Catholic lay opinion on the subject is measured in "U.S. Catholicism: Trends in the '90s," *National Catholic Reporter*, October 8, 1991; see also D'Antonio et al., *Laity, American and Catholic*, 103–105. The illicit ordination in Germany is described in "Some Women Seeking Ordination Won't Wait for Church's OK," *National Catholic Reporter*, January 27, 2006; other such ordinations have followed in Canada and the United States, with equally little effect.

67. The most complete biography is George Weigel's massive *Witness to Hope: The Biography of John Paul II* (New York: Cliff Street Books, 1999). For a less adulatory, though still favorable, treatment, see Tad Szulc, *Pope John Paul II: The Biography* (New York: Scribner, 1995). In addition to his four extended visits in the United States, John Paul twice stopped over in Alaska during trips to Asia.

68. See the coverage of this event in *New York Times,* August 16, 1993; *National Catholic Reporter,* August 27, 1993; and *Our Sunday Visitor,* September 5, 1993.

69. "Sign Post," *Sign* 48, no. 6 (January 1969): 33. For a sensible early discussion of "cafeteria Catholics," see Peter Steinfels, "Beliefs," *New York Times,* April 13, 1991.

70. As before, see the studies in Gallup and Castelli, *American Catholic People,* 1–9; D'Antonio et al., *Laity, American and Catholic,* 10–15; and Froehle and Gautier, *Catholicism U.S.A.,* 3–19.

71. The text of the encyclical *Mortalium Animos* is in Claudia Carlen, ed., *The Papal Encyclicals, 1903–1939* (Raleigh, N.C.: McGrath, 1981), 313–319. For a general survey written as the climate was changing, see Samuel M. Cavert, *Church Cooperation and Unity in America: A Historical Review,*

1900–1970 (New York: Association Press, 1970); see also John T. McGreevy, "Thinking on One's Own: Catholicism and the American Intellectual Tradition, 1928–1960," *Journal of American History* 84 (June 1997): 97–131.

72. "Sign Post," *Sign* 32, no. 3 (October 1952): 54; ibid., 34, no. 8 (March 1955): 62; ibid., 29, no. 11 (June 1950): 37; ibid., 29, no. 8 (March 1950): 33; and ibid., 29, no. 7 (February 1950): 59.

73. There is no comprehensive history of the Feeney episode, and, since most of the existing archival sources remain closed to scholars, there may not be for some time. In the meantime, see George Pepper, *The Boston Heresy Case in View of the Secularization of Religion: A Case Study in the Sociology of Religion* (Lewiston, N.Y.: Edwin Mellen, 1988); and Patrick W. Carey, "Avery Dulles, St. Benedict's Center, and No Salvation Outside the Church, 1940-1953," *Catholic Historical Review* 93 (July 2007): 553–575. Avery Dulles left the group well before the blow-up; he became a prominent Jesuit theologian and eventually a cardinal of the church.

74. The key texts are the Decree on Ecumenism ("Unitatis Redintegratio"), *Documents of Vatican II,* ed. Abbott, 341–366; Decree on Eastern Catholic Churches ("Orientalium Ecclesiarum"), ibid., 373–386; Declaration on the Relationship of the Church to Non-Christian Religions ("Nostra Aetate"), ibid., 660–668; and Declaration on Religious Freedom ("Dignitatis Humanae"), ibid., 675–696. On the significance of this shift, see John T. Noonan, Jr., *A Church That Can and Cannot Change: The Development of Catholic Moral Teaching* (Notre Dame, Ind.: University of Notre Dame Press, 2005), 145–158.

75. National Councils of Catholic Men and Women, *First Steps in Grass-Roots Ecumenism* (Washington, D.C.: NCCM, 1966), 55, 58; James J. Young, *Third Living Room Dialogues* (Paramus, N.J.: Paulist Press, 1970), 9; Archdiocese of Chicago, *Guidelines for Ecumenism* (Chicago: Archdiocese of Chicago, 1968), 25; O'Brien, *Faith and Friendship,* 367–368. See also the newsletter of the Boston Archdiocesan Ecumenical Commission, *Fellowship* 2, no. 1 (January 1965): 1–2, copy in O'Neill Library, Boston College, Chestnut Hill, Mass.

76. Thomas C. Donlan et al., *Toward Marriage in Christ: A College Text in Theology,* 2nd rev. ed. (Dubuque, Iowa: Priory Press, 1960), 91, 59. For the nineteenth-century experience, see James M. O'Toole, "Portrait of a

Parish: Race, Ethnicity, and Class in Boston's Cathedral of the Holy Cross, 1865–1880," *Boston's Histories: Essays in Honor of Thomas H. O'Connor,* ed. James M. O'Toole and David Quigley (Boston: Northeastern University Press, 2004), 99–100.

77. For the intermarriage rates in Detroit, see Leslie Woodcock Tentler, *Seasons of Grace: A History of the Catholic Archdiocese of Detroit* (Detroit: Wayne State University Press, 2001), 99–101, 475–477. For a summary of sociological data on this subject, see Dean R. Hoge and Kathleen M. Ferry, *Empirical Research on Interfaith Marriage in America* (Washington, D.C.: United States Catholic Conference, 1981), esp. 1–5; see also Joseph M. Champlin, *Together for Life: A Preparation for Marriage and for the Ceremony* (Notre Dame, Ind.: Ave Maria Press, 1975), 93–96.

78. On Liuzzo, see "4 Rights Leaders Attend Funeral," *New York Times,* March 31, 1965; on Reeb, see "Boston's Uncommon Tribute," *Boston Pilot,* March 20, 1965.

79. The fullest study of these tensions within the Catholic community is John T. McGreevy, *Parish Boundaries: The Catholic Encounter with Race in the Twentieth-Century Urban North* (Chicago: University of Chicago Press, 1996), esp. ch. 8; Groppi is discussed 198–205, quotations at 183 and 190. For the case of Saint Agnes parish, see Thomas C. Henthorn, "A Catholic Dilemma: White Flight in Northwest Flint," *Michigan Historical Review* 31, no. 2 (Fall 2005): 1–42.

80. McGreevy, *Parish Boundaries,* 190; J. Anthony Lukas, *Common Ground: A Turbulent Decade in the Lives of Three American Families* (New York: Knopf, 1985), 363. For another example of an antibusing prayer march, see ibid., 271–276.

81. Miller's case received extensive newspaper coverage from start to finish: see, for example, "Draft Protestor Is Seized by F.B.I. for Burning Card," *New York Times,* October 19, 1965; "David Miller and the Catholic Workers: A Study in Pacifism," ibid., October 24, 1965; and "Pacifist Gets Suspended Sentence for Destroying Draft Card," ibid., March 16, 1966. See also "7 War Protestors Beaten in Boston," ibid., April 1, 1966. Disapproval of this tactic was expressed in "Self-Defeating Martyrdom," *America* 116 (April 15, 1967): 548.

82. "Antiabortion Move Proposed," *New York Times,* February 1, 1973;

"Reversal of Abortion Ruling Sought," ibid., February 2, 1973; "Letters from '70s Reveal a Ted K with Sentiments against Abortion," *Boston Herald,* September 9, 1994; "Kennedy and Romney Blast Away," *Boston Globe,* October 26, 1994; John T. McGreevy, *Catholicism and American Freedom: A History* (New York: Norton, 2003), 280.

83. Catholics are frequently polled for their opinions on abortion; see, as examples, John Deedy, "Counter-Attack by the Bishops," *New York Times,* February 18, 1973; Gallup and Castelli, *American Catholic People,* 91–99; and Steinfels, *People Adrift,* 95–96.

84. For one early analysis of Cuomo's speech and the issues it raised, see Garry Wills, *Under God: Religion and American Politics* (New York: Simon and Schuster, 1990), ch. 27. For a more recent assessment of Catholics and electoral politics, see John T. McGreevy, "Shifting Allegiances: Catholics, Democrats, and the GOP," *Commonweal* 133, no. 16 (September 22, 2006): 14–19.

6. The Church in the Twenty-first Century

1. "Sex Charges against Priest Embroil Louisiana Parents," *New York Times,* June 20, 1985; "Rhode Island Priest Gets Year in Sex Assault Case," ibid., June 25, 1986; "Newark Priest Pleads Guilty to Sexual Assault on Youths," ibid., March 5, 1987; "Molestation of Child by Priest Stirring Furor and Anguish in Seattle Church," ibid., June 12, 1988. On Ritter, see Peter J. Wosh, *Covenant House: Journey of a Faith-Based Charity* (Philadelphia: University of Pennsylvania Press, 2005).

2. The literature describing these cases is now quite extensive. For Porter, see David France, *Our Fathers: The Secret Life of the Catholic Church in an Age of Scandal* (New York: Broadway Books, 2004), 206–217; Jason Berry, *Lead Us Not into Temptation: Catholic Priests and the Sexual Abuse of Children* (New York: Doubleday, 1992), 360; and Elinor Burkett and Frank Bruni, *A Gospel of Shame: Children, Sexual Abuse, and the Catholic Church* (New York: Viking, 1993), esp. 3–25. France's book is filled with minor factual errors but is still useful. See also the summary in Porter's obituary, *Boston Globe,* February 12, 2005. For an introduction to the psychological

dimensions of these cases, see Paul R. Dokecki, *The Clergy Sexual Abuse Crisis: Reform and Renewal in the Catholic Community* (Washington, D.C.: Georgetown University Press, 2004).

3. The Geoghan case is treated in France, *Our Fathers,* 129–140 and 328–330; see also Dokecki, *Clergy Sexual Abuse Crisis,* 70–80. The *Globe*'s investigative reports were subsequently compiled in book form: *Betrayal: The Crisis in the Catholic Church* (Boston: Little, Brown, 2002). Geoghan's death is reported in "Former Priest Geoghan Is Slain," *Boston Globe,* August 24, 2003. The settlement with victims is described in "Church in an $85M Accord," *Boston Globe,* September 10, 2003.

4. For examples of favorable coverage of Shanley, see "Catholic Gays Claim Diocese Ignores Them," *Boston Globe,* August 29, 1982; "After Eight Years' Ministry to Gays, Priest Recalled," *National Catholic Reporter,* March 2, 1979; and "Priests' Transfer Indicates Strife on Homosexuality," *New York Times,* April 25, 1979.

5. National Review Board for the Protection of Children and Young People, *A Report on the Crisis in the Catholic Church in the United States* (Washington, D.C.: United States Conference of Catholic Bishops, 2004), esp. 22–30; *The Nature and Scope of Sexual Abuse of Minors by Catholic Priests and Deacons in the United States, 1950–2002* (Washington, D.C.: United States Conference of Catholic Bishops, 2004), esp. 26–35, 208–215. For an assessment of how the rate among priests compared with that of the general population, see Stephen J. Rossetti, "The Catholic Church and Child Sexual Abuse," *America* 186, no. 13 (April 22, 2002), 8–15; a more detailed review of the professional literature on this subject is in Stephen J. Rossetti, "The Effects of Priest Perpetration of Child Sexual Abuse on the Trust of Catholics in the Priesthood, Church, and God" (Ph.D. diss.: Boston College, 1994), 1–16. See also Richard John Neuhaus, "Scandal Time III," *First Things* 125 (August/September 2002): 90; and "Scandal's Cure Lies in Tackling Deeper Issues," *National Catholic Reporter,* March 22, 2002. For a systematic critique of press coverage of clergy sexual abuse, see Philip Jenkins, *Pedophiles and Priests: Anatomy of a Contemporary Crisis* (New York: Oxford University Press, 1996), esp. ch. 4.

6. Kinsey and other studies are quoted in Stephen J. Rossetti, *A Tragic*

Grace: The Catholic Church and Child Sexual Abuse (Collegeville, Minn.: Liturgical Press, 1996), 3. Some of the fragmentary comparative studies are summarized in *Nature and Scope of Sexual Abuse of Minors*, 154–162.

7. Law's travails are chronicled in *Betrayal;* see the photo section of that volume for images of protestors. The resignations in Palm Beach are treated ibid., 101–104. On the Springfield case, see "Grand Jury Indicts Dupre," *Springfield Republican*, September 28, 2004. For the Los Angeles settlement, see *Los Angeles Times*, July 15, 2007. For one partial summary of the costs of these settlements, see "Spokane Diocese Reaches $48 Million Settlement," *Seattle Times*, January 5, 2007. See also the figures in *Nature and Scope of Sexual Abuse of Minors*, 103–120, esp. Table 6.1.1.

8. "Abuse Victims Lay Blame at Feet of Catholic Bishops" and "Extent of Priests' Accountability Debated," both *New York Times*, June 14, 2002; "Victims Take Bishops to Task," *Bergen County Record*, June 14, 2002. The texts of the Steinfels and Appleby addresses are in *Origins* 32, no. 7 (June 27, 2002): 110–117. The charter, together with documents governing its implementation, is in *Promise to Protect, Pledge to Heal* (Washington, D.C.: United States Conference of Catholic Bishops, 2003).

9. For early reports, see "Catholics Drawn to Splinter Group in Wellesley," *Boston Globe*, May 1, 2002, and "Laity Seeking Answers Find Their Voice in Group," *Boston Herald*, May 26, 2002.

10. "Lay Catholics Issue Call to Transform Their Church" and "Small Group Has Big Goals," both *Boston Globe*, July 21, 2002; "Laity Urge Vatican to Open Process of Governing Church," *Boston Herald*, July 22, 2002. VOTF took advantage of the Internet in spreading its message: see www.voiceofthefaithful.org.

11. For a sensible assessment of VOTF and other organized lay responses to the scandal, see David Gibson, *The Coming Catholic Church: How the Faithful Are Shaping a New American Catholicism* (New York: Harper Collins, 2003), 109–114. See also Margery Eagan, "Watch Out Law: The Church Ladies Are Now after You," *Boston Herald*, July 21, 2002; David O'Brien ("baptism or wake"), quoted in Gibson, *Coming Catholic Church*, 114; and "Law to Reject Donations from Voice of the Faithful," *Boston Globe*, July 23, 2002.

12. "Laity Urge Vatican to Open Up Process of Governing Church,"

Boston Herald, July 22, 2002; "New Catholic Reform Groups at a Crossroads," *Boston Globe,* July 17, 2002. See also James D. Davidson and Dean R. Hoge, "Catholics after the Council: A New Study's Major Findings," *Commonweal* 131, no. 20 (November 20, 2004): 13–19; and Paul Lakeland, *The Liberation of the Laity: In Search of an Accountable Church* (New York: Continuum, 2003). On the retention of Catholic loyalty, even in the face of disagreement with the church, see Michele Dillon, *Catholic Identity: Balancing Reason, Faith, and Power* (New York: Cambridge University Press, 1999).

13. For a general treatment of the problem, see Gerald Gamm, *Urban Exodus: Why the Jews Left Boston and the Catholics Stayed* (Cambridge, Mass.: Harvard University Press, 1999). The figures on Boston priests were compiled from the archdiocesan weekly newspaper, *The Pilot,* which reported all priestly deaths, retirements, and ordinations. National statistics for sisters are reported each year in *Official Catholic Directory* (New York: P. J. Kenedy); for a historical summary, see *Pilot,* May 21, 2004.

14. Compare the parish entries in the *Pittsburgh Catholic Directory, 1991* (Pittsburgh: Diocese of Pittsburgh, 1991), 29–115, and *Pittsburgh Catholic Directory, 2001* (Pittsburgh: Diocese of Pittsburgh, 2001), B20–B134.

15. On the Boston reconfiguration plans, see the reports in *Pilot,* January 16, May 28, and August 6, 2004. On the resistance see, for example, "Weymouth Parishioners Stage Sit-In to Protest Closing," *Boston Globe,* August 31, 2004; "Inside the Vigils," ibid., December 19, 2004; and "St. Albert's Wins Seven-Month, Round-the-Clock Battle to Reopen," ibid., April 1, 2005.

16. On Saint Dominic's, see the reports in *Newsday* in April, May, and June 2004, esp. "400 Parishioners Attend Angry Meeting," April 28, 2004; see also "Ripples from Scandal Disrupt a Catholic Church," *New York Times,* August 29, 2004. On the New Hampshire case, see "Some Grads Don't Want Bishop at N.H. Rite," *Boston Globe,* June 8, 2005.

17. R. Scott Appleby, "What Is at Stake in the Present Crisis?" *Origins* 32, no. 7 (June 27, 2002): 113; Gibson, *Coming Catholic Church,* ch. 9; Michael L. Papesh, "Farewell to 'the Club': On the Demise of Clerical Culture," *America* 186, no. 16 (May 13, 2002): 7–11.

18. Mary Jo Bane, "A Challenge to Lay Catholics," *Boston Globe,* Febru-

ary 3, 2002; Margaret O'Brien Steinfels, "This Crisis through the Laity's Lens," *Origins* 32, no. 7 (June 27, 2002): 112.

19. The language in which the various Masses are said is specified in *Boston Catholic Directory, 2006* (Boston: Archdiocese of Boston, 2006), 61–78; and *Catholic Directory, Diocese of Galveston-Houston, 2001* (Houston: Diocese of Galveston-Houston, 2001), 106–145.

20. For evidence of these trends, see the summaries in Bryan T. Froehle and Mary L. Gauthier, *Catholicism USA: A Portrait of the Catholic Church in the United States* (Maryknoll, N.Y.: Orbis Books, 2000), esp. 17–18, 23, 57–59, 159–164. See also Philip J. Murnion and David DeLambo, *Parishes and Parish Ministers: A Study of Parish Lay Ministry* (New York: National Pastoral Life Center, 1999), ii. On the problematic nature of the term "Hispanic," see Richard Rodriguez, *Brown: The Last Discovery of America* (New York: Viking, 2002), ch. 5. On the broader trends in recent immigration, see David M. Reimers, *Other Immigrants: The Global Origins of the American People* (New York: New York University Press, 2005).

21. Gilberto M. Hinojosa, "Mexican-American Faith Communities in Texas and the Southwest," *Mexican Americans and the Catholic Church, 1900–1965,* ed. Jay P. Dolan and Gilberto M. Hinojosa (Notre Dame, Ind.: University of Notre Dame Press, 1994), 102, 99, 105–106.

22. In general, see Jeffrey M. Burns, "The Mexican Catholic Community in California," ibid., 127–233. On Chavez, see Susan Ferriss and Ricardo Sandoval, *Fight in the Fields: Cesar Chavez and the Farmworkers Movement* (New York: Harcourt Brace, 1997), esp. 142–146; and James T. Fisher, *Communion of Immigrants: A History of Catholics in America* (New York: Oxford University Press, 2000), 147–148, 151–153. Chavez's 1968 speech is in Timothy Matovina and Gerald E. Poyo, eds., *Presente! U.S. Latino Catholics from Colonial Origins to the Present* (Maryknoll, N.Y.: Orbis Books, 2000), 206–209.

23. On the experience of some of these groups, see Lisandro Perez, "Cuban Catholics in the United States," *Puerto Rican and Cuban Catholics in the U.S., 1900–1965,* ed. Jay P. Dolan and Jaime R. Vidal (Notre Dame, Ind.: University of Notre Dame Press, 1994), 145–208, esp. 194–207; and Jaime R. Vidal, "Citizens Yet Strangers: The Puerto Rican Experience," ibid., 9–143.

See also Thomas A. Tweed, *Our Lady of the Exile: Diasporic Religion at a Cuban Catholic Shrine in Miami* (New York: Oxford University Press, 1997), esp. 28.

24. Burns, "Mexican Catholic Community," 93, 178; Kristy Nabhan-Warren, *The Virgin of the Barrio: Marian Apparitions, Catholic Evangelizing, and Mexican American Activism* (New York: New York University Press, 2005); Vidal, "Citizens Yet Strangers," 206–207. See also the rich descriptions and analyses of the Chicago processions in Karen Mary Davalos, "'The Real Way of Praying': The Via Crucis, *Mexicano* Sacred Space, and the Architecture of Domination," *Horizons of the Sacred: Mexican Traditions in U.S. Catholicism,* ed. Timothy Matovina and Gary Reibe-Estrella (Ithaca, N.Y.: Cornell University Press, 2002), 41–68.

25. The fullest treatment of this devotion is Timothy Matovina, *Guadalupe and Her Faithful: Latino Catholics in San Antonio, from Colonial Origins to the Present* (Baltimore: Johns Hopkins University Press, 2005).

26. Matovina, *Guadalupe and Her Faithful,* 39; compare this with the stories in Robert A. Orsi, *Thank You, St. Jude: Women's Devotion to the Patron Saint of Hopeless Causes* (New Haven: Yale University Press, 1996), esp. ch. 6.

27. The sharp assessment of earlier devotional practices is quoted in Orsi, *Thank You, St. Jude,* 33. On the decline of Peyton's popularity, see James P. McCartin, "'The Love of Things Unseen': Catholic Prayer and the Moral Imagination in the Twentieth-Century United States" (Ph.D. diss.: University of Notre Dame, 2003), 134–136. On devotional practices among young Hispanics, see Dean R. Hoge et al., *Young Adult Catholics: Religion in the Culture of Choice* (Notre Dame, Ind.: University of Notre Dame Press, 2001), ch. 5; see esp. Table 5.2.

28. "Pope Offers Apology to Victims of Sex Abuse by Priests," *New York Times,* April 24, 2002; "Pope Tells Crowd of 'Shame' Caused by Abusive Priests," ibid., July 29, 2002.

29. For a useful summary of the changes in this process, see Gerald P. Fogarty, "Introduction," *Patterns of Episcopal Leadership,* ed. Gerald P. Fogarty (New York: Macmillan, 1989), xxi–xlvi.

30. The succession of bishops, together with the previous assignments of

each man, is summarized in the annual listings in the *Official Catholic Directory* (New York: P. J. Kenedy); these examples were compiled from the 2005 edition.

31. For a discussion of some of these organizational issues, see the essays in Jean M. Bartunek et al., *Church Ethics and Its Organizational Context: Learning from the Sex Abuse Scandal in the Catholic Church* (Lanham, Md.: Rowman and Littlefield, 2006).

32. See George M. Mardsen, *The Soul of the American University: From Protestant Establishment to Established Nonbelief* (New York: Oxford University Press, 1994). For a sustained, at times hysterical, critique of Catholic colleges, see James Tunstead Burtchaell, *The Dying of the Light: The Disengagement of Colleges and Universities from Their Christian Churches* (Grand Rapids, Mich.: Eerdmans, 1998), esp. ch. 6. Calmer consideration is given in Robert E. Sullivan, ed., *Higher Learning and Catholic Traditions* (Notre Dame, Ind.: University of Notre Dame Press, 2001). For a general picture of American Catholic higher education, see Froehle and Gautier, *Catholicism USA,* 79–85.

33. For the critique, see Burtchaell, *Dying of the Light,* 563 and 627. Detailed descriptions of the negotiations between American bishops and the Vatican are given in Charlotte Allen, "Crossroads: The Identity Crisis of Catholic Colleges," *The New Republic* (February 15, 1999): 16–21; and Steinfels, *A People Adrift,* 131–133, 142–144. See also *"Ex Corde Ecclesiae": An Application to the United States* (Washington, D.C.: National Conference of Catholic Bishops, 1999); and "Catholic Campuses Face a Showdown on Ties to Church," *New York Times,* February 5, 1999.

34. J. Donald Monan and Edward A. Malloy, "*'Ex Corde Ecclesiae'* Creates an Impasse," *America* 180, no. 3 (January 30–Feburary 6, 1999): 6–12; Lakeland, *Liberation of the Laity,* 280; Gibson, *Coming Catholic Church,* 283.

35. On the sales of John Paul's books, see Tad Szulc, *Pope John Paul II: The Biography* (New York: Scribner, 1994), 465–466.

36. "Signal Calling: Former UB Quarterback Forgoes Family and Career," *Buffalo News,* July 3, 2005; "A Small, Sturdy Band of 'John Paul Priests,'" *Christian Science Monitor,* April 8, 2005; "The Divine Experience," *Syracuse Post-Standard,* August 19, 2006; Felix Klein, "John Paul II Priests," *Commonweal* 132, no. 14 (August 12, 2005): 25; "More Men Choosing Priest-

hood," *Pittsburgh Post-Gazette,* September 12, 2002; "Young Catholics Seek to Restore Old Values," *New York Times,* April 14, 2002; "Hope for the Future: Formation at the North American College in Rome," *National Catholic Register,* January 19–25, 2003.

37. Jonathan Englert, *The Collar: A Year of Striving and Faith inside a Catholic Seminary* (Boston: Houghton Mifflin, 2006), 59; Dean R. Hoge and Jacqueline E. Wenger, *Evolving Visions of the Priesthood: Changes from Vatican II to the Turn of the New Century* (Collegeville, Minn.: Liturgical Press, 2003), 64; "A Small, Sturdy Band of 'John Paul Priests'"; Paul Stanosz, "Seminarians Today," *Commonweal* 132, no. 4 (August 12, 2005): 22; Andrew Greeley, "Young Fogeys," *Atlantic Monthly* 293, no. 1 (January–February 2004): 40–41.

38. Stanosz, "Seminarians Today," 21–22; Hoge and Wenger, *Evolving Visions of the Priesthood,* 68; Klein, "John Paul II Priests," 24; Dean R. Hoge, *The First Five Years of Priesthood: A Study of Newly Ordained Catholic Priests* (Collegeville, Minn.: Liturgical Press, 2002), 57; Charles R. Morris, *American Catholic* (New York: Times Books, 1997), 384. Long-term trends in favor of married priests are charted in George Gallup, Jr., and Jim Castelli, *The American Catholic People: Their Beliefs, Practices, and Values* (Garden City, N.Y.: Doubleday, 1987), 53–56.

39. Hoge, *First Five Years of Priesthood,* Table 2.9; Klein, "John Paul II Priests," 25; Morris, *American Catholic,* 385.

40. These statistics have been compiled from the several diocesan websites and from the *Official Catholic Directory* (New York: P. J. Kenedy) for the relevant years.

41. "How Americans Voted: A Political Portrait," *New York Times,* November 7, 2004. See also Congressional Quarterly Electronic Library, Voting and Elections Collection, at www.cqpress.com/electronic-products .html. On the Communion dispute in 2004, see "Cardinal Cautions Catholic Politicians," *Boston Globe,* April 24, 2004; "Bishops Rebuke 'Evil' Pols," *Boston Herald,* June 19, 2004; and Ellen Goodman, "Putting Kerry on the 'Wafer Watch,'" *Boston Globe,* April 15, 2004.

Acknowledgments

Archivists and librarians remain the scholar's best friends and collaborators. In preparing this book, I have been helped by many of them, renewing old friendships and making some new ones. In particular, the staff of the John J. Burns Library at Boston College opened their treasures of books, pamphlets, catechisms, and other things that Catholic lay people used in living out their faith over more than two centuries. Thanks, too, to the staff of the American Catholic History Research Center at the Catholic University of America; working there is not only profitable but also an immense personal pleasure. I am also grateful to the staffs of the Thomas P. O'Neill, Jr., Library at Boston College, the Bentley Historical Library of the University of Michigan, the Associated Archives of Saint Mary's Seminary and University in Baltimore, and the diocesan archives in Boston, Charleston, Galveston-Houston, Milwaukee, and Pittsburgh.

Colleagues and friends are also essential to researching, thinking, and writing. They ask probing questions; they point out the obvious topics you have managed to ignore; they push you along just by asking how it's going; they tell you when the sentences you really liked are awful. Some or all of this book has been seen by many eyes, and I am particularly indebted to those of Richard Cox, Andrew Finstuen, Kevin Kenny, David McCowin, and Timothy Meagher. Paul Ginnetty gets special mention for applying his sense of style in a line-by-line reading that took far too much time away from his own responsibilities. Students quickly become friends and colleagues, too, and I thank the religious history reading group of graduate students at Boston College for an early assessment of the opening chapters. I have also been fortunate, through the generosity of Dean Joseph Quinn of the College of Arts and Sciences at Boston College, to have had the help of two undergraduate research assistants: Matthew Gaudette (class of 2004) and Courtney Tincher (class of 2008). Their work was indispensable in writing Chapters two and five, respectively. Editors also become friends, and I am happy to have had the chance to work with Joyce Seltzer. The book was her idea in the first place, and I am glad now that she talked me into putting off other things to do it. She was an ideal editor, pushing when I needed it, leaving me alone when I needed that, too.

My deepest thanks go to a very special group of lay people from Saint Ignatius of Loyola parish in Chestnut Hill, Massachusetts. The book is dedicated to them, the members of my "small faith group." The first word in that phrase modifies the last one, not the second—only the group is small. That we came together at all more than a decade ago seems now like evidence for the Holy Spirit, since the only thing we apparently had in common was that we could meet on Tuesdays. They have taught me many things about how to live in the world and somewhere else at the same time.

Index

abortion, 244, 261–263, 303
abstinence from meat, 23, 224
Adams, John, 12, 42, 44
adulthood, imagery of, 201, 210–211, 215,
  251–252, 265, 276, 283
Advent, observance of, 28–29
African American Catholics, 25–27, 66,
  157–158, 167–168, 279
Alabama, Catholics in, 54, 139, 157
altar rail, 112–113, 119, 204
altar servers, 78, 113, 117–118, 119, 211–212
America, Catholic relationship to, 7–8,
  38–44, 139–144, 261–263, 302–304
America magazine, 171, 245–246, 261
anti-Catholicism, 7–8, 38–41, 89–93, 98–
  99, 139–141, 194–195, 306
anti-communism, 157, 162, 187–188, 195–
  196
anti-Semitism, 169, 254, 255
Appleby, Scott, 274–275, 282
Association of Catholic Trade Unionists,
  146, 166, 191
Assumption of Mary (doctrine), 131

Baker, Pacificus, 28–30
Baltimore, Catholics in, 14, 33, 104, 115,
  143, 242
Baltimore Catechism, 4, 223–224
Bane, Mary Jo, 282–283

baptism: practice of, 12, 17, 25–26, 82–83,
  235; theology of, 82–83
Bedini, Gaetano, 86–87, 131
Beecher, Lyman, 90
Benedict XVI, Pope, 301–302
Benediction of the Blessed Sacrament, 75,
  77, 122, 149, 222–223
Bible, 29, 34, 91–92, 135, 224–225
bishops, American Catholic, 60–64, 72–
  73, 87, 88, 121, 137–138, 161–162, 175,
  181, 228, 245, 248, 262, 268, 274–275,
  293–295, 297
Blanshard, Paul, 194–195
Boisi, Geoffrey, 281
Boston, Catholics in, 12, 14–15, 27, 39, 42,
  55, 56–57, 76, 81, 83, 109, 110, 111, 121,
  128–129, 142, 148, 155, 187–188, 208, 217,
  235, 256, 257, 258, 260, 261, 270–272,
  274, 276–277, 284–285
boxing, 143, 155, 158
Brooklyn, Catholics in, 116, 126, 193
Buffalo, Catholics in, 55, 57, 117, 138

California, Catholics in, 132, 173, 194, 210,
  235, 240, 246, 249, 286–287. See also
  Los Angeles, Catholics in
Callahan, Patrick Henry, 156–157
Call to Action, 243–244
Calvert family, 23, 39–40

Carey, Mathew, 33–35
Carroll, Charles, of Carrollton, 22, 36, 43, 126
Carroll, John, 13–14, 18, 20–22, 31, 35, 46–48, 56, 61–62, 79, 88, 134, 138, 203
Casey, Robert, 244
catechisms, 4, 12, 31–33, 48, 133, 134. *See also* Baltimore Catechism
Catholic Action, 146–148, 158, 162, 169, 171, 173, 190–191, 198, 210, 307
Catholic Interracial Council, 167, 258
Catholics for a Free Choice, 244
Catholics United for the Faith, 243
Catholic Traditionalist Movement, 243
Catholic Worker Movement, 145–146, 162–163, 166, 168, 260–261
Catholic Youth Organization, 146, 155
Challoner, Richard, 28–29, 33, 34, 79, 134
chapels, private, 19–21, 24–25
charismatic movement, 227–230
Charleston: Catholics in, 15–16, 50–52, 64–72, 74, 89–90; diocesan constitution, 65–73
Chavez, Cesar, 286–287
Cheverus, John, 11–13, 44, 46, 125, 138
Chicago, Catholics in, 102–103, 106, 142, 155, 176, 209, 220, 240, 253, 289
childhood, imagery of, 63, 210–211
Christian Family Movement, 171–174, 175, 189
Christmas, observance of, 28, 30, 235
church buildings, 11, 42, 73–74, 95, 117, 127, 152; design of, 111–115, 212–213
church year, observance of, 28–29, 77
Cincinnati, Catholics in, 27, 56, 102, 152, 216
Civil Rights Movement, 258–259
Civil War, 98, 100, 105, 114, 141, 150
clericalism, 18, 63, 282–283, 300–301
Cleveland, Catholics in, 94–95, 116, 235, 237, 259
colleges, Catholic, 160, 168, 295–297
Common Ground Initiative, 244–245
Commonweal magazine, 169, 262, 274
Communion. *See* Eucharist

confession, 12, 16, 21–22, 30–31, 103, 113–114, 181–185, 216–219, 224, 240, 264–265
confirmation, 15
Connecticut, Catholics in, 156, 215
contraception, 200–201, 239–242, 250, 251, 264–265, 300
convents, 90–91, 103–104
conversion: to Catholicism, 26–27, 86, 145, 162, 166; to Protestantism, 107–108
Coolidge, Calvin, 152–153
Corbett, James J., 143
Cort, John C., 166
Coughlin, Charles, 168–169
Crowley, Patricia Caron, 173, 199–201, 241–242, 307
Cuban Catholics, 287–288
Cuomo, Mario, 263
cursillo, 225–226

Day, Dorothy, 145–146, 162–163, 306
deacons, 234–236
Democratic Party, 142, 168, 195, 197, 261, 262–263, 303
Denver, Catholics in, 108, 152, 173, 250–251
Detroit, Catholics in, 101, 138, 152, 165, 168, 236, 247–248, 257, 258
devotions, private, 5, 12–13, 27–38, 119, 124, 223, 288, 290–291
dialogue Mass, 203–204
Dornin, Bernard, 33
Dulles, Avery, 254

Easter, observance of, 23, 27, 29
England, John, 64–71, 85–86, 109
ethnicity, Catholicism and, 57–58, 95–96, 102, 105–107, 266–267, 284–292. *See also individual ethnic groups*
Eucharist: devotion to, 123–124, 126, 223, 299; frequency of, 30, 120–121, 178–179, 213–214; reception of, 15, 21, 27, 30, 177, 204, 210, 214–216, 232, 303–304; theology of, 18, 30, 32, 113, 123, 177–178, 214–215. *See also* First Communion
Eucharistic fast, 179–180, 213–214

examination of conscience, 30–31, 35, 183, 184
Ex Corde Ecclesiae, 296–297
Extreme Unction, 219–220

Family Rosary Crusade, 187–188
fasting, 21, 23, 134
Feeney, Leonard, 254–255
Fernandez, John Oliveira, 57
Ferraro, Geraldine, 263
Fichter, Joseph, 176–177, 182, 184
First Amendment to U.S. Constitution, 41–42, 59, 195
First Communion, 32, 180–181, 218
First Vatican Council (1869–1870), 46
Fitzgerald, John F., 124
Florida, Catholics in, 274, 287–288, 294
Ford, Henry II, 196
French Catholics, 27, 55, 58
Friedan, Betty, 212

Garden of the Soul, 28, 134
Gaston, Margaret, 20
Geoghan, John, 270–271, 281
Georgia, Catholics in, 15–16, 17, 20, 32–33, 67–68, 70, 76, 303
German Catholics, 16, 55, 58, 98–99, 102–103, 115, 121, 131, 142, 157
Glendon, Mary Ann, 244
Gother, John, 28–30
Grail Movement, 164–165
Gregory XVI, Pope, 88–89

Hague, Frank, 142–143
Haly, James, 33
Hanly, Roger, 11–13, 14, 32, 50, 95, 305
Hispanic Catholics, 100, 226, 266, 285–292, 303–304
Holy Days of Obligation, 121–122
Holy Name Society, 149–153, 155, 189
Holy Orders. *See* priesthood, theology of
homosexuality, 244, 273, 304
Houston, Catholics in, 206, 285, 291, 302–303
Hughes, John, 61

Humanae Vitae, 242, 262, 272
Hurban, Anna, 94–95, 306

Illinois, Catholics in, 54, 210, 218, 229. *See also* Chicago, Catholics in
Immaculate Conception (doctrine), 130, 139
immigrants, Catholic, 95–96, 97–100, 140, 266–267, 284–285, 290–292, 306
immigration, 97–99, 284–285
Indian tribes, 14–15, 79, 100
indulgences, 48, 133–136, 138
infallibility, papal, 46, 131, 138–139, 249
interfaith activity, 255–256
Irish Catholics, 11, 17, 27, 58, 97–99, 102–103, 121, 260, 279, 290
Italian Catholics, 98, 99, 106, 107–108, 290
ius patronatus, 60, 62–63

Jay, John, 41
Jefferson, Thomas, 9, 41
Jesuit priests, 16, 24–25, 39, 135, 160, 189, 254, 255
John XXIII, Pope, 199, 202, 209, 238, 241
John Paul II, Pope, 239, 248–251, 289, 292–294, 296, 298–299, 301

Kennedy, Edward, 261–262
Kennedy, John Fitzgerald, 197–198
Kennedy, Rose Fitzgerald, 124
Kentucky, Catholics in, 19–20, 54, 131, 150, 156, 249
Kerry, John, 303–304
Knights of Columbus, 155–157
Knights of Lithuania, 157
Knights of Saint George, 157
Knights of Saint Mary of Czechstochowa, 157
Knights of Saint Peter Claver, 157–158
Know Nothings, 140
Ku Klux Klan, 8, 140, 152, 258

labor movement, Catholics in, 143, 159–160, 165–166

laity, relationship to priests, 53–64, 68–71,
113, 117–118, 128–129, 146, 147–148, 150,
154–155, 174–175, 210–211, 233, 239–240,
264–265, 282–283, 295, 307
Law, Bernard, 274, 280, 294
Legion of Decency, 170–171
Lent, observance of, 23, 28–29, 30, 78–
79, 123
Leo XIII, Pope, 136–137, 143
limbo, 83
litanies, 37, 125
Lithuanian Catholics, 100, 103, 157
liturgical movement, 203–204
Liuzzo, Viola, 258
Los Angeles, Catholics in, 173, 192, 266–
267, 274
Louisiana, Catholics in, 55, 269. *See also*
New Orleans, Catholics in
Loyola, Ignatius, 25, 230
Luce, Clare Booth, 196
Lueken, Veronica, 243
Lynah, Edward, 68, 71

Mack, Connie, 143
Maine, Catholics in, 11–13, 14–15, 32, 79,
125, 139, 246
marriage, 17, 22, 25–26, 226–227, 304; interfaith, 22, 26–27, 256–258
Marriage Encounter, 226–227
Mary, Blessed Virgin, 37–38, 114, 124, 125–
126, 130, 148, 186, 289–290. *See also* Our
Lady of Guadalupe
Maryland, Catholics in, 13–14, 19, 20, 23–
27, 39–40, 42. *See also* Baltimore, Catholics in
Mass: attendance, 74–76, 84, 110, 115–116,
122, 148, 176–177, 190, 221–222, 278,
285; availability of, 19, 28, 74–76, 115–
116, 119, 121, 176, 279; celebration of, 2,
12, 15–17, 21, 30, 46, 120, 202–205, 207–
210, 220–221, 285; description of, 4, 42,
74–80, 116–120, 204–205, 207–210, 299;
prayers after, 136–137, 204; on Saturday,
205–207
Massachusetts, Catholics in, 15, 39, 80,
89–90, 140, 155, 159, 182, 209, 252–253,

254–255, 270–272, 274, 275, 280–281,
304. *See also* Boston, Catholics in
Maurin, Peter, 145–146, 161–162
McCarthy, Joseph, 195–196
McDonald, James, 50–51, 69, 95, 305
McKenna, Charles Hyacincth, 150
Michigan, Catholics in, 149, 181–182, 240,
246, 259. *See also* Detroit, Catholics in
Miller, David, 260–261
Milwaukee, Catholics in, 105, 115–116, 121–
122, 259
ministers, lay, 232–234, 285
Minnesota, Catholics in, 115, 208, 211, 213,
233
missals, 78–79, 84, 118–119, 205. *See also*
prayer books
Missouri, Catholics in, 16–17, 117. *See also*
St. Louis, Catholics in
Monk, Maria, 8, 90–91
monsignors, 6, 137–138
movies, Catholics and, 8, 165, 170–171, 236
Moynihan, Daniel Patrick, 196
Murray, John Courtney, 255
Murray, Philip, 165–166
music, liturgical, 79–82, 122, 133, 164, 203–
204, 211

Napoleon, 5, 47, 87
National Catholic Rural Life Conference,
146, 163–164
National Catholic Welfare Council, 161
National Council of Catholic Women,
161–162, 175
nativism. *See* anti-Catholicism
New Hampshire, Catholics in, 12, 15, 81–
82, 210, 218, 251, 281
New Jersey, Catholics in, 207, 208, 218,
246
New Orleans, Catholics in, 55, 63, 76,
176–177, 179, 182, 251
New York (state), Catholics in, 19, 41, 54–
55, 57, 131–132, 139, 149, 193–194, 217,
247, 256, 281. *See also* Buffalo, Catholics
in; New York City, Catholics in
New York City, Catholics in, 13, 27, 33, 48,
58, 80, 115, 126, 128, 132, 142, 150, 154,

237, 239, 240–241, 243, 260, 269. *See also* Bronx, Catholics in

North Carolina, Catholics in, 20, 70, 253

Noonan, John, 241

nuns. *See* sisters, religious

Ohio, Catholics in, 27, 173, 249, 254, 302. *See also* Cincinnati, Catholics in; Cleveland, Catholics in

O'Malley, Sean, 280, 294

ordinary time, 2, 29

O'Reilly, John Boyle, 143

Ostinelli, Liugi, 81–82

Our Lady of Guadalupe, 289–290

Pacelli, Eugenio. *See* Pius XII, Pope

Papal States, 45, 47, 86, 87, 131–132, 137, 139

parishes: closing of, 278–281, 305; finances of, 108–111, 153–154; formation of, 27, 52–55, 66–68, 101–103, 126, 193–194, 229, 267–268

Paul VI, Pope, 200, 238–239, 241–242, 243

Pennsylvania, Catholics in, 13, 16, 42, 54, 55, 189, 254. *See also* Philadelphia, Catholics in; Pittsburgh, Catholics in

Peter's Pence, 6, 132, 138

pew sales, 109–110

Peyton, Patrick, 187, 196, 227, 290

Philadelphia, Catholics in, 33, 42, 52, 54, 56, 60, 86, 91–92, 110, 132, 176, 189, 225

pilgrimages, 6, 191–192

Pittsburgh, Catholics in, 54, 106, 138, 206, 233, 279

Pius VI, Pope, 47, 87

Pius VII, Pope, 85, 87

Pius IX, Pope, 92, 129–132, 134–135, 138, 139, 249

Pius X, Pope, 179, 181

Pius XI, Pope, 146, 158, 191

Pius XII, Pope, 191–192, 202

Polish Catholics, 98, 100, 103, 106–107, 115–116, 157, 259, 279, 289, 290

politics, American Catholics and, 7–8, 142–143, 261–263, 302, 303–304

pope: American Catholics and, 5–7, 44–48, 84–89, 130–139, 190–192, 238–242, 292–293; non-Catholic attitudes toward, 41, 44, 46, 86, 130. *See also individual popes*

population, American Catholic, 4, 43–44, 54, 100–101, 160, 222, 285–286, 302

Porter, James, 270, 282

prayer books, 27–38, 48, 77, 84, 118–119, 135–136. *See also* missals

prayers, 12, 25, 28, 29–30, 36–38, 48, 78–79, 118–119, 120, 123–125, 133–137, 148, 183, 185–188

preaching, 75, 76, 103, 110, 205

priesthood, theology of, 17–18, 63, 300–301

priests: characteristics of, 18, 20, 236, 298–300; circuit riding, 14–18, 31, 279, 305; numbers of, 4, 13–14, 96, 116, 236–238, 267, 305; relationship to lay people, 53–64, 68–71, 113, 116, 128–129, 148, 174–175, 210–211, 300–301. *See also* Jesuit priests

Propaganda Fide, Congregation de, 46–47

Protestant churches, 12, 14, 34, 39–40, 42, 59–60, 61–62, 96, 101, 107–108, 110, 147, 171, 177, 183, 227, 229–230, 245, 253–254

Protestants, Catholic relationship to, 22, 32, 197, 252–258

Raccoltà, 135–136

racial segregation, 76, 157–158, 167–168, 176, 258–260

radio, 168–169, 191, 196

Reagan, Ronald, 263

Reed, Rebecca, 90–91

Regan, Alice, 161–162

Republican Party, 195, 262–263, 303

retreats, lay, 188–190, 225

Rhode Island, Catholics in, 40, 229

Roe v. Wade, 261–262, 304

Roosevelt, Franklin D., 168–169, 191

rosary, 38, 119, 136, 148–149, 187, 220, 223, 290–291

Ruth, George Herman ("Babe"), 143

Ryan, Mary Perkins, 210

Sacco and Vanzetti, 159
St. Louis, Catholics in, 76, 101, 105, 142,
    153, 154
St. Vincent de Paul Society, 153–155, 159
saints, devotion to, 37–38, 124–125, 186,
    290–291
Savannah, Catholics in, 15, 32–33
schools, Catholic, 4, 7–8, 66, 104–105, 151
Second Vatican Council (1962–1965), 64,
    175, 199–201, 243, 246, 299, 307
Seton, Elizabeth, 104
sexual abuse, 1, 268–278, 292–293, 297,
    299
Shanley, Paul, 271–272
Sheen, Fulton, 196–197
sin, 182–184, 217–218, 241–242
sisters, religious, 4, 90–91, 96, 141, 160,
    212; numbers of, 103–106, 267
slaves, Catholic, 13, 25–26, 66
Slovak Catholics, 94–95
Smith, Alfred E., 143–144, 197
social welfare agencies, Catholic, 4, 7–8,
    153–155, 158–159, 161–162, 307
South Carolina, Catholics in, 15–16, 20–
    21, 33, 50–52, 64–72, 85. *See also*
    Charleston
Spanish American War, 141–142
Spellman, Francis, 163, 192
spiritual direction, 230–232
spirituality, lay, 35–38, 119, 120–121, 126–
    127, 175–176, 178, 189–190, 223–225,
    263–264
Stations of the Cross, 114, 123, 124, 126,
    188
Steinfels, Margaret O'Brien, 274–275, 283
suburbanization, 193–194, 223, 252, 267–
    268, 302–303
Sunday, observance of, 74–75, 205–207
Sweeney, John, 244

television, 196
Tennessee, Catholics in, 219, 230, 294
Texas, Catholics in, 132, 220, 286, 289,
    302–303. *See also* Houston, Catholics in
Timon, John, 16–17, 117
Tocqueville, Alexis de, 72–73, 158
toleration, religious, 40–43, 89
trustees, parish, 53–64, 66–68, 87, 283, 306

United States Catholic Miscellany, 68, 71
Ursuline Convent, Charlestown, Massa-
    chusetts, 89–90
Utah, Catholics in, 142, 153–154, 191

Vatican I. *See* First Vatican Council
Vatican II. *See* Second Vatican Council
Vermont, Catholics in, 114–115
Vespers, 75, 76, 81, 122, 222–223
vestry. *See* trustees, parish
Vietnam War, 260–261
Virginia, Catholics in, 14, 41, 55, 57, 58–59,
    251
Voice of the Faithful, 1, 275–278, 283, 291,
    305

Washington, D.C., Catholics in, 16, 54,
    152
Wisconsin, Catholics in, 132, 208, 209. *See
    also* Milwaukee, Catholics in
women, Catholic, 29, 66, 122, 148–149,
    160, 161–162, 164–165, 211–212, 216, 242,
    282, 283–284; ordination of, 245–250,
    264, 277, 282
women religious. *See* sisters, religious
World War I, 156–157, 161
World War II, 152, 163, 177, 187, 193
World Youth Day, 250–251, 193, 298